THE WALKS
By John Powell and Peter Ma[tthews]

Competitive race walking has a long and proud history in Britain, wi[th?] the annals of British Athletics. Such a list is headed by the Olympic Harold Whitlock, Don Thompson and Ken Matthews. But the last of Britain has declined very considerably in that last half century so th[at?] small and frankly rather poor fields and the 50 kilometres event scarc[e.] of the walking fraternity, and it would be hard to find a more devoted following all be it mostly of advancing years, deplore the way that techniques of international walkers have evolved so that their style is so very different to the traditionalists of old. Nonetheless one most recognise the intense work that today's world elite put into their training and racing, and while all too many athletics commentators and followers belittle race walking (and it is true that athletes could go quicker if they did not stick to the rules of walking), one must admire its practitioners – it may be weird to some but it can be wonderful.

But whatever may be one's views on this sport, the purpose of this booklet is to honour its past and to record the deeds of British walkers. All well as all international results, John Powell has done a huge amount of work in producing the top sixes for all national and inter-counties championships, with winners of area championships and of other major races in Britain. We also show the progression of British records and finally have all-time lists for the standard distances. Information has been included up June 2014, and that includes the IAAF World Cup of Race Walking, held in Taicang, China on 3-4 May 2014, where there was a wondrous depth of top-class performance and Britain had four representatives.

There are some gaps in our information, both of winners of some events and of first names of various walkers, so we would be very pleased to hear of additions and corrections so that these can be added to our collection of information. Any such amendments will be posted on the NUTS website.

Peter Matthews

ACKNOWLEDGEMENTS
With thanks to Colin Young and Norma Blaine for filling in some of our missing first names.

Cover: (left) Don Thompson, Britain's last Olympic champion, seen here during the second of his record eight London to Brighton (86km) walk wins, (right) Paul Nihill, winner of a record number of national titles, seen in action at Crystal Palace in London.

Contents
AAA/AAC Championships 35	European Indoor Champs 19	Scottish champions 86
Age-group champions 107	European U23/Juniors 19	Southern Championships 95
All time lists 109	International Matches 22, 27	UK Championships 44, 54
Annual bests and Statistics 10	Junior internationals 25, 29	UK and World Merit Rankings 14
CAU champions 46, 80	Lugano Trophy 19	WAAA Championships 66
Commonwealth Games 18	Winners of Major British Races 99	Welsh Champions 87
Directory of internationals 31	Midland Championships 88	Women's Championships 64
England internationals 27, 30	Most national titles 107	Women's name changes 16
English Championships 27	Northern Championships 92	Women's World Games 19
Eschborn Trophy 21	Olympic Games 18	World Championships 18
European Championships 18	Progressive UK records 2	World Cup 19
European Cup 22	RWA Championships 45, 74	World Junior/Youth Champs 19
		World University Games 22

Series editor: Peter Matthews, 10 Madgeways Close, Great Amwell, Ware, Herts SG12 9RU
e-mail: p.matthews121@btinternet.com
Copyright © National Union of Track Statisticians 2014

Other Titles in this Series – this book is No.15
No.1 – Men's 400 Metres *by Peter Matthews* (1999)
No.2 – Javelin (men and women) *by Ian Tempest* (1999)
No.3 – High Jump (men and women) *by Ian Tempest* (2001)
No.4 – Triple Jump (men and women) *by Ian Tempest* (2002)
No.5 – Men's 1500 Metres and 1 Mile *by Peter Matthews* (2002)
No.6 – Discus (men and women) *by Ian Tempest* (2003)
No.7 – AAA Championships 1880-1939 *by Ian Buchanan* (2003)
No.8 – Women's Hurdles *by Stuart Mazdon and Peter Matthews* (2003)
No.9 – Long Jump (men and women) *by Ian Tempest* (2004)
No.10 – Shot Put (men and women) *by Ian Tempest* (2006)
No.11 – 1930-1939 UK Men's Ranking Lists *by Ian Buchanan, David Thurlow and Keith Morbey (2007)*
No.12 – Pole Vault (men and women) *by Ian Tempest* (2008)
No.13 – Hammer (men and women) *by Ian Tempest* (2010)
No.14 – Decathlon (men) by *Alan Lindop (2011)*
No.15 – Women's Multi-events *by Stuart Mazdon* (2012)

BRITISH RECORDS and BEST PERFORMANCES

1 MILE WALK   Professional marks
6:42.0+	Joe	Stockwell	21.1.1844	1	in 4M	London (BH)	20 May 1865
6:39.0+	William	Spooner	c.1831	1	in 15M	London (BH)	10 Jul 1865
6:25.0+	Joe	Stockwell	21.1.1844	1	in 2M	Fulham	26 May 1873
6:23.0p	William	Perkins	16.9.1852	1	in 3M	London (LB)	1 Jun 1874
6:20.0p	William	Perkins	16.9.1852	1	in 1Hr	Brighton	29 Jul 1876

Amateurs
7:37.0	Walter	Rye	31.10.1843	1hc		London (BH)	24 Nov 1866
7:15.0+	Walter	Rye	31.10.1843	1hc	in 2M	London (BH)	30 Nov 1867
6:55.0+	Walter	Rye	31.10.1843	1hc	in 2M hc	London (BH)	30 Apr 1868
6:48.0+	Thomas	Griffith	c.1839	1	in 2M	Leeds	6 Aug 1870
6:47 ¼	Harry	Webster	14.5.1854	1		Wilmslow	26 Jun 1875
6:41.0	Harry	Webster	14.5.1854	1		Stoke-on-Trent	6 Aug 1878
6:36.0+	Harry	Webster	14.5.1854	1	in 2M	Preston	12 Jun 1879
6:33.6	William	Sturgess	2.4.1871	1		London (SB)	26 Sep 1896
6:32.4	William	Sturgess	2.4.1871	1		London (SB)	22 Jun 1897
6:26.0+	George	Larner	7.3.1875	1	in 2M	Manchester	13 Jul 1904
6:25.8	Robert	Bridge	16.4.1883	1		Manchester	1912
6:22.2	Robert	Bridge	16.4.1883	1		Royton	1912
6:17.0	Paul	Nihill	5.9.39	1		London (CP)	5 Sep 1970
6:08.9	Roger	Mills	11.2.48	1		London (CP)	13 Sep 1974
5:59.1	Darrell	Stone	2.2.68	1		Portsmouth	2 Jul 1989
5:58.9	Andrew	Penn	31.3.67	1		Rugby	13 Aug 1997
5:58.4	Alex	Wright	19.12.90	1		Leeds	5 Oct 2011

Uncertain performances
6:15.0	Alfred	Yeoumans	4.11.1876	1		Builth Wells	1903
6:00.0exh	Alfred	Yeoumans	4.11.1876	1		Swansea	1 Sep 1906

3000 METRES WALK
12:46.6	Albert	Cooper	29.6.10	1		London (VP)	19 Aug 1933
12:38.2+	Albert	Cooper	29.6.10	1	in 2M	London (BP)	20 Jul 1935
12:09.0	Paul	Nihill	5.9.39	1		Motspur Park	7 Jul 1969
11:55.0 u	Phil	Embleton	20.12.48	1		Enfield	24 May 1971
11:51.1	Paul	Nihill	5.9.39	1	Surrey	Motspur Park	5 Jun 1971
11:44.68	Roger	Mills	11.2.48	1	AAA	London (CP)	7 Aug 1981
11:28.4 u	Phil	Vesty	5.1.63	1		Leicester	9 May 1984
11:42.94	Phil	Vesty	5.1.63	1	AAA	London (CP)	23 Jun 1984
11:41.73	Ian	McCombie	11.1.61	1	AAA	London (CP)	13 Jun 1985
11:35.2	Phil	Vesty	5.1.63	1		Melbourne (Box Hill)	13 Feb 1986
11:34.9	Mark	Easton	24.5.63	1		Woodford	19 Aug 1987
11:32.2	Ian	McCombie	11.1.61	1		Derby	20 Jul 1988
11:24.4	Mark	Easton	24.5.63	1		Tonbridge	10 May 1989

Estimated times
12:20.0+p	John	Raby		1	in 1Hr	London (LB)	20 Aug 1883
12:28.8+	William	Sturgess	2.4.1871	1	in 2M	London (Putney)	10 Jul 1897
12:17.0+	George	Larner	7.3.1875	1	in 2M	Manchester	12 Jul 1904

2 MILES WALK
Professional marks
14:36.0+	Charles	Westhall	6.3.1823	1	in 10M	Islington	8 Dec 1851
13:53.0+	James	Jones	c.1831	1	in 7M	Woolwich	29 Aug 1853
13:50.0+	Joe	Stockwell	21.1.1844	1	in 4M	London (BH)	20 May 1865
13:30.0+	William	Perkins	16.9.1852	1	in 3M	London (LB)	1 Jun 1874
13:14.0+	John	Raby		1	in 1 Hr	London (LB)	20 Aug 1883

Amateurs
17:34.0+	Leslie	Stephen	28.11.1832	1	in 1Hr	Cambridge	29 Mar 1862
16:45.0	Leslie	Stephen	28.11.1832	1		Cambridge	21 Feb 1863
16:29.0+	Horace	Petherick	1838	1		London (Bow)	11 Mar 1865
16:28.0	Walter	Rye	31.10.1843	1		London (BH)	28 Oct 1865
16:22.0+	J	Westell		1	in 4M hc	London (BH)	16 Mar 1867
16:10.0+	R.M.	Williams		1	in 7M	London (BH)	15 Apr 1867
15:53.0+	Walter	Rye	31.10.1843	1	in 7M	London (BH)	30 Aug 1867
15:40.0	Samuel	Smith		1hc		London (BH)	30 Nov 1867
15:42.0	Walter	Rye	31.10.1843	2hc		London (BH)	30 Nov 1867

Smith won this handicap race in 15:15.0 with a 25 second start. Rye's time was from scratch.

15:20.0+	Walter	Rye	31.10.1843	1	in 3M hc	London (BH)	25 Apr 1868
14:54.0	Walter	Rye	31.10.1843	1		London (BH)	30 Apr 1868
14:46.0	Thomas	Griffith	c.1839	1		Bideford	30 Aug 1869
14:34.5	Thomas	Griffith	c.1839	1		Leeds	6 Aug 1870
14:34.0+	William	Morgan	1845	1	in AAC 7M	London (LB)	20 Aug 1883
14:14.4	Harry	Curtis	5.10.1865	1		London (Pa)	2 Aug 1890
14:10.4	Harry	Curtis	5.10.1865	1		London	18 Apr 1891
14:02.6	Harry	Curtis	5.10.1865	2hc		London (Highgate)	25 Apr 1891
14:02.4	Harry	Curtis	5.10.1865	1		London (SB)	4 Jul 1891
13:48.4	William	Sturgess	2.4.1871	1		London (Oval)	14 Sep 1895
13:44.0	William	Sturgess	2.4.1871	1		Windsor	26 Sep 1895
13:33.0	William	Sturgess	2.4.1871	1		London (W)	20 Jun 1896
13:24.2	William	Sturgess	2.4.1871	1		London (Putney)	10 Jul 1897
13:11.4	George	Larner	7.3.1875	1		Manchester	12 Jul 1904
13:11.4	Stan	Vickers	18.6.32	1		Peterborough	2 Jul 1960
13:02.4	Stan	Vickers	18.6.32	1		London (WC)	16 Jul 1960
12:52.6	Brian	Adams	13.3.49	1		Leicester	28 Aug 1976

Notable Times not accepted by the AAA

14:20.0	Thomas	Griffith	c.1839	1		Ealing	27 Apr 1872
14:18.5	Harry	Webster	14.5.1854	1		Widnes	16 Jun 1877
14:17.0	Harry	Webster	14.5.1854	1		St Helens	21 Jul 1877
14:15.0	Harry	Webster	14.5.1854	1		Rainhill	28 Jul 1877
13:47.25	Harry	Webster	14.5.1854	1		Heywood	7 Aug 1877
13:54.8	Harry	Webster	14.5.1854	1		Preston	12 Jul 1879
13:29.6	William	Sturgess	2.4.1871	1			5 Oct 1895
12:53.2	Alfred	Yeoumans	4.11.1876	1		Swansea	8 Sep 1906

5000 METRES WALK

21:09.4+	George	Larner	7.3.1875	1	in 4M	Brighton	19 Aug 1905
20:44.0	Paul	Nihill	5.9.39	1		London (CP)	14 May 1969
20:14.2	Paul	Nihill	5.9.39	1		Östersund	12 Jul 1972
20:14.17	Sean	Martindale	8.11.66	2		Cwmbran	9 Jul 1988
19:35.0	Darrell	Stone	2.2.68	1		Brighton	16 May 1989
19:29.87	Tom	Bosworth	17.1.90	1	UK	Birmingham	31 Jul 2011
19:27.39	Alex	Wright	30.3.90	1	UK	Birmingham	14 Jul 2013
19:16.82	Tom	Bosworth	17.1.90	2	1 UK	Birmingham	29 Jun 2014

Indoors

20:08.04	Steve	Barry	25.10.50	4	EI	Budapest	5 Mar 1983
20:05.82	Andrew	Drake	6.2.65	3		Glasgow	10 Mar 1989
19:36.92	Andrew	Drake	6.2.65	1		Cosford	3 Feb 1991
19:28.20	Andrew	Drake	6.2.65	3		Turin	13 Feb 1991
19:22.29	Martin	Rush	25.12.64	1		Birmingham	8 Feb 1992

5 MILES WALK

Professional marks

38:00.0+	William	Spooner	c.1831	1	in 10M	Islington	8 Dec 1851
37:43.0+	William	Spooner	c.1831	1	in 7M	Islington	24 Feb 1852
37:06.0+	Wlliam	Spooner	c.1831	1	in 10M	Woolwich	20 Jun 1853
36:32.0+	William	Perkins	16.9.1852	1	in 8M	London (LB)	20 Sep 1875
36:18.0+	William	Griffin	1861	1	in 1Hr	London (LB)	4 Oct 1881
35:10.0+	John	Raby		1	in 1Hr	London (LB)	20 Aug 1883

Amateurs

44:48.0+	Leslie	Stephen	28.11.1832	1	in 1Hr	Cambridge	29 Mar 1862
42:30.0+	Frederic	Pace	1841	1	in 10M	London (Bow)	11 Mar 1865
41:35.0+	John	Chambers	12.2.1843	1	in AAC 7M	London (BH)	15 Apr 1867
41:05.0+	Thomas	Griffith	c.1839	1	in 7M	Clifton	26 Oct 1867
40:07.0	R.M.	Williams		1hc		London (BH)	30 May 1868
39:03.8+	Thomas	Griffith	c.1839	1	in AAC 7M	London (LB)	9 Apr 1870
38:12.0+	William	Morgan	1845	1	in AAC 7M	London (LB)	22 Mar 1875
37:22.0+	Harry	Webster	14.5.1854	1	in AAC 7M	London (LB)	7 Apr 1879
37:17.0+	Harry	Curtis	5.10.1865	1	in AAA 7M	Birmingham	12 Jul 1890
36:27.0+	William	Sturgess	2.4.1871	1	in 1Hr	London (SB)	19 Oct 1895
36:00.5+	George	Larner	7.3.1875	1	in 1Hr hc	London (SB)	30 Sep 1905
35:47.2+	Alfred	Pope	24.3.04	1	in 1Hr	London (WC)	31 Aug 1932
35:43.4	Harry	Churcher	21.11.10	1		Motspur Park	5 Jun 1948
35:33.0	Harry	Churcher	21.11.10	1		London (WC)	16 Jun 1949

3

35:24.0+	Roland	Hardy	3.12.27	1	in 10k	London (WC)	15 Jul 1950
35:15.0+	Roland	Hardy	3.12.27	1	in 7M	London (WC)	31 May 1952
34:26.6	Ken	Matthews	21.6.34	1		London (WC)	28 Sep 1959
34:21.2	Ken	Matthews	21.6.34	1		London (WC)	28 Sep 1960
33:43+ u	Phil	Embleton	20.12.48	1	in 10k	London (Nh)	14 Apr 1971

Time not accepted by the AAA

36:49.0+	Harry	Venn	1856			London (LB)	15 Apr 1878

10,000 METRES WALK

44:58.4e	George	Larner	7.2.1875	1	in 1Hr	London (SB)	30 Sep 1905
45:15.6	Ernest	Webb	25.4.1874	1		London (Herne Hill)	20 Dec 1912
44:42.4+	Alfred	Pope	24.3.04	1	in 1Hr	London (WC)	31 Aug 1932
44:37.4+	Roland	Hardy	3.12.27	1	in 7M	London (WC)	15 Jul 1950
43:42.4+e	Roland	Hardy	3.12.27	1	in 7M	London (WC)	31 May 1952
42:35.6	Ken	Matthews	21.6.34	1		London (WC)	1 Aug 1960
41:55.5	Phil	Embleton	20.12.48	1	Essex	London (Nh)	14 Apr 1971
41:14.7	Steve	Barry	25.10.50	1	AAA	London (WL)	20 Mar 1982
41:13.62	Steve	Barry	25.10.50	3	vGDR	London (CP)	19 Jun 1982
40:54.7	Steve	Barry	25.10.50	1	AAA	Kirkby	19 Mar 1983

Note: track short - 4cm/lap but Barry walked full distance due to constant lapping of field of 55+ competitors on outside or in 2nd lane.

40:53.60	Phil	Vesty	5.1.63	1	UK	Cwmbran	28 May 1984
40:45.87	Ian	McCombie	11.1.61	1	UK	Derby	25 May 1987
40:39.77	Ian	McCombie	11.1.61	1	UK	Derby	5 Jun 1988
40:06.65	Ian	McCombie	11.1.61	1	UK	Jarrow	4 Jun 1989

10 KILOMETRES WALK Where superior to track bests above

40:35+	Steve	Barry	25.10.50	1	in 20k	Southport	14 May 1983

7 MILES WALK
Professional marks

57:30.0	Charles	Westhall	6.3.1823	1		Gravesend	1 Sep 1848
57:30.0+	Charles	Westhall	6.3.1823	1		Bayswater	12 Aug 1850
56:00.0	William	Spooner	c.1831	1		Islington	22 Sep 1851
54:58.0+	William	Spooner	c.1831	1	in 10M	Islington	8 Dec 1851
54:30.0	James	Miles	24.7.1840	1		Liverpool	25 Jul 1864
54:10.0	George	Davison	2.9.1844	1	in 3 Hr	London (HW)	6 Dec 1869
51:51.0	William	Perkins	16.9.1852	1		London (LB)	20 Sep 1875
51:29.0+	William	Griffin	1861	1	in 1Hr	London (LB)	4 Oct 1881
51:04.0+	John	Raby		1	in 1Hr	London (LB)	20 Aug 1883

Amateurs

59:52.0+	Frederick	Pace	1841	1	in 10M	London (Bow)	11 Mar 1865
59:32.0	John	Chambers	12.2.1843	1	AAC	London (BH)	23 Mar 1866
59:31.0	Walter	Rye	31.10.1843	1		London (BH)	2 Mar 1867
58:12.0	Thomas	Farnworth		1	AAC	London (BH)	15 Apr 1867
57:30.0	Thomas	Farnworth		1		Clifton	26 Oct 1867
55:30.0	Thomas	Griffith	c.1839	1	AAC	London (LB)	9 Apr 1870
54:57.0	William	Morgan	1845	1	AAC	London (LB)	5 Apr 1873
53:47.0	William	Morgan	1845	1	AAC	London (LB)	22 Mar 1875
52:34.0	Harry	Webster	14.5.1854	1	AAC	London (LB)	7 Apr 1879
52:28.4	Harry	Curtis	5.10.1865	1	AAA	Birmingham	12 Jul 1890
51:27.0+	William	Sturgess	2.4.1871	1	in 1Hr	London (SB)	19 Oct 1895
50:50.8+	George	Larner	7.3.1875	1	in 1Hr hc	London (SB)	30 Sep 1905
50:28.8+	Alfred	Pope	24.3.04	1	in 1Hr	London (WC)	31 Aug 1932
50:11.6	Roland	Hardy	3.12.27	1	AAA	London (WC)	15 Jul 1950
49:28.6	Roland	Hardy	3.12.27	1	BG	London (WC)	31 May 1952
48:53.0+	Ken	Matthews	21.6.34	1	in 1Hr	London (PH)	24 Sep 1960
48:24.0	Ken	Matthews	21.6.34	1	CAU	London (WC)	20 May 1961
48:23.0	Ken	Matthews	21.6.34	1	AAA	London (Hu)	28 Mar 1964
48:22.2+	Ken	Matthews	21.6.34	1		Walton-on-Thames	6 Jun 1984

Notable performances disregarded as records

53:43.0p	William	Bassett		1		Woolwich	18 Apr 1853
51:19.0p	William	Spooner	1831	1		London (BH)	10 Jul 1865
50:52.0p	George	Topley	20.10.1845	1		London (BH)	12 Mar 1866
52:25.0	Harry	Venn		1		London (LB)	15 Apr 1878

1 HOUR WALK
Professional marks
11,476+	William	Gale	21.4.1832	1		Neath	4 Sep 1855
12,527+	George	Davison	2.9.1844	1		London (HW)	6 Dec 1869
12,875	William	Perkins	16.9.1852	1	in 8M	London (LB)	20 Sep 1875
12,875	William	Perkins	16.9.1852	1	in 8M	Brighton	29 Jul 1876
13,022	William	Perkins	16.9.1852	1		London (LB)	5 Oct 1876
13,032	William	Griffin	1861	1	in 1Hr	London (LB)	4 Oct 1881
13,188	Harry	Thatcher		1		London (LB)	1 May 1882

Amateurs
10,794m	Leslie	Stephen	28.11.1832	1		Cambridge	29 Mar 1862
11,265+	Frederick	Pace	1841	1		London (Bow)	11 Mar 1865
	(several others equalled this by walking 7 miles inside the hour)						
12,625	Harry	Curtis	5.10.1865	1		London (Pa)	27 Dec 1890
13,123	William	Sturgess	2.4.1871	1		London (SB)	19 Oct 1895
13,125u	William	Sturgess	2.4.1871	1		London	19 Sep 1896
13,275	George	Larner	7.3.1875	1hc		London (SB)	30 Sep 1905
13,308	Alfred	Pope	24.3.04	1		London (WC)	31 Aug 1932
13,517	Stan	Vickers	18.6.32	1		London (PH)	27 Sep 1958
13,805	Ken	Matthews	21.6.34	1		London (PH)	24 Sep 1960
13,927	Ken	Matthews	21.6.34	1		Walton-on-Thames	6 Jun 1964
13,960	Phil	Embleton	20.12.48	1		Ilford	2 Aug 1972
13,987+	Steve	Barry	25.10.50	3	in 20k	Brighton	28 Jun 1981
14,324+	Ian	McCombie	11.1.61	1	in 20k	London (SP)	7 Jul 1985

Notable performances disregarded as records
12,875p	William	Spooner	1831	1		London (BH)	10 Jul 1865
12,875p	George	Topley	20.10.1845	1		London (BH)	12 Mar 1866
12,875p	George	Topley	20.10.1845	1		London (BH)	30 Jul 1866

10 MILES WALK
Professional marks
1:25:18+	Charles	Westhall	6.3.1823	1		Bayswater	12 Aug 1850
1:23:05+	James	Smith	.8.1816	1	In 20M	Manchester	25 May 1850
1:22:05	William	Spooner	c.1831	1		Islington	8 Dec 1851
1:21:58+u	William	Spooner	c.1831	1	in 20M	Islington	23 Dec 1851
1:21:04	William	Spooner	c.1831	1	in 14M	London (BH)	19 Feb 1862
1:17:33+	George	Davison	2.9.1844	1	in 3Hr	London (HW)	6 Dec 1869
1:15:58+	William	Perkins	16.9.1852	1		London (LB)	20 Sep 1875
1:14:45+	John	Raby		1	in 3Hr	London (LB)	3 Dec 1883

Amateurs
1:26:37	Frederick	Pace	1841	1		London (Bow)	11 Mar 1865
1:19:50	Christopher	Clarke		1hc		Richmond, Surrey	5 Mar 1887
1:19:27.2	Harry	Curtis	5.10.1865	1		Tufnell Park	27 Dec 1890
1:17:38.8+	William	Sturgess	2.4.1871	1	in 14M	London (SB)	3 Oct 1896
1:16:57.0+	William	Sturgess	2.4.1871	1		London (W)	14 Oct 1899
1:15:57.4	George	Larner	7.3.1875	1	OG	London (WC)	17 Jul 1908
1:15:55.0+	Harold	Ross	25.3.1882			Milan	20 Nov 1910
1:14:30.6	Fred	Redman		1		London (WC)	26 May 1934
1:14:06+	George	Coleman	21.11.16	1		Alperton	29 Sep 1956
1:13:44	Stan	Vickers	18.6.32	1	RWA	London (VP)	15 Mar 1958
1:11:00.4	Ken	Matthews	21.6.34	1	RWA	Sheffield	21 Mar 1959
1:10:57	Ken	Matthews	21.6.34	1	RWA	London (He)	19 Mar 1960
1:09:40.6	Ken	Matthews	21.6.34	1		Walton-on-Thames	6 Jun 1984

10 MILES ROAD WALK
1:08:18+	Paul	Nihill	5.9.39	1	in 20k	Douglas IOM	30 Jul 1972
1:07:58	Phil	Vesty	5.1.63	1		Basingstoke	19 Feb 1983
1:06:15+	Steve	Barry	25.10.50	1	in 20k	Douglas, IOM	26 Feb 1983

20 KILOMETRES TRACK WALK
Professional marks
1:34:04.3e	John	Raby		1		London (LB)	3 Dec 1883

Amateurs
1:45:28 e	Christopher	Clarke		1		Balham	26 Dec 1885
1:38:12.2e	William	Sturgess	2.4.1871	1		London (Putney)	30 Oct 1897
1:38:45.3	Thomas	Green	30.3.94	3		Riga	1 Jun 1933
1:34:00.6	George	Coleman	21.11.16	1		Alperton	29 Sep 1956

1:30:00.8	Ken	Matthews	21.6.34	1		London (RP)	11 Apr 1959
1:28:45.8+	Ken	Matthews	21.6.34	1	in 2Hr	Walton-on-Thames	6 Jun 1964
1:26:22.0	Steve	Barry	25.10.50	3	v2N	Brighton	28 Jun 1981
1:24:07.6u	Phil	Vesty	5.1.63	1		Leicester	1. Dec 1984
1:24:21.3u	Ian	McCombie	11.1.61	1	No kerb	London (SP)	7 Jun 1985
1:25:53.6	Sean	Martindale	11.1.61	4		Fana, NOR	28 Apr 1989
1:23:26.5	Ian	McCombie	11.1.61	8		Fana, NOR	26 May 1990

20 KILOMETRES ROAD WALK

1:37:55.4	Lloyd	Johnson	7.4.00	3		Riga	1934
1:36:02	Harold	Whitlock	16.12.03	2		Munich	8 May 1938
1:35:37	Roland	Hardy	3.12.27	1		Manchester	4 Aug 1956
1:32:24.2	Stan	Vickers	18.6.32	5	OG	Melbourne	28 Nov 1956
1:30:00.8	Ken	Matthews	21.6.34	1		London (Regents Park)	11 Apr 1959
1:28:15	Ken	Matthews	21.6.34	1		London (VP)	23 Apr 1960
1:27:59	Phil	Embleton	20.12.48	1		London (BP)	3 Apr 1971
1:27:34.8	Paul	Nihill	5.9.39	3	EC	Helsinki	10 Aug 1971
1:26:55	Paul	Nihill	5.9.39	1		Douglas IOM	27 Feb 1972
1:24:50	Paul	Nihill	5.9.39	1		Douglas IOM	30 Jul 1972
1:22:51	Steve	Barry	25.10.50	1		Douglas, IOM	26 Feb 1983
1:22:37	Ian	McCombie	11.1.61	1	RWA	Thamesmead	11 May 1985
1:22:03	Ian	McCombie	11.1.61	13	OG	Seoul	23 Sep 1988

Short course

| 1:33:31 | Harold | Whitlock | 16.12.03 | 2 | | Stockholm | 1 Aug 1937 |
| 1:26:05 | Ken | Matthews | 21.6.34 | 2 | | Moskva | 6 Sep 1959 |

2 HOURS WALK

Professional marks

22,530m	Charles	Westhall	6.3.1823	1		Bayswater	23 Jul 1849
22,520	William	Spooner	c.1831	1	in 14M	London (BH)	19 Feb 1862
23.738	James	Miles	24.7.1840	14.75M in 1:59:14		Liverpool	21 Jul 1865
24,605+	George	Davison	2.9.1844	1	in 3 Hr	London (HW)	6 Dec 1869
24,894+	William	Perkins	16.9.1852	1	in 3 Hr	London (LB)	16 Jul 1877

Amateurs

20,583+	J	Berry		1	in 25M	London (LB)	6 May 1876
22,128e+	W.E.N.	Costin		1	in 30M	London (SB)	27 Dec 1880
22,128e	Christopher	Clarke		1	in 30M	Balham	26 Dec 1885
22,530+	William	Sturgess	2.4.1871	14M in 1:52:49.4		London (SB)	3 Oct 1896
23,438+e	Jack	Butler	.1871	1	in 3 Hr	London (Putney)	23 Oct 1897
24,256	Harold	Ross	25.3.1882	1		Liverpool	20 May 1911
24,598+	Robert	Bridge	16.4.1883	1	in 12 Hr	London (SB)	2 May 1914
25,563	Ken	Matthews	21.6.34	1		Walton-on-Thames	6 Jun 1984
26,037	Ron	Wallwork	26.5.41	1		Blackburn	31 Jul 1971
27,262 irr	Chris	Maddocks	28.3.57	1		Plymouth	31 Dec 1989

30 KILOMETRES WALK

2:39:03.6t	Jack	Butler	.1871	1	in 3 Hr	London (Putney)	23 Oct 1897
2:37:28.8t	Harold	Ross	25.3.1882	1	in 3 Hr	London (SB)	12 Jun 1913
2:30:21.5t+	Don	Thompson	20.1.33	1	in 50k	Walton-on-Thames	14 Oct 1960
2:28:44.0t+	Paul	Nihill	5.9.39	1	in 20M	Leicester	9 Apr 1972
2:24:18.2t+	Roy	Thorpe	18.5.34	1	in 20M	Hamburg	25 May 1974
2:19:42R	Murray	Lambden	14.10.56	1		Douglas, IOM	28 Feb 1981
2:15:11R	Steve	Barry	25.10.50	1		Douglas, IOM	27 Feb 1982
2:10:16R	Steve	Barry	25.10.50	1	CG	Brisbane	7 Oct 1982
2:07:56R	Ian	McCombie	11.1.61	1		Edinburgh	27 Apr 1986

More track bests

2:22:54.7+	Dennis	Jackson	29.6.45	2	in 35k	Brighton	27 Jun 1981
2:19:18.0+	Chris	Maddocks	28.3.57	1	in 50k	Birmingham	22 Sep 1984
2:11:54 irr	Chris	Maddocks	28.3.57	1		Plymouth	31 Dec 1989

20 MILES WALK

Professional marks

2:57:55+	Charles	Westhall	6.3.1823	1	in 3 Hr	Bayswater	1 Apr 1850
2:54:17+	Charles	Westhall	6.3.1823	1	in 3 Hr	Bayswater	20 Aug 1850
2:42:48+	George	Davison	2.9.1844	1	in 3 Hr	London (HW)	6 Dec 1869
2:39:57+	William	Perkins	16.9.1852	1	in 3 Hr	London (LB)	16 Jul 1877

Amateurs

2:47:52+	Thomas	Griffith	c.1839	1	in 21M	London (LB)	3 Dec 1870
2:47:17.5	Fred	Poynton		1	RWA	Windsor Park	26 Apr 1924
2:46:30.4	Albert	Plumb	14.11.02	1	RWA	Derby	10 May 1930
2:43:38.6	Albert	Plumb	14.11.02	1	RWA	Birmingham	7 May 1932
2:40:08	George	Coleman	21.11.16	1		Wimbledon	14 May 1955
2:35:58	Roland	Hardy	3.12.27	1	North	Manchester	28 Apr 1956
2:30:35	Paul	Nihill	5.9.39	1	RWA	Douglas, IOM	12 Jun 1971
2:29:40+	Chris	Maddocks	28.3.57	1	in 50k	Birmingham	22 Sep 1984

More track bests

2:46:10	George	Galloway	14.12/07	1		London (WC)	26 May 1934
2:42:25.2+	Don	Thompson	20.1.33	1	in 3 Hr	London (Alperton)	6 Jun 1959
2:41:43.8	Don	Thompson	20.1.33	1	in 50k	Walton-on-Thames	14 Oct 1960
2:40:42.6	Paul	Nihill	5.9.39	1		Leicester	9 Apr 1972
2:34:25.4	John	Warhurst	28.3.57	3	vFRG	Hamburg	25 May 1974

35 KILOMETRES WALK

2:52:30	David	Cotton	16.9.56	1		Sutton Coldfield	1 Jul 1978
2:52:08	Roger	Mills	11.2.48	1	RWA	Leicester	16 Jun 1979
2:47:24.7t	Dennis	Jackson	29.6.45	2		Brighton	27 Jun 1981
2:46:15+	Chris	Maddocks	28.3.57	1	in 50k	Bergen	25 Sep 1983
2:43:12+	Chris	Maddocks	28.3.57	1	in 50k	Birmingham	22 Sep 1984

50 KILOMETRES TRACK WALK

4:40:23t	Jack	Butler	.1871	1		London (Putney)	13 Jun 1905
4:29:38.6	Don	Thompson	20.1.33	1		London (Alperton)	29 Sep 1956
4:17:29.8	Don	Thompson	20.1.33	1		Walton-on-Thames	14 Oct 1960
4:11:22.0	Bob	Dobson	4.11.42	1		Saint-Denis	10 Aug 1974
4:05:47.3	Chris	Maddocks	28.3.57	1		Birmingham	22 Sep 1984
4:05:44.6	Paul	Blagg	23.1.60	3	SGP	Bergen (Fana)	26 May 1990

50 KILOMETRES ROAD WALK

4:35:36	Thomas	Green	30.3.94	1	RWA	Croydon	12 Jul 1930
4:30:38	Harold	Whitlock	16.12.03	1	RWA	Derby	4 Jul 1936
4:24:39	Don	Thompson	20.1.33	1	RWA	Enfield	16 Jun 1956
4:22:58	Don	Thompson	20.1.33	8		Podebrady	26 Aug 1956
4:21:50	Don	Thompson	20.1.33	1	RWA	Wimbledon	21 Jun 1958
4:20:31.8	Tom	Misson	11.5.30	4	EC	Stockholm	22 Aug 1958
4:12:19	Don	Thompson	20.1.33	1	RWA	Baddesley	20 Jun 1959
4:11:31.2	Paul	Nihill	5,9.39	2	OG	Tokyo	18 Oct 1964
4:10:20	Bob	Dobson	4.11.42	13	WCh	Malmö	18 Sep 1976
4:09:39	Bob	Dobson	4.11.42	1		Aigen	24 Oct 1976
4:08:39.2	Bob	Dobson	4.11.42	2		Aigen	28 Oct 1978
4:07:22.4	Bob	Dobson	4.11.42	1		Lassing	20 Oct 1979
4:06:43	Chris	Maddocks	28.3.57	1	POL Ch	Gdynia	20 Apr 1980
4:05:14	Chris	Maddocks	28.3.57	1	vFra,Spa	Paris	13 Sep 1980
4:02:37.6	Chris	Maddocks	28.3.57	9	WCp	Bergen	25 Sep 1983
4:02:00	Chris	Maddocks	28.3.57	6	ESP Ch	Vilanova	18 Mar 1984
4:00:05	Les	Morton	1.7.58	5	ESP Ch	Madrid	16 Mar 1986
3:59:55	Paul	Blagg	23.1.60	19	WCh	Rome	5 Sep 1987
3:58:25	Les	Morton	1.7.58	5		Puerto Pollensa	21 Mar 1988
3:57:48	Les	Morton	1.7.58	1		Burrator	30 Apr 1989
3:51:37	Chris	Maddocks	28.3.57	1		Burrator	28 Oct 1990

Probably short course

4:09:14.2	Don	Thompson	20.1.33	4	LT	Pescara	10 Oct 1965

100 KILOMETRES ROAD WALK

9:34:25	Tony	Geal	28.7.52	1		Grand-Quévilly	2 Jun 1979

Short course

9:04:48	Thomas	Misson	11.5.30	1		Seregno	1 Nov 1958

WOMEN

1 MILE TRACK WALK

8:27 2/5	Lily	Howes	8.12.07	1	WAAA	London (SB)	14 Jul 1928
8:18.0	Lily	Howes	8.12.07	1	WAAA	London (SB)	13 Jul 1929
8.12 1/5	Lily	Howes	8.12.07	1		London (SB)	21 Jun 1930
7.53 4/5	Constance	Mason	.07	1		Hampton on Thames	13 Jun 1931

7

7:45 3/5	Constance	Mason		1	WAAA	London (SB)	11 Jul 31
7:40.8	Jeanne	Probekk		1	WAAA	London (Herne Hill)	30 Jun 34
7:38.4	Beryl	Randle	16.12.28	1	WAAA	London (WC)	19 Jun 54
7:36.2	Judy	Farr	24.1.42	1	South	London (Cambridge H)	5 Jun 65
7:29.1+	Marion	Fawkes	3.12.48	1		Copenhagen	14 Aug 76
7:14.3+ u	Carol	Tyson	15.12.57	1k		London (PH)	17 Sep 77
7:14.4+	Marion	Fawkes	3.12.48	1		Östersund	30 Jun 79
6:56.2	Johanna	Jackson	17.1.85	1		Leeds	7 Oct 09

3000 METRES TRACK WALK

16:03.2	Judy	Farr	24.1.42	3		Malmö	7 Jun 64
15:49.8+	Judy	Farr	24.1.42	1+		Solihull	28 Sep 68
15:28.0	Betty	Jenkins	13.1.38	1		Birmingham (PB)	30 Nov 69
15:24.4	Betty	Jenkins	13.1.38	1	Mid	Birmingham (PB)	3 Jun 72
15:00.6	Sally	Wish	15.4.58	1		Warley	16 Sep 72
14:58.0	Christine	Coleman	14.1.47	1	Middx	Welwyn Garden City	18 Jul 73
14:46.0	Marion	Fawkes	3.12.48	1	NthIC	Blackburn	23 Jun 74
14:33.50	Marion	Fawkes	3.12.48	1	WAAA	London (CP)	20 Jul 74
14:28.8	Marion	Fawkes	3.12.48	1	North	Kirkby	28 Jun 75
14:24.4	Marion	Fawkes	3.12.48	1	NthIC	Cudworth	17 Aug 75
14:14.8	Marion	Fawkes	3.12.48	1		Gateshead	29 May 76
14:10.2	Carol	Tyson	15.12.57	1		Gateshead	5 Sep 76
14:00.0	Carol	Tyson	15.12.57	1	North	Kirkby	19 Jun 77
13:46.4	Carol	Tyson	15.12.57	1		Stretford	6 Aug 77
13:40.0	Carol	Tyson	15.12.57	1		London (PH)	17 Sep 77
13:40.0	Carol	Tyson	15.12.57	1	North	Kirkby	23 Jul 78
13:25.2	Carol	Tyson	15.12.57	1		Östersund	6 Jul 79
13:17.56+	Lisa	Langford	15.3.67	1m	UK	Derby	25 May 87
12:59.1	Betty	Sworowski	22.7.61	1		Leamington Spa	19 Aug 89
12:49.16	Betty	Sworowski	22.7.61	1	WG	Wrexham	28 Jul 90
12:40.98	Johanna	Jackson	17.1.85	1	CAU	Bedford	26 May 08
12:22.62	Johanna	Jackson	17.1.85	1	in 5k	Sydney	14 Feb 09

5000 METRES TRACK WALK

26:30.6	Betty	Franklin/Jenkins	13.1.38	1	vDEN	Copenhagen	27 Sep 59
26:27.0	Barbara	Fisk	11.8.50	5	v3N	Le Neubourg	24 Aug 69
25:09.2	Betty	Jenkins	13.1.38	3	v5N	Warley	16 Sep 72
25:02.0	Marion	Fawkes	3.12.48	1		Warley	4 Aug 74
24:59.2	Marion	Fawkes	3.12.48	3		Stockholm	24 Aug 74
24:47.8	Marion	Fawkes	3.12.48	1		Warley	7 Sep 75
24:24.0	Marion	Fawkes	3.12.48	2	v5N	Copenhagen	14 Aug 76
24:10.0	Marion	Fawkes	3.12.48	1	WAAA	London (CP)	21 Aug 76
23:59.62	Marion	Fawkes	3.12.48	4	vSWE, POL	Stockholm	26 Jul 77
23:58.4	Carol	Tyson	15.12.57	1		Manchester (Stretford)	21Aug 77
23:42.4	Carol	Tyson	15.12.57	1		Drachten	1 Oct 77
23:31.5	Marion	Fawkes	3.12.48	1	WAAA	Birmingham (A)	16 Jun 79
23:11.2	Carol	Tyson	15.12.57	1	vSWE, NOR	Östersund	30 Jun 79
22:19.04	Lisa	Langford	15.3.67	1	UK	Derby	25 May 87
22:02.06	Betty	Sworowski	22.7.61	1	EvITA	Gateshead	28 Aug 89
21:57.68	Lisa	Langford	15.3.67	2		Antrim	25 Jun 90
21:52.38	Vicky	Lupton	17.4.72	1		Sheffield	9 Aug 95
21:42.51	Lisa	Kehler (Langford)	15.3.67	1	AAA	Birmingham	13 Jul 02
21:30.75	Johanna	Jackson	17.1.85	1	UK	Birmingham	14 Jul 08
21:01.24	Johanna	Jackson	17.1.85	1		Brisbane	9 Feb 09
20:46.58	Johanna	Jackson	17.1.85	1	NSW Ch	Sydney	14 Feb 09

5 KILOMETRES ROAD WALK
Where superior to track bests above

26:09.8	Judy	Farr	24.1.42	1		London	24 Sep 66
24:15	Carol	Tyson	15.12.57	1		London (Lambeth)	31 Jul 77
22:51	Marion	Fawkes	3.12.48	1	EscCp	Eschborn	29 Sep 79
22:37+	Lisa	Langford	15.3.67		WCp	New York	3 May 87
22:09	Lisa	Langford	15.3.67	1		Redditch	8 Apr 89
22:01	Lisa	Langford	15.3.67	1		Birmingham	9 Dec 89
21:50	Betty	Sworowski	22.7.61	7		L'Hospitalet	6 May 90
21:36	Vicky	Lupton	17.4.72	1		Sheffield	18 Jul 92

10,000 METRES TRACK WALK

52:50.0	Christine	Coleman	14.1.47	1mx		Welwyn GC	21 Aug 73
50:03.0	Marion	Fawkes	3.12.48	1		London (WL)	26 Mar 77
49:59.0	Carol	Tyson	15.12.57	1	WAAA	London (WL)	25 Mar 78
48:37.6	Marion	Fawkes	3.12.48	1	WAAA	Hornchurch	31 Mar 79
48:11.4	Marion	Fawkes	3.12.48	1		Härnösand	8 Jul 79
47:56.3	Virginia	Birch	1.7.55	4	v3N	Borås	15 Jun 85
46:36.1	Betty	Sworowski	22.7.61	1	vNOR, SWE	Moss	17 Sep 89
45:53.9	Julie	Drake	21.5.69	5	SGP	Bergen (Fana)	26 May 90
45:18.8	Vicky	Lupton	17.4.72	1	AAA	Watford	2 Sep 95
45:09.57	Lisa	Kehler	15.3.67	1	AAA	Birmingham	13 Aug 00

10 KILOMETRES ROAD WALK
Where superior to track bests above

53:20	Judy	Farr	24.1.42	1		Birmingham	18 Apr 64
49:27	Carol	Tyson	15.12.57	1		Aigen	28 Oct 78
47:54	Lisa	Langford	15.3.67	1		Douglas	28 Feb 87
46:37	Lisa	Langford	15.3.67	1	RWA	Ham	14 Mar 87
46:09	Lisa	Langford	15.3.67	1	vHUN	Békéscsaba	5 Apr 87
45:42	Lisa	Langford	15.3.67	11	WCp	New York	3 May 87
45:18	Lisa	Kehler (Lamgford)	15.3.67	1		Rotterdam	15 May 98
45:03	Lisa	Kehler	15.3.67	3	CG	Kuala Lumpur	19 Sep 98
44:52	Johanna	Jackson	17.1.85	1		Sheffield	17 Apr 08
43:52	Johanna	Jackson	17.1.85	1	IC	Coventry	6 Mar 09

20 KILOMETRES ROAD WALK

1:58:37.8t	Margaret	Lewis	19.6.37	1		Sotteville	15 Sep 71
1:53:16	Irene	Corlett	18.1.43	1	Manx	Peel, IoM	26 Aug 81
1:47:35	Lillian	Millen	5.3.45	1		Southwick	17 Apr 82
1:44:42	Lillian	Millen	5.3.45	1		London (BP)	2 Apr 83
1:40:45	Irene	Bateman	13.11.47	1		Basildon	9 Apr 83
1:40:12	Niobe	Menendez	1.9.66	2	RWA	Leamington	21 Mar 99
1:37:44	Vicky	Lupton	17.4.72	1		Leamington	27 Jun 99
1:37:31	Sarah-Jane	Cattermole	20.1.77	1		Perth	23 Jan 00
1:36:40	Sarah-Jane	Cattermole	20.1.77	1		Perth	4 Mar 00
1:35:35	Lisa	Kehler	15.3.67	14	EAA GP	Leamington	23 Apr 00
1:33:57	Lisa	Kehler	15.3.67	23	ECp	Eisenhüttenstadt	17 Jun 00
1:31:40	Johanna	Jackson	17.1.85	1	AUS Ch	Melbourne	23 Feb 08
1:31:33	Johanna	Jackson	17.1.85	22	OG	Beijing	21 Aug 08
1:31:16	Johanna	Jackson	17.1.85	1		Lugano	8 Mar 09
1:30:41	Johanna	Jackson	17.1.85	7		La Coruña	20 Jun 10

50 KILOMETRES ROAD WALK

5:09:41	Lillian	Millen	5.3.45	1		Sleaford	18 Jul 81
5:01:52	Lillian	Millen	5.3.45	1		York	16 Apr 83
4:50:51	Sandra	Brown	1.4.49	1		Basildon	13 Jul 91

100 KILOMETRES ROAD WALK

11:17:42+	Sandra	Brown	1.4.49	1	in 24Hr	Etréchy, FRA	27-28 Oct 90

UK INDOOR WALKS RECORDS

Men

1 Mile	5:56.39	Tim	Berrett	23.1.65	3		New York	2 Feb 90
3000m	11:23.99	Alex	Wright	19.12.90	2		Athlone	27 Jan 13
5000m	19:22.29	Martin	Rush	25.12.64	1		Birmingham	8 Feb 92

Women

3000m	13:08.64	Niobe	Menendez	1.9.66	2	AAA	Cardiff	2 Feb 02

UK JUNIOR WALKS RECORDS

Men

3000m	11:53.23	Tim	Berrett	23.1.65	2	AAA	London (CP)	23 Jun 84
10,0000m	41:52.13	Darrell	Stone	2.2.68	4	EJ	Birmingham	7 Aug 87
20km road	1:26:13	Tim	Berrett	23.1.65	2	Kent Ch	Dartford	25 Feb 84
50km road	4:18:18	Gordon	Vale	12.1.82	7		Lassing	24 Oct 81

Women

3000m	13:03.4	Vicky	Lupton	17.4.72	2	Yorks	Sheffield	18 May 91
5000m	22:36.81	Vicky	Lupton	17.4.72	3	v3N-j	Espoo	15 Jun 91
10,000m	47:04.0	Vicky	Lupton	17.4.72	1		Sheffield	30 Mar 91
20km road	1:52:03	Vicky	Lupton	17.4.72	1		Sheffield	13 Oct 91

UK WALKS STATISTICS OVER THE YEARS

20 KILOMETRES WALK   50 KILOMETRES WALK

Year Best   10th   50th   1:40+W100 Best   10th   50th 5:00+ W100

In final column for each event is number of UK athletes in world top 100, or (in brackets) in world top 50

Year	Best	Name	10th	50th	1:40+	W100	Best	Name	10th	50th	5:00+	W100
1958	1:32:38	Vickers	1:40:42		6	2	4:20:32	Misson	4:47:07		?	(3)
1959	1:30:08	Matthews	1:41:42		7	3	4:12:19	Thompson	4:47:02		16	(2)
1960	1:28:15	Matthews	1:39:51		10	3	4:17:30	Thompson	5:00:08		9	(3)
1961	1:29:11	Matthews	1:41:21		8	5?	4:22:31	Thompson	4:48:14		19	(2)
1962	1:31:02	Matthews	1:38:02		13	1	4:27:26	Thompson	4:51:32		14	(2)
1963	1:30:10	Matthews	1:40:47		8	2	4:16:44	Middleton	4:41:59		20+	(5)
1964	1:28:46	Matthews	1:37:36		16	5	4:11:32	Nihill	4:41:55		25	(6)
1965	1:31:52	Fullager	1:38:15		13	3	4:17:23	Middleton	4:49:48		19	(3)
1966	1:31:35	Fullager	1:38:16		15	3	4:23:01	Middleton	4:56:25		14	4
1967	1:31:14	Nihill	1:38:24		16	3	4:25:21	Thompson	4:50:24		16	4
1968	1:29:59	Webb	1:34:51		27	4	4:18:59	Nihill	4:46:58		17	5
1969	1:28:29	Nihill	1:34:27		30+	7	4:19:13	Eley	4:37:03		29	(2)
1970	1:30:35	Fullager	1:34:13		30+	6	4:19:58	Middleton	4:41:20		22	(2)
1971	1:27:35	Nihill	1:34:08		30	4	4:15:05	Nihill	4:37:34		31+	(4)
1972	1:24:50	Nihill	1:33:50		36	4	4:12:37	Warhurst	4:34:08		34	(3)
1973	1:29:37	Warhurst	1:33:20		41	5	4:14:29	Dobson	4:32:39		38+	7
1974	1:28:50	Seddon	1:33:26		37	6	4:11:22	Dobson	4:35:19		29	3
1975	1:27:46	Adams	1:34:07		36	4	4:14:35	Warhurst	4:39:56		35	2
1976	1:27:35	Flynn	1:33:50		46	4	4:09:39	Dobson	4:32:05		38	2
1977	1:28:42	Flynn	1:32:53	1:39:08	59	2	4:15:52	Dobson	4:34:05		41	2
1978	1:28:44	Flynn	1:33:47	1:40:02	49	3	4:08:39	Dobson	4:28:56		45	3
1979	1:27:25	Mills	1:33:23		43	0	4:07:23	Dobson	4:26:50		41	1
1980	1:27:00	Mills	1:30:22	1:38:46	55	0	4:05:14	Maddocks	4:24:13	4:58:17	50	2
1981	1:26:18	Barry	1:32:28	1:40:10e	48	1	4:10:46	Graham	4:25:45		46	3
1982	1:25:00	Barry	1:32:10	1:41e	45	2	4:12:27	Graham	4:31:14		31	0
1983	1:22:51	Barry	1:32:34	1:38:34	59	1	4:02:38	Maddocks	4:28:59		42	1
1984	1:24:14	McCombie	1:32:01	1:39:42	52	3	4:02:00	Maddocks	4:29:03	4:59:51	50	1
1985	1:22:37	McCombie	1:29:44	1:39:48	50	2	4:06:14	Graham	4:27:33		29	2
1986	1:23:24	McCombie	1:30:31	1:40:xx	45	2	4:03:08	Jackson	4:26:53		33	3
1987	1:23:26	McCombie	1:30:52		36	4	3:59:55	Vesty	4:28:24		28	2
1988	1:22:03	McCombie	1:29:48		37	2	3:58:25	Morton	4:30:19		26	2
1989	1:22:35	Maddocks	1:29:44		29	3	3:57:48	Morton	4:39:30		21	1
1990	1:23:27	McCombie	1:30:31		26	2	3:51:37	Maddocks	4:34:18		19	3
1991	1:24:06	Rush	1:31:21		33	0	4:02:11	Morton	4:32:17		20	2
1992	1:22:12	Maddocks	1:29:20		27	4	3:58:36	Morton	4:38:12		15	2
1993	1:25:57	Penn	1:34:28		29	0	4:03:55	Morton	4:48:51		14	1
1994	1:26:11	Bell	1:34:28		19	0	4:32:25	Morton	5:00:00+		9	0
1995	1:24:49	Stone	1:34:22		19	0	3:53.14	Maddocks	4:49:40		12	2
1996	1:23:58	Stone	1:34:27		21	0	4:18:41	Maddocks	4:48:01		17	0
1997	1:25:53	Stone	1:32:22		24	0	4:05:42	Maddocks	4:46:54		12	1
1998	1:26:37	Stone	1:33:00		22	0	4:03:53	Easton	4:55:36		11	1
1999	1:25:10	Stone	1:31:45		20	0	4:07:49	Cheeseman	--		6	0
2000	1:25:56	Drake	1:32:33		13	0	3:57:10	Maddocks	4:51:31		13	1
2001	1:28:18	Penn	1:35:03		14	0	4:09:27	Hollier	4:55:53		10	0
2002	1:24:43	Drake	1:33:11		16	0	4:11:29	Easton	4:56:55		11	0
2003	1:28:52	Penn	1:40:++		8	0	4:24:54	Penn	--		1	0
2004	1:27:51	Daniel King	1:39:04		11	0	4:26:06	Partington	--		3	0
2005	1:29:13	Penn	1:40:+		8	0	4:17:40	Partington	--		4	0
2006	1:29:35	Partington	1:38:45		10	0	4:25:39	Partington	5:49:48		2	0
2007	1:28:26	Daniel King	1:47:32		6	0	4:13:36	Daniel King	5:37:01		2	0
2008	1:26:14	Daniel King	1:42:19		7	0	4:04:49	Daniel King	5:27:52		4	1
2009	1:28:31	Luke Finch	1:45:39		6	0	4:22:22	Davis	over 6hr		2	0
2010	1:25:46	Wright	1:35:29		10	0	4:28:29	Davis	5:57:25		3	0
2011	1:26:45	Wright	1:45:21		7	0	4:14:55	Dominic King	5:37:27		3	0
2012	1:24:49	Bosworth	1:49:52		5	0	4:08:34	Dominic King	–		4	0
2013	1:23:05	Wright	1:45:23		5	1	4:05:36	Daniel King	5:27:03		5	1

50kmW: 1958- 10 men to 4:47:07, 1963 - 20 to 4:51:30, 1971- 31 to 4:56:20, 1973- 38 to 4:55
WOMEN
10 KILOMETRES WALK 20 KILOMETRES WALK

Year	Best	10th	50th	To 58:00	Wld 100	Best	10th	To 1:55	Wld 100

In final column for each event is number of UK athletes in world top 100, or (in brackets) in world top 50

Year	Best	Name	10th/50th	To	Wld	Best	Name	10th	Wld
1977	50:03t	Fawkes	57:33	10					
1978	49:27	Tyson	54:23	12					
1979	48:11.4	Fawkes	56:29	11					
1980	49:30.4	Tyson	57:17	11					
1981	48:34.5	Tyson	53:49	19	14	1:53:16	Corlett		1
1982	48:57.6	Bateman	54:39	23	(2)	1:47:35	Millen		2
1983	48:52.5	Bateman	53:58	22	5	1:40:45	Bateman		4
1984	49:35	Millen	52:36	28	5	1:53:27	Brown		2
1985	47:56.3	Birch	53:29	26	1	1:46:32	Millen		1 x
1986	47:58.3	Allen	53:00	25	1	1:56:29	B Lupton		0 x
1987	45:42	Langford	51:52	29	3	1:55:57	Millen		0 x
1988	47:52	Langford	53:55	28	1	1:43:50	Sworowski		3
1989	46:02	Langford	52:18	26	2	1:54:38	Sandra Brown		2
1990	45:53.9	Drake	50:51	28	2	1:53:16	Reader		1
1991	45:59	Sworowski	50:56	28	1	1:48:29	S Brown		3
1992	46:04	V Lupton	50:33	28	0	1:48:22	Reader		2
1993	45:59	Drake	52:15	27	1	1:45:11	Callanin		7
1994	45:48	V Lupton	51:31	27	3	1:44:48	V Lupton		5
1995	45:18.8	V Lupton	51:09	28	2	1:42:47	V Lupton		4
1996	47:05	V Lupton	52:23	21	0	1:43:57	V Lupton		7
1997	47:16	V Lupton	52:49	29	0	1:43:52	Black		3
1998	45:03	Kehler	51:20	24	1	1:44:25	V Lupton		2
1999	47:51.2	Charnock	52:37	21	0	1:37:44	V Lupton	1:49:12	12 0
2000	45:09.57	Kehler	53:35	17	1	1:33:57	Kehler	1:54:46	10 1
2001	47:05	Cattermole	53:18	20	0	1:39:10	Cattermole	–	8 0
2002	45:53	Kehler	52:25	20	2	1:36:45	Kehler	1:51:12	10 1
2003	48:54	Cattermole	54:15	14	0	1:41:04	Cattermole	2:+	8 0
2004	49:19	Cattermole	54:19	14	x	1:42:02	Cattermole	2:+	5 0
2005	48:02	Cattermole	52:59	18	x	1:38:00	Cattermole	1:53:25	10 0
2006	47:25	Jackson	53:16	18	x	1:41:00	Jackson	2:07:16	5 0
2007	47:49	Jackson	56:46	11	x	1:36:28	Jackson	2:13:31	3 0
2008	44:52	Jackson	56:16	12	x	1:31:33	Jackson	2:15:26	3 1
2009	45:39	Jackson	56:57	11	x	1:31:16	Jackson	2:11:49	4 1
2010	43:53	Jackson	54:44	11	x	1:30:41	Jackson	2:05:20	5 1
2011	44:59	Jackson	56:20	10	x	1:31:50	Jackson	2:03:44	6 1
2012	46:17	Jackson	55:54	11+	x	1:35:25	Jackson	2:16:05	3 0
2013	49:03.99	Davies	56:06	9+	x	1:43:25	Lewis	2:09:35	4 0

Kehler née Langford.
Note: women's 20km walk replaced the 10 kilometres as the standard international distance in 1999. Uniquely for this period at any event: mother and daughter headed UK rankings with Brenda and Vicky Lupton at 20km walk.

ANNUAL UK MEN'S WALK BESTS EACH YEAR 1930-2013

Year	20 Kilometres	50 Kilometres	10,000m track
1930		4:35:36 Thomas Green	
1931		4:39:59 Frank Rickards	
1932		4:43:35 Lloyd Johnson	44:42.4 Alfred Pope
1933	1:48:45.3t Thomas Green	4:39:17 Harold Whitlock	47:03.0 Thomas Green
1934	1:37:55.4 Lloyd Johnson	4:36:30 Lloyd Johnson	
1935		4:39:08 Harold Whitlock	
1936		4:30:38 Harold Whitlock	
1937		4:38:43 Harold Whitlock	
1938	1:36:02.0 Harold Whitlock	4:41:51 Harold Whitlock	
1939		4:40:43 Harold Whitlock	
1940		5:02:41 Harold Whitlock	
1945		4:48:59 Harry Forbes	
1946		4:42:58 Harry Forbes	

Year	2 Miles Track		7 Miles		20 Miles Road	
1947			4:40:06	Harry Forbes	45:31.6	Harry Churcher
1948			4:35:35.8	Rex Whitlock	45:10.4	James Morris
1949			4:51:50	Lloyd Johnson	45:38.8	Harry Churcher
1950			4:43:04	John Proctor	44:33.4	Roland Hardy
1951			4:45:34	Donald Tunbridge	44:38.2	Roland Hardy
1952			4:32:21	Rex Whitlock	43:42.4	Roland Hardy
1953			4:46:10	Frank Bailey		
1954			4:34:34	Albert Johnson	45:27.0	George Coleman
1955			4:31:32	Albert Johnson	46:44.4	George Coleman
1956	1:32:34.2	Stan Vickers	4:22:58	Don Thompson	44:07.0	George Coleman
1957			4:30:10	Don Thompson	46:02.4	Stan Vickers
Year	2 Miles Track		7 Miles		20 Miles Road	
1920	14:32.0	Charles Dowson	51:20	R Ricketts	2:51:59.6	Harold Ross
1921	14:40.2	John Evans	55:22.4	William Hehir	2:58:56.4	William Hehir
1922	14:31.8	J Dowse	53:24.2	Gordon Watts	2:49:55	Reg Goodwin
1923	14:24.0	Gordon Watts	54:35.4	Gordon Watts	2:50:01.4	Lloyd Johnson
1924	14:11.2	Reg Goodwin	52:00.6	Reg Goodwin	2:47:12	Fred Poynton
1925	14:07.4	Reg Goodwin	51:52.4	Colin McClellan	2:48:17.4	Fred Poynton
1926	14:32.4	Wilf Cowley	53:56.0	Reg Goodwin	none	
1927	14:21.6	Alfred Pope	53:15	Harold King	2:55:53	Lloyd Johnson
1928	14:04.8	Alfred Pope	51:02	Cecil Hyde	2:49:17	Lloyd Johnson
1929	13:57.6	Alfred Pope	51:56	Cecil Hyde	2:49:32	Dick Edge
1930	13:46.8	Cecil Hyde	50:24	Cecil Hyde	2:40:47sh?	Dick Edge
1931	13:52.6	Alfred Pope	51:28	Albert Fletcher	2:40:56	Thomas Green
1932	13:44.6	Albert Cooper	50:33	Albert Plumb	2:40:00sh?	Harry Taylor
1933	13:39.8	Albert Cooper	51:22	Fred Redman	2:40:02	Lloyd Johnson
1934	13:41.0	Albert Cooper	52:10.4	Johnny Johnson	2:38:45	Stan Fletcher
1935	13:30.2	Albert Cooper	52:39	Albert Cooper	2:39:41	Dick Edge
1936	13:50.0	Albert Cooper	50:55	Don Brown	2:42:02	Lloyd Johnson
1937	13:45.0	Albert Cooper	51:13.0	Harry Churcher	2:42:43	Stan Fletcher
1938	13:57.4	David Richards	52:01	Harry Churcher	2:46:45	Stan Fletcher
1939	13:50.0	Harry Churcher	52:37.0	Harry Churcher	2:39:43	Stan Fletcher
1940						
1945						
1946	14:04.6	Harry Churcher	52:19	Jack Rutland	2:50:45	Harry Forbes
1947	13:56.0	Harry Churcher	52:48.4t	Harry Churcher	2:47:40	Harry Forbes
1948	13:49.3	Harry Churcher	51:43	Harry Churcher	2:46:59	Johnny Henderson
1949	14:02.0	Harry Churcher	51:02.2t	Harry Churcher	2:49:42	Lawrence Allen
1950	13:42.0	Roland Hardy	50:11.6t	Roland Hardy	2:43:20	John Proctor
1951	13:43.2	Roland Hardy	51:09.8	Roland Hardy	2:45:01	Lloyd Johnson
1952	13:27.8	Roland Hardy	49:28.6	Roland Hardy	2:49:28	John Proctor
1953	14:02.2	George Coleman	51:47.0	Roland Hardy	2:49:58	Don Tunbridge
1954	13:48.2	George Coleman	51:22.98	George Coleman	2:41:40	Roland Hardy
1955	13:37.6	Gareth Howell	51:52.6	Roland Hardy	2:40:08	George Coleman
1956	13:54.0	Joe Barraclough	50:19.0	George Coleman	2:38:27	Roland Hardy
1957	13:41.4	Gareth Howell	51:34.4	Stan Vickers	2:44:01	Don Thompson
1958	13:33.4	Stan Vickers	50:09.0	Stan Vickers	2:43:21	Lawrence Allen
1959	13:19.4	Ken Matthews	49:47,4	Ken Matthews	2:37:30	Tom Misson
1960	13:02.4	Stan Vickers	48:53.0+	Ken Matthews	2:38:48	Don Thompson
1861	13:24.6	Ken Matthews	48:24.0	Ken Matthews	2:42:47	Don Thompson
1962	13:15.0	Ken Matthews	52:05.0	Colin Wlliams	2:38:39	Ken Matthews
1963	13:18.2	Ken Matthews	49:52.8	Ken Matthews	2:39:43	Paul Nihlll
1964	13:19.45	Ken Matthews	48:22.2+	Ken Matthews	2:38:21	Paul Nihlll
1965	13:19.6	Paul Nihlll	49:45.0	Paul Nihlll	2:42:28	Don Thompson
1966	13:24.6	Paul Nihlll	49:50.0+	Ron Wallwork	2:39:08	Paul Nihlll
1967	13:34.2	Geoffrey Toone	51:26.0+	Arthur Jones	2:42:43	Roy Lodge
1968	13:16.0	Geoffrey Toone	49:55.0	Paul Nihlll	2:35:07	Paul Nihlll
	3000 Metres Track		10,000 Metres Track			
1969	12:09.0	Paul Nihlll	43:20.4	Paul Nihlll	2:38:33	Brian Eley
1970	12:13.8	Paul Nihlll	43:54.4	Geoffrey Toone	2:37:22	Ron Wallwork
1971	11:51.2	Paul Nihlll	41:55.6	Phil Embleton	2:30:35	Paul Nihlll
1972	12:12.0	Paul Nihlll	42:34.6	Paul Nihlll	2:35:19	Ron Wallwork
1973	12:16.8	Roger Mills	43:51.2	Roger Mills	2:32:34	John Warhurst
1974	12:08.2	Roger Mills	43:50.4	Roger Mills	2:34:25.4t	John Warhurst
1975	12:13.2	Roger Mills	42:40.0	Brian Adams	2:36:26	Bob Dobson
1976	12:02.2+*	Brian Adams (12:52.6M)	42:58.0	Brian Adams	2:32:13	Roger Mills

	3000 Metres Track			10,000 Metres Track		30 Kilometres Track	
1977	12:08.36	Roger Mills	43:25.0	Brian Adams	2:34:45	Brian Adams
1978	11:59.10	Roger Mills	43:44.0	Brian Adams	2:52:30	David Cotton (35km)
1979	12:09.07	Roger Mills	43:14.2	Roger Mills	2:29:08	Amos Seddon
1980	11:59.1	Roger Mills	42:41.6	Mick Greasley	2:23:04	George Nibre
1981	11:44.68	Roger Mills	42:06.35	Gordon Vale	2:19:42	Murray Lambden
1982	11:53.46	Steve Barry	41:13.62	Steve Barry	2:10:16	Steve Barry
1983	11:48.03	Phl Vesty	40:54.7	Steve Barry	2:28:43	Chris Maddocks (31.5k)
1984	11:28.4	Phil Vesty	40:53.60	Phil Vesty	2:19:18t	Chris Maddocks
1985	11:41.73	Ian McCombie	41:05.8	Ian McCombie	2:11:09	Chris Maddocks
1986	11:35.2	Phil Vesty	41:24.7	Martin Rush	2:07:56	Ian McCombie
1987	11:34.9	Mark Easton	40:45.87	Ian McCombie	2:23:17	Les Morton
1988	11:32.2	Ian McCombie	40:39.77	Ian McCombie	2:19:26	Paul Blagg
1989	11:24.4	Mark Easton	40:06.65	Ian McCombie	2:11:38	Chris Maddocks
1990	11:31.0	Andi Drake	40:47.5+	Ian McCombie	2:09:20	Ian McCombie
1991	11:39.54	Andrew Penn	40:55.6	Martin Rush		
1992	11:42.5	Steve Partington	41:22.0+	Ian McCombie	2:19:58	Steve Partington
1993	11:40.54i	Martin Rush	41:33.0	Darrell Stone	2:16:52	Steve Partington
1994	11:52.2	Steve Partington	42:23.0	Steve Partington	2:11:30	Darrell Stone
1995	11:33.4	Steve Partington	41:10.11	Darrell Stone	2:18:41	Chris Maddocks
1996	11:52.6	Steve Partington	42:29.73	Steve Partington		
1997	11:35.5	Andrew Penn	42:21.89	Andrew Penn	2:29:45	Allan King
1998	11:59.47	Martin Bell	41:48.81	Martin Bell	2:30:25	Allan King
1999	11:56.72i	Andi Drake	42:14.69	Andi Drake	2:21:09	Allan King
2000	11:58.0	Andi Drake	43:12.85	Matthew Hales	2:20:04+	Chris Maddocks
2001	12:02.24i	Andi Drake	43:21.0	Andi Drake	2:18:31	Steve Hollier
2002	11:55.7	Steve Hollier	42:17.1	Dominic King	2:26:47	Martin Young
2003	11:54.39	Dominic King	43:08.59	Daniel King	2:21:06+	Andi Drake
2004	11:48.72	Andi Drake	43:52.86	Daniel King	2:36:14	Matthew Hales
2005	11:34.62	Daniel King	44:40.35	Daniel King	2:34:19	Matthew Hales
2006	11:50.55	Nicholas Ball	43:50.94	Nicholas Ball	2:24:18	Andrew Penn
2007	11:58.50	Daniel King	46:31.0	Mark Williams	2:24:25+	Daniel King
2008	12:28.18	Daniel King	-		2:22:30+	Daniel King
2009	12:51.93	Alex Wright	45:26.0	Alex Wright	–	
2010	11:38.16	Alex Wright	46:15.0	Tommy Taylor	2:38:58	Tommy Taylor
2011	11:51.19	Tom Bosworth	42:07.11	Tom Bosworth	2:24:50	Daniel King
2012	11:46:05	Tom Bosworth	43:58.54	Tom Bosworth	2:26:23+	Dominic King
2013	11:23.99i	Alex Wright	42:25.06	Jamie Higgins	–	

	35 Kilometres Walk		10000 Metres Walk additions	
1991	2:36:19	Chris Maddocks	1960 42:35.6	Ken Matthews
1992	2:38:11	Martin Rush	1961 43:02.6	Ken Matthews
1993	2:42:13	Mark Easton	1963 43:23.0	Ken Matthews
1994	2:48:50	Graham White	1964 42:52.0	Ken Matthews
1995	2:40:49	Darrell Stone	1965 44:09.8	Paul Nihill
1996	2:56:03	Les Morton	1966 44:09.0	Ron Wallwork
1997	--		1967 44:48.2	Bob Hughes
1998	2:47:28	Mark Easton	1968 45:28.0	Arthur Jones
1999	2:49:45	Darrell Stone		
2000	2:46:26+	Andrew Drake		
2001	2:50:00	Mark Easton		
3002	2:34:09	Chris Cheeseman		
2003	2:41:09	Chris Cheeseman		
2004	3:06:25	Nathan Adams		
2005	–			
2006	–			
2007	2:51:59	Daniel King		
2008	–			
2009	–			
2010	–			
2011	–			
2012	2:52:21+	Dominic King		
2013	–			

BRITISH MERIT RANKINGS (1968-2013)

Columns show: Name, Points (from 12 for 1st to 1 for 12th each year), Years ranked at No.1, Years ranked in top 12, All ranking positions. Note that while 12 athletes were ranked originally each year, now only a few are each year due to the severe decline in British walking. + indicates would also rank pre-1968.

Name	Pts	Top	Years	Rankings
Men's 20 Kilometres				
Chris Maddocks	172	5	18	83-7, 84-4, 85-3, 86-2, 87-2, 88-2, 89-1, 90-6, 91-9, 92-1, 93-1, 94-6, 95-2, 96-3, 97-7, 98-4, 99-1, 00-1
Andrew Penn	168	4	17	88-5, 90-7, 91-4=, 92-2, 93-2=, 95-5, 96-4, 97-1, 98-5, 00-2, 01-1, 02-1, 03-1, 04-4, 05-2, 06-4, 07-2
Roger Mills	143.5	4	16	69-10, 70-6, 72-3, 73-1, 74-1, 75-3, 76-3=, 77-2, 78-3, 79-1, 80-1 81-3, 82-5, 83-4, 84-8, 85-10
Ian McCombie	135	6	12	81-2, 82-2, 83-3, 84-2, 85-1, 86-1, 87-1, 88-1, 89-2, 90-1, 91-1, 92-4
Darrell Stone	134	4	14	88-4, 89-4, 91-6=, 92-7, 93-2=, 94-1, 95-1, 96-1, 97-2, 98-1, 99-4, 00=-3, 01-7, 10-5
Steve Partington	134	1	18	85-9, 87-12, 88-11, 89-8=, 90-4=, 91-4=, 92-6, 93-4, 94-3, 95-3, 96-2, 97-4, 98-6, 00-7, 01-4, 02-2, 04-6, 06-1
Mark Easton	121	0	15	85-4=, 87-5, 89-3, 90-2, 91-2, 92-8=, 93-6, 94-5, 97-3, 99-7, 00-7, 01-5, 02-6, 03-5, 04-5
Andrew Drake	111.5	0	13	86-11, 87-4, 88-4, 89-6, 90-3, 91-6=, 98-3, 99-3, 00-4, 02-3, 03-2, 04-3. 05-5
Daniel King	104.5	4	10	03-3=, 04-1, 05-1, 06-2, 07-1, 08-1, 09-3, 10-7, 11-3, 13-3
Dominic King	92.5	0	10	02-4, 03-3=, 04-2, 05-3, 06-3, 07-3, 09-2, 10-8, 11-5, 13-4
Amos Seddon	85.5	0	11	72-11, 73-4, 74-2, 75-4, 76-5, 77-7=, 78-4, 79-3, 80-2=, 81-7, 82-7
Olly Flynn	79.5	3+1T	8	72-12, 74-3, 75-1=, 76-1, 77-1, 78-1, 79-2, 80-2=
Paul Nihill +	75	4	7	68-1, 69-1, 70-2=, 71-1, 72-1, 75-6, 76-3=
Shaun Lightman	68.5	0	10	68-4, 69-4, 70-4, 71-3, 72-7, 73-6, 75-12=, 76-9, 77-4, 78-8
Martin Rush	63.5	0	9	83-10, 84-6, 85-4=, 86-3, 87-7, 90-10, 91-3, 92-3, 93-7
Phil Vesty	62.5	1	7	81-10, 82-3, 83-2, 84-1, 85-2, 86-4=, 87-6
Martin Bell	60	0	9	89-12, 91-12, 92-5, 93-8, 94-2, 95-4, 97-6, 98-2, 99-6
Les Morton	59	0	12	85-8, 86-6, 87-3, 88-9, 89-8=, 90-12, 91-8, 92-8=, 93-5, 95-9, 97-11, 98-9
Steve Barry	57	3	6	79-12, 80-2=, 81-1, 82-1, 83-1, 84-3
Chris Cheeseman	56	0	8	94-4, 95-6, 96-5, 97-9, 98-7, 99-2, 01-6, 02-9
John Warhurst	46.5	0	9	68-6, 69-7, 72-4=, 73-2, 74-8=, 75-10, 76-11, 77-9=, 78-11
Alex Wright	45	2	4	10-3, 11-1, 12-2, 13-1
Tom Bosworth	45	1	4	10-2, 11-2, 12-1, 13-2
Ben Wears	39	0	4	08-2, 10-4, 11-4, 12-3
Allan King	37.5	0	8	79-7=, 80-9, 81-11, 82-8-, 83-5, 85-6=, 93-9, 99-10
Bill Sutherland	35.5	0	5	68-10, 69-5, 70-5, 71-5, 72-4=
John Webb	35	0	5	68-2, 69-3, 70-1, 71-11, 73-7
Steve Hollier	33	0	5	98-8, 99-9, 00-6, 01-2, 02-7
Peter Fullager (to AUS)	31.5	0	4	68-3, 69-2, 70-2=
Ron Wallwork	31	1	5	68-9, 70-1, 71-4, 72-10, 73-10
Phil Embleton	30	0	4	69-9, 70-9, 71-2, 72-2
Jimmy Ball	29.5	0	9	84-11, 85-12, 86-8, 87-8, 88-7=, 89-11, 90-8, 91-10, 92-12
Peter Kaneen	29	0	4	03-7, 05-6, 06-6, 07-4
Matthew Hales	26	0	4	99-8, 00-5, 01-3, 02-10
Chris Harvey	25.5	0	4	77-9=, 78-6, 79-4, 80-5=
Luke Finch	24	2	2	09-1, 10-1
Graham Morris	23.5	0	5	77-9=, 78-10, 79-6, 80-11, 81-4
Sean Martindale	22.5	0	3	88-7=, 89-5, 90-4=
Paul Blagg	21	0	6	82-4, 83-11, 84-10, 85-11, 86-9, 88-12
Tim Berrett (to CAN)	21	0	3	84-5, 88-6, 89-7
Jamie O'Rawe	20	0	5	95-10, 97-10, 98-12, 99-5, 00-8
Men's 50 Kilometres				
Bob Dobson	183.5	2	26	69-9, 70-2, 71-2, 72-4, 73-2, 74-1, 75-2, 76-1, 77-3, 78-4, 79-3, 80-7, 81-3, 82-4, 83-9, 84-8=, 85-10, 86-10, 87-9=, 88-6, 89-5, 90-7 91-12=, 92-11, 93-9, 97-10
Les Morton	163	9	15	84-8=, 85-1, 86-1, 87-2, 88-1, 89-1, 90-1, 91-1, 92-1, 93-1, 94-1 95-2, 97-3, 98-5. 99-2
Chris Maddocks	131.5	6+1T	12	78-6, 79-4, 80-1=, 83-1, 84-1, 90-2, 91-3, 92-2, 95-1, 96-1, 97-1, 00-1
Dennis Jackson	102	0	11	80-4, 81-4, 83-2, 84-5, 85-2, 86-3, 87-3, 91-4, 92-8, 93-3, 96-4
Chris Berwick	101.5	0	16	84-12=, 85-5, 86-6=, 87-7, 88-5, 89-3, 90-6, 91-5, 92-6, 93-6, 94-3, 95-8, 96-9, 97-9, 98-10, 99-5

14

Name	Score			Details
Paul Blagg	94	1	9	83-4, 84-2, 85-3, 86-3, 87-1, 88-2, 90-3, 91-2, 92-3
John Warhurst	85.5	1	11	69-4, 70-4, 71-6, 72-2, 74-2, 75-1, 76-9, 77-2, 78-11, 81-7=, 82-9
Michael Smith	85	0	12	85-10, 86-5, 87-6, 89-2, 91-8, 98-9, 99-4, 00-10, 01-5, 02-7, 03-2, 03-3
Ray Middleton +	76.5	1	9	68-4, 69-2=, 70-1, 71-5, 72-5, 73-3, 74-5=, 75-7, 77-7=
Scott Davis	76	2	7	05-3, 06-2, 07-2, 08-3, 09-1, 10-1, 11-3
Barry Graham	72.5	1T	8	81-2, 82-1=, 83-3, 84-4, 85-4, 86-4, 87-4. 88-9
Chris Cheeseman	72	1	7	96-2, 97-4, 98-3, 99-1, 00-3, 01-2. 02-4
Adrian James	70	1+1T	12	76-10=, 77-12, 78-5, 79-1, 80-3, 81-5, 82-1=, 83-11, 84-11, 85-8, 87-9=. 88-7
Steve Hollier	64	1	6	98-2, 99-3, 00-2, 01-1, 02-2. 05-4
Mark Easton	63	2	6	92-4, 95-3, 97-2, 98-1, 00-4, 02-1
Daniel King	58	3	5	07-1, 08-1, 11-2, 12-2, 13-1
Shaun Lightman	53	7	1	68-3, 69-2=, 72-8, 73-1, 76-10=, 77-4=, 78-7
Brian Adams	47	2	7	73-11, 74-5=, 77-1, 78-1, 79-9=, 80-8, 82-8
Steve Partington	46	3	5	93-10, 96-6, 04-1, 05-1, 06-1
Allan King	43.5	0	7	83-5, 84-6=, 85-9, 92-5, 96-8, 97-7, 98-7
Peter Kaneen	40	0	5	00-7, 01-6, 02-6, 04-2, 05-2
Karl Atton	39	0	5	96-7, 97-5, 98-6, 01-3, 02-5
Tim Watt	37	0	5	94-2, 95-4, 97-8, 98-8, 00-65
Paul Nihill +	36	3	3	68-1, 71-1, 72-1
Graham White	36	0	4	94-4, 95-5, 96-3, 98-4
Gordon Vale	35	0	5	81-10, 82-7, 83-6, 84-3, 88-4
Ken Harding	31	0	7	69-10, 70-6, 71-8, 72-9, 73-7, 74-9, 75-11
Darren Thorn	31	0	5	85-11=, 86-6=, 89-4, 90-5, 91-7
Gareth Brown	31	0	4	95-6, 96-5, 00-6, 02-10
Alec Banyard	29.5	0	6	71-11, 72-10, 73-6, 74-4, 75-6, 76-10=
Charles Fogg	26.5	-	5	69-6, 70-10, 74-12=, 75-4, 76-6
Darrell Stone	26	0	3	90-4, 00-5, 01-4
Brian Eley	23	1	2	68-2, 69-1
Dominic King	35	2	3	08-2, 11-1, 12-1
George Chaplin	21	0	4	68-8, 69-5, 70-12, 72-6
Ed Shillabeer	20.5	0	7	85=11=, 86=11=, 88-12=, 89-6. 90-10, 91-1, 93-8
Ron Wallwork	20	0	2	70-3, 71-3

Women ranked from 1973

Name	Score			Details
Lisa Langford/Kehler	258	9	25	83-9, 84-7, 85-3, 86-3, 87-1, 88-2, 89-1, 90-1, 92-3, 94-2, 95-1, 96-3, 97-1, 98-1, 00-1, 01-6, 02-1, 03-3, 05-7, 07-2, 08-3, 09-2, 10-2, 11-1, 12-2
Victoria Lupton	115	5	11	88-10, 90-5, 91-2, 92-1, 93-1, 94-1, 95-2, 96-1, 97-2, 98-2, 99-1,
Johanna Jackson	102	8	9	04-7, 05-1, 06-1, 07-1, 08-1, 09-1, 10-1, 11-1, 12-1
Niobe Menendez	101	2	10	98-10, 99-3, 00-2, 01-1, 02-2, 04-1, 05-2, 06-4, 08-2, 10-3
Sylvia Saunders/Black	98.5	0	14	74-3, 75-6, 76-5, 77- 5, 78- 8=, 89-9, 90-6, 91-5, 92-4, 93-4, 94-7, 95-8, 96-10, 97-3
Virginia Lovell/Birch	93.5	1	12	73-5, 75-2=, 77-6, 78-5, 79-8, 81-10, 82-5, 83-3, 84-2, 85-1, 86-4, 87-11
Verity Larby/Snook	82	0	11	89-11, 90-7, 91-6, 92-6, 93-3, 94-3, 95-4, 96-2, 97-4, 05-10, 07-5
Julie Drake	78	0	10	85-11=, 86-8, 87-7, 88-3, 89-3, 90-3, 91-4, 92-7, 93-2, 11-3
Marion Fawkes	76	3	7	73-7, 74-1, 75-1, 76-1, 77-2, 78-2, 79-1
Irene Bateman	75.5	2+1T	8	76-10, 77- 4, 78-6, 79-3, 80-2, 81-1=, 82-1, 83-1
Helen Elleker	74.5	0	8	83-7, 84-4=, 85-2, 86-2, 87-3, 89-4, 90-4, 91-3
Sarah Brown	72	0	12	80-7, 81-7, 82-4, 83-8, 85-8, 86-6, 87-5.=, 88-5, 89-6, 90-8, 91-8, 92-10
Sarah-Jane Cattermole	71	0	8	99-4, 00-3, 01-3, 02-4, 03-4, 04-3, 05-4, 06-8
Carol Tyson	69.5	3+1T	6	76-2, 77-1, 78-1, 79-2, 80-1, 81-1=
Betty Sworowski	67	2	7	86-7, 87-9, 88-1, 89-2, 90-2, 91-1, 92-2
Elaine Cox/Callinan	66.5	0	12	74-10, 75-10, 76-8, 77-10, 78-8=, 79-5, 80-3, 81-5, 93-4, 94-8, 95-7, 00-8
Beverley Francis/Allen	65	1	12	75-12, 76-11, 77-7=, 78-7, 79-7, 80-8, 81-11, 83-10, 84-10, 85-4, 86-1, 87-2
Kim Baird/Braznell	61	0	9	93-9, 94-10, 95-6, 96-6, 97-6, 98-4, 99-5, 00-5, 02-5
Sharon Tonks	58	0	8	98-8, 99-12, 00-4, 01-2, 02-3, 03-2, 04-10, 05-5
Carolyn Partington	53	0	7	93-6, 94-4, 95-3, 96-5, 97-10, 98-3, 02-7
Nicola Jackson	51	0	7	84-3, 85-7, 86-5, 87-4, 88-4, 89-5, 94-12
Melanie Brookes/Wright	50	0	8	90-9, 91-9, 92-5, 93-5, 94-6, 95-5, 96-4, 98-11
Sophie Hales	42	0	6	02-8, 03-5, 04-5, 05-11, 06-4, 07-3
Karen Keale/Ratcliffe	38	0	7	94-9, 95-9, 96-7, 97-7, 98-7, 01-8, 02-6

Joanne Hesketh	34	0	5	01-7, 02-10, 03-6, 04-4, 11-4
Katie Stones	34	0	5	02-11, 03-7, 04-8, 05-3, 06-2
Catherine Charnock	31	0	5	97-8, 98-5, 99-2, 00-10, 0-9
Pamela Branson	31	0	4	74-3, 75-4, 76-6, 77-4=
Diane Bradley	30	0	4	08-4, 09-3, 10-5, 11-6
Rebecca Mersh	27	0	4	04-6, 05-8, 06-5, 07-6
Heather Lewis	27	0	3	11-7, 12-3, 13-2
Lisa Simpson	25	0	6	85-9, 86-11, 87-8, 88-6, 89-7, 90-12
Bethan Davies	21	1	2	12-4, 13-1
Jane Kennaugh/Gibson	21	0	4	99-9, 00-6, 01-4, 02-12

WORLD RANKINGS (*TRACK AND FIELD NEWS*)
Men – ranked from 1970
Paul Nihill   20km: 1971-3, 1972-5; 50km: 1971-9
Phil Embleton   20km: 1971-6
Roger Mills   20km: 1974-4
Brian Adams   20km: 1975-10
Women – ranked from 1987: None

UK Venue abbreviations
London (xx)
BH   Beaufort House, Brompton
BP   Battersea Park
CP   Crystal Palace
Cr   Croydon
Elt   Sutcliffe Park, Eltham
Ha   Haringey
He   Copthall Stadium, Hendon
Isl   Islington
LB   Liilie Bridge
LV   Lea Valley, Enfield
Pa   Paddington
RP   Regent's Park
QC   Queen's Club
SB   London (SB)
TB   Tooting Bec
WC   White City
WF   Waltham Forest
WL   West London
Belfast   M   Mary Peters
Cardiff   L   Leckwith
                    M   Maindy
Dublin   S   Santry
Edinburgh   G   Goldenacre
                    M   Meadowbank
                    Mf   Murrayfeild
Glasgow   S   Scotstoun
Manchester C   City
                    F   Fallowfield
                    SC   Sports City
                    Str   Stretford

Women Name Changes
Marion Adamson	Fawkes
Kim Baird	Braznell
Susan Booth	Howard
Melanie Brookes	Wright
Sarah Brown	Sowerby
Claire Childs	Walker
Elaine Cox	Calinan
Catherine Duhig	Reader
Maureen Eyre	Graham
Judy Farr	Woodsford
Beverley Francis	Allen
Betty Franklin	Jenkins
Audrey Hackett	Price
Joyce Holmes	Heath
Jessie Howes	Jones
Johanna Jackson	Atkinson
Jane Kennaugh	Gibson
Lisa Langford	Kehler
Verity Larby	Snook
Marie Latham	Jackson
Nellie Loines	Batson
Virginia Lovell	Birch
Sheila Martin	Jennings
Helen Milne	Vincent
Roma Phillips	Joyce
Jeanne Probekk	Williams
Beryl Randle	Day
Fiona Rose	Edgington
Sylvia Saunders	Black
Karen Smith	Ratcliffe
Dilys Williams	Rayworth

PERFORMANCES IN MAJOR CHAMPIONSHIPS

OLYMPIC GAMES – Track Walks

1906 Athens
1500m and 3000m: dq Richard Wilkinson
1908 London 3500m heats July 13, final July 14
1	George Larner	14:55.0	1h1 15:32.0
2	Ernest Webb	15:07.4	1h2 15:17.2
dnf	William Palmer	–	3h1 16:33.0
dq	Richard Harrison	–	2h3 16:04.4
	Ernest Larner		4h3 16:10.0
	John Butler		5h3 16:17.0
	Sydney Sarel		5h1 17:06.0
	William Brown		dq h1(16:10.0)
	Alfred Yeoumans		dq h1
	Richard Quinn		dq h2
	John Reid		dq h2

10 Miles heats July 15, final July 17
1	George Larner	1:15:57.4	1h2 1:18.19.0
2	Ernest Webb	1:17:31.0	1h1 1:20:18.8
3	Edward Spencer	1:21:20.2	2=h1 1:21:25.4
4	Frank Carter	1:21:26.2	2=h1 1:21:25.4
5	Ernest Larner	1:21:26.2	2=h1 1:21:25.4
dnf	Richard Harrison	–	2h2 1:18:21.2
dnf	William Palmer	–	4h2 1:19:04.0
	Godwin Withers		5h2 1:19:22.4
	Sydney Schofield		6h2 1:21:07.4
	Tommy Hammond		6h1 1:23.44.0
	Alfred Yeoumans		dq h1
	Jack Butler		dnf h2

20 KILOMETRES ROAD

1956 Melbourne November 28
5	Stan Vickers	1:32:34.2
7	George Coleman	1:34:01.8
8	Roland Hardy	1:34:40.4

1960 Rome September 2
3	Stan Vickers	1:34:56.4
10	Eric Hall	1:38:54.0
dnf	Ken Matthews	–

1964 Tokyo October 10
1	Ken Matthews	1:29:34.0
8	John Edgington	1:32:46.0
10	John Paddick	1:33:28.4

1968 Mexico City October 14
11	Arthur Jones	1:37:32.0
22	John Webb	1:42:51
24	Robert Hughes	1:43:50

1972 Munich August 31
6	Paul Nihill	1:28:44.4
14	Phil Embleton	1:33:22.2
17	Peter Marlow	1:35:38.8

1976 Montreal July 23
11	Brian Adams	1:30:46.2
14	Olly Flynn	1:31:42.4
30	Paul Nihill	1:36:40.4

1980 Moscow July 24
10	Roger Mills	1:32:37.8

1984 Los Angeles August 3
13	Phil Vesty	1:27:28
19	Ian McCombie	1:28:53
24	Steve Barry	1:30:46

1988 Seoul September 23
13	Ian McCombie	1:22:03
24	Chris Maddocks	1:23:46

1992 Barcelona July 31
16	Chris Maddocks	1:28:45

23	Andrew Penn	1:31:40
24	Martin Rush	1:31:56

50 KILOMETRES

1932 Los Angeles August 3
1	Tommy Green	4:50:10

1936 Berlin August 5
1	Harold Whitlock	4:30:41.4
17	Lloyd Johnson	4:54:56.0
dnf	Joseph Hopkins	

1948 London July 31
3	Lloyd Johnson	4:48:31
5	Bert Martineau	4:53:58
dnf	Rex Whitlock	

1952 Helsinki July 31
4	Rex Whitlock	4:32:21.0
11	Harold Whitlock	4:45:12.6
15	Don Tunbridge	4:50:40.4

1956 Melbourne November 24
8	Albert Johnson	5:02:19
9	Eric Hall	5:03.59

1960 Rome September 7
1	Don Thompson	4:25:30.0
5	Thomas Misson	4:33:03.0
dq	Albert Johnson	–

1964 Tokyo October 18
2	Paul Nihill	4:11:31.2
10	Don Thompson	4:22:39.4
13	Ray Middleton	4:25:49.2

1968 Mexico City October 17
7	Bryan Eley	4:37:32.2
18	Shaun Lightman	4:52:20.0
dnf	Paul Nihill	–

1972 Munich September 3
9	Paul Nihill	4:14:09.4
18	John Warhurst	4:23:21.6
25	Howard Timms	4:34:43.8

1912 Stockholm 10,000m heats July 8, final July 12
2	Ernest Webb	46:50.4	2h1 47:25.4
dnf	William Palmer	–	5h1 51:21.0
dq	George Yates	–	1h2 49:43.6
dq	Thomas Dumbill	–	3h2 50:57.6
	Robert Bridge		dnf h2

1920 Antwerp 3000m heats Aug 19, final Aug 20
6	Charles Dowson	13:28.0e	4h1 13:54.9e
7	William Hehir	13:29.8e	5= ht2
10	Charles Gunn	13:34.0e	5= h2

10,000m heats Aug 15, final Aug 16
3	Charles Gunn	49:43.9e	5h1 48:22.0
5	William Hehir	50:11.8	1h2 51:33.8
	Charles Dowson		dnf h1

1924 Paris 10,000m heats July 9, final July 13
2	Reg Goodwin	48:37.9	1h1 49:04.0
6	Fred Clark	49:59.2	5h2 ntt
	Gordon Watts		dq h2

1948 London 10,000m heats Aug 3, final Aug 7
4	James Morris	46:04.0	2h1 45:10.4
5	Harry Churcher	46:28.0	1h2 46:26.4
7	Ronald West	–	3h2 47:11.6

1952 Helsinki 10,000m heats July 25, final July 27
5	George Coleman	46:06.8	1h2 46:12.4
	Roland Hardy		dq h1
	Lawrence Allen		dq h2

1980 Moscow July 31
11	Ian Richards	4:22:57

1984 Los Angeles August 11
16	Chris Maddocks	4:26:33

1988 Seoul September 30
27	Les Morton	3:59:30
28	Paul Blagg	4:00:07

1992 Barcelona August 7
21	Les Morton	4:09:34
30	Paul Blagg	4:23:10

1996 Atlanta August 2
34	Chris Maddocks	4:18:41

2000 Sydney September 29
39	Chris Maddocks	4:52:12

2012 London August 11
51	Dominic King	4:15:05

WOMEN – 10 KILOMETRES

1992 Barcelona August 3
32	Betty Sworowski	50:14
35	Lisa Langford	51:44
dq	Vicky Lupton	–

1996 Atlanta July 29
33	Vicky Lupton	47:05

WOMEN – 20 KILOMETRES

2000 Sydney September 29
33	Lisa Kehler	1:37:47

2008 Beijing August 21
22	Johanna Jackson	1:31:33

2012 London August 11
dq	Johanna Jackson	–

WORLD CHAMPIONSHIPS
20 KILOMETRES

1983 Helsinki August 7
25	Phii Vesty	1:27:20
37	Roger Mills	1:30:25

41	Ian McCombie	1:31:14	9	Ron Wallwork	1:34:31.0		**20 MILES**	
1987	Rome August 30		13	John Webb	1:34:52.0	1966	1 Ron Wallwork E	2:44:42.8
9	Ian McCombie	1:23:51	**1969**	1 Paul Nihill	1:30:48.0		2 Ray Middleton E	2:45:19.0
34	Chris Maddocks	1:32:36	8	John Webb	1:35:51.0		4 Don Thompson E	2:46 43.0
1991	Tokyo August 24		13	Peter Fullager	1:38:24.0		7 Phil Bannan M	3:06:11.2
27	Ian McCombie	1:25:30	**1971**	3 Paul Nihill	1:27:34.8		8 Albert Johnson M	3:08:05.8
1993	Stuttgart August 21		6	Phil Embleton	1:29:31.6		9 Roy Hart W	3:15:02.6
26	Chris Maddocks	1:29:22	13	Bill Sutherland	1:34:15.0		dnf Howard Gawne M	–
30	Darrell Stone	1:32:55	**1974**	3 Roger Mills	1:32:33.8	1970	3 Bill Sutherland S	2:37 24
dnf	Andrew Penn	–	6	Amos Seddon	1:34:17.6		4 Bob Dobson E	2:39:55
1995	Gothenburg August 10		**1978**	21 Roger Mills	1:31:52.5		5 Ron Wallwork E	2:40:10
25	Darrell Stone	1:28:48	25	Brian Adams	1:33 08.2		6 Len Duquemin G	2:42:48
2013	Moscow August 21		26	Amos Seddon	1:34:17.8		7 Shaun Lightman E	2:44:50
31	Alex Wright	1:26:40	**1982**	11 Steve Barry	1:31:00		10 John Moullin G	2:48:07
	50 KILOMETRES		13	Ian McCombie	1:32:36		11 Dave Rosser W	2:49:41
1976	Malmö September 18		**1990**	16 Mark Easton	1:31:06		13 Allan Callow M	2:51:21
13	Bob Dobson	4:10:20	dq	Andi Drake	–		14 Dave Smyth Ni	2:53:49
32	Roy Thorpe	4:35:57	**2002**	dq Andi Drake	–		15 John Cannell M	2:56:19
dnf	Carl Lawton			**50 KILOMETRES**			16 Dave Dorey G	3:03:41
1987	Rome September 5		**1938**	1 Harold Whitlock	4:41:51	1974	1 John Warhurst E	2:35 23.0
19	Paul Blagg	3:59:55	dnf	Frank Bentley	–		2 Roy Thorpe E	2:39:02.2
1991	Tokyo August 31		**1946**	2 Harry Forbes	4:42:58		4 Graham Young M	2:42:55.2
10	Les Morton	4:09:18	3	Charles Megnin	4:57:04		8 Allan Callow M	2:53:12.2
22	Paul Blagg	4:35:22	**1950**	5 John Proctor	4:48:01		9 Len Duquemin G	2:53:37.4
24	Chris Maddocks	4:39:15	6	Alfred Cotton	5:03:30		10 John Moullin G	2:57:27.2
1993	Stuttgart August 21		**1954**	6 Frank Bailey	4:46:06.4		11 Robin Waterman G	
23	Les Morton	4:06:56	dnf	Albert Johnson	–			3:00:14.2
1995	Gothenburg August 10		**1958**	4 Tom Misson	4:20:31.8		12 Derek Harrison M	
dq	Les Morton	–	5	Don Thompson	4:25:09.0			3:00:32.4
	WOMEN – 10 KILOMETRES		**1962**	3 Don Thompson	4:29:00.2		dnf Carl Lawton E	–
1987	Rome September 1		13	Ray Hall	4:55:47.0		**30 KILOMETRES**	
13	Lisa Langford	46:23	dq	Ray Middleton	–	1978	1 Olly Flynn E	2:22:03.7
25	Beverley Allen	48:50	**1966**	5 Ray Middleton	4:23:01.0		2 Brian Adams E	2:29:14.5
1991	Tokyo August 24		9	Don Thompson	4:27:11.2		5 Amos Seddon E	2:29:57.5
20	Betty Sworowski	45:59	**1969**	5 Ray Middleton	4:27:00		8 Graham Young M	2:33:14.9
38	Helen Elleker	48:56	dnf	Bryan Eley	–		dnf Allan Callow M	–
39	Julie Drake	49:47	dnf	Shaun Lightman	–		dnf Robbie Lambie M	–
1993	Stuttgart August 14		**1971**	16 Bob Dobson	4:21:15.0	1982	1 Steve Barry W	2:10:16
23	Vicky Lupton	47:03	dnf	Ron Wallwork	–		7 Roger Mills E	2:21:54
29	Verity Larby	47:54	dnf	Carl Lawton	–		8 Murray Lambden M	2:22:12
42	Julie Drake	50:22	**1974**	11 John Warhurst	4:26 34.6		10 Rob Elliott G	2:24:28
1995	Gothenburg August 10		14	Bob Dobson	4:35:26.4		12 Graham Young M	2:27:04
35	Lisa Langford	46:06	**1978**	23 Ian Richards	4:27:09.3		13 Paul Blagg E	2:30:42
	WOMEN – 20 KILOMETRES		dnf	David Cotton	–		dq Robbie Lambie M	–
2007	Osaka August 31		**1986**	18 Dennis Jackson	4:16:52	1986	3 Ian McCombie E	2:10:36
25	Johanna Jackson	1:39:34	dq	Les Morton	–		4 Chris Maddocks E	2:12:42
2009	Berlin August 16		**1990**	dnf Paul Blagg	–		7 Martin Rush E	2:16:01
dq	Johanna Jackson	–	dnf	Darrell Stone	–		8 Steve Johnson W	2:21:05
2011	Daegu August 31			**WOMEN – 10 KILOMETRES**			10 St. Partington M	2:23:05
23	Johanna Jackson	1:35:32	**1986**	14 Lisa Langford	49:21	1990	3 Ian McCombie E	2:09:20
			15	Beverley Allen	49:50		5 Mark Easton E	2:14:52
	EUROPEAN		dq	Helen Elleker	–		6 Chris Maddocks E	2:15:07
	CHAMPIONSHIPS		**1990**	10 Lisa Langford	46:33		9 St. Partington M	2:20:11
	10,000 METRES TRACK		15	Betty Sworowski	47:37	1994	4 Darrell Stone E	2:11:30
1950	dq Lawrence Allen	–	20	Julie Drake	49:26		7 St. Partington M	2:14:15
	dq Roland Hardy	–	**1994**	20 Vicky Lupton	46:30		12 Chris Maddocks E	2:18:14
1954	5 Bryan Hawkins	46:52.8	23	Verity Snook	47:23		13 Mark Easton E	2:20:10
	9 George Coleman	47:37.4	dq	Lisa Langford	–		14 Steve Taylor M	2:21:34
	20 KILOMETRES		**1998**	18 Lisa Kehler	45:42		**30 KILOMETRES**	
1958	1 Stan Vickers	1:33:09.0		**WOMEN – 20 KILOMETRES**		1998	4 Darrell Stone E	1:26:37
	11 Albert Johnson	1:41:54.4	2010	10 Johanna Jackson	1:33:33		7 Martin Bell S	1:28:20
1962	1 Ken Matthews	1:35:54.8		**COMMONWEALTH GAMES**			10 Chris Maddocks E	1:30:21
	11 Bob Clark	1:41:30.0	E England, G Guernsey				12 Andi Drake E	1:32:04
	15 Arthur Thomson	1:50:08.2	M Isle of Man, N Northern Ireland,				13 St. Partington M	1:32:15
1966	7 Peter Fullager	1:33:02.4	S Scotland, W Wales			2002	4 Andy Penn E	1:29:15
							dq Dominic King E	–

	dq	Steve Partington M	–
2006	6	Daniel King E	1:31:17
	7	Dominic King E	1:32:21
	8	Andy Penn E	1:32:54
2010	10	Luke Finch E	1:29:37
	11	Tom Bosworth E	1:30:44
	13	Alex Wright E	1:34:26

50 KILOMETRES

1998	4	Steve Hollier E	4:18:41
	5	Mark Easton E	4:22:23
	6	Graham White S	4:30:17
	8	Ch Cheeseman E	4:38:36
2002	6	Steve Hollier E	4:16:46
	7	Gareth Brown E	4:40:07
	dq	Mark Easton E	–
2006	6	St. Partington M	4:25:39

WOMEN – 10 KILOMETRES

1990	3	Lisa Langford E	47:23
	7	Helen Elleker E	49:51
	dnf	Betty Sworowski E	–
1994	5	Vicky Lupton E	45:58
	6	Lisa Langford E	46:01
	7	Verity Snook S	46:06
	9	Cal Partington M	47:21
	11	Karen Smith E	48:25
1998	3	Lisa Kehler E	45:03
	6	Cal Partington M	48:09
	7	Vicky Lupton E	48:27
	8	Kim Braznell E	51:15
	10	Karen Kneale M	52:25

WOMEN – 20 KILOMETRES

2002	2	Lisa Kehler E	1:36 45
	7	Niobe Menendez E	1:46:16
	8	Sharon Tonks E	1:49:21
	9	S-J Cattermole S	1:50 29
	dnf	Cal Partington M	–
2006	7	Jo Jackson E	1:42:04
	8	Niobe Menendez E	1:47:35
2010	1	Jo Jackson E	1:34:22
	4	Lisa Kehler E	1:40:33

EUROPEAN INDOOR CHAMPIONSHIPS

5000 METRES TRACK
1990 12 Andi Drake 20:10.83

WOMEN 3000 METRES TRACK
1988 12 Lisa Langford 13:32.30
1990 9h1 Sylvia Black 13:35.52

WORLD JUNIOR CHAMPIONSHIPS

10,000 METRES TRACK
1986 19 Darrell Stone 44:57.50
2002 dq Dominic King –

WOMEN 5000 METRES TRACK
1986	13	Julie Drake	24:39.11
	21	Vicky Lawrence	26:36.70
1988	11	Julie Drake	24:37.42
1990	5	Vicky Lupton	22:51.24
1994	21	Nina Howley	25:12.23

WORLD YOUTH CHAMPIONSHIPS

10,000 METRES TRACK
2001 23 Cameron Smith 47:42.76

	dnf	Luke Finch	–
2005	15	Nick Ball	47:15.51
2007	dnf	Ben Wears	dnf

WOMEN 5000 METRES TRACK
1999	15	Amy Hales	24:52.61
2001	15	Sophie Hales	26:35.46
2005	16	Rebecca Mersh	25:21.79

EUROPEAN U23 CHAMPIONSHIPS

20 KILOMETRES
2001 dq Matt Hales –

WOMEN 20 KILOMETRES
2007 7 Jo Jackson 1:36:28

EUROPEAN JUNIOR CHAMPIONSHIPS

10.000 METRES TRACK
1970	12	Chris Eyre	47:10.0
	18	Peter Dallow	49:45.2
1973	14	Jacky Lord	48:50.8
1977	12	Graham Morris	47:07.2
1979	6	Gordon Vale	43:31.98
1981	7	Gordon Vale	43:05.57
1983	4	Tim Berrett	43:04.09
1987	4	Darrell Stone	41:52.13
	9	Gareth Brown	43:54.25
1991	17	Phil King	46:49.40
2001	dq	Lloyd Finch	–

WOMEN 5000 METRES TRACK
1985	7	Lisa Langford	23:21.67
	17	Susan Ashforth	25:40.96
1987	10	Julie Drake	24:13.50
	13	Vicky Lawrence	24:53.86
1991	4	Vicky Lupton	22:41.10
	dq	Sarah Brown	–
	dnf	Theresa Ashman	–
1997	25	Nikki Huckerby	25:56.82

WOMEN'S WORLD GAMES

1000 METRES TRACK
1926 1 Daisy Crossley 5:10.0

WORLD CUP

From its inception in Lugano, Switzerland in 1961, there was a team and individual competition of race walking for men for the Lugano Trophy. From 1975 a Women's race was held in conjunction for the Eschborn Cup (named after its first venue in Germany). From 1979 the IAAF have run the event as the IAAF World Race Walking Cup.

LUGANO TROPHY

1961 Qual. London (WP) 12 Aug 20 Km
1	Ken Matthews	1:32:12.4
5	George Williams	1:32:04.2
6	Robert Clark	1:38:19.0

50 Km
1	Don Thompson	4:25:19.2
3	Ray Middleton	4:41:03.2
5	Charles Fogg	4:47:04.4

Team: GB 41, FRG 39, BEL 12
FINAL – Rancate/Lugano ITA

50 Km Oct 15 Rancare
2	Don Thompson	4:30 35.0
4	Ray Middleton	4:39:24.0
9	Charles Fogg	4:49:22.0

20 Km Oct 16 Lugano
1	Ken Matthews	1:30:54.2
3	George Williams	1:34:02.0
7	Robert Clark	1:36 51.2

GB 54, SWE 54, ITA 28, HUN 23

1963 Qual. Challes-les-Eaux
Sept 14 20 Km
1	Ken Matthews	1:33 07.4
3	Paul Nihill	1:35:04.0
4	Vaughan Thomas	1:41:04.2

Sept 15 50 Km
1	Ray Middleton	4:27:06.0
4	Charles Fogg	4:45:07.0
6	Ron Wallwork	4:48:14.0

GB 25, FRA 19
FINAL Varese
Oct 12 50 Km
2	Ray Middleton	4:17:15.4
5	Ron Wallwork	4:23:46.4
6	Charles Fogg	4:30:15.2

Oct 13:20 Km
1	Ken Matthews	1:30:10.2
2	Paul Nihill	1:33:18.4
6	John Edgington	1:35:27.0

GB 93, HUN 64, SWE 63, ITA 51, TCH 44, FRG 26

1965 Pescara
Oct 9 20 Km
4	Peter Fullager	1:31:52.0
6	Ron Wallwork	1:32:41.2
14	Malcolm Tolley	1:37:34.8

Oct 10 50 Km
4	Don Thompson	4:09.14.2
7	Ray Middleton	4:19:14.8
10	Charles Fogg	4:23:23.6

GDR 117, GB 89, HUN 64, SWE 59, ITA 54 FRG 43, FRA 39

1967 Bad Saarow
Oct 15 20 Km
6	Peter Fullager	1:31:33.4
8	John Webb	1:33:55.6
9	Ron Wallwork	1:34:53.2

Oct 15 50 Km
6	Don Thompson	4:25:21.0
8	Ray Middleton	4:29:23.0
9	Shaun Lightman	4:31:23.8

GDR 128, USSR 107, GB 104, FRG 73, SWE 52, USA 50, HUN 46, ITA 40

1970 Eschborn
Oct 10 20 Km
11	Ron Wallwork	1:31:35.8
15	Paul Nihill	1:33:09.8
18	Shaun Lightman	1:34:37.8
28	Bob Hughes	1:41:40.4

Oct 11 50 Km
11	Ray Middleton	4:19:57.2
15	Bob Dobson	4:26:58.8
21	John Warhurst	4:34:31.0
24	Ken Harding	4:42:03.2

GDR 134, USSR 125, FRG 88, GB

65, ITA 59, USA 59, SWE 40, HUN 31

1973 Qual. Borås
Sept 8 20 Km
2   Roger Mills   1:31:48.0
3   Roy Thorpe   1:33:12.0
4   John Warhurst   1:33:33.0
5   Amos Seddon   1:34:37.0
Sept 9 50 Km
1   Shaun Lightman   4:18:27.0
2   Bob Dobson   4:19:00.0
7   Ray Middleton   4:30:12.0
12 Mike Holmes   4:41:19.0
GB 97, SWE 84, FRA 70, NOR 34, DEN 31, IRL 28
FINAL Oct 12 20 Km – Lugano
8   Roger Mils   1:32:44.4
18 John Warhurst   1:34:58.0
20 Amos Seddon   1:35:17.0
24 Roy Thorpe   1:37 40.0
Oct 13 50 Km – Rancate
12 Shaun Lightman   4:15:13.4
19 Ray Middleton   4:22:25.0
23 Bob Dobson   4:27:31.4
30 Mike Holmes   4:37:54.0
GDR 139, USSR 134, ITA 104, FRG 95, USA 95, GB 81, POL 52, SWE 40, CAN 18

1975 Qual. – Odense
Sept 20 50 Km
3   Roy Thorpe   4:25:17.0
5   Charles Fogg   4:30:16.0
6   John Warhurst   4:32:24.0
9   John Lees   4:42:59.0
Sept 21 20 Km
2   Brian Adams   1:30:18.0
3   Roger Mills   1:32:56.0
5   Amos Seddon   1:35 41.0
8   Peter Marlow   1:35:16.0
GB 90, SWE 80, POL 74, BEL 53, NOR 23
FINAL - Grand Quévilly
Oct 11 20 Km
6   Brian Adams   1:27:46
8   Olly Flynn   1:28:08
17 Roger Mills   1:30:42
28 Amos Seddon   1:35:23
Oct 12 50 Km
4   John Warhurst   4:14:35
15 Roy Thorpe   4:26:28
19 Alec Banyard   4:30:25
20 Charles Fogg   4:31:15
USSR 117, GDR 105, FRG 102, GB 102, ITA 100, HUN 76, SWE 69, FRA 59, USA 24

1977 Milton Keynes
Sept 24 20 Km
30 Mike Holmes   1:33:06
32 Mick Greasley   1:33:13
33 Roger Mills   1:33:22
39 Amos Seddon   1:34:31
Sept 25 50 Km
17 Brian Adams   4:23:54
27 Bob Dobson   4:26:09
28 John Warhurst   4:26 47
33 Peter Hodkinson   4:29:27

MEX 185, GDR 180, ITA 160,...
11 GB 69

1979 Qual. - Hove
Sept 2 20 Km
2   Roger Mills   1:27:50
3   Amos Seddon   1:29:04
5   Chris Harvey   1:29:37
9   Graham Morris   1:31:59
Sept 2 50 Km
3   Adrian James   4:09:33
9   Chris Maddocks   4:23:46
11 George Nibre   4:25 57
12 Peter Hodkinson   4:29:37
FRG 68, SWE 66, GB 65, BEL 29, NED 14
FINAL – Eschborn
Sept 29 20 Km
26 Roger Mills   1:27 25
27 Olly Flynn   1:27 49
29 Chris Harvey   1:28:26
32 Amos Seddon   1:28:56
Sept 30 50 Km
31 Adrian James   4:09:52
37 Ian Richards   4:14:47
39 George Nibre   4:18:19
43 Chris Maddocks   4:27:03
MEX 240, USSR 235, GDR 201,...
12 GB 89

1981 Qual. – Helsinki
Aug 29 20 Km
1   Steve Barry   1:26 44
2   Ian McCombie   1:28:02
7   Roger Mills   1:30:12
10 Graham Morris   1:34:22
Aug 30 50 Km
4   Dennis Jackson   4:11:16
6   Ian Richards   4:17:03
10 Barry Graham   4:22:48
11 Bob Dobson   4:23:29
GB 49, NOR 44, FRG 37, FIN 28
FINAL – Valencia
Oct 3 20 Km
17 Steve Barry   1:29:56
19 Ian McCombie   1:30:03
30 Roger Mills   1:33:30
33 Amos Seddon   1:33:52
Oct 4 50 Km
20 Ian Richards   4:21:04
28 Barry Graham   4:34:34
31 Bob Dobson   4:36:13
34 Dennis Jackson   4:39:37
ITA 227, USSR 227, MEX 221,...
8 GB 137

1983 Qual. London (SP)
June 11 20 Km Track
3   Phil Vesty   1:27 26.3
4   Ian McCombie   1:27:34.5
6   Roger Mills   1:29:44.5
dq Steve Barry   –
June 11 50 Km Track
7   Chris Maddocks   4:18:25
8   Paul Blagg   4:22:03
9   Dennis Jackson   4:22:38
10 Allan King   4:28:19
GB 41, ESP 39, FIN 38, SWE 37
FINAL - Bergen

Sept 24 20 Km
21 Phil Vesty   1:26 29.8
32 Ian McCombie   1:28:27.8
33 Roger Mills   1:28:32.6
40 Allan King   1:30:29.1
Sept 25 50 Km
9   Chris Maddocks   4:02:37.6
16 Dennis Jackson   4:07:58.0
22 Barry Graham   4:12:17.2
30 Paul Blagg   4:19:16.3
USSR 231, ITA 189, MEX 146, TCH 138, GB 137

1985 St.John's, Isle of Man
Sept 29 20 Km
20 Ian McCombie   1:27:15
23 Martin Rush   1:28:12
36 Phil Vesty   1:31:38
41 Mark Easton   1:33:24
Sept 28 50 Km
17 Les Morton   4:11:32
18 Dennis Jackson   4:12:11
29 Paul Blagg   4:26 21
39 Barry Graham   4:48:27
GDR 234, USSR 234, ITA 233,...
7 GB 141

1987 New York
May 3 20 Km
23 Ian McCombie   1:24:13
27 Chris Maddocks   1:24:33
61 Phil Vesty   1:29:04
65 Andi Drake   1:29:45
May 2 50 Km
27 Paul Blagg   4:06:22
35 Dennis Jackson   4:11:05
42 Les Morton   4:14:48
58 Barry Graham   4:25 37
USSR 607, ITA 569, GDR 518,...
11 GB 445

1989 L'Hospitalet de Llobregat
May 27 20 Km
15 Chris Maddocks   1:22:35
18 Ian McCombie   1:22:58
42 Darrell Stone   1:26:55
46 Mark Easton   1:27:50
52 Steve Partington   1:28:54
May 28 50 Km
25 Les Morton   4:03:30
38 Mike Smith   4:11:04
61 Darren Thorn   4:28:45
70 Chris Berwick   4:35:23
USSR 585, ITA 534, FRA 516,...
8 GB 425

1991 San Jose, California, USA
June 1 20 Km
38 Ian McCombie   1:25:20
42 Martin Rush   1:25:42
53 Mark Easton   1:27:57
58 Andy Penn   1:28:28
June 6 50 Km
20 Les Morton   4:02:11
25 Paul Blagg   4:04:09
45 Chris Maddocks   4:20:05
55 Dennis Jackson   4 26:08
ITA 517, GER 491, MEX 487,...
9 GB 363

1993 Monterrey, MEX
Apr 24 20 Km
37	Chris Maddocks	1:31:04
46	Andy Penn	1:31:57
50	Steve Partington	1:32:45
61	Darrell Stone	1:35:57

Apr 25 50 Km
41	Les Morton	4:19:29
44	Dennis Jackson	4:22:12
dq	Allan King	–
dnf	Mark Easton	–

MEX 540, ESP 491, ITA 497,...
13 GB 286

1995 Beijing
Apr 29 20 Km
29	Darrell Stone	1:24:49
58	Steve Partington	1:30:02
70	Andy Penn	1:31:46
80	Chris Cheeseman	1:34 23

Apr 30 50 Km
42	Mark Easton	4:06:01
44	Les Morton	4:02:52
72	Graham White	4:29:41

MEX 846, ITA 815, CHN 805...
14 GB 625

1997 Podebrady
Apr 19 20 Km
79	Andy Penn	1:26 49
85	Mark Easton	1:28:02
92	Graham White	1:29:27
dnf	Darrell Stone	–

Apr 20 50 Km
42	Chris Maddocks	4:05:42
56	Chris Cheeseman	4:10 23
66	Les Morton	4:16:12
67	Karl Atton	4:16:20

RUS 865, MEX 802, BLR 801,...
18 GB 549

ESCHBORN TROPHY
1979 Eschborn Sept 29 5 Km
1	Marion Fawkes	22:51
2	Carol Tyson	22:59
6	Irene Bateman	23:25
13	Elaine Cox	24:18

GB 85, SWE 74, NOR 69

1981 Valencia Oct 3 5 Km
13	Irene Bateman	24:40.0
15	Lillian Millen	24:47.4
18	Jill Barrett	25:05.1
19	Carol Tyson	25:10.9

USSR 105, SWE 104, AUS 90, GB 76

1983 Bergen Sep 24 10 Km
19	Irene Bateman	48:59.8
25	Jill Barrett	49:47.0
26	Virginia Birch	49:51.2
42	Brenda Lupton	51:53.5

CHN 132, USSR 130, AUS 126,...
7 GB 82

1985 St.Johns, IoM Sep 24 10 Km
25	Lisa Langford	49:45
28	Helen Elleker	50:28
39	Beverley Allen	52:16
43	Karen Nipper	53:53

CHN 104, USSR 98, CAN 74,... 12

GB 29

1987 New York May 3 10 Km
11	Lisa Langford	45:42
37	Beverley Allen	48:45
42	Helen Elleker	49:11
dq	Nicky Jackson	–

USSR 203, ESP 174, AUS 167,... 8
GB 135

1989 Barcelona May 27 10 Km
15	Lisa Langford	46:02
49	Betty Sworowski	48:50
51	Helen Elleker	48:56
63	Julie Drake	50:57
66	Nicky Jackson	51:07

USSR 218, CHN 212,... 11 GB 140

1991 San Jose June 1 10 Km
21	Betty Sworowski	46:38
39	Vicky Lupton	48:57
43	Helen Elleker	49:12
60	Julie Drake	52:05

USSR 203, ITA 180, MEX 162,...12
GB 115

1993 Monterrey Apr 24 10 Km
35	Julie Drake	50:58
57	Verity Larby	52:18
67	Vicky Lupton	53:39
81	Sylvia Black	56:28

ITA 196, CHN 193, RUS 193,... 21
GB 72

1995 Beijing Apr 29 10 Km
35	Lisa Langford	46:00
50	Vicky Lupton	47:04
59	Cal Partington	42:17
68	Verity Snook	48:42
81	Melanie Wright	50:50

CHN 443, ITA 429, RUS 424,... 15
GB 326

1997 Podebrady Apr 19 10 Km
58	Vicky Lupton	47:16
80	Sylvia Black	49:00
94	Verity Snook	50:14
101	Lisa Crump	51:20

RUS 440, ITA 435, CHN 425,... 20
GB 270

WORLD CUP
1999 Mézidon-Canon
May 1 20 Km
74	Jamie O'Rawe	1:33:16
77	Chris Maddocks	1:33:25
82	Karl Atton	1:34:36
83	Andi Drake	1:34:53
101	Matt Hales	1:40 23

21 GB 233

May 2 50 Km
57	Chris Cheeseman	4:07 49
69	Les Morton	4:15 43
74	Steve Hollier	4:20 35
dnf	Mark Easton	–
dq	Allan King	–

16 GB 200

May 2 Women's 20 Km
74	Vicky Lupton	1:42:31
76	Catherine Charnock	1:43:57
77	Niobe Menendez	1:44:17
90	Kim Braznell	1:47 22

dnf	Lisa Crump	–

18 GB 227

2002 Turin
Oct 12 20 Km
46	Steve Partington	1:31:41
63	Steve Hollier	1:35:18
66	Andi Drake	1:36:06
68	Dominic King	1:37:40

15 GB 175
50km: No British competitors
Oct 12 Women's 20 Km
71	Sharon Tonks	1:48:33
75	S. Jane Cattermole	1:52:44
dq	Lisa Kehler	–

2004 Naumburg
May 2 20 Km
61	Dominic King	1:28:12
73	Andi Drake	1:29:40
dq	Daniel King	–

May 1 Junior 10 Km
27	Luke Finch	45:18
41	Nick Ball	47:08

9 GB 68
May 1 Junior Women's 10 Km
12	Katie Stones	50:29
27	Sophie Hales	52:29
38	Jenny Gagg	54:14

7 GB 39
2006 La Coruña
May 13 Women's 20 Km
54	Johanna Jackson	1:41:47
dnf	Katie Stones	–

May 13 Junior 10 Km
11	Nick Ball	43:36
43	Ben Wears	47:07

12 GB 54
May 14 Junior Women's 10 Km
39	Sarah Foster	55:42
dq	Rebecca Mersh	–

2008 Cheboksary
May 11 50 Km
59	Dominic King	4:25:26
dq	Daniel King	–

May 11 Women's 20 Km
45	Johanna Jackson	1:37:56

May 10 Junior 10 Km
38	Ben Wears	45:22

2010 Chihuahua (A)
May 15 Women's 20 Km
46	Johanna Jackson	1:47:12

2012 Saransk
May 12 20 Km
53	Alex Wright	1:26:38
71	Tom Bosworth	1:28:45
93	Ben Wears	1:34:18

18 GB 217
May 13 50 Km
50	Dominic King	4:13:25
60	Daniel King	4:29:49

May 12 Women's 20 Km
42	Johanna Jackson	1:38:29

May 12 Junior 10 Km
dnf	Jamie Higgins	–

May 12 Junior Women 10 Km
23	Heather Lewis	50:38
dnf	Ellie Dooley	—

dnf Tasha Webster	–	
2014 Taicang		
May 3 20 Km		
43 Tom Bosworth	1:22:53	
May 3 Women's 20 Km		
48 Johanna Atkinson	1:33:55	
May 4 Junior Women 10 Km		
27 Ellie Dooley	49:53	
32 Emma Achurch	50:20	
12 GBR 59		

EUROPEAN CUP
1998 Dudince April 25
20 Km 39 Martin Bell 1:29:18
50 Km 28 Mark Easton 4:03:53
Apr 25 Women's 10 Km
27 Lisa Langford 45:54
2000 Eisenhüttenstadt
June 17 20 Km
50 Chris Maddocks 1:31:39
51 Andy Penn 1:33:10
dq Andi Drake –
dq Darrell Stone –
June 18 50 Km
28 Steve Hollier 4:07:18
43 Chris Cheeseman 4:23:19
45 Don Bearman 4:36:15
dnf Tim Watt –
FRA 12, 12 GB 116
June 17 Women's 20 Km
23 Lisa Kehler 1:33:57
46 Niobe Menendez 1:43:18
50 Kim Braznell 1:46:24
dnf Sara-Jane Cattermole –
ITA 11, 11 GB 119
June 18 Junior Women's 10 Km
36 Claire Reeves 59:13
2001 Dudince May 19
20 Km 45 Matt Hales 1:30:08
50 Km
33 Steve Hollier 4:20:50
37 Chris Cheeseman 4:24:48

RUS 11, ESP 21, FRA 24
Junior 10 Km
29 Lloyd Finch 45:35
36 Andrew Parker 46:17
43 Cameron Smith 50:33
RUS 3, 14 GB 65
2003 Cheboksary May 18
20 Km
43 Daniel King 1:33:08
48 Dominic King 1:35:16
dq Andi Drake –
Junior 10 Km
15 Luke Finch 44:05
dq Neil Bates –
Junior Women's 10 Km
20 Sophie Hales 52:20
21 Katie Stones 52:44
RUS 3, 9 GB 41
2005 Miskolc May 21
20 Km dq Dominic King –
Women's 20 Km
46 Johanna Jackson 1:53:34
Junior 10 Km
18 Nick Ball 44:58
Junior Women's 10 Km
dq Rebecca Mersh –
2007 Leamington Spa May 20
20 Km 48 Daniel King 1:30:59
Women's 20 Km
38 Johanna Jackson 1:38:56
43 Lisa Kehler 1:41:00
Junior 10 Km
36 Ben Wears 44:41
Junior women's 10 Km
32 Rebecca Mersh 52:44
2009 Metz May 24
20 Km 25 Luke Finch 1:36:30
50 Km
dq Daniel King, Dominic King
Women's 20 Km
27 Johanna Jackson 1:45:05

Junior 10 Km
24 Mark O'Kane 46:04
39 Tom Bosworth 52:01
dq Ben Wears –
2011 Olhão May 21
20 Km
25 Alex Wright 1:30:36
31 Tom Bosworth 1:32:48
dq Daniel King –
dnf Ben Wears –
50 Km 25 Dominic King 4:18:56
Women's 20 Km
12 Johanna Jackson 1:33:53
44 Lisa Kehler 1:47:58
Junior 10 Km
30 Jamie Higgins 47:28
Junior Women's 10 Km
22 Heather Lewis 52:56
25 Lauren Whelan 54:20
1 RUS 3, 9 GB 47
2013 Dudince May 19
20 Km
31 Tom Bosworth 1:27:34
43 Alex Wright 1:31:17
50 Km dq Dominic King –
Women's 20 Km
45 Bethan Davies 1:54:11
Junior 10 Km
10 Jamie Higgins 44:08
41 Cameron Corbishley 48:19

WORLD UNIVERSITY GAMES
20 KILOMETRES
1983 11 Phil Vesty 1:29:08.3
1987 9 Martin Rush 1:32:34
1989 dq Tim Berrett –
WOMEN 5000 METRES
1987 7 Lisa Langford 23:01.73t
1989 10 Lisa Langford 22:10R
WOMEN 10 KILOMETRES
1991 dq Vicky Lupton –

INTERNATIONAL MATCHES – MEN t = track
1947 Sep 7 v FRA Paris 10,000mt: 1 Harry Churcher 45:31.6, 3. Jim Morris 46:12.4 (non-scoring)
1949 Aug 1 v FRA London (WC) 10,000mt: 1 Churcher 45:38.8, 2. Morris 46:40.8 (non-scoring)
1950 Sep 9 v FRA Paris 10,000mt: 1 Roland Hardy 46:32.8, 3. Lawrence Allen 48:00.6 (Ns)
1959 May 24 v SUI Lugano 20km: 1 Ken Matthews 1:31:44, 2 Tom Misson 1:35:19, 3 George
 Williams 1:38:18, 6 Eric Hall 1:42:17. GB 14, SUI 22
 Sep 6 v USSR Moscow 20km: 2 Matthews 1:26:05.2, 4 Stan Vickers 1:28:43.6
 Sep 27 v ITA , SWE Varese 20km: 1 Vickers 1:31:56.2, 2 Matthews 1:33:50.6
1960 May 29 V GDR, DEN Berlin 25km: 1 Matthews 1:52:31, 5 Eric Hall 1:59:55, 6 Don Thompson 2:00:11
 Aug 1 v FRA London (WC) 10,000mt: 1 Matthews 42:35.6, 2 Vickers 43:43.6
1961 Sep 24 v FRA Colombes 20km: 1 John Godbeer 1:38:32, 2 Robert Clark 1:38:32 (non-scoring)
1964 Sep 11 v FRA London (BP) 20km: 1 Matthews 1:31:22, 3 John Edgington 1:35:09, 4 John Paddick
 1:35:38
1966 Jun 18 v USSR London (BP) 20km: 2 Paul Nihill 1:33:03, 4 Ron Wallwork 1:34:50
 Oct 2 v FRA Paris n/s 10,000mt: 2 Peter Fullager 45:13.0, 3 Wallwork 45:56.4, 4 John Webb 46:09.6
1967 Aug 12 v USA London (BP) 10km: 2 Arthur Jones 43:56.8, 3 Bob Hughes 44:48.0
1968 May 18 v 3N Spremburg 20km: 4 Webb 1:29:59.4, 6 Fullager 1:31:32.8, 8 Phil Thorn 1:34:17.0
 Jun 1 v FRG, TCH Kleinaspach 20km: 3 Hughes 1:33:35, 7 Wallwork 1:36:42, 8 Bill Sutherland
 1:37:02, 10 John Warhurst 1:39:14. GBR 37, FRG 35, CZE 20
 35km: 1 Nihill 2:54:21, 2 Ray Middleton 2:55:23, 3 Shaun Lightman 2:56:38, 10 George Chaplin 3:06:05
1969 May 3 v FRG Bexley 20km: 1 Nihill 1:30:18.4, 2 Fullager 1:30:49.0, 4 Webb 1:36:06.0, 5
 Hughes 1:37:10.0. GB 25, FRG 19
 35km: 2 Middleton 3:03:51.0, 3 Lightman 3:05:47.8, 6 Sutherland 3:10:30.0, 7 Chaplin 3:12:24.2
 Jul 6 v TCH Brno 20km: 1 Nihill 1:31:22.2, 2 Fullager 1:35:30.6

	Aug 12	v USA London (BP)	20km: 2 Fullager 1:33:47. 3 Sutherland 1:34:39
	Aug 16	v ITA, TCH Verona	20km: 1 Nihill 1:31:22.2, 2 Fullager 1:32:07.0
	Aug 30	v FRA London (BP)	20km: 1 Sutherland 1:31:10, 2 Webb 1:35:55, 3 Hughes 1:37:12
1971	Sep 25	v FRG Hillingdon	20km: 1 Phil Embleton 1:31:20, 3 Wallwork 1:32:25, 5 Steve Gower 1:33:55, 7 Tony Taylor 1:36:09. GB 19, FRG 25
			35km: 4 Warhurst 2:50:55, 5 Carl Lawton 2:54:35, 6 Ian Brooks 2:58:16, 7 Middleton 2:58:44
1972	May 27	v FRG Bremen	20km: 1 Roger Mills 1:30:09.8, 5 Sutherland 1:40:16.6, dnf Peter Marlow
		(FRG 32, GB 11)	50km: 4 Warhurst 4:12:36.8, 5 Middleton 4:15:51.2, 6 Chaplin 4:20:05.0
	Oct 1	v FRA Colombes	20,000mt: 1 Mills 1:34:16.0, 2 Nihill 1:35:55.2 (non-scoring)
1973	May 27	v FRG Warley	20km: 2 Warhurst 1:32:40.2, 3 Mills 1:34:44,2, 5 Webb 1:37:10.2, 7 Mike Holmes 1:40:44.2 FRG 24, GB 20
			35km: 3 Bob Dobson 2:55:59.0, 4 Eric Taylor 2:59:11.4, 5 Roy Thorpe 2:59:37.2, 8 Lightman 3:20:28.2
	Jul 1	v GDR, BUL Leipzig	20,000mt: 4 Mills 1:34:18.2, 5 Warhurst 1:35:29.8
	Sep 22	v SWE London (CP)	10,000mt: 1 Mills 43:51.2, 2 Warhurst 44:33.8, 4 Thorpe 45:13.4 (n/s)
1974	May 25	v FRG Hamburg	20,000mt: 2 Mills 1:31:24.2, 4 Olly Flynn 1:32:15.8, 5 Marlow 1:32:28.8, 6 Taylor 1:34:21.2. FRG 26, GB 18
		20 Miles t: 3 Warhurst 2:34:25.4, 4 Thorpe 2:35:44.0, 5 Amos Seddon 1:37:35.4, 6 Mike Holmes 2:42:01.4
	Jun 20	v GDR London (CP)	20,000mt: 2 Flynn 1:33:47.2, 3 Marlow 1:35:26.6 (non-scoring)
	Jun 29	v POL, CAN Warsaw	20,000mt: 2 Mills 1:34:12.6, 4 Brian Adams 1:41:16.6
	Jul 30	v SWE Stockholm	10,000mt: 2 Lightman 44:43.0, 3 Carl Lawton 45:16.4 (non-scoring)
1975	Jun 1	v FRG, MEX Woodford	20,000mt: 3 Adams 1:29:51, 4 Flynn 1:30:31, 7 Mills 1:33:11, 9 Seddon 1:34:37. MEX 36, FRG 29, GB 26
			50,000mt: 5 Bob Dobson 4:19:03, 6 Charles Fogg 4:22:41, 9 John Lees 4:31:46, 10 Thorpe 4:36:56
	Jun 21	v GDR Dresden	20,000mt: 2 Mills 1:34:00.4, 4 Adams 1:36:25.0
	Sep 13	v SWE Edinburgh	10,000mt: 1 Nihill 44:23.20, 3 David Cotton 45:26.69 (non-scoring)
1976	Jun 16	v FRG Salzgitter	20km: 3 Mills 1:29:55.4, 4 Adams 1:31:32.4, 5 Seddon 1:32:32.0, 6 Lawton 1:33:31.0. FRG 25 GB 19
		35k: 1 Thorpe 2:51:02.8, 5 Stuart Elms 2:54:47.0, 7 John Lees 3:00:27.0, 8 Barry Ingarfield 3:03:10.0
	Jul 3	v POL London (CP)	20,000mt: 2 Mills 1:39:17, 3 Seddon (non-scoring) 1:40:16
	Oct 3	v ITA Blackpool	20km: 1 Flynn 1:27:35, 4 Mills 1:30:21, 6 Adams 1:31:12, 7 Seddon 1:34:18
1977	Jul 3	v ITA Luino	20km: 2 Mills 1:34:43.8, 4 Seddon 1:36:51.6, 6 Mick Greasley 1:42:28.2
	Jul 10	v FIN Oulu	10,000mt: 2 Mills 43:42.1, 4 Seddon 45:50.3
	Jul 26	v3N Stockholm	20km: 9 Lawton 1:34:29.0, 10 Seddon 1:35:23.2
	Aug 26	v USSR Edinburgh	20,000mt: 2 Holmes 1:32:30.10, 3 Warhurst 1:33:19.58, 4 Adams 1:33:54.58
1978	Jun 10	v GDR London (CP)	20,000mt: 2 Steve Gower 1:30:27.38, 4 Seddon 1:30:53.64
	Aug 6	v ITA Hove	20km: 1 Barry 1:30:18, 6 Chris Harvey 1:34:10, 7 Gower 1:36:16, 8 Ken Carter 1:38:05. ITA 42, ITA 21
			35km: 4 Cotton 2:53:25, 5 Lightman 2:54:43, 6 Dobson 2:58:55, 8 Ian Richards 3:02:27
	Sep 17	v FRG Sheffield	20km: 1 Flynn 1:32:26, 2 Harvey 1:33:40, 4 Seddon 1:35:08, 7 Gower 1:37:38. GB 38, FRG 28
			50km: 3 Adams 4:15:22, 5 Chris Maddocks 4:21:06, 6 Lightman 4:24:09, 7 Adrian James 4:24:32
1979	May 20	v ITA Gradisca d'Isonzo	20km: 1 Flynn 1:33:19, 4 Harvey 1:36:51, 7 Graham Morris 1:39:01 8 Holmes 1:40:16. ITA 42, GB 25
			35km: 3. Adams 2:34:25, 5 James 2:56:54, 6 Mills 3:04:30, 7 Lawton 3:04:47
	Jun 2	Eur Comm. Grand Quévilly	35km: 8 Seddon 2:52:04, 14 Allan King 3:06:25
	Sep 22	v RUS London (CP)	10,000mt: 4 Mills 43:14.70, 5 Gordon Vale 44:21.17, 6 Seddon 44:32.41
1980	May 31	v GRE, HUN Athens	10,000mt: 2 Harvey 43:48.2, 4 George Nibre 45:03.6
	Sep 12	v SWE Edinburgh	10.000mt: 3 King 44:43.00, 4 Holmes 45:27.72
	Sep 13	v 3N Colombes	50km: 1 Maddocks 4:05:14, 3 Dennis Jackson 4:21:58, 5 Adams 4:30:26 dnf Ian Richards. GB 87, FRA 66, ESP 58, SUI 25
	Sep 14		20km: 2 Steve Barry 1:29:17.1, 3 Seddon 1:30:37.3, 5 Nibre 1:33:57.6, 7 Greasley 1:38:25.7
1981	Jun 14	v GDR Dresden	20,000mt: 3 Barry 1:30:20.8, 4 Seddon 1:35:32.9
	Jun 28	v ESP, FRA Brighton	20,000mt: 2 Barry 1:26:22.0, 5 Morris 1:31:29.6, 6 Vale 1:31:34.4, 8 David Jarman 1:32:34.5. GB 53, ESP 52, FRA 22
			35,000mt: 2 Jackson 2:47:34.7, 4 Murray Lambden 2:51:14.1, 6 Seddon 2:51:09.0, 9 Mills 3:01:45.7
	Jul 17	v USSR Gateshead	20,000mt: 3 Barry 1:27:41.4, 4 Morris 1:30:54.7
	Sep 23	v ITA Cagliari	10,000mt: 4 Barry 43:11.10, 5 Ian McCombie 43:34.75, 6 Phil Vesty 45:30.42
1982	May 8	v3 N Valencia	20km: 3 Barry 1:26:09.6, 6 Mike Parker 1:29:47.1, 7 Vesty 1:30:49.9 9 Adams 1:32:06.7. ESP 81, GB 76, FRA 38, SUI 24
	May 9		35km: 2 Paul Blagg 2:48:08, 3 Lambden 2:49:37, 4 Jarman 2:50:28. 6 Vale 2:54:34
	Jun 19	v GDR London (CP)	10,000mt: 3 Barry 41:13.62, 4 Vesty 42:55.00
	Jun 27	v 3N Rome	20km: 7 Mills 1:32:16, 9 Vesty 1:35:04, 10 Lambden 1:35:36, 12 Blagg 1:35:53, 13 Parker 1:39:35, 14 Barry Graham 1:40:06, ITA 15, FRA 38, ESP 41, GB 42
	Jul 18	v 4N Bielefeld	20km: 2 Barry 1:25:00, 5 McCombie 1:27:48, 9 Vesty 1:29:10, 14 Blagg 1:32:17. FRG 65, SWE 53, USA 50, GB 45, NOR 27
			50km: 11 Lambden 4:20:51, 13 Dobson 4:21:44, 15 Richards 4:24:36, dnf Vale

1983 Jun 5   v USSR Birmingham   10,000mt: 2 Roy Sheppard 44:48.87, 3 Tim Berrett J 45:10.70, 4 Graham
                                    White 45:26.80
       Jun 19 v FIN,SUI Lappeenranta 10,000mt: 2 Vesty 43:22.14, 4 Mills 44:03.08
1985 Feb 16 v ITA, YUG Genoa   Indoor 5000mt: 3 Vesty 20:30.62, 4 McCombie 20:33.20
       Oct 13 v FRA Flers   20km: 1 Chris Smith 1:31:58, 4 King 1:34:03, 5 Steve Johnson 1:34:26
                                    8 Andrew Drake 1:39:41. GB 68, FRA 64
                 35km: 4 Mike Smith 2:54:49, 5 Chris Berwick 2:58:58, 8 Darren Thorn 3:03:24, 8 Harvey 3:09:00
1986 May 24 v 5N Potsdam   20km: 5 McCombie 1:23:24; 12 Martin Rush 1:27:28, 19 Parker 1:31:18
                                    21 King 1:31:23. GDR 177, ITA 154, SWE 105, ESP 87, FRA 77, GB 77
       May 25   50km: 13 Jackson 4:04:44, 13 Les Morton 4:05:53, 14 Blagg 4:06:36, 17 Thorn 4:19:39
       Sep 27 v FRA Brighton   20km: 1 Maddocks 1:28:07.9, 2 Vesty 1:28:30.9, 5 Jimmy Ball 1:33:08.2,
                                    dq Drake. GB 75, FRA 50
                 35km: 2 Graham 2:50:16.6, 3 Berwick 2:54:19.6, 6 Andrew Trigg 2:56:50.8, dq M Smith
1987 Apr 5   v HUN Békéscsaba   20km: 2, Maddocks 1:23:50, 5 Morton 1:28:12, 6 Drake 1:28:20, ...
                                    Andrew Penn 1:36:26, dq Blagg. HUN 34, GB 20
                 50km: 5 Trigg 4:27:36, (6g Ed Shillabeer 4:28:24), 7 Berwick 4:29:46, dnf M Smith
       Jun 6   v 5N Saluzzo   35km: 17 Blagg 2:49:13, 18 Jackson 2:55:24, 19 Graham 2:55:24, 20 C
                                    Smith 3:14:41. 1 ITA 180, GDR 146, ESP 139, FRA 84, SWE 81, GB 64
       Jun 7 20km: 9 McCombie 1:25:25.1, 15 Morton 1:28:40.8, 18 Drake 1:30:56.8, 20 Steve Johnson 1:31:21.0
       Sep 26 v FRA, FRG Paris   20km: 1 Mark Easton 1:29:16, 3 Drake 1:30:15, 5 Rush 1:31:01
                 35km: 7 C Smith 2:59:42, 8 Graham 3:01:03, 9 Berwick 3:04:11
1988 Mar 20 v ESP Puerto Pollensa 50km: 4 Morton 3:58:25, dnf Maddocks & M Smith
       May 5   v 5N Trnava   20km: 4 McCombie 1:24:33, 7 Stone 1:26:57, 11 Drake 1:29:49, 17
                                    Penn 1:33:33. CZE 97, POL 68, GB 55, HUN 54, FRG 48, SUI 21
                 30km: 8 Blagg 2:23:00, 12 Jackson 2:26:39, 19 Graham 2:37:07, dnf Maddocks
       Jun 19 v FRA Portsmouth   10,000mt: 4 McCombie 41:37.29, dq Drake
1989 Mar 10 v USA, USSR Glasgow Indoor 5000mt: 3 Drake 20:05.82, 4 Martin Bell 20:26.36
       Jun 24 v FRG, USA, USSR Birmingham 10,000mt: 3 McCombie 40:52.49, 5 Martindale 42:12.62
       Jun 25 v 5N Laval   20km: 15 Stone 1:30:55. 16 Steve Partington 1:31:49, dq Drake, Easton.
                 Inc women: ESP 245 ITA 223 FRA 182 GDR 157 SWE 136 FRG 108 GB 99
1990 Feb 23 v GDR Glasgow   Indoor 5000m: 2 Easton 20:01.65, 3 Drake 20:19.84
       Mar 18 v USA/USSR Cosford   Indoor 5000mt: 3 Drake 19:57.72, 6 Rush 21:13.73
       Jun 16 8N Munich   20km: 18 Easton 1:26:30, 19 Martindale 1:26:46, 23 Maddocks 1:28:10,
                                    27 Penn 1:30:31. GDR 283 ESP 267 ITA 230 ,... 7 GB 134
                 35km: 14 Morton 2:40:38, 15 Stone 2:41:53, 23 Rush 2:50:21, dnf Thorn
       Jun 29 v GDR/CAN Gateshead 10,000mt: 5 McCombie 41:16.36, 6 Drake 42:00.31
1991 Feb 13 v ITA, YUG Turin   Indoor 10,000mt: 3 Drake 19:28.20, 5 Rush 20:28.74
       Mar 3   v USA   Indoor 3000m: 2 Easton 11:43.57, 4 Partington 11:47.36
       Jun 29 8N Örnsköldsvik   20km: 11 Rush 1:24:06, 14 Easton 1:24:25, 15 Partington 1:24:28, dq
                                    Stone. GER 258 ITA 229 ESP 199 FRA 147 SWE 147 GB 143 AUS 18
                 35km: 5 Maddocks 2:36:19, 7 Morton 2:37:27, 18 Jackson 2:51:44, 22 Stuart Phillips 3:01:05
1992 Jun 6   8N La Coruña   20km: 14 Stone 1:25:05, Gareth Holloway 1:31:59, dnf, Bell, McCombie
  (ITA 231, ESP 229, 7 GB 115)   35km: 6 Rush 2:38:11, 7 Maddocks 2:38:46, 17 King 2:47:36, dq Morton
1993 Feb 13 v USA Birmingham   Indoor 3000m: 1 Rush 11:40.54, 2 Stone 11:51.04, 3 Bell 11:54.96
       Mar 20 v 5N Békéscsaba   20km: 18 Partington 1:28:26, 21 Bell 1:29:12, 25 Holloway 1:32:39, 29
                                    Brian Dowrick 1:36:02. HUN 44 GB 24 POL 23.5 CZE 16 ROM 15 SVK 14
                 35km: 11 Maddocks (g) 2:42:50, 15 King 2:45:20, 20 Phillips 2:52:15, 21 Jackson 2:53:12, dnf Morton
       Jun 12 Eschborn   20km: 33 Stone 1:26:59, 35 Partington 1:27:22, 40 Penn 1:28:38
  (11 GB 113) 35km: 25 Easton 2:42:13, 34 Morton 2:47:40, 41 Karl Atton 2:56:41, 42 Dowrick 3:03:18
       Jul 10   v 3N Livorno   20km (short?): 11 Stone 1:23:37, 15 Morton 1:26:31, 17 Easton 1:28:43
                                    (ITA 46... 4 GB 87)
1994 Jun 12 Livorno   20km: 20 Stone 1:26:53, 22 Bell 1:27:18, 31 Partington 1:29:48, 34
                                    Chris Cheeseman 1:30:37. 1 RUS 445, 2 ESP 405,... 10 GB 153
                 35km: 30 White 2:48:50, 32 Morton 2:50:01, 39 Atton 2:55:38
1995 May 27 v 3N Özd   20km: 11 Phil King 1:36:25, 13 Jamie O'Rawe 1:37:37, 15 Steve Taylor
                                    1:41:22. HUN 61, UKR 42, SVK 37, GB 18
       Jun 11 6N Fougères   20km: 19 Maddocks 1:28:11, 20 Partington 1:28:35, 22 Penn 1:32:28
                 35km: 11 Stone 2:40:49, 17 Easton 2:45:58, 18 Morton 2:49:15, 19 White 2:55:01
1996 Apr 27 6N Podebrady   50km: 12 Gareth Brown 4:27:22, 16 Jonathan Cocker 4:58:08 (6th GB)
       Jun 1   6N Moscow   20km: 15 Stone 1:24:30, 19 Partington 1:27:12, 21 Penn 1:28:38, 25
                                    Richard Oldale 1:33:40. RUS 134 ITA 108 GER 79 BLR 68 FRA 64 GB 9?
                 35km: 21 Morton 2:56:03, 22 Brown 2:58:13. dnf Cocker
1998 May 30 8N Senigallia   20km: 10 Drake 1:28:01, 15 Steve Hollier 1:34:26. dnf Bell
  May 31 (1 FRA 626..5 GBR 314?) 35km: 14 Easton 2:47:28, 19 Cheeseman 2:56:13, dq, Morton, dnf White
1999 May 30 8N Catania   20km: 8 Maddocks 1:27:19, 12 Drake 1:28:32, 16 O'Rawe 1:30:25, 18
                                    Bell 1:31:14, dq Stone. ITA 311 RUS 197 FRA 189 GB 166...

```
                        35km: 9 Hollier 2:52:47, 10 Atton 2:55:20, 12 Morton 2:58:48, 12 King 3:02:03
2000  Apr 23  10N Leamington      20km: 17 Penn 1:30:26, 18 Maddocks 1:31:10, 20 Matt Hales 1:31:57
              50km: 9 Hollier 4:15:18, 10 Cheeseman 4:17:57, 11 Tim Watt 4:23:18, dnf Drake, 1 ESP 659, 2 GB 588
2001  Apr 21  Leamington          20km: 8 Hales 1:28:40, 12 Partington 1:33:00, 13 Don Bearman 1:34.05,
                                  17 Mark Williams 1:38:48. 1 GB 216, 2 NOR 184...
```

GB A or B INTERNATIONAL MATCHES
```
1967  Jul 23   v FRA La Baule     20km: 1= Roy Lodge & Arthur Jones 1:38:39.4, dnf Ken Bobbett (n/s)
1970  Aug 1    v FRA Cwmbran      20km: 1 Roger Mills 1:37:12, 2 Phil Embleton 1:38:48, 8 Chris Eyre 1:47:38
1975  Jul 12   v FRA Dieppe 20,000mt: 1 Olly Flynn 1:30:31.0, 3 Don Cox 1:33:56.6, 5 Bob Dobson 1:34:26.6
1977  16 Jul   v FRA Nice   10000mt: 2 Carl Lawton 45:33.1, 4 David Cotton 47:04.2, 5 Peter Selby 47:28.0
1999  Aug 28   v FRA Ashford 5000mt: 2 Darrell Stone 20:03.27, 3 Martin Bell 20:35.07, 6 Matt Hales 21:58.59
2001  Aug 11   v FRA Ashford      5000mt: (n/s) 4 Andrew Goudie 22:10.13
2003  Jul 11   v ITA, Catalonia Barcelona  5000mt: 3 Dominic King 20:24.75, 5 Daniel King 21:16.83
```

GB U23 INTERNATIONALS
```
1990  Jul 22    v 3N Denia              10,000mt: 3 Darrell Stone 42:21.26, 5 Gareth Holloway 47:20.36
1991  Aug 17   v ESP/GER/FRA Vigo 10,000mt: 5 Holloway 47:52.0
1995  Jul 29    v FRA/ESP/ITA Narbonne 5000mt: 4 Phil King 20:05.7, 8 Gary Witton 22:14.0
1996  Jul 14    v GER/RUS Hexham  5000mt: 5 King 21:58.57, 6 David Keown 22:47.37
1997  Mar 1     v FRA/ITA/BEN Liévin Indoor 5000m: 6 Scott Davis 22:45.48
      Jun 14    v FRA/GER Hexham   5000mt: 2 Hollier 21:52.29
1998  Jun 14 v FRA Hexham          5000mt: 3 Hollier 21:42.44, 4 Scott Taylor 23:31.15
      Aug 1     v FRA/GER Dessau   10,000mt: 4 Hollier 46:35.30, 6 Taylor 50:03.69
1999  Feb 6     v FRA Birmingham   Indoor 5000m: 3 Taylor 23:10.01, 4 Michael Kemp 23:16.41
      Jul 18    v FRA/GER Hexham   5000m: 3 Matt Hales 21:21.58, 4 Andrew Goudie 23:00.24
2001  Mar 10    v FRA Cardiff      Indoor 3000m: 2 Lloyd Finch 12:26.0, dnf Dominic King
2002  Jul 20    v GER Newport      10,000mt: 2 Daniel King 45:33.32, 4 Nathan Adams 47:47.50
      Aug 3     v FRA/ESP Niort    5000mt: 5 Daniel King 22:43.97, 6 Luke Finch 23:33.94
2004  Jul 24 v GER/ITA Manchester 5000mt: 1 Dominic King 19:57.91, 2 Daniel King 19:57.95
2005  Aug 6     4-N Manchester     5000mt: 2 Dominic King 20:14.76, 3 Daniel King 20:14.86
```

GB JUNIORS
```
1965  Jul 10    v 5N Berlin             10.000mt: 4 Dave Watts 47:15.6, 8 Ian Brooks 48:44.4. 3. GB 18
1967  Jul 27    v FRA Portsmouth        10,000mt: 4 Brian Armstrong 49:46.2, 5 Brian Adams 50:26.6, 6 Steve
                                        Fish 51:04.6
1968  Jun 23    v ITA,FRG,SUI Gradisca d'Isonzo  15km: 3 Phil Bannan 1:13:42, 8 Phil Embleton 1:16:04, 10
                                        Adams 1:17:13, dq John Norman. ITA 30, FRG 21, GB 19, SUI 9
      Sep 7     v FRG                   10.000mt: 1 Adams 49:06.8, 4 Geoff Saxty 52:39.2
1969  Jun 22    v FRG, ITA Dortmund  15km: 4 Mike Holmes 1:12:18, 6 Adams 1:12:43, 11 Jeff Ford 1:14:36,
                                     12 John Mullen 1:15:40. ITA 22, FRG 13, GB 11
      Jul 27    v FRA Dôle (n/s) 10,000mt: 2 Geoff Hunwicks 52:01.4, 3 Richard Evans 52:06.0, dnf Olly Flynn
      Sep 14    v FRG Herford           10,000mt: 2 Evans 51:32.4, 3 Mike Holmes 53:22.4
1970  Jun 20    v FRG,ITA London (BP)  15km: 2 Chris Eyre 1:10:22.6, 7 Holmes 1:13:39.6, 8 Tony Malone
                                        1:14:17.2, 12 Steve Crow 1:18:08.4
      Sep 26 v FRG Leicester            10,000mt: 1 Eyre 49:08.09, 4 Peter Dallow 49:51.8
1971  Jun 6     v 6N Husum              10,000mt: 10 Brian Laver 50:10.2, 14 Paul Sturdy 54:05.6
1973  Sep 19    v SWE Warley            10,000mt: 1 Jacky Lord 46:06.0, 4 Robert Chaplain 48:48.6
1974  Jul 30    v SWE Stockholm         10,000mt: 2 Barry Lines 46:03.2, 3 Lord 46:34.4 (non-match)
      Sep 14    v FRG Warley            10,000mt: 1 Lord 46:18.2, 2 Lines 47:13.0
1975  Aug 9     v FRA Warley            10,000mt: 1 David Cotton 45:35.4, 2 Mike Dunion 47:32.2, 3 Mike
                                        Angrove 48:23.8
      Sep 13 v  SWE Edinburgh           10.000mt: 3 Dunion 46:09.0, 4 Angove 49:16.6 (n/s)
      Oct 1     v ITA Blackpool         10,000mt: 4 Dunion 45:10, 6 George Nibre 46:08, 7 Colin Wilkes 46:53,
                                        8 Graham Morris 47:25
1977  Jul 3     v ITA Luino             10km: 2 Morris 46:33.2, 6 Nibre 48:16.2, 7 Chris Harvey 49:32.0, 8
                                        Dunion 51:05.4
      Jul 25    v 3N Stockholm          10,000mt: 7 Dunion 47:22.6, 8 Morris 47:24.6
      Aug 7     v FRA Dôle              10,000mt: 1 Morris 47:31.8, 2 Julian Robinson 47:33.6
1978  Jul 11    v FRG, USA Lubeck       1 Morris 45:43.6, 2 Mark Wordsworth 46:16.5
      Aug 6     v ITA Hove              10km: 3 Morris 44:55, 5 Michael Miley 45:41, 6 Wordsworth 47:30
                                        7 Ian McCombie 47:35
      Aug 20 v FRG London (CP)          1 Miley 47:41.85, 4 Paul Blagg 49:58.57
      Sep 17    v FRG Sheffield         10km: 1 Miley 47:14, 2 Wordsworth 47:15, 3 McCombie 48:11, 6 Roy
                                        Sheppard 49:19
1979  May 20 v ITA Gradisca d'Isonzo  10km: 4, Gordon Vale 46:19, 5 Miley 46:52, 7 Niall Troy 48:36
                                        8 Richard Dorman 49:06
      Aug 1     v CAN/ITA Wolverhampton  10,000mt: 4 Vale 43:57.6, 5 Dorman 46:39.0
```

Year	Date	Match	Results
1980	Jul 5	v FRG Grangemouth	10,000mt: 2 Vale 45:24.0, 3 Phil Vesty 46:39.7
	Sep 14	v 3N Colombes	5000mt: 2 Vesty 22:00.8, 4 Russell Bestley 23:09.5, 6 Tim Berrett 23:36.4, 14 Chris Dark 24:47.2
1981	Jun 13	v FRG Oldenburg	10,000mt: 2 Vale 43:14.84, 4 Vesty 47:38.98
	Jun 28	v ESP, FRA Brighton	5000mt: 2 Vesty 21:28.3, 4 Jimmy Ball 22:44.6, 5 Berrett 22:53.7, 7 Mike Smith 23:07.1. ESP 20, UK 19, FRA 7
1982	May 9	v3N Valencia (U18)	5km: 4 Neil Corbett 22:56.7, 5 Andi Drake 23:22.4, 8 Donald Bearman 24:09.2 11 Simon Moore 25:17.6
	Aug 14	v FRG Birmingham	10,000mt: 2 Berrrett 46:48.10, 3 Drake 48:32.27
1983	Jul 16	v FRG Koblenz	10,000mt: 1 Berrett 45:25.65, 2 Martin Rush 45:43.65
1984	Jun 3	v 3N Barcelona	10km: 4 Berrett 45:14, 9 Drake 47:03, 10 Steve Partington 47:41, 15 David Hucks 51:46. U18 5km: 5 Nathan Kavanagh 22:20, 10 Ian Ashforth 23:01, 11 Andy Penn 23:20, 15 Gareth Brown 23:35
	Jul 7	v FRG/ITA London (He)	10,000mt: 2 Kavanagh 47:07.9, 6 Ashforth 49:30.4
	Jul 24	v NOR/ITA Haugesund	10,000mt: 1 Berrett 43:32.06, 3 Drake 45:14.05
1985	May 5	v 3N Pisa	10km: 5 Kavanagh 44:07.1, 8 Pat Chichester 44:34.6, 9 Simon Moore 44:41.8, 10 Penn 44:55.3, ITA 31, ESP 22, GB 17
		U18 5km: 3 Ashforth 20:54.3, 6 Kirk Taylor 21:52.9, 9 Paul Nunn 22:18.9. ESP 28, ITA & GB 22	
	Jul 6	v FRG Kamen	10.000mt: 1 Chichester 45:22.2, 4 Penn 46:10.2
	Oct 13	v FRA Flers	U18 5km: 1 Ashforth 22:04, 2 K Taylor 22:23, 4 Darrell Stone 22:33. 6 Brown 23:04
1986	May 24	6 Nations Potsdam	10km: 11 Stone 44:55, 13 Ashforth 45:43, 14 K Taylor 45:57 15 Brown 45:58
	Jun 14/15	v ESP, ITA Alcalá (ESP 69, ITA 44, GB 25)	10km: 9 Stone 46:12, 10 Ashforth 46:44, 11 Taylor 47:08, 12 Brown 49:12 U18 5km: 5 Jonathan Vincent 22:56, 7 Russell Hutchings 23:03, 13 Gareth Holloway 23:29, 12 Jonathan Bott 25:16
	Aug 16	v FRG Göttingen	10,000mt: 2 Ashforth 47:56.5, 4 Brown 50:03.9
	Sep 27	v FRA Brighton	10,000mt: 1 Stone 44:50.7. 4 Penn 46:52.0, 6 Nunn 48:45.1, dq Taylor U18 5000mt: 1 Hutchings 22:17.5, 2 Holloway 22:32.5, 3 Bott 22:37.0, dq Vincent
1987	Apr 5	v HUN Békéscsaba	10km: 2 Stone 42:53, 4 Brown 44:52, 6 Taylor 45:38
	Jun 7	v 5N Saluzzo	10km: 4 Stone 43:02.9, 13 Andrew Pryor 48:55.5, dnf Taylor, Bott
	Jun 27	v FRG/POL Ipswich	10,000mt: 2 Brown 45:37.29, 5 Bott 46:28.50
	Aug 22	v FRG/SUI Lage	10,000mt: 2 Holloway 46:54.46, 4 Leigh Taylor 49:43.34
	Sep 26	v FRA, FRG Paris	10km: 1 Stone 41:46, 2 Brown 44:06, 6 Nunn 45:40, 9 Pryor 46:54 U18 5km: 2 Vincent 21:46, 4 L Taylor 21:51, 6 Holloway 22:01
1988	Jun 19	v TCH Prague	10,000mt: 3 Holloway 44:40.8, 4 Vincent 45:07.8
	Aug 20	v IRL/SUI Cwmbran	5000mt: 1 Holloway 22:19.15, 2 Vincent 22:40.20
1989	Jun 25	v 5N Laval	10km: 16 Vincent 47:20, 19 Holloway 48:57, 20 Karl Atton 49:12, dq L Taylor
	Jul 7	v FRG, SWE U23	10,000mt: 2 Holloway 45:13.40, 5 Vincent 46:08.21
	Aug 5	v ITA/HUN Calamaggiore	10,000mt: 4 Holloway 46:14.72, 6 Martin Young 50:24.22
	Sep 2	v GRE U23/HUN U23	10,000mt: 3 Young 49:52.49, dq Atton
1990	Jun 16	8N Munich	10,000mt: 13 Philip King 45:54, 26 Carl Warmsley 47:39, 27 Guy Jackson 47:41, 29 Kieron Butler 48:49
	Jul 7	v FIN/FRG Lübeck	10,000mt: 4 Young 47:02.32, 5 Warmsley 47:20.84
	Jul 28	v AUS/ITA Horsham	5000mt: 5 Young 22:47.40, 6 Jackson 22:52.29
	Aug 4	v FRA/ITA/FRG Saarguemines	10,000mt: 3 King 47:52.0, 7 Young 51:02.4
1991	Jun 15	v FIN/USSR Espoo	10,000mt: 7 Stuart Tilbury 46:04.79, 8 Young 46:31.96
	Jun 29	8N Örnsköldsvik	10km: 10 King 43:49, 17 Tilbury 46:20, 20 Butler 47:32, 25 Matt Pryor 50:21
	Jul 19	8N Salamanca	5000mt: 7 Brown 26:22.62, 10,000mt: 6 Tilbury 47:38.44
	Aug 24	v GER/HUN Gladbach	10,000mt: 2 King 43:59.9, 6 Scott Davis 48:13.0
1992	Jun 6	8N La Coruña	10km: 13 Davis 45:03, 19 Pryor 46:26, 20 Jamie O'Rawe 46:53, 21 James Chamberlain 48:06
	Aug 9	v ITA/EUN San Giuliano	10,000mt: 4 Davis 46:20.29, dq Chamberlain
	Aug 29	v FRA/ESP Horsham	10,000mt: 3 Davis 45:35.54, 4 O'Rawe 45:49.07
1993	Jun 12	Eschborn	10km: 17 King 43:36, 29 Chamberlain 45:30, 35 David Keown 48:08, 37 Robert Watson 49:22
	Jun 26	GER/RUS Lübeck	5000mt: 1 King 20:16.41, 5 Davis 22:33.62
1994	Jun 12	Livorno	10km: 22 Davis 44:50, 27 Chamberlain 46:17
	Jun 18	v POL/GER/RUS	10,000mt: 7 Chamberlain 47:42.90
	Aug 6	v ITA, TCH Schio	10,000mt: 5 Steve Hollier 55:05.92
1995	Feb 25	v GER, RUS Erfurt	Indoor 5000m: 5 Stuart Monk 22:23.53, 6 Hollier 23:19.09
	Jun 11	6N Fougères	10km: dq Hollier
	Aug 6	v FRA/BEN Belfort	5000mW: dq Hollier, Monk
1996	Mar 2	v FRA/GER/ITA Liévin	Indoor 5000m: 7 Scott Taylor 24:16.01, dq Monk
	Jun 1	6N Moscow	10km: 21 Monk 48:23.8, 22 Michael Kemp 49:35.2, 23 S Taylor 50:35.6
	Aug 3	v ITA/FRA/ESP Nembro	8 Matthew Hales 48:06.0, 9 S Taylor 51:39.2
1997	Mar 1	v FRA, GER Chemnitz	Indoor 5000m: 4 Michael Kemp 23:52.66, dq Hales

```
         Jun 7    v GER Bad Homburg  10,000mt: 4 Kemp 49:20.0, 5 S Taylor 51:59.0
1998  Feb 28   v FRA, GER Birmingham  Indoor 5000m: 4 Kemp 22:11.44, 5 Thomas Taylor 23:27.28
         May 30  8N Senigallia          10km: 8 T Taylor 45:03, 19 Nigel Whorlow 50:24, dq Kemp
         Jul 18   v ESP/FRA Alicante    10,000mt: 3 T Taylor 47:31.97, 5 Kemp 48:30.78
         Sep 5   Budapest  4 GB 48 10km: 8 Hales 46:44, 12 T Taylor 47:45, 13 Kemp 48:02, 19 Whorlow 50:57
1999  Feb 27   v 3N Nogent-sur-Oise Indoor 5000m: 7 Nathan Adams 24:58.66
         May 30  8N Catania            10,000mt: 18 Adams 52:19, dq Lloyd Finch
         Jul 24   v FRA/ESP/ITA Albertville  3000nt: 7 Adams 24:25.50, dq Finch
         Aug 21  v3N (U19) Neubrandenburg  10,000mt: 6 Finch 45:57.08, 8 Adams 50:18.58
         Sep 4   v 6N Budapest          10km: 16 Dominic King 49:27, 19 Adams 50:01, 26 Daniel King 52:34
2000  Mar 4    v GER, FRA Neubrandenburg  Indoor 5000m: 3 Dominic King 21:25.17, 5 Finch 22:23.45
         Apr 23   10N Leamington        10km: 5 T Taylor 45:20, 6 Finch 45:20, 9 Dominic King 45:53
         Sep 2   Budapest              10km: 5 Andrew Parker 48:33, 15 James Davis 50:56, 16 Adams 51:01
         Oct 7    4N (U19) Grossetto    10,000mt: 6 Dominic King 47:29.37, 7 Parker 49:12.46
2001  Mar 3    v FRA,GER,ITA Vittel    Indoor 5000m: 6 Cameron Smith 23:31.82, dq Finch
         Jul 29   FRA (U19) Dôle        5000mt: 1 Finch 21:47.8, 2 Dominic King 22:24.6
         Sep 9   v 4N Budapest          10km: 1 Finch 43:49, 7 Dominic King 45:45, 11 Parker 47:44
2002  Jul 7    v ITA/ESP Gorizia       5000mt: 4 Daniel King 21:46.29, dnf Parker
2003  Jul 5    v ITA Nove              5000mt: 2 Luke Finch 21:45.21. 6 Nick Ball 23:54.06
2004  Mar 20  v5N Leamington          10km: 3 Luke Finch 46:02, 6 Ball 47:20, 10 Robert Bain 51:37
2005  Apr 16  v3N Leamington          10km: 1 Ball 44:05, 7 Bain 49:42, 8 Simon Hambridge  50:03
2006  Jun 17   Leamngton (& B team)  10km: 2 Ben Wears 48:48, 6 S Hambridge 51:58, 8 Jack Tomlin 53:48,
                                                        dnf Mark Hambridge, dq Ball
```

ENGLAND (v Overseas countries)
```
1961  Sep 20  v RUS   London (WC)   20km: 1 Ken Matthews 1:30:17.4, 2 George Williams 1:36:01.2
1963  Aug 14  v ITA  London (WC)    10,000mt: 1 Matthews 43:22.84, 3 Paul Nihill 45:44.2 (non-scoring)
1965  Aug 30  v CZE  London (BP)    20km: 3 Ron Wallwork 1:37:01.6, 4 Dave Watts 1:41:42.4
1977  Jun 21  v ITA Turin            10,000mt: 4 Roger Mills 43:40.0, 5 Brian Adams 44:26.6
1979  Jun 6   v CAN Gateshead        10,000mt: 1 Adams 44:14.7, 4 Graham Morris 45:06.07
1987  Jun 20  v TCH/ITA  Portsmouth  10,000mt: 4 Chris Maddocks 41:06.57, 5 Andrew Drake 43:03.28
1988  Jul 9   'B' v 3N Cwmbran       5000mt: 2 Sean Martindale 20:14.17
1989  Jul 22  v POR/ESP/WAL          10,000mt: 5 Martindale 42:37.66, 6 Patrick Chichester (W) 44:50.00, 7
                 Swansea              Kirk Taylor (W) 45:25.20
         Aug 28  v OCE/ITA Gateshead  10,000mt: 3 Ian McCombie 40:42.53, 4 Paul Blagg 42:08.57
1993  Feb 7   v BEL Gent             Indoor 5000mt: 1 Martin Rush 20:17.94, 3 Andrew Penn 21:36.01
         Aug 28  v UKR Kiev             10,000mt: 3 Maddocks 42:22.72, 4 Mark Easton 42:59.02
1997  Sep 27  v 5N Dublin 20km: 3 Darrell Stone 1:25:53, 3 Partington IOM 1:27:44, 6 Les Morton 1:32:22
1998  Sep 13  v IRL,NED,IOM Dublin  20km: 3 Gareth Brown 1:33:07, 5 Morton 1:34:32, 6 Andy O'Rawe 1:34:35
2006  Jun 17  Leamngton  20km: 12 Williams 1:42:32, 14 Trevor Jones 1:46:37, dq Daniel King, Dominic King
```

ENGLAND A
```
2000  Sep 2   v FRA Vittel  5000mt: 3 Matt Hales 20:06.66, 5 Dominic King 22:22.45, 8 Andrew Goudie
                              22:39.26
```

ENGLAND U23
```
1990  Sep 15  v TCH, POL Jablonec 10,000mt: 4 Andrew Penn 43:46.44, 5 Gareth Brown 44:34.82
1994  Jul 7   v AUS U20/NIR King's Lynn  5000mt: 2 Phil King 20:49.27, 4 Kieron Butler 22:18.53
```

ULTRA DISTANCE
```
1978  v5N      Compiègne           85km: 4 John Eddershaw 8:13:35, 7 Ken Harding 8:15:45, 10 David
                                             Boxall 8:24:35, 17 Peter Worth 8:41:30.. 1 FRA 4, 2 GB 9, 3 NED 30...
1979  Jun 2    Eur Comm. Grand Quévilly  100km: 1 Tony Geal 9:34:25, 2 Boxall 9:53:31, 3 John Lees
                                             10:03:25, 6 Eddershaw 10:24:59
```

WOMEN – GB INTERNATIONALS
```
1974  Jul 30   v SWE Stockholm      3000mt: 3, Marion Fawkes 14:40.4, 4 Betty Jenkins 15:16.4 (n/s)
1975  Oct 11   v 7N Grand Quévilly  5km: 5 Fawkes 25:14, 9 Virginia Lovell 26:16, 11 Sylvia Saunders 27:05,
                                             dq Farr. 1 USA 70, 2 GB 49, 3 FRA 45, 4 SWE 70
1977  Jul 25   v3N Stockholm        5000mt: 4 Fawkes 23:59.62, 5 Carol Tyson 24:17.72
1979  May 26 v3N St-Aubin-les-Elbeuf 5000mt: 1 Fawkes 24:36.5, 2 Irene Bateman 24:43.4, 3 Tyson
                                             24:53.5, 4 Farr 25:12.5, 7 Virginia Birch (née Lovell) 26:33.0
         Jun 2    Eur Comm. Grand Quévilly  10km: 1 Fawkes 49:18, 2 Bateman 50:08, 3 Farr 50:52, 12
                                             Beverley Francis 57:42
         Jun 30  v NOR, SWE Östersund  1 Tyson 23:11.2, 2 Fawkes 23:19.2, 6 Bateman 23:44.0, 10
                                             Farr 25:11.0. GB 22, SWE 14, NOR 10
1980  Jun 28  v NOR, SWE Cwmbran 3000mt: 2 Tyson 13:46.3, 8 Karen Eden 14:53.0, 9 Jll Barrett 15:07.2 .
                                             SWE 32, NOR 23, GB 21
                                   5000mt: 4 Bateman 24:21.0, 5 Elaine Cox 24:23.8, 9 Elaine Worth 26:01.9
```

	Sep 12	v SWE Edinburgh	5000mt: 2 Tyson 24:05.02, 4 Bateman 24:29.79
1981	May 10	v ESP, NOR Barcelona	5km: 2 Bateman 24:04, 3 Tyson 24:13. 1 NOR, 2 GB, 3 ESP
	May 28	v SWE, NOR Fana	3000mt: 2 Tyson 13:55, 4 Gillian Edgar 14:18, 5 Barrett 14:23
	(SWE 16, GB 14, NOR 14)		5000mt: 3 Bateman 23:57, 5 Lillian Millen 24:12, 8 Cox 25:49.0
1982	May 9	v3N Valencia	5km: 1 Bateman 23:53.2, 3 Millen 24:32.8, 6 Sarah Brown 25:45.5
			7 Birch 25:52.1
	May 30	v 3N Lomello	5km: 2 Bateman 24:28, 6 Birch 25:24, 7 Millen 25:34, 11 Brown 26:22
	Jun 19	vSWE,NOR Västerås	5000m: 2 Millen 24:59.3, 7 Helen Ringshaw 26:28.2, 9 Lisa Langford 28:55.5.
	(SWE 17, NOR 16, GB 11)		10000m: 3 Bateman 50:40.5, 7 Brenda Lupton 54:45.8, 8 Brown 57:34.0
1983	Jun 11	v SWE,NOR London (SP)	3000mt: 2 Barrett 14:12.0, 4 Birch 14:27.4, 9 Brown 15:33.5
			5000mt: 2 Bateman 24:02.8, 5 Millen 25:10.6, dnf Lupton
	Jun 19	v FIN,SUI Lappeenranta	5000mt: 1 Bateman 24:11.05, 3 Karen Nipper 25:30.14
1984	May 5	v3N Bergen (Fana)	5000mt: 14 Barrett 23:51.1, 17 Birch 24:11,1, 19 Lupton 24:18.6
1985	Jun 15	vSWE, NOR Borås	10,000mt: 4 Birch 47:56.3, 8 Helen Elleker 49:46.2, 12 Allen (Francis)
			50:41.2
	Oct 13	v FRA Flers	10km: 2 Allen 49:54, 3 Birch 51:40, 5 Nipper 53:05, 6 Lisa Simpson 53:20
1986	May 24	v 5N Potsdam	10km: 11 Allen 48:23, 13 Elleker 49:00, 20 Nicky Jackson 51:16
			21 Brown 51:28
	Jun 21	v SWE,NOR Plymouth	10,000mt: 3 Allen 47:58.3, 5 Elleker 48:58.3, 6 Langford 49:07.8, 9
			Jackson 49:54.6. SWE 19, NOR 14. GB 11
	Sep 27	v FRA Brighton	10,000mt: 1 Birch 51:08.6, 2 Betty Sworowski 51:16.6, 3 Simpson
			51:54.5, 7 Lupton 54:58.1
1987	Apr 5	v HUN Békéscsaba	10km: 1 Langford 46:09, 4 Allen 48:30, 7 Jackson 49:18
	Jun 6	v 5N Saluzzo	10km: 15 Elleker 50:42, 18 Jackson 51:58, 19 Simpson 52:08, 21 Allen
			52:47, 24 Brown 55:18
	Sep 26	v FRA, FRG Paris	10km: 1 Langford 47:57, 4 Allen 52:03, 7 Brown 52:40, 11 Jackson 55:08
1988	Mar 20	v ESP Puerto Pollensa	10km: 3 Drake 51:16, 6 Sworowski 52:15, 10 Jackson 53:39
	May 5	v 5N Trnava	10km: 9 Drake 50:43, 11 Sworowski 51:07, 16 Jackson 52:13, 18
			Simpson 53:15. HUN 49, POL 45, FRG 32, GB 23, TCH 17, SUI 6
	Jun 19	v FRA Portsmouth	6000mt: 3 Sworowski 23:55.51, 6 Jackson 25:01.58
	Sep 3	v SWE, NOR Göteborg	10,000mt: 2 Sworowski 49:41.3, 4 Drake 50:58.3, 6 Karen Dunster
			54:16.0. SWE 19, NOR 14, GB 11
1989	Jun 24	v FRG, USA, USSR Birmingham	10,000mt: 3 Sworowski 22:39.59, 6 Drake 23:40.56
	Jun 25	v 5N Laval	10km: 18 Elleker 50:18, 21 Jackson 50:56, 24 Brown 53:04
	Sep 17	v NOR, SWE Moss	10km: 1 Sworowski 46:36.1, 3 Elleker 49:52.6, 4 Brown 50:25.8
1990	Jun 16	8N Munich	10km: 10 Langford 46:26, 11 Sworowski 47:02, 13 Drake 47:15, 15
			Elleker 47:47
	Jun 29	v GDR/CAN Gateshead	5000mt: 2 Sworowski 22:11.30, 6 Drake 23:11.21
1991	Feb 13	v ITA, YUG Turin	Indoor 5000m: 3 Julie Drake 13:43.71, 4 Verity Larby 14:09.76
	Mar 3	v USA Glasgow	Indoor 3000m: 2 Drake 13:29.73, 4 Larby 13:50.80
	Jun 29	8N Örnsköldsvik	10km: 15 Sworowski 46:48, 19 Elleker 47:49, 20 Drake 48:11, 25 Sylvia
			Black (Saunders) 49:18
1992	Jun 6	8N La Coruña	10km: 11 Lupton 46:28, 14 Sworowski 46:42, 22 Black 48:20, 24
			Melanie Brookes 48:29
1993	Mar 20	v 5N Békéscsaba	10km: 7 Drake 45:59, 12 Vicky Lupton 47:53, 14 Black 48:01, 22
			Brookes 49:36
	Jun 12	Eschborn	10km: 22 V Lupton 46:21, 28 Larby 47:01, 32 Drake 47:48, 39 Brookes 48:40
	Jul 10	v 3N Livorno	10km: 12 V Lupton 45:28, 13 Brookes 47:40, 15 Black 48:01, 16 Karen Smith 48:56
1994	Jun 12	Livorno	10km: 25 Snook (Larby) 47:24, 26 Langford 47:34, 28 Cal Partington
			47:46, 31 V Lupton 48:07, 34 Wright (née Brookes) 49:04
1995	May 27	v 3N Özd	10km: 9 Kim Baird 51:06, 10 Elaine Callinan (née Cox) 51:32, 11 Karen
			Kneale 52:56, 14 Black 56:15
	Jun 11	6N Fougères	10km: 15 V.Lupton 46:40, 16 Langford 47:13, 17 Partington 47:21, 21
			Wright 48:48
1996	Apr 27	6N Podebrady	10km: 11 V Lupton 47:19, 12 Snook 47:54, 16 Wright 49:51 (5th GB)
	Jun 1	6N Moscow	10km: 27 Snook 47:12, 31 Wright 49:15, 32 Braznell (Baird) 51:28, dq Lupton
1998	May 31	8N Senigallia	10km: 17 Braznell 49:10, 19 Lisa Crump 49:51, 20 Kneale 52:05, dq Lupton
1999	May 30	8N Catania	10kmt: 8 Menendez 49:10, 10 Braznell 51:37, dq Charnock & Lupton
2000	Apr 23	10N Leamington	20km: 14 Kehler (née Langford) 1:35:35, 19 Niobe Menendez 1:45:48,
			21 Sara-Jane Cattermole 1:48:43
2001	Apr 21	Leamington	20km: 4 Menendez 1:45:19, 5 Sharon Tonks 1:46:15, 6 Cattermole 1:47:35

GB A or B INTERNATIONAL MATCHES

1999	Aug 28	v FRA Ashford	3000mt: 2 Catherine Charnock 13:40.93, 3 Kate Horwill 13:59.89, 5 Amy
			Hales 14:24.58
2001	Aug 11	v FRA Ashford	3000mt: 1 Niobe Menendez 13:14.73, 5 Wendy Bennett 14:37.53, 6
			Sophie Hales (U23) 14:48.50

2003 Jul 11 v ITA, Catalonia Barcelona 5000mt: 5 Sharon Tonks 25:00.02, 6 Bennett 25:36.04

GB U23 INTERNATIONALS
1990 Jul 22 v 3N Denia   5000mt: 5 Verity Larby 24:17.33, 7 Joanne Pope 25:33.91
1991 Aug 17 v ESP/GER/FRA Vigo 5000mt: dq Sarah Brown, dnf Theresa Ashman
1995 Jul 29 v FRA/ESP/ITA Narbonne 3000mt: 7 Catherine Charnock 14:49.3, 8 Kath Horwill 15:05.2
1996 Jul 14 v GER/RUS Hexham   3000mt: 5 Charnock 14:22,51, 6 Horwill 14:52.78
1997 Jun 14 v FRA/GER Hexham   3000mt: 3 Charnock 14:07.32, 4 Helen Ford-Dunn 16:11.18
1998 Jun 14 v FRA Hexham   3000mt: 2 Debbie Wallen 14:23.48, 3 Sally Warren 15:06.06
     Aug 1   v FRA/GER Dessau   5000mt: 4 Warren 25:36.61, dq Wallen
1999 Feb 6   v FRA Birmingham   Indoor 3000m: 3 Nikki Huckerby 15:05.12
     Jul 18 v FRA/GER Hexham   5000m: 2 Huckerby 14:30.94, 4 Katie Ford 14:49.73
2000 Jul 22 v FRA/GER Liverpool 5000mt: 4 Warren 25:11.33, 5 Huckerby 25:33.09
2002 Jul 20 v GER Newport   5000mt: 2 Sophie Hales 24:19.06
     Aug 3   v FRA/ESP Niort   3000mt: 5 Claire Reeves 15:12.76, 6 Nicola Phillips 15:21.67
2004 Jul 24 v GER/ITA Manchester 3000mt: 4 Rebecca Mersh 14:18.93, 5 Johanna Jackson 14:25.96
2005 Aug 6   4-N Manchester   5000mt: 1 Jackson 22:46.07, 4 Katie Stones 24:18.19

GB JUNIORS
1979 May 26 v3N St-Aubin-les-Elbeuf 5000mt: 1 Karen Eden 26:33.3, 3 Susan Till 26:56;00, 4 Jane Lewis 28:01.5, 5 Linda Nichols 28:32.6, 10 Joanna Wickham 29:18.6
1984 May 5   v 3N Bergen (Fana) 3000mt: 4 Nicky Jackson 14:12.8, 8 Helen Ringshaw 14:31.7, 13 Elizabeth Ryan 15:31.7. Inc. senior: CHN 32, SWE 18, NOR 13, GB 11
     Jun 3   v 3N Barcelona   5km: 3 Jackson 24:28, 6 Lisa Langford 25:34, 7 Elizabeth Ryan 25:41 12 Ruth Sugg 26:34
     Jul 7   v FRG London (He) 5000mt: 1 Langford 25:00.6, 2 Kim Macadam 26:36.9
     Jul 29 v NOR/ITA Haugesund 5000mt: 1 Langford 24:42.84, 2 Ringshaw 24:59.04
1985 May 5   v 3N Pisa   5km: 5 Susan Ashforth 23:57.2, 6 Macadam 25:12.8, 8 Julie Drake 25:35.8, 10 Lisa Simpson 25:55.2. ESP 34, GB 23, ITA 12
     Jun 15 v SWE, NOR Borås   5000mt: 2 Ashforth 14:07.9, 7 Macadam 14:32.9, 9 Victoria Lawrence 14:45.7
     Jul 6   v FRG Kamen   5000mt: 1 Langford 23:54.2, 3 Drake 25:43.2
     Oct 13 v FRA Flers   5km: 1 Langford 24:09, 2 Lawrence 25:07, 4 Drake 25:21, 7 Ashforth 26:54
1986 Jun 15 v ESP, ITA Alcalá 5km: 5 Angela Hodd 25:13, 6 Macadam 25:36, 9 Drake 26:06, 11 Simpson 26:46
     Jun 21 v SWE,NOR Plymouth 5000mt: 3 Lawrence 14:22.3, 8 Suzie Pratt 26:11.7, 9 Joanne Clarke 26:41.8
     Aug 16 v FRG Göttingen   5000mt: 1 Lawrence 26:39.4, 2 Hodd 27:05.3
     Sep 27 v FRA Brighton   5000mt: 1 Drake 25:26.2, 3 Macadam 25:56.1, 4 Hodd 26:25.7, 5 Pratt 26:26.0
1987 Apr 5   v HUN Békéscsaba   5km: 1 Drake 24:44, 2 Lawrence 24:52, 4 Hodd 25:44
     Jun 27 v FRG/POL Ipswich 5000mt: 1 Lawrence 24:23.34, 4 Drake 25:09.10
     Aug 22 v FRG/SUI Lage   5000mt: 1 Andrea Crofts 26:50.59, 3 Joanne Pope 27:59.00
     Sep 26 v FRA, FRG Paris   5km: 1 Lawrence 23:54, 3 Drake 24:25, 4 Karen Dunster 24:49, 6 Crofts 25:25
1988 Jun 19 v TCH Prague   5000mt: 3 Drake 24:54.0, 4 Dunster 25:53.0
     Aug 20 v IRL/SUI Cwmbran 3000mt: 1 Vicky Lupton 14:45.84, 2 Tracey Devlin 14:54.41
     Sep 3   v SWE, NOR Göteborg 5000mt: 6 Lupton 25:15.3, 7 Crofts 25:42.6, 9 Devlin 27:15.3
1989 Jun 25 v 5N Laval   5km: 12 Pope 25:06, 14 Verity Larby 25:14, 18 Sharon Tonks 25:49, 19 Lupton 26:03
     Jul 1   v FRG, SWE U23   5000mt: 3 Crofts 25:14.75, 6 Zena Lindley 25:40.32
     Aug 6   v ITA/HUN Calamaggiore 5000mt: 5 Pope 25:34.61, 6 Larby 25:39.55
     Sep 3   v GRE U23/HUN U23 Athens 5000mt: 1 Lupton 24:59.25, 5 Lindley 26:23.75
     Sep 17 v NOR, SWE Moss   5000mt: 2 Devlin 24:34.6, 4 Larby 24:44.1, 5 Lupton 24:48.1
1990 Jun 16 8N Munich   5km: 15 Pope 26:47, 28 Theresa Ashman 26:19; 29 Philippa Savage 26:19, dq Lupton
     Jul 7   v FIN/FRG Lübeck   5000mt: 1 Lupton 23:45.70, 6 Michelle Venables 27:48.21
     Jul 28 v AUS/ITA Horsham 3000mt:1 Lupton 13:29.18, 6 Pope 14:28.56
     Aug 4   v FRA/ITA/FRG Saarguemines 5000mt: 7 Kerry Woodcock 26:26.1, 8 Venables 26:50.1
1991 Jun 15 v FIN/USSR Espoo   5000mt: 3 Lupton 22:36.77, 8 Ashman 25:30.17
     Jun 29 8N Örnsköldsvik   5km: 1 Lupton 22:43, 19 Carolyn Brown 24:54, 23 Kath Horwill 25:05, 24 Carla Jarvis 25:41
     Jul 19 8N Salamanca   5000mt: 7 Brown 26:22.52
     Aug 24 v GER/HUN Gladbach 5000mt: 4 Jarvis 25:18.0, 8 Horwill 25:54.1
1992 Jun 6   8N La Coruña   5km: 21 Brown 24:39, 23 Jarvis 25:01, 24 Ashman 25:07, 25 Horwill 25:08
     Aug 9   v ITA/EUN San Giuliano 5000mt: 5 Brown 27:13.85, 6 Horwill 27:46.75
     Aug 29 v FRA/ESP Horsham 5000mt: 4 Brown 24:27,73, 6 Ashman 26:21.48
1993 Jun 12 Eschborn   5km: 33 Brown 25:46, 34 Nina Howley 25:58, 40 Clare Ellis 26:39

29

	Jun 26	v GER/RUS Lübeck	3000mt: 5 Brown 15:15.24, 6 Lynsey Tozer 15:47.85
1994	Jun 12	Livorno	5km: 31 Tozer 26:58
	Jun 18	v POL/GER/RUS	5000mt: 7 Horwill 25:25.96, 8 Nikki Huckerby 27:25.38
	Aug 6	v ITA, TCH Schio	5000mt: 2 Howley 25:38.51, 5 Huckerby 26:57.88
1995	Feb 25	v GER, RUS Erfurt	Indoor 3000m: 5 Sarah Bennett 15:35.65, 6 Helen Ford-Dunn 16:29.41
	Jun 11	6N Fougères	5km: 18 Huckerby 26:15, 20 Howley 26:51, 21 Sally Warren 26:54, 22 Ellis 27:34
1995	Aug 6	v FRA/BEN Belfort	3 Howley 15:10.0, 4 Huckerby 15:15.0
1996	Mar 2	v FRA/GER/ITA Liévin	Indoor 3000m: 7 Bennett 14:39.24, 8 Debbie Wallen 15:30.16
	Jun 1	6N Moscow	10km: 16 Huckerby 25:21.3, 19 Howley 26:01.2, dq Wallen
	Aug 3	v ITA/FRA/ESP Nembro	5000mt: 7, Huckerby 26:32.2, 8 Bennett 26:53.9
1997	Mar 1	v FRA, GER Chemnitz	Indoor 3000m: 5 Becky Tisshaw 14:51.86, dq Bennett
	Jun 7	v GER Bad Homburg	5000mt: 5 Huckerby 25:18.0, 6 Bennett 26:28.0
1998	Feb 28	v FRA, GER Birmingham	Indoor 3000m: 3 Katie Ford 14:17.96, 6 Amy Hales 14:44.35
	May 30	8N Senigallia	5km: 16 Ford 24:48, 19 Bennett 24:59, 21 A Hales 25:17, 25 Wallen 25:50
	Jul 18	v ESP/FRA Alicante	5000mt: 4 Ford 25:25.4, 6 Bennett 26:01.4
	Sep 5	Budapest 3 GB 40	5km: 8 Wallen 25:11, 9 Bennett 25:15, 12 Ford 25:38, 16 A Hales 26:17
1999	Feb 27	v 3N Nogent-sur-Oise	Indoor 3000m: 6 Ford 15:13.58, 8 Nicola Phillips 15:25.75
	May 29	8N Catania	5000mt: 10 A Hales 25:22.0, 11 Ford 25:42.0, 14 Phillips 26:25.0, 15 Bennett 27:23.0.
	Jul 24	v FRA/ESP/ITA Albertville	3000mt: 7 Phillips 14:52.67, 8 Ford 15:21.68
	Aug 21	v3N (U19) Neubrandenburg	5000mt:8 A Hales 24:47.99, 8 Phillips 25:11.46
	Sep 4	v 6N Budapest	5km: 5 Phillips 25:28, 7 A Hales 25:47, 14 Kelly Mann 26:19
2000	Mar 4	v GER, FRA Neubrandenburg	Indoor 3000m: 4 Phillips 14:29.37, 6 Laura Fryer 16:29.82
	Apr 23	10N Leamington	10km: 8 Phillips 51:36, 10 Claire Reeves 55:53, 11 Ford 56:28
	Sep 2	Budapest	5km: 11 Sophie Hales 26:47, 14 Phillips 27:05, 22 Natalie Evans 28:31
	Oct 7	4N (U19) Grossetto	5000mt: 7 Natalie Evans 29:00.58
2001	Mar 3	v FRA,GER,ITA Vittel	Indoor 3000m: 5 S Hales 14:38.18, 7 Phillips 14:49.40
	Jul 29	FRA (U19) Dôle	3000mt: 2 Katie Stones 14:25.91, 4 Reeves 16:31.41
	Sep 9	v 4N Budapest	5km: 4 S Hales 25:10, 8 Katie Hales 25:47, 15 Bryna Christmas 27:58
2002	Jul 7	v ITA/ESP Gorizia	5000mt: 5 S Hales 24:35.56, 6 Stones 27:34.98
2003	Jul 5	v ITA Nove	5000mt: 3 S Hales 24:51.30, 4 Stones 25:23.13
2004	Mar 20	v5N Leamington	10km: 1 S Hales 51:16, 2 Stones 51:20, 5 Jenny Gagg 53:12
2005	Apr 16	v3N Leamington	10km: 1 Rebecca Mersh 51:38, 3 Sarah Foster 56:02, 4 Fiona McGorum 56:13

ENGLAND (v Overseas countries)

1959	Sep 27	v DEN Copenhagen	5000mt: 1. Betty Franklin 26:30.6, 2 Beryl Randle 26:32.0, 3 Nellie Batson 27:58.2, 5 Helen Vincent 27:58.2. ENG 7, DEN 15
1964	Jun 7	v DEN, SWE Malmö	5000mt: 3 Judy Farr 27:53.4, 4 Audrey Hackett 28:10.01. SWE, ENG, DEN
1966	Sep 17	v DEN London (He)	c.5.4km: 1 Farr 28:55.6, 3 Sheila Jennings 28:52.0, 4 Hackett 29:11.4, 6 Betty Jenkins 30:04.0, 9 Margaret Lewis 30:46.0
1968	Aug 31	v DEN, SWE Odense	5000mt: 6 Jenkins 27:26.8, 7 Doris Froome 27:27.0, 8 Farr 27:27.2, 11 Barbara Fisk 28:11,4, 14 Diane Cotterill 29:34.4
1969	Aug 24	v 3N Le Neubourg	5000mt: 5 Fisk 26:27.0, 6 Farr 26:28.0, 9 Jenkins 27:17.0, 14 Marian Hindley 28:34.0, 16 Jennifer Peck 28:54.0
1970	Sep 5	v 4N Borås	5000mt: 12 Margaret Lewis 27:54.0, 13 Barbara Cook 28:12.0, 14 Jenny Peck 28:18.0, 17 Jean Wallis 28:50.0, 19 Barbara Brown 29:15.0
1972	Sep 16	v 4N Warley	5000mt: 3 Jenkins 25:09.2, 5 Brenda Cook 25:58.4, 7 Margaret Lewis SWE 72 ENG 61 NOR 37 DEN 22 FRA 19 26:21.2, 8 Barbara Cook 26:21.4, 14 Virginia Lovell 27:36.4
1973	Sep 1	v 5N Copenhagen (1 NOR 76, 2 SWE 75, 3 ENG 67 ...)	5000mt: 5 Sally Wish 25:34.0, 6 Jenkins 25:38.0, 9 Marion Fawkes 26:26.0, 14 Lovell 26:59.0, 18 Pam Branson 27:58.0
1974	Aug 24	Stockholm	5000mt: 3 Fawkes 24:59.2, 23 Wish 28:11.0
	Sep 22	v 4N Grand Quévilly	5km: 1 Fawkes 25:01, 3 Branson 26:02, 6 Sylvia Saunders 26:06, 10 Wish 27:09. ENG 37 SWE 35 FRA 28 SUI 11 ESP 10
1976	Aug 14	Lyngby 'World Ch'	5000mt: 2, Fawkes 24:24.0, 5 Carol Tyson 24:53.0, 7 Farr 25:07.0, 6 Saunders 26:31.0. SWE 70, ENG 70, NOR 59.... Nobody at 10km
1978	Aug 12	Fredrikstad 'World Ch'	5000mt: 3 Fawkes 23:31.7, 4 Tyson 23:35.2, 12 Irene Bateman 25:21.0, dq, Karen Eden
1985	Jul 13	v 3N Budapest	10,000mt: 1 Virginia Birch 50:58.4, 1 Helen Elleker 52:29.8
1989	Jul 22	v POR/ESP/WAL Swansea	5000mt: 2 Lisa Langford 23:05.10, 4 Julie Drake 24:06.29
	Aug 28	v OCE, ITA Gateshead	5000mt: 1 Betty Sworowski 22:02.06, 4 Elleker 24:17.42
1990	Aug 11	v HUN, TCH Miskolc	5000mt: 3 Drake 23:08.03, 4 Elleker 23:21.28
1993	Feb 7	v BEL Gent	Indoor 3000m: 1 Drake 13:54.05, 2 Melanie Brookes 14:13.65
	Aug 28	v UKR Kiev	5000mt: 3 Brookes 24:12.50, 4 Black (Saunders) 25:01.00
1997	Sep 27	v 5N Dublin	10km: 2 Sylvia Black 49:08, 3 Kim Braznell 49:47 (M+W: 1 ENG 126)
1998	Sep 12	v IRL,NED,IOM Dublin	10km: 2 Catherine Charnock 49:14, 4 Sharon Tonks 51:55

ENGLAND A
2000 Sep 2 v FRA Vittel 3000mt: 3 Charnock 13:58.96, 4 Niobe Menendez 14:08.52, 6 S Warren 14:54.39
ENGLAND U23
1990 Sep 15 v TCH, POL Jablonec   3000mt:1 Lisa Langford 22:44.88, 5 Vicky Lupton 23:26.27
1994 Jul 7   v AUS U20/NIR King's Lynn   3000mt: 3 Lupton 13:20.23, 4 Claire Walker 15:11.65

GREAT BRITAIN & NI WALKS INTERNATIONALS
Shown for each athlete: Surname, full names (if known), dates of birth (and death, where known), clubs, number of senior internationals (years), plus major Games and Championships contested (including Commonwealth Games for home countries).
Diminutives, where widely used, included in quotes here, with shortened versions of names underlined.
Men
ADAMS, Brian (13.3.49) Leicester WC	15 (1974-82)	OG 76, EC & CG 78
ALLEN, Laurence 'Lol' (25.4.21) Sheffield United H	3 (1950-2)	OG 52, EC 50
ATTON, Karl (14.9.71) Leicester WC, Road Hoggs	5 (1993-9)	
BAILEY, Frank G (14.4.28) Polytechnic H	1 (1954)	EC 54
BALL, James R 'Jimmy' (17.2.63) Southampton AC	1 (1986)	
BENTLEY, Frank Edward (18.8.09 - .8.95) Belgrave H	1 (1938)	EC 38
BANYARD, Alec Williams (27.2.42) Southend on Sea	1 (1975)	
BARRY, Steven John (25.10.50) Roath Labour	13 (1980-3)	OG 84, EC & CG 82
BEARMAN, Donald (16.4.66) Steyning	2 (2000-01)	
BELL, Martin (9.4.61) Splott Conservative	8 (1989-98)	CG 98
BERWICK, Christopher (1.5.46) Leicester WC	5 (1985-9)	
BLAGG, Paul (23.1.60) Cambridge H	16 (1982-92)	OG 88/92, WC 87/91, EC 90, CG 82
BOSWORTH, Thomas 'Tom' (17.1.90) Tonbridge	4 (2011-14)	CG 10
BRIDGE, Robert 'Bobby' (16.4.1883 - 17.7.53) Lancashire WC	1 (1912)	OG 12
BROOKS, Ian (21.4.45) Surrey WC	1 (1971)	
BROWN, Gareth James (10.5.68) Steyning	2 (1996)	CG 02
BROWN, William C. 'Bill' (?) Surrey WC	1 (1908)	OG 08
BUTLER, John 'Jack' (?) Polytechnic H	1 (1908)	OG 08
CARTER, Frank T. (.1878) Queens Park H	1 (1908)	OG 08
CARTER, Kenneth Reginald John (7.3.47) Southend AC	1 (1978)	
CHAPLIN, George E (18.2.31) Coventry Godiva	3 (1968-72)	
CHEESEMAN, Christopher (11.12.58) Surrey WC	8 (1994-01)	CG 98
CHURCHER, Harry George (21.11.10 - 24.6.72)	3 (1947-9)	OG 48
CLARK, Frederick Ernest (25.3.1898 – 1960s?) Surrey WC	1 (1924)	OG 24
CLARK, Robert Alfred 'Bob' (15.5.35 - .11.07) Polytechnic H	4 (1961-2)	EC 62
COCKER, Jonathan (26.9.71) York CIU	2 (1996)	
COLEMAN, George William (21.11.16 - .1.05) Highgate H	3 (1920-6)	OG 52/56, EC 54
COTTON, Alfred (21.8.14 - .7.97) Woodford Green	1 (1950)	EC 50
COTTON, David (16.9.56) Holloway Polytechnic	3 (1975-8)	EC 86
DOBSON, Robert William 'Bob' (4.11.42) Basildon, Southend on Sea, Ilford	13 (1970-82)	WC 76, EC 71/74, CG 70
DOWRICK, Brian (20.1.63) Splott Conservative	2 (1993)	
DOWSON, Charles Samuel (16.11.1889 – 5.2.80) Queens Park H	1 (1920)	OG 20
DRAKE, Andrew Paul 'Andi' (6.2.65) Coventry RWC	23 (1985-02)	EC 90/02, CG 98, EI 90
DUMBILL, Thomas Henry (23.9.1884) Lancashire WC	1 (1912)	OG 12
EASTON, Mark Jonathan (24.5.63) Surrey WC	15 (1985-99)	EC 90, CG 90/94/98/02
EDGINGTON, John William (5.4.36 - .2.93) Coventry Godiva	3 (1963-4)	OG 64
ELEY, Bryan (28.1.39) Bristol WC, Trowbridge	2 (1968-9)	OG 68, EC 69
ELMS, Stuart George (30.4.46) Brighton & Hove	1 (1976)	
EMBLETON, Philip Bruce (28.12.48 - 22.5.74) Metropolitan WC	5 (1971-2)	OG 72, EC 71
FINCH, Luke (21.9.85) Leicester WC, Colchester H	1 (2009)	CG 10
FLYNN, Oliver Thomas 'Olly' (30.6.50) Basildon	9 (1974-9)	OG 76, CG 78
FOGG, Charles William 'Charlie' (14.3.34) Enfield AC/Borough of Enfield H	8 (1961-75)	
FORBES, Harry John (1.3.13) Birmingham H	1 (1946)	EC 46
FULLAGER, Peter Edward (19.4.43) Surrey WC, Basildon. Later AUS	10 (1966-9)	EC 66, 69
GODBEER, John F () Cambridge H	1 (1961)	
GOODWIN, Gordon Reginald (17.12.1895 - .2.84) Surrey WC	1 (1924)	OG 24
GOWER, Stephen 'Steve' (7.10.50 - 21.8.02) Essex Beagles	4 (1971-8)	
GRAHAM, Barry (16.8.46) York Postal	11 (1981-8)	
GREASLEY, Michael 'Mick' (26.4.54) Sheffield United	3 (1977-80)	
GREEN, Thomas William 'Tommy' (30.3.1894 – 29.3.73) Belgrave H	1 (1932)	OG 32
GUNN, Charles Edward James 'Charlie' (14.8.1885 – 30.12.83) Railway Clearing House	1 (1920)	OG 20

31

HALES, Matthew (6.10.79) Steyning   3 (1999-01)
HALL, Eric William (15.9.32) Belgrave H   4 (1956-60)   OG 56/60
HALL, Raymond Charles (25.6.33) Belgrave H   1 (1962)   EC 62
HAMMOND, Thomas Edgar 'Tommy' (18.6.1878 - 18.12.45) Surrey WC   1 (1908)   OG 08
HARDING, Kenneth (23.6.29) Royal Sutton Coldfield   1 (1970)
HARDY, Roland (11.6.26) Sheffield United H   4 (1950-6)   OG 52/56, EC 50
HARRISON, Richard (1885) North Shields Poly/WC   1 (1908)   OG 08
HARVEY, Christopher (14.10.56) Lancashire WC   7 (1978-85)
HAWKINS, Bryan (16.4.28) Metropolitan WC   1 (1954)   EC 54
HEHIR, William (21.1.1887) Surrey WC, Herne Hill H, IRL   1 (1920)   OG 20
HODKINSON, Peter (5.11.44) Cambridge H   2 (1977-9)
HOLLIER, Steven (27.2.76) Wolverhampton & Bilston   7 (1998-02)   CG 98/02
HOLLOWAY, Gareth Paul (2.2.70) Splott Conservative   1 (1992-3)
HOLMES, Michael Stephen 'Mike' (26.8.51) Yorkshire RWC   8 (1973-80)
HOPKINS, Joseph 'Joe' (19.2.02 - .74) Lancashire WC   1 (1936)   OG 36
HUGHES, Robert 'Bob' (27.10.47) Royal Sutton Coldfield   6 (1967-70)   OG 68
INGARFIELD, Barry (13.8.38) Metropolitan WC   1 (1976)
JACKSON, Dennis (29.6.45) York Postal   16 (1980-93)   EC 86
JAMES, Adrian Howard (23.9.46) Borough of Enfield H   4 (1978-9)
JARMAN, David (2.2.50) Surrey WC   2 (1982)
JOHNSON, Albert H (1.5.31 - 20.5.09) Sheffield United   4 (1954-60)   OG 56/60, EC 54/58
                                                                                          CG 66
JOHNSON, Stephen Lyndon 'Ossie' (10.6.60) Wales, Splott Conservative   2 (1985-7)   CG 86
JOHNSON, Tebbs Lloyd (7.4.00 – 26.12.84) Leicester WC, Surrey AC   2 (1936-48)   OG 36/48
JONES, Arthur John (5.10.38) Brighton & Hove   2 (1967-8)   OG 68
JONES, Trevor (2.10.56) Steyning   1 (2006)
KING, Allan (3.13.56) Leicester WC, Road Hoggs   11 (1979-99)
KING, Daniel (30.5.83) Colchester H   8 (2003-12)   CG 06
KING, Dominic (30.5.83) Colchester H   11 (2002-13)   OG 12, CG 02/06
KING, Philip (25.11.74) Brighton & Hove   1 (1995)
LAMBDEN, Murray (14.10.56) Isle of Man, Boundary H   4 (1981-2)   CG 1982
LARNER, Ernest Edward (25.6.1880) Highgate H   1 (1908)   OG 08
LARNER, George Edward (7.2.1875 - 4.3.49) Brighton & Co H, Highgate H   1 (1908)   OG 08
LAWTON, Carl Philip (20.1.48) Belgrave H   8 (1971-9)   WC 76, EC 71, CG 74
LEES, John (23.2.45) Brighton & Hove   3 (1975-6)
LIGHTMAN, Shaun (15.4.43) Metropolitan WC   12 (1967-79)   OG 68, EC 69, CG 70
McCOMBIE, Ian Peter (11.1.61) Cambridge H   24 (1981-92)   OG 84/88, WC 83/87/91,
                                                                                          EC 82, CG 86/90

MADDOCKS, Christopher Lloyd (28.3.57) Dawlish & SD, City of Plymouth   32 (1978-00)   OG 84/88/92/96/00,
                                                                                          WC 87/91/93, CG 86/90/94/98

MARLOW, Peter (20.4.41) Southend on Sea   5 (1972-5)   OG 72
MARTINDALE, Sean (8.11.66) York Postal   1 (1989)
MARTINEAU, Harold Albert (24.12.14 - 3.5.94) Surrey WC   1 (1948)   OG 48
MATTHEWS, Kenneth Joseph (21.6.36) Royal Sutton Coldfield   15 (1959-64)   OG 60/64, EC 62
MEGNIN, Charles E 'Charlie' (1.4.15 - 2.11.03) Highgate H   1 (1946)   EC 46
MIDDLETON, Raymond Christopher (9.8.36) Belgrave H   17 (1961-73)   OG 64, EC62/66/69
                                                                                          CG 66
MILLS, Roger G (11.2.48) Ilford   34 (1972-83)   OG 80, WC 83, EC
                                                                                          74/78, CG 82
MISSON, Thomas William 'Tom' (11.5.30) Metropolitan WC   3 (1958-60)   OG 60, EC 58
MORRIS, Charles James 'Jim' (2.1.15) Surrey AC   3 (1947-9)   OG 48
MORRIS, Graham Barry (19.1.58) Steyning   5 (1979-81)
MORTON, Leslie (1.7.58) Sheffield United H/WC   27 (1985-99)   OG 88/92, WC 91/93/95,
                                                                                          EC 86

NIBRE, George (9.2.57) Ilford   4 (1979-80)
NIHILL, Vincent Paul (5.9.39) Surrey WC   16 (1963-76)   OG 64/68/72/76
                                                                                          EC 69/71

OLDALE, Richard (26.1.66) Sheffield United/RWC   1 (1996)
O'RAWE, James 'Jamie' (3.2.73) Road Hoggs   3 (1995-9)
PADDICK, John Chester (31.8.43) Royal Sutton Coldfield   2 (1964)   OG 64
PALMER, William James (19.4.1882 – 21.12.67) Herne Hill H   2 (1908-12)   OG 08/12
PARKER, Michael Graham 'Mike' (21.4.53) Brighton & Hove. Later NZL.   3 (1982-6)
PARTINGTON, Stephen Wyand 'Steve' (17.9.65) Isle of Man, Manx H   12 (1989-02)   CG 86/90/94/98/02/06
PENN, Andrew Shaun 'Andy' (31.3.67) Coventry RWC   14 (1987-00)   OG 92, WC 93
                                                                                          CG 02/06

PHILLIPS, Stuart (15.4.63) Ilford   2 (1991-3)

PROCTOR, John Wilson Grange (3.9.23 - 26.10.00) Sheffield United	1 (1950)	EC 50
QUINN, Richard (3.12.1882) Motherwell H, Bellahouston H	1 (1908)	OG 08
REID, John J. (?) Clonliffe H (IRL)	1 (1908)	OG 08
RICHARDS, Ian William (12.4.48) Coventry Godiva	8 (1978-82)	OG 80, EC 78
RUSH, Martin Gavin Anthony (25.12.64) Cockermouth, Lakeland, Loughborough Un.	11 (1985-93)	OG 92, CG 86
SAREL, Sydney Lancaster (18.6.1872 - 23.12.50) London AC, Oxford Un.	1 (1908)	OG 08
SCHOFIELD, Sidney Charles Apps (7.2.1883 – 24.3.56) Surrey WC	1 (1908)	OG 08
SEDDON, Amos (22.1.41) Borough of Enfield H	25 (1973-81)	EC 74/78, CG 78
SHILLABEER, Edmund Harrold (2.8.39) Dawlish & South Devon	1 (1987)	
SMITH, Michael John 'Mike' (20.4.63) Coventry RWC	3 (1985-9)	
SPENCER, Edward Adams (5.11.1881 – 6.5.65) Polytechnic H	1 (1908)	OG 08
STONE, Darrell Richard (2.2.68) Steyning	20 (1988-00)	WC 93/95, EC 90 CG 94/98
SUTHERLAND, William Mackintosh Saunders 'Bill' (6.4.45) Highgate H	6 (1968-72)	EC 71, CG 70
TAYLOR, Anthony J 'Tony' (3.6.47) Lancashire WC	2 (1971-4)	
TAYLOR, Eric (9.6.39) Hinckley, Nomads, Bromsgrove, Coventry Godiva	1 (1973)	
TAYLOR, Stephen M 'Steve' (19.3.66) Isle of Man, Manx H.	1 (1995)	CG 94
THOMAS, Vaughan (?)	1 (1963)	
THOMPSON, Donald James (20.1.33 - 4.10.06) Metropolitan WC	11 (1956-67)	OG 56/60/64 EC 58/62/66, CG 66
THOMSON, Arthur G R (22.4.36) Metropolitan WC, Enfield & Haringey	1 (1962)	EC 62
THORN, Darren Michael (17.7.62) Coventry RWC	4 (1985-90)	
THORN, Philip W (19.11.38) Trowbridge	1 (1968)	
THORPE, Roy S (18.5.34) Sheffield United	10 (1973-6)	WC 76, CG 74
TIMMS, Howard William (9.7.44) Surrey WC	1 (1972)	OG 72
TOLLEY, Malcolm Robert (15.4.44) Sheffield United	1 (1965)	
TRIGG, Andrew David 'Andy' (23.6.82) Leicester WC	1 (1986-7)	
TUNBRIDGE, Donald Arthur (28.10.20 - .3.99) Highgate H	1 (1952)	OG 52
VALE, Gordon (12.1.62) Surrey WC	4 (1979-82)	
VESTY, Philip John (5.1.63) Leicester WC	14 (1981-7)	OG 84, WC 83
VICKERS, Stanley Frank (18.6.32) Belgrave H	6 (1956-60)	OG 56/60, EC 58
WALLWORK, Ronald Edward (26.5.41) Lancashire WC	10 (1963-71)	EC 66/71, CG 70/74
WARHURST, John 'Jake' (1.10.44) Shefield United H	15 (1968-77)	OG 72, EC & CG 74
WATT, Timothy (19.9.66) Steyning	2 (2000)	
WATTS, Hubert Gordon A (8.12.1893 - .3.86) Surrey WC	1 (1924)	OG 24
WEARS, Ben (4.7.90) Redcar RW	2 (2011-12)	
WEBB, Ernest James (25.4.1874 – 24.2.37) Herne Hill H	2 (1908-12)	OG 08/12
WEBB, John Albert (21.12.36) Basildon	9 (1966-73)	OG 68, EC 66/69
WEST, Richard A. 'Ron' (27.4.14) Cambridge H	1 (1948)	OG 48
WHITE, Graham (28.3.59) Brighton & Hove	6 (1983-98)	CG 98
WHITLOCK, George Bernard Rex (8.9.10– 26.6.82) Metropolitan WC	2 (1948-52)	OG 48/52
WHITLOCK, Hector Harold (1.12.03 – 27.12.85) Metropolitan WC	3 (1936-52)	OG 36/52, EC 50
WILLIAMS, George (?) Belgrave H	3 (1959-61)	
WILLIAMS, Mark (7.9.64) Tamworth	2 (2001-06)	
WITHERS, Godwin Robert James (28.9.1884 – 5.2.76) Railway Clearing House	1 (1908)	OG 08
WRIGHT, Alex (19.12.90) Belgrave H	3 (2011-13)	CG 10
YATES, William George (5.8.1880 – 27.12.67) Salford H	1 (1912)	OG 12
YEOUMANS, Alfred Thomas (4.11.1876 – 21.8.42) Swansea A & CC, Highgate H	1 (1908)	OG 08

Not including ultra distance events
Commonwealth Games but not GB

BANNAN, Philip G (3.1.48) Isle of Man	CG 66
CALLOW, John Allan (4.9.45) Isle of Man. Boundary H.	CG 70/74/78
CANNELL, John (29.11.45) Isle of Man	CG 70
DOREY, David R A 'Dave' (29.11.35) Guernsey	CG 70/74
DUQUEMIN, Leonard 'Len' (28.11.30) Guernsey, Belgrave H	CG 70
ELLIOTT, Robert (31.3.59) Guernsey, Sarnia	CG 82
HARRISON, Derek (22.1.35) Isle of Man, Boundary H	CG 74
HART, Roy Alfred (23.1.36) Wales, Roath Labour	CG 66
LAMBIE, Robert 'Robbie' (6.7.54) Isle of Man	CG 78/82
MOULLIN, John (8.9.41) Guernsey	CG 70/74
ROSSER, Richard David 'Dave' () Wales	CG 70
SMYTH, David J R A 'Dave' (29.11.35 - 7.6.06) N.Ireland, Bristol	CG 70
WATERMAN, Robin () Guernsey	CG 74
YOUNG, Graham (30.5.45) Isle of Man	CG 74/78/82

England Internationals only
O'RAWE, Andrew 'Andy' (8.9.63) Road Hoggs — 1998
WATTS, David J 'Dave' (11.2.45) Metropolitan WC — 1965

WOMEN
ADAMSON/FAWKES, Marion (3.12.48) North Shields Poly — 7 (1974-9)
BAIRD/BRAZNELL, Kim (28.2.56) Dudley & Stourbridge — 5 (1995-00) CG 98
BARRETT, Jill (13.7.64) Verlea — 6 (1980-4)
BATEMAN, Irene Lillian (13.11.47) Basildon — 15 (1979-83)
BROOKES/WRIGHT, Melanie (5.4.64) Nuneaton H — 6 (1992-6)
BROWN, Sarah Jean (28.9.64) Steyning — 8 (1982-9)
CATTERMOLE, Sara-Jane (29.1.77) Dartford H — 4 (2000-02) CG 02
CHARNOCK, Catherine (3.5.75) Barrow & Fylde — 1 (1999)
COX/CALLINAN, Elaine Valerie (13.9.60) Solihull & Small Heath — 4 (1979-95)
CRUMP, Lisa (30.3.76) Sheffield United — 3 (1997-9)
DAVIES, Bethan (7.11.90) Cardiff, Leeds University — 1 (2013)
DRAKE, Julie Elizabeth (21.5.69) Brighton & Hove — 17 (1989-93) WC 91/93, EC 90
DUNSTER, Karen Lynn (18.5.69) Aldershot, Farnham & District — 1 (1988)
EDEN, Karen (4.11.62) Solihull AC — 1 (1980)
EDGAR, Gillian (26.6.64) Lakeland AC — 1 (1981)
ELLEKER, Helen (21.3.56) Sheffield United — 14 (1985-91) WC 91, EC 86, CG 90
FRANCIS/ALLEN, Beverley Colleen (16.3.59) Brighton & Hove — 11 (1979-87) WC 87, EC 86
JACKSON/ATKINSON, Johanna Frances (17.1.85) Redcar RWC — 15 (2005-14) OG 08/12, WC 07/09/11, CG 06/10

JACKSON, Nicola Sally (1.5.65) Trowbridge — 11 (1986-9)
KNEALE, Karen (23.4.69) Isle of Man, Manx H — 2 (1995-8) CG 98
LANGFORD/KEHLER, Lisa Martine (15.3.67) Wolverhampton & Bilston — 26 (1982-11) OG 92/00, WC 87/95 EC 86/90/94/98, CG 90/94/98/02/10, EI 88

LARBY/SNOOK, Verity A (13.11.70) Aldershot, Farnham & District — 10 (1991-7) WC 93, EC & CG 94
LOVELL/BIRCH, Virginia Claire 'Ginny' (1.7.55) Brighton & Hove — 10 (1975-86)
LUPTON, Brenda (5.10.52) Sheffield United — 6 (1982-92)
LUPTON/WHITE, Victoria Anne 'Vicky' (17.4.72) Sheffield United/RWC — 17 (1991-9) OG 92/96, WC 93 EC 94, CG 94/98

MENENDEZ, Niobe (1.9.66) Steyning — 3 (1999-01) CG 02/06
MILLEN, Lillian (5.3.45) Lakeland AC — 6 (1981-3)
NIPPER, Karen Lesley (22.12.64) Roath Labour — 3 (1983-5)
PARTINGTON, Carolyn 'Cal' (27.6.66) Manx H — 2 (1994-5) CG 94/98/02
RINGSHAW, Helen (22.7.66) Steyning — 1 (1982)
SAUNDERS/BLACK, Sylvia (16.4.58) Harborne H, Birchfield H — 9 (1975-97) EI 90
SIMPSON, Lisa Alison Marie (18.4.68) Mitcham AC — 4 (1985-8)
SMITH/WORTH, Elaine (15.1.58) Bolehall Swifts — 1 (1980)
SMITH, Karen (1.6.61) Coventry RWC — 1 (1993) CG 94
STONES, Katherine (22.11.85) Kingston upon Hull — 1 (2006)
SWOROWSKI, Elizabeth 'Betty' (11.3.61) Sheffield United — 16 (1986-92) OG 92, WC 91 EC & CG 90

TONKS, Sharon Jayne (18.4.70) Dudley & Stourbridge — 2 (2001-02) CG 02
TYSON, Carol Joan (15.12.57 - 24.6.05) Lakeland AC — 9 (1977-81)

England Internationals only
BATSON/LOINES, Nellie (12.2.27) Small Heath H — 1959
BILLINGSLEY/LEWIS, Margaret (19.6.37) Harborne H, Birchfield H — 1966-72
BRANSON, Pamela (10.3.58) Harborne H — 1973-4
DAY/RANDLE, Beryl E M (16.12.28) Birchfield H — 1959
EDGE/COOK, Brenda Joyce (17.10.35) Wolverhampton & Bilston — 1972
FISK/COOK, Barbara (11.8.50) Redhill & Reigate — 1968-72
FRANKLIN/JENKINS, Betty Ann (13.1.38) Birchfield H — 1959-72
FROOME, Doris () Harborne H — 1968
KNIGHT/HINDLEY, Marian (2.6.36) Birchfield H — 1969
MOORE/COTTTERILL, Diane N (27.3.45) South Shields H — 1968
PECK/FINCH, Jennifer (25.7.49) Selsonia Ladies — 1969-70
VINCENT/MILNE, Helen M (19.12.32) London Olympiades — 1959
WISH, Sallyanne (15.4.58) Solihull AC — 1973-4
WOODSFORD/FARR, Judith Undine 'Judy' (24.1.42) Trowbridge — 1964-9

AAA TRACK CHAMPIONSHIPS

2 MILES
1901 July 6 Huddersfield
George Deyermond Ireland   14:17.4
H.Simpson Polytechnic H
W.Martindale Polytechnic H
Jack Butler Polytechnic H
1902 July 5 London (SB)
William Sturgess Polytechnic H   14:46.6
G.Bush Northampton Institute H
W.Endean Polytechnic H
R.Watson London AC
H.Simpson Borough Polytechnic H
1903 July 4 Northampton
Edward Negus Northampton   14:44.4
G.Bush Northampton Institute H   14:51.0
Thomas O'Gorman Polytechnic H   15:04.0
W.Martindale Polytechnic H   15:05.0
W.Endean Polytechnic H   15:19.0
1904 July 2 London (SB)
George Larner Brighton & County H   13:57.6
George Deyermond Ireland
Frank Carter Queens Park H
S.Winterbottom Salford H
1905 July 1 London (SB)
George Larner Brighton & County   13:50.0
Robert Wilkinson Sefton H
W.Martindale Polytechnic H
Frank Carter Polytechnic H
1906 July 7 London (SB)
Alfred Yeoumans Swansea A & CC   14:20.4
Frank Creasey United H
Richard Harrison North Shields WC
Frederick Thompson Ranelagh H
Jack Butler Polytechnic H
Sydney Sarel London AC
1907 July 6 Manchester (Fallowfield)
Richard Harrison North Shields WC   14:01.8
Johnny Johnson Salford H   14:10.4
William Yates Salford H   14:24.2
1908 July 4 London (WC)
George Larner Brighton & County H   13:58.4
Ernest Webb Herne Hill H   14:05.6
Richard Harrison North Shields WC   14:14.6
Harry Kerr NZL   14:24.0
William Palmer Herne Hill H   14:24.0
Frank Creasey United H   14:25.0
1909 July 3 London (SB)
Ernest Webb Herne Hill H   13:56.4
A.Rowland NZL   14:26.6
T.Eaton Polytechnic H   14:40.6
Godwin Withers Railway Clearing House   14:47.6
A.Bennison Sheffield United H   14:55.0
E.Tudor Polytechnic H   14:56.0
1910 July 2 London (SB)
Ernest Webb Herne Hill H   13:54.4
Harold Ross Tooting AC   13:58.6
R.Steels North Shields Polytechnic   14:21.0
William Palmer Herne Hill H   14:27.0
D.Trotter Ashcombe AC   14:28.0
Frank Creasey Highgate H   14:29.0
1911 July 1 London (SB)
Harold Ross Middlesex WC   13:55.4
Will Ovens Herne Hill H
William Yates Salford AC
Godwin Withers Railway Clearing House AC

Richard Harrison North Shields Polytechnic
D.Trotter Ashcombe AC
1912 June 22 London (SB)
Bobby Bridge Lancashire WC   13:55.4
Ernest Webb Herne Hill H
Thomas Dumbill Lancashire WC
Harold Ross Middlesex WC
Will Ovens Herne Hill H
Godwin Withers Railway Clearing House
1913 July 5 London (SB)
Bobby Bridge Lancashire WC   13:51.8
Harold Ross Uxbridge & W Middlesex   14:01.8
Jack Lynch Polytechnic H   14:18.8
Will Ovens Herne Hill H   14:27.0
Godwin Withers Railway Clearing House   14:30.0
William Hehir Herne Hill H   14:31.0
1914 July 4 London (SB)
Bobby Bridge Lancashire WC   13:57.2
William Hehir Surrey WC   14:20.0
Jack Lynch Polytechnic H   14:25.0
H.Brockhurst Cavendish H   14:27.0
A.Taylor Surrey WC   14:28.0
1919 July 5 London (SB)
Bobby Bridge Lancashire WC   14:18.4
Gunnar Rasmussen DEN   14:28.8
J.Dowse Uxbridge & W Middlesex   14:29.8
G.Rounce unattached, Grays   14:55.4
Harold Ross Uxbridge & W Middlesex   14:56.6
W.Draper Surrey AC   15:05.0
1920 July 3 London (SB)
Charles Dowson Queens Park H   14:32.0
William Hehir Surrey AC   14:43.0
Charles Gunn Railway Clearing House   14:49.0
D.Trotter Ashcombe AC   14:59.0
E.McMullen Ashcombe AC
Harold Ross Herne Hill H
1921 July 2 London (SB)
John Evans Metropolitan Police AC   14:40.2
Charles Gunn Railway Clearing House   14:49.2
Fred Poynton Leicester WC   14:51.0
J.Dowse Finchley H   14:57.4
E.McMullen Ashcombe AC   15:07.2
R.Brew Southend H   15:09.2
1922 July 1 London (SB)
Ugo Frigerio ITA   14:30.0
J.Dowse Finchley H   14:31.8
Bobby Bridge Salford H   14:39.4
Gordon Watts Surrrey WC
Reg Goodwin Surrey WC
Harold Ross Herne Hill H
1923 July 7 London (SB)
Gordon Watts Surrey WC   14:24.0
Reg Goodwin Surrey WC   14:31.2
Fred Poynton Leicester WC   14:51.0
C.Ward Finchley H   14:53.0
J.Dowse Finchley H
Harold King Belgrave H
1924 Aug 9 Northampton
Reg Goodwin Surrey WC   14:11.2
C.Coulson Sheffield United H   14:19.2
Gordon Watts Surrey WC   14:22.0
Wilf Cowley Surrey AC
Cecil McMasters South Africa
1925 July 18 London (SB)
Reg Goodwin Surrey WC   14:07.4

35

Wilf Cowley Surrey AC	14:21.8	Paul Bernhard LAT		
C.Cater Port of London A Police	14:32.2	**1936** July 10 London (WC)		
Fred Clark Surrey AC	14:38.4	Bert Cooper Woodford Green		13:50.0
C.Coulson Sheffield United H	14:38.6	Paul Bernhard LAT		14:01.4
L.Sandy Surrey AC	14:55.2	Harry Churcher Belgrave H		14:02.8
1926 July 2 London (SB)		**1937** July 16 London (WC)		
Wilf Cowley Surrey AC	14:32.4	Bert Cooper Woodford Green		13:58.2
C.Cater PLA Police AC	14:40.0	Eddie Staker Highgate H		14:24.4
Lloyd Johnson Surrey AC	14:43.0	Don Brown Belgrave H		14:33.4
Dave McMullen Belgrave AC		Percy Wright Belgrave H		
G.Booker Surrey WC		Andrew Galloway Surrey WC		
E.Sharman Southern Railway		Dai Richards Newport H		
1927 July 1 London (SB)		**1938** July 15 London (WC)		
Alf Pope Woodford Green	14:21.6	Bert Cooper Woodford Green		14:02.2
Albert Fletcher Belgrave H		Eddie Staker Highgate H		14:07.6
C.Coulson Sheffield United H		Harry Churcher Highgate H		14:11.4
E.Sharman Southern Railway		Percy Wright Belgrave H		
C.Cater PLA Police AC		Hew Neilson Polytechnic H		
Wilf Cowley Surrey AC		Don Brown Victoria A & NAA		
1928 July 6 London (SB)		**1939** July 7 London (WC)		
Alf Pope Woodford Green	14:04.8	Harry Churcher Belgrave H		13:50.0
Cecil Hyde Enfield AC	14:16.2	Bert Cooper Woodford Green		14:05.4
John Wilson Sheffield United H	14:24.6	Hew Neilson Woodford Green		14:11.2
Albert Fletcher Belgrave H		Eddie Staker Highgate H		
H.Glover Ashcombe AC		Dai Richards Newport H		
C.Cater PLA Police AC		Percy Wright Belgrave H		
1929 July 5 London (SB)		**1946** July 19 London (WC)		
Alf Pope Woodford Green	13:57.6	Lars Hindmer SWE		13:59.0
Bert Cooper Woodford Green	14:00.2	Harry Churcher Belgrave H		14:04.6
Cecil Hyde Enfield AC	14:10.0	Eddie Staker Highgate H		14:16.0
Albert Fletcher Belgrave H		Frank Brown Portsmouth Police		14:35.8
John Reddish Herne Hill H		Alfred 'Tich' Marler Enfield AC		14:45.2
Dick Edge Derby W & AC		David Christie Murray Surrey WC		14:50.2
1930 July 4 London (SB)		**1947** July 19 London (WC)		
Cecil Hyde Enfield AC	13:56.4	Lasse Hindmer SWE		13:54.4
Bert Cooper Woodford Green	14:07.2	Harry Churcher Belgrave H		13:56.0
George Galloway Queens Park H		Giuseppe Kressevich ITA		14:09.6
Dick Edge Derby W&AC		Giuseppe Dordoni ITA		14:20.0
1931 July 3 London (SB)		Eddie Staker Highgate H		14:35.0
Alf Pope Woodford Green	13:52.6	Allan Furniss Sheffield Unted H		14:54.0
Bert Cooper Woodford Green	13:57.8	**1948** July 10 London (WC)		
Janis Dalins LAT	14:10.0	Harry Churcher Belgrave H		13:49.0
Dick Edge Derby W&AC		Jim Morris Surrey AC		13:57.0
1932 July 1 London (WC)		Ron West Cambridge H		14:27.0
Bert Cooper Woodford Green	13:44.6	Dave McMullen Cambridge H		14:37.0
Dick Edge Birmingham WC		Eddie Staker Highgate H		14:55.0
Leslie Dickinson Lancashire WC		**1949** July 30 Birmingham		
W.Sandy Valentines SC		Arne Borjesson SWE		14:06.6
J.Gardiner Cambridge H		Harry Churcher Belgrave H		14:09.6e
Bill Trew Cambridge H		Lol Allen Sheffield United H		
1933 July 7 London (WC)		**1950** July 22 Reading		
Bert Cooper Woodford Green	13:39.8	Roland Hardy Sheffield United H		13:46.8
Janis Dalins LAT		Percy Wright Belgrave H		15:09.8
Leslie Dickinson Lancashire WC		**1951** July 13 London (WC)		
Dick Edge Birmingham WC		Roland Hardy Sheffield United H		13:43.2
1934 July 13 London (WC)		Gerald Gregory Belgrave H		14:00.8
Bert Cooper Woodford Green	13:41.0	George Coleman Highgate H		14:15.6
Dick Edge Birmingham WC	13:45.0	Lol Allen Sheffield United H		14:33.4
Don Brown Belgrave H		Dave McMullen Belgrave H		14:35.6
Leslie Dickinson Lancashire WC		William Anderson Cambridge H		14:36.8
1935 July 12 London (WC)		**1952** June 20 London (WC)		
Bert Cooper Woodford Green	13:46.6	Roland Hardy Sheffield United H		13:27.8
Don Brown Belgrave H	13:53.8	Gerald Gregory Belgrave H		14:26.0
Leslie Dickinson Lancashire WC	14:19.4	Terry Whitlock Metropolitan WC		14:49.0
R.Edon Darlington H		Ted Barnes Highgate H		15:02.0
Harry Churcher Belgrave H				

1953 July 10 London (WC)
George Coleman Highgate H   14:02.2
Bryan Hawkins Metropolitan WC   14:05.8
Bob Richards Cambridge H   14:10.2
Terry Whitlock Metropolitan WC   14:31.6
Bob Goodall Woodford Green   14:32.5
Alec Mash Woodford Green   14:34.4
1954 July 10 London (WC)
George Coleman Highgate H   13:52.6
Bob Richards Cambridge H   14:06.6
Terry Whitlock Metropolitan WC   14:17.6
Joe Barraclough Lancashire WC   14:18.2
Bob Goodall Woodford Green   14:19.0
John Proctor Sheffield United H   14:25.2
1955 July 16 London (WC)
George Coleman Highgate H   14:01.0
Alf Poole Worcester H   14:15.8
George Williams Worcester H   14:47.0
Bob Goodall Woodford Green   14:50.6
Alec Mash Woodford Green   15:25.2
1956 July 14 London (WC)
Bob Goodall Woodford Green   14:20.8
Gareth Howell Highgate H   14:25.0
George Williams Worcester H   14:34.8
Colin Williams Ilford   14:46.2
Stan Vickers Belgrave H   14:51.6
Maurice Greasley Sheffield Utd H   14:59.4
1957 July 13 London (WC)
Stan Vickers Belgrave H   14:05.6
Bob Goodall Woodford Green   14:12.0
Colin Williams Ilford   14:17.8
Ted Smith Belgrave H   14:36.2
Alf Poole Worcester H   14:37.6
Eric Hall Belgrave H   14:40.4
1958 July 12 London (WC)
Stan Vickers Belgrave H   13:33.4
Ken Matthews R.Sutton Coldfield   13:45.2
Bob Goodall Woodford Green   14:09.2
Eric Hall Belgrave H   14:16.4
George Williams Worcester H   14:27.4
Colin Williams Ilford   14:36.6
1959 July 11 London (WC)
Ken Matthews R.Sutton Coldfield   13:19.4
Stan Vickers Belgrave H   13:47.1
George Williams Belgrave H   14:00.4
Bob Goodall Woodford Green   14:15.6
Bob Clark Polytechnic H   14:19.0
John Northcott Highgate H   14:33.6
1960 July 16 London (WC)
Stan Vickers Belgrave H   13:02.4
Ken Matthews R.Sutton Coldfield   13:09.6
Dieter Lindner GDR   13:44.4
Eric Hall Belgrave H   13:51.8
Colin Williams Ilford   14:05.4
Bob Goodall Woodford Green   14:13.2
1961 July 15 London (WC)
Ken Matthews R.Sutton Coldfield   13:24.6
Giuseppe Dordoni ITA   13:45.0
Colin Williams Ilford   14:12.8
Ray Middleton Belgrave H   14:22.4
John Northcott Highgate H   14:29.4
Ken Harding R.Sutton Coldfield   14:31.2
1962 July 14 London (WC)
Ken Matthews R.Sutton Coldfield   13:59.0
Colin Williams Ilford   14:26.2
John Northcott Highgate H   14:32.0

John Paddick R.Sutton Coldfield   14:40.4
Ray Middleton Belgrave H   14:47.4
Peter Stapleford Leicester WC   15:02.0
1963 July 13 London (WC)
Ken Matthews R.Sutton Coldfield   13:18.2
Abdon Pamich ITA   13:41.4
Paul Nihill Surrey WC   14:03.8
Ray Middleton Belgrave H   14:42.8
Peter Stapleford Leicester WC   14:43.0
Malcolm Tolley Sheffield Utd H   14:44.8
1964 July 11 London (WC)
Ken Matthews R.Sutton Coldfield   13:22.4
Colin Williams Ilford   14:44.8
Malcolm Tolley Sheffield Utd H   14:49.2
Peter Selby Surrey WC   14:51.4
1965 July 10 London (WC)
Paul Nihill Surrey WC   13:20.0
Malcolm Tolley Sheffield Utd H   13:50.0
Ron Wallwork Lancashire WC   13:54.6
Neil Munro Southampton AC   14:17.4
Norman Read Steyning   14:19.0
Ken Easlea Enfield H   14:23.6
1966 July 9 London (WC)
Ron Wallwork Lancashire WC   13:35.0
Malcolm Tolley Sheffield Utd H   13:46.4
John Webb Basildon   13:54.6
Peter Marlow Southend on Sea   14:05.0
Bob Hughes Smethwick H   14:15.2
1967 July 15 London (WC)
Ron Wallwork Lancashire WC   13:44.8
Arthur Jones Brighton & Hove   13:51.0
Bob Hughes R.Sutton Coldfield   13:54.2
Ken Easlea Enfield H   14:16.8
Bill Sutherland Highgate H   14:24.2
Colin Williams Surrey WC   14:33.4
1968 July 13 London (WC)
Arthur Jones Brighton & Hove   13:35.6
Bob Hughes R.Sutton Coldfield   13:41.4
Arthur Thomson Metropolitan WC   13:47.8
Ron Wallwork Lancashire WC   13:55.6
Ken Easlea Enfield H   14:24.6
Roger Mills Ilford   14:25.2

3000 METRES
1969 Aug 2 London (WC)
Roger Mills Ilford   12:57.0
Peter Marlow Southend on Sea   12:58.2
Phil Embleton Metropolitan WC   13:11.6
Ken Easlea Enfield H   13:42.6
Brian Armstrong Ilford   13:42.6
Dave Rosser Southend on Sea   13:51.4
1970 Aug 8 London (WC)
Paul Nihill Surrey WC   12:13.8
Roger Mills Ilford   12:35.0
Phil Embleton Metropolitan WC   12:35.8
Bob Dobson Basildon   12:40.4
Bill Sutherland Highgate H   12:55.0
Alan Smallwood Harborne H   13:04.0
1971 July 24 London (CP)
Paul Nihill Surrey WC   12:08.4
Phil Embleton Metropolitan WC   12:30.2
Bill Sutherland Highgate H   12:52.0
Alan Smallwood Halesowen AC   12:55.6
Bob Dobson Basildon   13:04.4
Don Cox Southend on Sea   13:07.4
1972 July 15 London (CP)
Roger Mills Ilford   12:31.54

Phil Embleton Metropolitan WC	12:39.76	Ray Hankin Sheffield United H	12:47.54
Peter Marlow Southend on Sea	12:45.68	Andy Trigg Leicester WC	12:49.51
Alan Smallwood Halesowen AC	13:02.23	**1982** July 24 London (CP)	
Don Cox Southend on Sea	13:07.38	Roger Mills Ilford	11:58.18
Mike Holmes Yorkshire WC	13:24.8	Phil Vesty Leicester WC	12:02.04
1973 July 14 London (CP)		Gordon Vale Surrey WC	12:16.41
Roger Mills Ilford	12:16.8	Brian Adams Leicester WC	12:27.12
Paul Nihill Surrey WC	12:18.6	Tim Berrett Tonbridge AC	12:32.98
Peter Marlow Southend on Sea	12:28.8	Chris Smith Leicester WC	12:33.08
Olly Flynn Basildon	12:52.4	**1983** July 23 London (CP)	
Alan Smallwood Halesowen AC	12:58.2	Dave Smith AUS	11:36.04
Ken Carter Southend on Sea	13:09.4	Phil Vesty Leicester WC	11:48.03
1974 July 13 London (CP)		Roger Mills Ilford	12:03.58
Roger Mills Ilford	12:27.0	Roy Sheppard Anglia Striders	12:30.72
Peter Marlow Southend on Sea	12:28.4	Tim Berrett Tonbridge AC	12:37.68
Brian Adams Leicester WC	12:40.2	Chris Smith Leicester WC	12:38.65
Ken Carter Southend on Sea	12:51.4	**1984** June 23 London (CP)	
Carl Lawton Belgrave H	12:53.8	Phil Vesty Leicester WC	11:42.94
Alan Smallwood Halesowen AC	12:56.8	Tim Berrett Tonbridge AC	11:54.23
1975 Aug 2 London (CP)		Roger Mills Ilford	12:13.56
Paul Nihill Surrey WC	12:43.14	Gordon Vale Surrey WC	12:18.91
Peter Marlow Southend on Sea	12:51.09	Adrian James Enfield H	12:38.33
Amos Seddon Enfield H	12:59.40	Andi Drake Coventry RWC	12:39.25
Alan Buchanan Brighton & Hove	13:15.42	**1985** July 13 London (CP)	
Dave Stevens Steyning	13:32.31	Ian McCombie Cambridge H	11:41.73
Alec Banyard Southend on Sea	13:35.52	Phil Vesty Leicester WC	11:54.57
1976 Aug 14 London (CP)		Martin Rush Cockermouth AC	12:04.28
Roger Mills Ilford	12:22.6	Murray Day Belgrave H	12:28.81
Graham Seatter Belgrave H/NZL	13:01.4	Steve Johnson Splott Conservative	12:32.77
Ken Carter Southend on Sea	13:06.0	Paul Blagg Cambridge H	12:44.56
Bob Dobson Southend on Sea	13:12.2	**1986** June 1, London (He) (RWA Champs)	
John Hall Belgrave H	13:17.4	Murray Day Belgrave H	12:04.0
Alan Buchanan Brighton & Hove	13:23.2	Chris Smith Leicester WC	12:23.0
1977 July 22 London (CP)		Les Morton Sheffield	12:45.2

7 MILES

Roger Mills Ilford	12:08.36	**1880** July 3 London (LB)	
Graham Seatter Belgrave H/NZL	12:14.91	George Beckley London AC	56:40.0
Brian Adams Leicester WC	12:39.81	T.Murphy Highgate H	56:57.0
Carl Lawton Belgrave H	12:56.70	James Squires London AC	58:29.0
Amos Seddon Enfield H	12:12.55	**1881** July 1 Birmingham	
Graham Morris Steyning	13:13.98	James Raby Elland	54:48.4
1978 June 23 London (CP)		**1882** July 5 Stoke on Trent	
Roger Mills Ilford	12:05.83	Henry Whyatt Nottingham Forest FC	55:56.5
Brian Adams Leicester WC	12:24.72	George Beckley London AC	56:09.0
Carl Lawton Belgrave H	12:41.12	R.Parry Liverpool AC	56:55.5
Graham Seatter Belgrave H/NZL	12:41.42	W.Howard Bromsborough CC	57:35.0
Graham Morris Steyning	12:44.44	G.Cooper Norwich	57:58.0
Peter Fox Steyning	12:52.00	**1883** June 30 London (LB)	
1979 July 13 London (CP)		Henry Whyatt Nottingham Forest FC	59:15.0
Roger Mills Ilford	12:09.07	J.Pritchard Birchfield H	59:20.0
Mike Parker Brighton & Hove	12:22.76	George Beckley London AC	59:55.0
Carl Lawton Belgrave H	12:37.69	**1884** June 21 Birmingham	
Gordon Vale Surrey WC	12:44.82	William Henry Meek USA	54:27.0
Mike Holmes York Postal RWC	12:44.84	James Jervis Liverpool H	57:53.2
Amos Seddon Enfield H	12:52.76	**1885** June 27 Southport	
1980 Sept 5 London (CP)		James Jervis Liverpool H	56:10.6
Steve Barry Roath Labour WC	12:00.44	Michael Hayes IRL	57:17.2
Richard Dorman Belgrave H	12:24.45	J.Lewis Newtown FC	
Ian Richards Coventry Godiva H	12:26.47	**1886** July 3 London (SB)	
Amos Seddon Enfield H	12:28.88	Joseph Jullie Finchley H	56:30.5
Mike Holmes Bingley H	12:40.65	William Wheeler Southampton AC	
Graham Morris Steyning	12:41.40	**1887** July 2 Stourbridge	
1981 Aug 7 London (CP)		C.Clarke Spartan H/USA	56:59.8
Roger Mills Ilford	11:44.68	Edward Lange USA	57:00.0
Phil Vesty Leicester WC	12:17.96	J.Lewis Newtown FC	57:52.5
Brian Adams Leicester WC	12:40.87	**1888** June 30 Crewe	
Richard Dorman Belgrave H	12:46.31		

C.Clarke USA	57:08.6
J.Lewis Newtown FC	57:41.0
1889 June 29 London (SB)	
William Wheeler Southampton AC	
Harry Curtis St.Pauls H	56:29.4
W.Curtis Belgrave H	57:00.2
	57:22.4
Joseph Jullie Finchley H	58:03.6
H.Hilsden Highgate H	59:03.6
E.Bates Beaumont H	59:07.8
1890 July 12 Birmingham	
Harry Curtis Highgate H	52:28.4
William Wheeler Southampton AC	54:29.2
John Wells Reading	54:58.6
J.Davenport Finchley H	56:54.0
1891 June 27 Manchester	
Harry Curtis Highgate H	54:00.2
John Wells Reading	56:24.4
Charles Nicoll USA?	56:34.2
1892 July 2 London (SB)	
Harry Curtis Highgate H	55:56.2
David Fenton Essex Beagles	57:06.2
A.Wooll Highgate H	57:34.2
G.Clamp Highgate H	
F.Kimber Walthamstow H	
1893 July 1 Northampton	
Harry Curtis Highgate H	56:37.2
William Sturgess Polytechnic H	60:07.0
F.Kimber Walthamstow H	63 19.0
W.Poole unattached, Towcester	63 26.8

4 MILES

1894 July 7 Huddersfield	
Harry Curtis Highgate H	30:05.8
David Fenton Essex Beagles	30:26.2
William Sturgess Polytechnic H	30:38.8
H.Cheverton Essex Beagles	
H.Clarke Harrogate H	
1895 July 6 London (SB)	
William Sturgess Polytechnic H	30:17.4
M.Forrester Polytechnic H	
W.Cryer Highgate H – awarded 3rd place 1 lap short as crowd invasion prevented him finishing.	
1896 July 4 Northampton	
William Sturgess Polytechnic H	28:57.6
Harry Curtis Highgate H	29:27.4
M.Forrester Polytechnic H	30:02.4
David Fenton Essex Beagles	30:18.0
W.Endean Polytechnic H	31:06.4
1897 July 3 Manchester	
William Sturgess Polytechnic H	28:24.8
E.Topple Polytechnic H	29:40.0
M.Forrester Polytechnic H	29:47.0
W.Endean Polytechnic H	29:59.0
E.Dover Essex Beagles	30:23.6
1898 July 2 London (SB)	
William Sturgess Polytechnic H	29:10.0
Jack Butler Polytechnic H	30:15.8?
G.Topliss Highgate H	30:41.0
W.Endean Polytechnic H	30:54.0
E.Dover Essex Beagles	31:03.4
R.Watson London AC	31:15.0
1899 July 1 Wolverhampton	
William Sturgess Polytechnic H	29:20.6
Jack Butler Polytechnic H	29:47.0
E.Middleton Polytechnic H	31:07.4
W.Endean Polytechnic H	
E.Dover Essex Beagles	

1900 July 7 London (SB)	
William Sturgess Polytechnic H	30:20.8
Jack Butler Polytechnic H	30:35.0
E.Middleton Polytechnic H	31:31.0
R.Watson London AC	31:25.0

7 MILES

1901 Apr 27 Crewe	
Jack Butler Polytechnic H	54:37.0
H.Simpson Polytechnic H	55:40.0
W.Martindale Polytechnic H	56:30.0
T.Hill Polytechnic H	59:00.2
1902 Apr 5 London (SB)	
William Sturgess Polytechnic H	52:49.4
Jack Butler Polytechnic H	52:58.0
H.Hartley Cambridge H	55:52.5
G.Bush Northampton Institute	56:51.0
S.Smith Cambridge H	56:58.0
W.Barnes Highgate H & H.Otway HHH	57:50.0
1903 Apr 25 Northampton	
Jack Butler Polytechnic H	56:17.2
W.Martindale Polytechnic H	58:17.4
W.Endean Polytechnic H	58:36.8
G.Lansley Finchley H	60:08.4
William Palmer Northampton Institute	61:25.0
F.Street Polytechnic H	64:21.0
1904 Apr 9 Rochdale	
George Larner Brighton & County H	52:57.4
Frank Carter Queens Park H	
W.Martindale Polytechnic H	
J.McLachlan Liverpool H	
1905 Apr 8 London (CP)	
George Larner Brighton & County H	52:34.0
Frederick Thompson London AC	54:29.0
W.Martindale Polytechnic H	54:47.0
G.Lansley Finchley H	55:08.0
H.Montague Malden H	55:37.0
H.Robinson Herne Hill H	56:56.0
1906 Apr 7 London (SB)	
Frank Carter Queens Park H	53:20.2
Frederick Thompson London AC	53:43.0
W.Martindale Polytechnic H	54:19.0
Sydney Sarel London AC	54:35.0
William Palmer Herne Hill H	55:54.0
T.Norton Cambridge H	56:23.0
1907 Apr 13 Manchester	
Frederick Thompson London AC	52:46.6
C.Trippier Salford H	52:50.0
J.Bennett Manchester AC	53:00.0
Sydney Sarel London AC	53:01.0
Ernest Webb Herne Hill H	53:41.0
H.Morris Sparkhill H	54:08.8
1908 Apr 18 London (SB)	
Ernest Webb Herne Hill H	53:02.6
Frank Carter Queens Park H	53:43.0
William Palmer Herne Hill H	54:25.0
Edward Larner Highgate H	54:30.2
Godwin Withers Railway Clearing House	54:44.8
Sydney Sarel London AC	55:09.6
1909 Apr 17 London (SB)	
Ernest Webb Herne Hill H	52:37.0
Frank Carter Queens Park H	54:44.6
Alred Pateman United H	55:14.0
Godwin Withers Railway Clearing House	55:17.0
Will Ovens Herne Hill H	55:55.0
Jack Butler Polytechnic H	55:04.6

1910 Apr 16 London (SB)		Harold King Belgrave H		55:46.6
Ernest Webb Herne Hill H	51:37.0	J.Dowse Finchley H		55:53.8
Alred Pateman Herne Hill H	54:17.4	C.Ward Finchley H		56:35.2
Will Ovens Herne Hill H	54:21.0	B.Brew Southend H		56:51.2
Godwin Withers Railway Clearing House	54:27.4	**1924** Apr 5 London (SB)		
William Yates Salford H	54:38.4	Reg Goodwin Surrey WC		52:00.6
Jack Lynch Polytechnic H	54:38.6	Gordon Watts Surrey WC		52:13.2
1911 Apr 29 London (SB)		C.Ward Finchley H		54:03.0
George Larner Highgate H	52:08.0	Fred Clark Surrey AC		54:04.0
William Yates Salford H	52:24.4	Wilf Cowley Surrey AC		54:05.0
Harold Ross Middlesex WC	52:45.2	F.Easto Surrey AC		54:30.0
Alred Pateman Herne Hill H	53:00.6	**1925** Apr 4 London (SB)		
H.Morris Birmingham WC	53:10.2	Gordon Watts Surrey WC		52:53.8
Jack Lynch Polytechnic H	53:13.2	Wilf Cowley Surrey AC		54:08.0
1912 Apr 20 London (SB)		Fred Clark Garratt WC		54:39.8
Bobby Bridge Lancashire WC	52:45.6	Reg Goodwin Surrey WC		55:09.6
William Yates Salford H	52:59.8	A.Greening Surrey AC		56:05.0
Harold Ross Middlesex WC	54:20.8	T.Thwaites Surrey AC		56:27.6
Alred Pateman Herne Hill H	54:42.8	**1926** May 1 London (SB)		
D.Trotter Ashcombe AC	54:53.6	Reg Goodwin Surrey WC		53:56.0
Jack Lynch Polytechnic H	55:10.0	C.Coulson Sheffield United H		54:44.6
1913 Apr 19 London (SB)		Wilf Cowley Surrey AC		55:23.6
Bobby Bridge Lancashire WC		L.Sandy Surrey AC		56:29.8
& Harold Ross Herne Hill H	52:08.4	H.Devonshire Finchley H		56:38.0
Jack Lynch Polytechnic H	53:19.0	H.Lloyd Queens Park H		56:53.0
William Yates Salford H	54:21.4	**1927** July 4 London (SB)		
William Hehir Herne Hill H	54:21.8	Wilf Cowley Surrey AC		55:46.4
Alred Pateman Herne Hill H	54:43.0	L.Sandy Surrey AC		56:25.0
1914 Apr 18 London (SB)		Edward Presland Herne Hill H		56:59.0
Bobby Bridge Lancashire WC	52:32.0	L.Holland Surrey AC		
Jack Lynch Polytechnic H	53:06.6	E.Sharman Southern Railway AC		
William Hehir Surrey WC	55:14.6	G.Booker Surrey WC		
Alred Pateman Herne Hill H	55:32.6	**1928** July 14 Sheffield		
J.Dowse Uxbridge & W.Middlesex	56:06.0	Cecil Hyde Enfield AC		55:46.2
H.Devonshire Uxbridge & WM	56:07.6	Dick Edge North Staffordshire H		56:12.6
1919 Sept 20 London (SB)		John Wilson Sheffield United H		56:35.6
William Hehir Surrey WC	53:23.6	**1929** Sept 7 London (SB)		
Charles Dowson Queens Park H	53:31.2	Cecil Hyde Enfield AC		53:38.6
J.Dowse Finchley H	54:37.6	Alf Pope Woodford Green		55:17.6
W.Inns Surrey AC	57:36.6	John Reddish Herne Hill H		55:47.4
R.Ricketts Belgrave H	58:51.0	**1930** July 5 London (SB)		
C.Wells Belgrave H	58:52.0	Cecil Hyde Enfield AC		53:32.6
1920 Apr 10 London (SB)		Albert Plumb North London H		54:01.4
Charles Dowson Queens Park H	53:50.0	Tommy Green Belgrave H		54:16.4
William Hehir Surrey WC	55:54.2	Armando Valente ITA		54:52.2
James Belchamber Belgrave H	57:36.4	John Reddish Herne Hill H		55:14.0
Edgar Horton Surrey WC	57:53.0	Stan Smith Derby W&AC		55:25.0
W.Day Slough AC	58:05.0	**1931** July 4 London (SB)		
H.Hanger Belgrave H	58:22.0	Ugo Frigerio ITA		53:32.0
1921 Oct 1 London (SB)		Janis Dalins LAT		53:40.0
Harold Ross Herne Hill H	55:48.6	Alf Pope Woodford Green		54:09.0
William Hehir Surrey WC	56:21.6	Albert Fletcher Belgrave H		54:15.0
Reg Goodwin Surrey WC	56:21.8	Dick Edge Derby WC		54:16.8
Fred Poynton Leicester WC	56:48.0	George Galloway Queens Park H		54:28.0
Donato Pavesi ITA	57:02.0	**1932** July 2 London (WC)		
B.Brew Southend H	57:39.0	Alf Pope Woodford Green		51:25.4
1922 Sept 30 London (SB)		Dick Edge Birmingham WC		53:26.6
Gordon Watts Surrey WC	53:24.2	Albert Plumb North London H		53:30.4
Reg Goodwin Surrey WC	53:37.2	Cecil McMaster RSA		54:24.0
J.Dowse Finchley H	54:03.4	A.Hurst Cambridge H		54:29.0
F.Easto Surrey AC	54:10.6	L.Sandy Port of London Police A		54:33.0
Harold Ross Herne Hill H	54:21.8	**1933** July 8 London (WC)		
Godwin Withers Railway Clearing House	55:28.6	Johnny Johnson Enfield AC		53:01.6
1923 Sept 29 London (SB)		Janis Dalins LAT		53:35.0
Gordon Watts Surrey WC	54:35.4	Dick Edge Birmingham WC		53:55.4
Reg Goodwin Surrey WC	55:19.2	Alf Pope Woodford Green		54:11.6

A.Hurst Cambridge H	54:18.0	Harry Churcher Belgrave H	52:41.8
Fred Redman Metropolitan WC	54:45.0	Jim Morris Surrey AC	53:04.0
1934 July 14 London (WC)		Lol Allen Sheffield United H	54:31.0
Johnny Johnson Enfield AC	52:10.4	Fred Barrett Cambridge H	55:52.6
Leslie Dickinson Lancashire WC	52:18.4	Bill Wilson Highgate H	55:58.0
Fred Redman Metropolitan WC	52:22.4	Gordon Dick Highgate H	56:17.6
Henry Hake Surrey WC	52:35.4	**1950** July 15 London (WC)	
A.Hurst Cambridge H	53:43.0	Roland Hardy Sheffield United H	50:11.6
W.Burgess Herne Hill H	53:59.8	Lol Allen Sheffield United H	50:22.6
1935 July 13 London (WC)		Axel Thuresson SWE	53:42.2
Henry Hake Surrey WC	53:48.0	George Coleman Highgate H	53:52.0
Albert Plumb Enfield AC	55:33.0	Alf Readman Belgrave H	56:18.6
Alf Pope Woodford Green	56:04.0	Chris Shaw Highgate H	56:28.4
Norman Burt Surrey WC		**1951** July 14 London (WC)	
Tommy Richardson Woodford Green		Roland Hardy Sheffield United H	51:14.6
Leslie Dickinson Lancashire WC		Lol Allen Sheffield United H	52:54.4
1936 Apr 4 London (WC)		Harry Churcher Belgrave H	54:04.0
Vic Stone Polytechnic H	52:21.2	George Coleman Highgate H	54:30.0
Alf Pope Woodford Green	52:40.0	Bryan Hawkins Metropolitan WC	54:52.6
Fred Redman Metropolitan WC	53:04.4	George Ruston Sheffield United H	56:03.6
Albert Fletcher Belgrave H	53:11.0	**1952** June 21 London (WC)	
Harold Whitlock Metropolitan WC	53:51.2	Roland Hardy Sheffield United H	50:05.6
Don Brown Victoria AA	54:27.8	Lol Allen Sheffield United H	51:29.2
1937 Apr 3 London (WC)		George Coleman Highgate H	52:24.6
John Mikaelsson SWE	50:19.2	Bryan Hawkins Metropolitan WC	52:51.0
Harry Churcher Belgrave H	51:13.0	Fred Barrett Cambridge H	54:50.6
Fred Redman Metropolitan WC	51:55.0	Brian Shepherd Walton AC	55:23.6
Bert Cooper Woodford Green	52:57.0	**1953** June 27 Chesterfield	
Harold Whitlock Metropolitan WC	53:09.0	Roland Hardy Sheffield United H	51:47.0
A.Rayner Surrey AC	54:27.0	Bryan Hawkins Metropolitan WC	54:23.0
1938 Apr 23 London (WC)		John Proctor Sheffield United H	54:59.0
John Mikaelsson SWE	51:48.2	Ken Camp Derbyshire Sports	
Erik Hedberg SWE	53:23.0	**1954** July 9 London (WC)	
Joe Coleman Belgrave H	53:36.8	George Coleman Highgate H	51:22.8
Eddie Staker Highgate H	53:40.2	Bryan Hawkins Metropolitan WC	52:26.4
Harold Whitlock Metropolitan WC	54:06.0	Bob Goodall Woodford Green	54:18.4
Leslie Coleman Belgrave H	54:07.0	Joe Barraclough Lancashire WC	54:47.8
1939 Apr 22 London (WC)		John Goodall Woodford Green	55:51.4
Harry Churcher Belgrave H	52:37.0	Rod Hutchison Metropolitan WC	56:11.0
Eddie Staker Highgate H	53:31.4	**1955** July 15 London (WC)	
Joe Coleman Belgrave H	54:32.2	Roland Hardy Sheffield United H	53:04.6
Percy Wright Belgrave H	55:44.0	George Coleman Highgate H	53:32.2
Leslie Coleman Belgrave H	56:34.0	Alf Poole Worcester H	54:26.2
A.Foster Woodford Green	56:52.0	Bob Richards Cambridge H	54:54.6
1946 July 20 London (WC)		Bryan Hawkins MetropolitanWC	55:45.0
Lars Hindmar SWE	52:30.0	Joe Barraclough Lancashire WC	55:56.4
Eddie Staker Highgate H	53:39.0	**1956** July 13 London (WC)	
Harry Churcher Belgrave H	54:18.8	George Coleman Highgate H	50:19.0
Bert Cooper Woodford Green	54:41.0	Stan Vickers Belgrave H	52:45.2
Jim Morris Surrey AC	55:29.8	Alf Poole Worcester H	53:11.8
Alfred 'Tich' Marler Enfield AC	55:51.2	Bryan Hawkins Metropolitan WC	53:18.0
1947 Apr 5 London (WC)		Eric Hall Belgrave H	54:18.8
Harry Churcher Belgrave H	52:48.4	Rod Hutchison Metropolitan WC	54:59.8
Mario Di Salvo ITA	53:13.8	**1957** Aug 10 Watford	
Giuseppe Kressevich ITA	54:17.6	Stan Vickers Belgrave H	51:34.4
Jim Morris Surrey AC	54:37.0	Eric Hall Belgrave H	51:49.0
Jack Rutland Belgrave H	54:58.0	Bob Goodall Woodford Green	53:06.0
Dave McMullen Belgrave H	55:17.0	Tom Misson Metropolitan WC	54:38.0
1948 July 3 London (WC)		George Chaplin Coventry Godiva H	54:48.0
Harry Churcher Belgrave H	52:23.0	Folke Zackrisson SWE	54:53.0
Jim Morris Surrey AC	53:14.0	**1958** Apr 19 London (Hu)	
Ron West Cambridge H	53:23.0	Stan Vickers Belgrave H	51:10.2
Allan Furniss Sheffield United H	53:55.0	Eric Hall Belgrave H	52:14.3
Alex Jamieson Dundee Hawkhill H	55:20.0	Bob Goodall Woodford Green	53:28.0
Eddie Staker Highgate H	55:38.0	Tom Misson Metropolitan WC	53:56.0
1949 July 16 London (WC)		Colin Williams Ilford	54:25.2

George Meadows Highgate H	55:12.0	Shaun Lightman Metropolitan WC	51:45.0
1959 Apr 4 London (Hu)		Arthur Thomson Metropolitan WC	51:45.2
Ken Matthews R.Sutton Coldfield	50:28.8	John Warhurst Sheffield United H	51:48.0
Stan Vickers Belgrave H	51:08.6	Bill Sutherland Highgate H	51:50.2
Eric Hall Belgrave H	53:04.2	Ron Wallwork Lancashire WC	52:09.4
Colin Williams Ilford	53:23.8	**10,000 METRES**	
George Williams Belgrave H	53:41.8	**1969** Mar 29 London (BP)	
George Coleman Highgate H	53:54.2	Paul Nihill Surrey WC	44:07.0
1960 Apr 16 London (Hu)		Phil Embleton Metropolitan WC	46:31.0
Ken Matthews R.Sutton Coldfield	49:42.6	Bill Sutherland Highgate H	46:41.0
Siegfried Lefranczik GDR	51:01.2	Tony Taylor Lancashire WC	46:43.0
Max Weber GDR	51:01.5	Colin Young Essex Beagles	46:45.0
Hannes Koch GDR	51:17.6	Len Duquemin Belgrave H	46:55.0
Eric Hall Belgrave H	51:52.0	**1970** July 4 London (BP)	
Colin Williams Ilford	53:53.0	Bill Sutherland Highgate H	45:16.8
1961 Apr 15 London (Hu)		Roger Mills Ilford	46:47.0
Ken Matthews R.Sutton Coldfield	49:43.6	Tony Taylor Lancashire WC	46:51.2
Colin Williams Ilford	53:08.1	Bob Dobson Basildon	47:33.8
John Godbeer Cambridge H	53:20.0	Olly Flynn Basildon	48:32.0
Ray Middleton Belgrave H	54:03.2	Denis Holly Brighton & Hove	50:28.0
John Northcott Highgate H	55:29.4	**1971** July 3 Leicester	
Brian Russell Gosport AC	56:20.0	Phil Embleton Metropolitan WC	45:26.2
1962 Mar 31 London (Hu)		Carl Lawton Belgrave H	46:31.4
Colin Williams Ilford	52:15.0	Alan Smallwood Halesowen AC	48:04.6
Arthur Thomson Metropolitan WC	52:47.2	Olly Flynn Basildon	50:33.8
Ray Middleton Belgrave H	53:50.4	Brian Laver Essex Beagles	51:07.4
John Edgington Coventry Godiva	54:12.0	Mike Harcombe Bristol WC	51:45.6
Mike Shannon Highgate H	54:54.6	**1972** Mar 25 London (BP)	
John Northcott Highgate H	55:05.0	Phil Embleton Metropolitan WC	44:26.8
1963 Mar 30 London (Hu)		Peter Marlow Southend on Sea	45:37.0
Ken Matthews R.Sutton Coldfield	49:52.8	Olly Flynn Basildon	46:28.4
Vaughan Thomas Belgrave H	53:42.0	Brian Adams Leicester WC	46:32.0
John Godbeer Cambridge H	53:50.0	Malcolm Tolley Leicester WC	46:49.4
Ron Wallwork Lancashire WC	53:55.0	Les Dick Highgate H	47:26.0
Ray Middleton Belgrave H	54:05.0	**1973** Mar 31 London (BP)	
Peter Selby Surrey WC	54:32.0	Roger Mills Ilford	44:38.6
1964 Mar 28 London (Hu)		Olly Flynn Basildon	44:52.4
Ken Matthews R.Sutton Coldfield	48:23.0	Shaun Lightman Metropolitan WC	44:53.2
Paul Nihill Surrey WC	51:20.0	Ron Wallwork Lancashire WC	45:05.8
Roy Hart Roath Labour WC	53:56.0	Tony Taylor Blackburn H	45:18.0
Bob Clark Polytechnic H	53:56.0	Bob Dobson Basildon	45:28.0
Malcolm Tolley Sheffield United H	54:45.0	**1974** Mar 30 London (WL)	
Colin Williams Ilford	55:39.0	Peter Marlow Southend on Sea	44:58.4
1965 Mar 27 London (Hu)		Brian Adams Leicester WC	45:51.0
Paul Nihill Surrey WC	51:54.4	Shaun Lightman Metropolitan WC	46:30.0
Ron Wallwork Lancashire WC	52:42.0	Amos Seddon Enfield H	46:55.2
Peter Fullager Surrey WC	53:18.0	Mike Holmes Yorkshire RWC	47:08.2
Malcolm Tolley Sheffield United H	53:52.4	Jackie Lord Highgate H	47:41.6
Eric Hall Belgrave H	54:20.0	**1975** Mar 29 London (WL)	
Peter McCullagh Metropolitan WC	54:31.0	Brian Adams Leicester WC	42:40.0
1966 Mar 26 London (Hu)		Roger Mills Ilford	43:20.8
Paul Nihill Surrey WC	50:52.0	Olly Flynn Basildon	44:25.8
Ron Wallwork Lancashire WC	51:02.0	Amos Seddon Enfield H	44:59.0
Roy Hart Roath Labour WC	51:58.0	Alan Smallwood Halesowen AC	45:16.6
John Webb Basildon	52:14.0	Carl Lawton Belgrave H	46:20.0
Peter McCullagh Metropolitan WC	52:22.0	**1976** Mar 27 London (WL)	
Malcolm Tolley Sheffield United H	53:05.0	Brian Adams Leicester WC	42:58.0
1967 Mar 25 London (Hu)		Roger Mills Ilford	43:01.0
Malcolm Tolley Basildon	52:32.4	Carl Lawton Belgrave H	45:10.0
John Webb Basildon	52:49.2	Bill Wright Southampton AC	45:24.0
Bob Hughes R.Sutton Coldfield	53:01.8	Stuart Elms Brighton & Hove	46:09.0
Ken Bobbett Roath Labour WC	53:16.0	David Cotton Holloway Polytechnic	46:09.0
Shaun Lightman Metropolitan WC	53:47.6	**1977** Mar 26 London (WL)	
Arthur Jones Brighton & Hove	53:53.6	Brian Adams Leicester WC	44:10.0
1968 Mar 30 London (BP)		Roger Mills Ilford	44:42.0
Paul Nihill Surrey WC	51:10.4	Amos Seddon Enfield H	45:04.0

Carl Lawton Belgrave H	45:12.0	**1987** Aug 2 London (CP)	
Graham Seatter Belgrave H	45:18.0	Ian McCombie Cambridge H	41:16.14
Adrian James Enfield H	45:19.0	Andi Drake Coventry RWC	42:06.73
1978 Mar 25 London (WL)		Mark Easton Surrey WC	42:18.92
Brian Adams Leicester WC	43:44.0	Paul Blagg Cambridge H	42:32.84
Roger Mills Ilford	45:18.0	Francisco Reis Ilford/POR	42:51.98
George Nibre Ilford	45:40.0	Pat Chichester Splott Cons WC	44:18.84
Carl Lawton Belgrave H	45:41.0	**1988** Aug 6 Birmingham	
Mark Wordsworth Tonbridge AC	45:54.0	Ian McCombie Cambridge H	41:36.51
Peter Marlow Southend on Sea	46:20.0	Paul Blagg Cambridge H	42:57.06
1979 Mar 31 Hornchurch Stadium, Upminster		Chris Maddocks Dawlish & S D	43:23.56
Brian Adams Leicester WC	43:48.4	Martin Bell Splott Conservative	43:58.88
Graham Morris Steyning	44:09.2	Andy Penn Coventry RWC	44:06.94
Amos Seddon Enfield H	45:25.6	Les Morton Sheffield United RWC	44:25.03
Gordon Vale Surrey WC	45:37.2	**1989** Aug 13 Birmingham	
Carl Lawton Belgrave H	45:55	Mark Easton Surrey WC	41:39.93
Peter Marlow Brighton & Hove	46:05	Darrell Stone Steyning	42:08.44
1980 Mar 29 London (PH)		Paul Blagg Cambridge H	42:53.18
Roger Mills Ilford	43:21.2	Darren Thorn Coventry RWC	45:12.68
Mike Parker Brighton & Hove	43:39.6	Gareth Brown Steyning	46:57.65
Gordon Vale Surrey WC	43:57.6	**1990** Aug 4 Birmingham	
Brian Adams Leicester WC	44:08.0	Mark Easton Surrey WC	41:32.80
Allan King Leicester WC	44:19.0	Andi Drake Coventry RWC	41:40.84
Ian McCombie Cambridge H	44:38.0	Sean Martindale York Postal RWC	41:49.16
1981 Mar 28 London (PH)		Paul Blagg Cambridge H	42:48.78
Steve Barry Roath Labour WC	43:22.0	Martin Rush Lakeland AC	43:01.25
Mike Parker Brighton & Hove	44:11.0	Les Morton Sheffield Utd RWC	43:07.33
Ian McCombie Cambridge H	44:38.0	**1991** July 27 Birmingham	
Gordon Vale Surrey WC	45:21.0	Ian McCombie Cambridge H	41:24.69
Allan King Leicester WC	45:52.0	Andy Penn Coventry RWC	41:59.10
Phil Vesty Leicester WC	45:58.0	Paul Blagg Cambridge H	42:47.16
1982 Mar 20 London (WL)		Steve Partington Manx H	42:57.89
Steve Barry Roath Labour WC	41:14.7	Martin Bell Splott Conservative	43:43.81
Ian McCombie Cambridge H	42:32.8	Les Morton Sheffield United RWC	44:03.71
Phil Vesty Leicester WC	42:46.3	**1992** June 28 Birmingham	
Brian Adams Leicester WC	43:16.4	Martin Rush Loughborough Univ	41:46.42
Roger Mills Ilford	43:21.9	Martin Bell Splott Conservative	42:07.42
Gordon Vale Surrey WC	43:26.2	Andy Penn Coventry RWC	42:21.70
1983 Mar 19 Kirkby		Mark Easton Surrey WC	43:15.68
Steve Barry Roath Labour WC	40:54.7	Steve Partington Manx H	43:21.06
Phil Vesty Leicester WC	43:00.1	Michael Lane IRL	43:49.27
Roy Sheppard Anglia Striders	43:18.3	**1993** July 17 Birmingham	
Tim Berrett Tonbridge AC	43:35.8	Martin Bell Splott Conservative	42:29.63
Allan King Leicester WC	44:11.1	Mark Easton Surrey WC	42:38.47
Chris Smith Leicester WC	44:30.6	Andy Penn Coventry RWC	42:51.86
1984 Mar 17 Birmingham		Chris Maddocks Plymouth City W	43:00.50
Ian McCombie Cambridge H	41:33.0	Steve Partington Manx H	43:05.72
Martin Rush Cockermouth AC	42:54.3	Martin Rush Lakeland AC	43:38.40
Steve Johnson Splott Conservative	43:38.6	**1994** June 19 Horsham	
Brian Adams Leicester WC	44:35.9	Darrell Stone Steyning	43:09.28
Dave Staniforth Sheffield United H	45:17.7	Mark Easton Surrey WC	44:06.93
Mick Greasley Sheffield United H	45:31.3	Michael Casey IRL	45:24.83
1985 June 29 London (He)		Andy O'Rawe Southend on Sea	46:29.31
Murray Day Belgrave H	43:35.3	Tim Watt Steyning	47:51.21
Roger Mills Ilford	43:48.9	Dave Turner Yorkshire RWC	48:52.89
Adrian James Enfield H	44:58.1	**1995** July 16 Birmingham	
Dave Staniforth Sheffield Utd H	45:10.3	Darrell Stone Steyning	41:10.11
Darren Thorn Coventry G	45:57.7	Steve Partington Manx H	41:14.61
Ian Ashforth Sheffield	46:12.5	Martin Bell Splott Conservative	41:16.13
1986 June 21 London (CP)		Phil King Coventry RWC	42:33.30
Ian McCombie Cambridge H	41:42.27	Mark Easton Surrey WC	42:49.59
Murray Day Belgrave H	42:46.92	Chris Maddocks Plymouth City	42:51.50
Paul Blagg Cambridge H	42:58.20	**1996** June 15 Birmingham	
Graham Seatter Belgrave H	43:10.94	Steve Partington Manx H	42:29.73
Chris Smith Leicester WC	45:01.86	Chris Cheeseman Surrey WC	44:07.95
Roy Sheppard Medway	45:09.62	Richard Oldale Sheffield Utd RWC	44:15.75

Martin Young Road Hoggs	44:59.98
Jamie O'Rawe Southend on Sea	45:09.42
Andy O'Rawe Southend on Sea	46:41.93
1997 Aug 25 Birmingham	
Phil King Coventry RWC	42:32.32
Steve Partington Manx H	42:48.39
Pierce O'Callaghan UCD, IRL	45:35.02
Michael Kemp Leicester WC	45:51.70
Richard Oldale Sheffield United	46:09.41
Brian Adams Leicester WC	47:47.75
1998 July 26 Birmingham	
Martin Bell Splott Conservative	41:48.81
Steve Partington Manx H	42:27.21
Andi Drake Coventry RWC	42:26.26
Mark Easton Surrey WC	44:04.41
Martin Young Road Hoggs	44:21.63
Jamie O'Rawe Road Hoggs	44:32.81
1999 July 25 Birmingham	
Andi Drake Coventry RWC	42:14.69
Chris Cheeseman Surrey WC	44:27.54
Jamie O'Rawe Road Hoggs	45:35.58
Matt Hales Steyning	46:05.76
Andy O'Rawe Road Hoggs	46:10.91
Don Bearman Steyning	46:28.96
2000 Aug 12 Birmingham	
Matt Hales Steyning	43:12.85
Steve Partington Manx H	43:30.50
Jamie O'Rawe Road Hoggs	43:54.49
Chris Cheeseman Surrey WC	44:29.51
Andrew Parker Wolverhampton& B	47:47.95
Andrew Goudie Belgrave H	48:42.87

5000 METRES

2001 July 14 Birmingham	
Lloyd Finch Leicester WC	20:47.23
Steve Hollier Wolverhampton & Bilston	21:04.36
Chris Cheeseman Surrey WC	21:05.29
Andy Penn Coventry Godiva H	21:18.02
Andrew Goudie Belgrave H	21:49.63
Dominic King Colchester H	21:50.48
2002 July 13 Birmingham	
Steve Hollier Wolverhampton & Bilston	20:41.29
Don Bearman Steyning	21:55.07
Nathan Adams City of Sheffield	23:11.68
2003 July 26 Birmingham	
Steve Hollier Wolverhampton & Bilston	20:59.46
Mark Easton Surrey WC	22:14.82
Nick Ball Steyning	22:49.58
Nathan Adams City of Sheffield	23:13.18
Andrew Goudie Belgrave H	23:25.80
Dave Turner Yorkshire RWC	23:33.91
2004 July 11 Manchester (SC)	
Dominic King Colchester H	20:11.35
Daniel King Colchester H	20:47.19
Steve Hollier Wolverhampton & Bilston	21:02.39
Steve Partington Manx H	21:08 35
Nick Ball Steyning	21:28.26
Luke Finch Leicester WC	21:54.34
2005 July 10 Manchester (SC)	
Colin Griffin IRL	20:44.45
Dominic King Colchester H	21:07.50
Daniel King Colchester H	21:29.40
Steve Partington Manx H	22:20.71
Matt Hales Steyning	22:88.62
Mark Williams Tamworth	24:10.62
2006 July 16 Manchester (SC)	
Colin Griffin IRL	19:43.40

Jamie Costin IRL	19:54.72
Dominic King Colchester H	21:21.16
Daniel King Colchester H	21:28.87
Nick Ball Steyning	21:56.99
Luke Finch Colchester H	22:27.28

UK 5000 METRES TRACK CHAMPS

2007 July 29 Manchester (SC)	
Dominic King Colchester H	20:57.90
Ben Wears Redcar	22:11.85
Peter Kaneen Manx H	22:55.00
Mark Williams Tamworth	23:01.77
Paul Evenett York CIU	23:20.97
Nick Silvester Aldershot, Farnham & D	23:46.48
2008 July 13 Birmingham	
Daniel King Colchester	21:06.37
Mark Williams Tamworth	22:21.40
Alex Wright Belgrave H	22:58.21
Tom Bosworth Tonbridge	23:29.66
Mark O'Kane Coventry G	23:38.44
Jim Ball Steyning	24:04.49
2009 July 12 Birmingham	
Scott Davis Ilford	22:40.63
Alex Wright Belgrave H	23:20.13
Mark O'Kane Coventry G	23:52.69
Philip Barnard Castle Point	24:15.00
Michael George Manx H	24:24.05
Mark Williams Tamworth	24:49.52
2010 June 27 Birmingham	
Alex Wright Belgrave H	20 11.09
Tom Bosworth Tonbridge	20 50 01
Luke Finch Colchester	21 29.89
Dominic King Colchester	22 14.12
Mark O'Kane Coventry G	23 22.11
2011 July 31 Birmingham	
Tom Bosworth Tonbridge	19:29:87
Daniel King Colchester	21:10.10
Tommy Taylor Birchfield	23:22.30
Jamie Higgins Leeds City	23:23.33
2013 July 14 Birmingham	
Alex Wright Belgrave H	19:27.39
Tom Bosworth Tonbridge	19:38.62
Jamie Higgins Leeds City	20:37.19
Dominic King Colchester	21:31.26
Daniel King Colchester	21:48.98
Cameron Corbishley Medway & Maidstone	22:36.02
2014 June 29 Birmingham	
Dane Bird-Smith AUS (g)	19:14.53
Tom Bosworth Tonbridge	19:16.82
Quentin Rew NZL (g)	20:07.00
Jamie Higgins Leeds City	20:55.01
Callum Wilkinson Enfield & Haringey	21:52.01
Alex Eaton Manx H	22:27.73

UK 10,000 METRES TRACK CHAMPS

1980 June 14 London (CP)	
Adrian James Enfield H	43:26.21
Mike Holmes York Postal RWC	43:34.55
Allan King Leicester WC	43:47.67
Gordon Vale Surrey WC	44:21.0
Brian Adams Leicester WC	44:47.4
Carl Lawton Belgrave H	44:52.0
1981 May 24 Antrim	
Steve Barry Roath Labour WC	42:32.43
Roger Mills Ilford	43:46.16
Gordon Vale Surrey WC	43:52.52
Adrian James Enfield H	44:52.88

Carl Lawton Belgrave H	45:31.70
Mick Greasley Sheffield United H	45:32.75 |//

1982 May 31 Cwmbran
Steve Barry Roath Labour WC	42:30.72
Roger Mills Ilford	43:42.57
Phil Vesty Leicester WC	43:45.02
Brian Adams Leicester WC	45:32.58
Graham White York Postal RWC	46:00.09
Allan King Leicester WC	46:19.07

1983 May 29 Edinburgh
Steve Barry Roath Labour WC	41:14.38
Ian McCombie Cambridge H	42:24.61
Martin Rush Cockermouth AC	43:42.75
Roger Mills Ilford	43:54.13
Graham White York Postal RWC	44:33.00
Gordon Vale Surrey WC	44:42.95

1984 May 28 Cwmbran
Phil Vesty Leicester WC	40:53.60
Martin Rush Cumberland AC	41:49.63
Richard Dorman Belgrave H	43:34.30
Gordon Vale Surrey WC	43:38.24
Brian Adams Leicester WC	44:29.22
Darren Thorn Coventry Godiva H	45:22.18

1985 May 26 Antrim
Ian McCombie Cambridge H	41:25.90
Martin Rush Cumberland AC	43:43.42
David Hucks Cambridge H	44:19.69
Paul Blagg Cambridge H	45:02.45
Tim Berrett Tonbridge AC	45:27.16
Dave Staniforth Sheffield United H	45:35.30

1986 May 26 Cwmbran
Phil Vesty Leicester WC	41:54.87
Steve Johnson Splott Conseravtive	43:40.89
Chris Smith Leicester WC	44:51.52
Dave Staniforth Sheffield United H	45:01.95
Andi Drake Coventry Godiva H	45:25.81
Graham White York Postal RWC	45:47.89

1987 May 25 Derby
Ian McCombie Cambridge H	40:45.87
Chris Maddocks Dawlish & S D	41:11.66
Phil Vesty Leicester WC	41:18.94
Andi Drake Coventry RWC	41:51.55
Mark Easton Surrey WC	42:07.94
Steve Johnson Splott Conservative	42:51.42

1988 June 5 Derby
Ian McCombie Cambridge H	40:39.77
Andi Drake Coventry RWC	41:18.64
Darrell Stone Steyning	42:26.79
Steve Johnson Splott Conservative	42:42.18
Sean Martindale York Postal RWC	43:00.67
Martin Bell Splott Conservative	43:27.63

1989 June 4 Jarrow
Ian McCombie Cambridge H	40:06.65
Steve Partington Boundary H	42:40.16
Sean Martindale York Postal RWC	43:26.63
Gareth Brown Steyning	44:18.43
Gareth Holloway Splott Conservative	46:31.58
Karl Atton Leicester WC	47:06.10

1990 June 2 Cardiff
Ian McCombie Cambridge H	41:16.00
Mark Easton Surrey WC	41:35.39
Andy Penn Coventry RWC	44:10.67
Gareth Holloway Splott Conservative	44:41.65
Jimmy Ball Steyning	44:49.32
Pat Chichester Splott Conservative	45:40.94

1991 June 9 Cardiff
Steve Partington Manx H	42:46.28
Gareth Holloway Splott Conservative	43:17.85
Les Morton Sheffield United RWC	43:41.07
Steve Taylor Manx H	44:39.01
Noel Carmody Cambridge H	44:45.63
Carl Walmsley Coventry RWC	45:01.93

1997 July 12 Birmingham
Andy Penn Coventry RWC	42:21.89
Martin Bell Splott Conservative	42:31.19
Mark Easton Surrey WC	42:37.98
Steve Partington Manx H	42:48.59
Andy O'Rawe Road Hoggs	45:28.35
Martin Young Road Hoggs	45:58.59

RWA 10 KILOMETRES ROAD CHAMPS

2005 Jun 4 Sheffield
Dominic King Colchester H	45:01
Dwane Butterrley Leicester WC	51:07
Sean Martindale York Postal	52:23
Glen Blythman Redcar RWC	52:42
Simon Hambridge Nuneaton H	54:2?
Ben Wears Redcar RWC	54:47

2006 Sep 10 Earls Colne
Daniel King Colchester	43:49
Dominic King Colchester H	46:19
Luke Finch Colchester H	47:17
Mark Williams Tamworth	49:15
Chris Cheeseman Surrey WC	49:35
Simon Hambridge Nuneaton H	53:03

2007 Sep 9 Earls Colne
Daniel King Colchester	44:30
Dominic King Colchester H	46:16
Ben Wears Redcar	48:06
Mark Williams Tamworth	48;43
Paul Evenett York CIU	49:37
Nick Silvester Aldershot F&D	49:54

2008 Sep 9 London (LV)
Daniel King Colchester	43:52
Brendan Boyce IRL	44:26
Ben Wears Redcar	45:05
Luke Finch Colchester	46:23
Scott Davis Ilford	46:27
Mark O'Kane Coventry Godiva	47:51

2009 Sep 5 Leicester
Brendan Boyce IRL	44:40
Scott Davis Ilford	45:34
Thomas Taylor Birchfeld	46:33
Paul Evenett York CIU	47:35
Daniel King Colchester	48:06
Stephen Crane Surrey	50:31

2010 Sep 11 Coventry
Alex Wright Belgrave H	42:38
Brendan Boyce Coventry G	45:55
Daniel King Colchester H	46:25
Mark O'Kane Coventry G	48:05
Paul Evenett Redcar RWC	49:04
Jonathon Hobbs Ashford	52:00

2011 London VP RWA/UK & CAU
Tom Bosworth Tonbridge /Kent	42:44
Dominic King Colchester H /Essex	43:57
Jamie Higgins Leeds City /Yorkshire	46:41
Tommy Taylor Birchfield /Leicestershire	49:28
Francisco Reis Ilford/POR/Middlesex	50:06
Ian Richards Steyning /Sussex	51:08

2012 Sep 2 Hillingdon RWA/UK
Alex Wright Belgrave H	44:06

Alberto De Casa Ilford/ITA	47:41	Arthur Jones Brighton AC/Sussex	78:30
Fabian Deuter Hillingdon/POL	50:19	Sheffield 36 Woodford Green 64 Metropolitan 69	
Steve Uttley Ilford	52:58	**1954** Mar 6 Highgate. Also CAU	
Arthur Thomson Enfield & Haringey	55:49	Roland Hardy Sheffield United H/Derby	74:16
Steve Arnold Nuneaton	56:14	Lol Allen Sheffield United H/Yorkshire	75:54
2013 July 20 Hayes RWA/UK		George Coleman Highgate H/Bedfordshire	76:11
Tom Bosworth Tonbridge	41:56	Richard Holland Sheffield United H/Yorkshire	77:58
Daniel King Colchester H	45:35	Bob Goodall Woodford Green/Essex	78:14
Dominic King Colchester H	46:55	Joe Barraclough Lancashire WC	78:27
Francisco Reis Ilford/POR/Middlesex	50:25	Sheffield 20 Metropolitan 61 Woodford Green 63	
Ian Richards Steyning /Sussex	51:59	**1955** Mar 12 Southport. Also CAU	
Luc Legon Bexley	54:51	Roland Hardy Sheffield United H/Derby	74:47

RWA 10 MILES CHAMPIONSHIP
1947 Mar 29 Sheffield

		George Coleman Highgate H/Bedfordshire	76:42
		Albert Johnson Sheffield United H/Yorkshire	77:29
Harry Churcher Belgrave H	81:23	Bryan Hawkins Metropolitan WC/Middlesex	78:00
Jack Rutland Belgrave H	81:48	Alex Macfarlane Polytechnic H/Middlesex	78:13
Ernie Clay Sheffield United H	82:22	Alf Poole Worcester H/Worcs	78:43
Dave McMullan Belgrave H	82:30	Sheffield 31 Woodford Green 37 Belgrave 64	
Charlie Megnin Highgate H	82:33	**1956** Mar 10 London (Regents Park). Also CAU	
Joe Coleman Belgrave H	82:41	Roland Hardy Sheffield United H/Derby	74:31
Belgrave 13 Highgate 58 Sheffield 64		George Coleman Highgate H/Bedfordshire	75:07
1948 Mar 20 London (Hyde Park) Also CAU		Bryan Hawkins Metropolitan WC/Middlesex	75:40
Harry Churcher Belgrave H/Surrey	75:10.4	Bob Goodall Woodford Green/Essex	77:05
James Morris Surrey AC/Middlesex	77:26.8	Lol Allen Sheffield United H/Yorkshire	77:41
Fred Redman Metropolitan WC/Middlesex	79:04	Stan Vickers Belgrave H/Kent	78:07
Charlie Churcher Belgrave H/Surrey	79:16	Sheffield 21 Highgate 46 Metropolitan 49	
Bert Martineau Surrey WC/Surrey	79:44	**1957** Mar 9 Coventry. Also CAU	
Gordon Dick Highgate H/Middlesex	80:27	Stan Vickers Belgrave H/Kent	76:51
Belgrave 42 Woodford Green 52 Enfield 101		Eric Hall Belgrave H/Surrey	77:07
1949 Mar 19 Leicester. Also CAU		George Chaplin Coventry Godiva/Warwicks	77:49
Lol Allen Sheffield United H/Yorkshire	75:09	John Edgington Coventry Godiva/Warwicks	78:23
James Morris Surrey AC/Middlesex	76:58	Lol Allen Sheffield United H/Yorkshire	78:46
John Proctor Sheffield United H/Yorkshire	77:07	Alf Poole Worcester Harriers/Worcs	79:02
Gordon Dick Highgate H/Middlesex	77:59	Belgrave 42 Metropolitan 50 Sheffield 60	
Bill Wilson Highgate H/Bedfordshire	78:01	**1958** Mar 15 London (Regents Park). Also CAU	
Charlie Churcher Belgrave H/Surrey	79:14	Stan Vickers Belgrave H/Kent	73:44
Sheffield 34 Highgate 41 Belgrave 42		Eric Hall Belgrave H/Surrey	74:06
1950 Mar 18 London (Regents Park). Also CAU		Norman Read Steyning/Sussex	75:08
Lol Allen Sheffield United H/Yorkshire	74:38	George Meadows Highgate H/Essex	76:32
Harry Churcher Belgrave H/Surrey	76:45	Bob Goodall Woodford Green/Essex	76:39
Roland Hardy Sheffield United H	77:47	Ken Matthews R.Sutton Coldfield/Warwicks	76:53
Alf Cotton Woodford Green/Middlesex	80:40	Belgrave 42 Highgate 52 Sheffield 71	
Bill Leveridge Essex Beagles/Essex	81:20	**1959** Mar 21 Sheffield. Also CAU	
Charlie Churcher Belgrave H/Surrey	81:32	Ken Matthews R.Sutton Coldfield/Warwicks	71:00
1951 Mar 17 Sutton near Macclesfield. Also CAU		Stan Vickers Belgrave H/Kent	73:03
Lol Allen Sheffield United H/Yorkshire	75:41	Eric Hall Belgrave H/Surrey	74:01
George Coleman Highgate H	77:48	Tom Misson Metropolitan WC/Middlesex	74:59
Harry Churcher Belgrave H/Surrey	79:08	George Williams Belgrave H/Surrey	76:12
Bill Allen Sheffield United H/Yorkshire	79:34	Colin Williams Ilford/Essex	76:14
Don Bott Sheffield United H/Yorkshire	80:26	Belgrave 28 Metropolitan 52 Highgate 73	
Dave McMullen Belgrave H/Surrey	80:34	**1960** Mar 19 Colindale. Also CAU	
Sheffield 21 Belgrave 37 Woodford Green 59		Ken Matthews R.Sutton Coldfield/Warwicks	70:57
1952 Mar 15 Imber Court, East Molesey. Also CAU		Stan Vickers Belgrave H/Kent	74:09
Roland Hardy Sheffield United H	73:16	Eric Hall Belgrave H/Surrey	74:59
Lol Allen Sheffield United H/Yorkshire	75:28	Don Thompson Metropolitan WC/Middlesex	76:11
George Coleman Highgate H	76:56	Tom Misson Metropolitan WC/Middlesex	76:23
Bryan Hawkins Metropolitan WC/Middlesex	77:37	John Godbeer Cambridge H/Kent	77:01
Paddy Woods Surrey AC/Surrey	77:52	Belgrave 23 Sheffield 91 Leicester 95	
Fred Barrett Cambridge H/Kent	78:52	**1961** Mar 18 Loughborough. Also CAU	
Sheffield 42 Highgate 54 Woodford Green 76		Ken Matthews R.Sutton Coldfield/Warwicks	74:21
1953 Mar 14 Cheltenham. Also CAU		Eric Hall Belgrave H/Surrey	76:54
Roland Hardy Sheffield United H	74:53.4	Bob Clark Polytechnic H/Kent	77:14
Richard Holland Sheffield Utd H	77:10	Don Thompson Metropolitan WC/Middlesex	77:48
Bryan Hawkins Metropolitan WC/Middlesex	77:27	Ray Middleton Belgrave H/Surrey	78:15
George Coleman Highgate H	77:57	John Godbeer Cambridge H/Kent	78:55
Fred Barrett Cambridge H/Kent	78:05	Sheffield 90 Lancashire WC 95 Canbridge H 104	

1962 Mar 17 Southgate. Also CAU
Ken Matthews R.Sutton Coldfield/Warwicks	76:10
Bob Clark Polytechnic H/Kent	77:40
Colin Williams Ilford/Essex	78:10
Don Thompson Metropolitan WC/Middlesex	78:21
Paul Nihill Surrey WC	79:09
Ray Middleton Belgrave H/Surrey	79:18

Belgrave 62 Sheffield 80 Surrey WC 80
1963 Mar 16 Manchester. Also CAU
Ken Matthews R.Sutton Coldfield/Warwicks	73:00
Paul Nihill Surrey WC/Surrey	73:34
John Edgington Coventry Godiva/Warwicks	75:12
Vaughan Thomas Belgrave H/Surrey	75:42
Ron Wallwork Lancashire WC/Lancashire	75:48
Bob Clark Polytechnic H/Kent	76:17

Belgrave 62 Sheffield 80 Surrey WC 80
1964 Mar 21 Morden. Also CAU
Ken Matthews R.Sutton Coldfield/Warwicks	70:22
Paul Nihill Surrey WC/Surrey	72:03
John Edgington Coventry Godiva/Warwicks	74:11
Roy Hart Roath Labour WC	74:56
Malcolm Tolley Sheffield Utd H/Yorkshire	75:06
George Chaplin Coventry Godiva/Warwicks	75:10

Surrey WC 43 Belgrave 56 Metropolitan 61
1965 Mar 20 Leicester. Also CAU
Paul Nihill Surrey WC/Surrey	74:55
Ron Wallwork Lancashire WC/Lancashire	75:52
Ken Harding R.Sutton Coldfield/Staffs	76:35
Malcolm Tolley Sheffield Utd H/Yorkshire	76:48
Peter Fullager Surrey WC/Kent	77:00
Eric Hall Belgrave H/Cheshire	77:38

Surrey WC 30 Belgrave 51 Metropolitan 91
1966 Mar 19 Hendon. Also CAU
Peter McCullagh Metropolitan WC/Oxford	74:05
Malcolm Tolley Sheffield Utd H/Yorkshire	74:23
Ron Wallwork Lancashire WC/Lancashire	74:30
Paul Nihill Surrey WC/Surrey	74:59
John Webb Basildon/Essex	76:08
John Paddick R.Sutton Coldfield/Staffs	77:10

Metropolitan 48 Sheffield 65 Surrey WC 77
1967 Mar 18 Bolton. Also CAU
Ron Wallwork Lancashire WC/Lancashire	75:06
Shaun Lightman Metropolitan WC/Middlesex	75:43
Arthur Jones Brighton & Hove/Sussex	76:10
Malcolm Tolley Basildon/Yorkshire	76:43
Eric Taylor Hinckley College/Leicestershire	76:48
Bill Sutherland Highgate H/Middlesex	76:54

Metropolitan 43 Belgrave 72 Wakefield 76
1968 Mar 18 Leicester. Also CAU
Paul Nihill Surrey WC/Surrey	72:28
John Webb Basildon/Essex	73:01
John Kirk Trowbridge	73:22
Bob Hughes R.Sutton Coldfield/Worcs	73:28
Arthur Thomson Metropolitan WC/Middlesex	73:38
Shaun Lightman Metropolitan WC/Middlesex	74:25

Metropolitan 46 Belgrave 55 Sheffield 77
1969 Mar 15 Morden. Also CAU
Paul Nihill Surrey WC.Surrey	71:14
John Webb Basildon/Essex	73:05
Bob Hughes R.Sutton Coldfield/Worcs	73:27
Brian Eley Bristol WC/Somerset	74:02
Malcolm Tolley Leicester WC/Leicestershire	74:20
George Chaplin Coventry Godiva/Warwicks	74:22

Leicester 67 Belgrave 91 Highgate 103
1970 Mar 21 Kirkby. Also CAU
Wlford Wesch Belgrave H/FRG/Surrey	72:07
Ron Wallwork Lancashire WC/Lancashire	72:13
Bernhard Nermerich FRG	72:43
Shaun Lightman Metropolitan WC/Middlesex	72:44
Phil Embleton Metropolitan WC/Essex	73:42
Tony Taylor Lancashire WC/Lancashire	74:07

Belgrave 35 Lancashire WC 65 Leicester 75
1971 Mar 20 Redditch. Also CAU
Phil Embleton Metropolitan WC/Essex	69:29
Paul Nihill Surrey WC/Surrey	71:42
Ron Wallwork Lancashire WC/Lancashire	72:49
Shaun Lightman Metropolitan WC/Middlesex	72:59
Wlford Wesch Belgrave H/FRG/Surrey	74:04
John Webb Basildon/Essex	74:22

Belgrave 53 Lancashire WC 65 Southend 68
1972 Mar 18 London (CP). Also CAU
Paul Nihill Surrey WC/Surrey	73:33
Phil Embleton Metropolitan WC/Essex	73:54
Peter Marlow Southend on Sea/Essex	74:06
Shaun Lightman Metropolitan WC/Middlesex	74:38
Bill Sutherland Highgate H/Middlesex	74:45
John Webb Basildon/Essex	74:54

Belgrave 62 Surrey WC 73 Sheffield 93
1973 Mar 17 Leyland. Also CAU
John Webb Basildon/Essex	72:43
Roger Mills Ilford/Essex	73:06
John Warhurst Sheffield Utd H/Yorkshire	73:20
Olly Flynn Basildon/Essex	74:01
Ron Wallwork Blackburn/Lancashire	74:11
Roy Thorpe Sheffield United H/Yorkshire	74:28

Sheffield 43 Belgrave 50 South 84
1974 Mar 16 Leicester. Also CAU
Peter Marlow Southend on Sea/Essex	72:58
Roy Thorpe Sheffield United H. Yorkshire	73:32
Eric Taylor Nomads WC/Leicestershire	73:42
Brian Adams Leicester WC/Leicestershire	73:55
John Webb Basildon/Essex	74:04
Ron Wallwork Blackburn/Lancashire	74:16

Belgrave 78 Brighton 88 Sheffield 91
1975 Mar 15 Southwick. Also CAU
Olly Flynn Basildon/Essex	71:15
Brian Adams Leicester WC/Leicestershire	71:38
Roger Mills Ilford/Essex	71:59
Carl Lawton Belgrave H/Surrey	74:10
Bob Dobson Southend on Sea/Essex	75:00
Stuart Maidment Yeovil Olympiads	75:04

Ilford 40 Southend 51 Brighton 82
1976 Mar 20 York Also CAU
Olly Flynn Basildon/Essex	69:59
Brian Adams Leicester WC/Leicestershire	71:00
Roger Mills Ilford/Essex	71:09
Paul Nihill Surrey WC/Surrey	71:33
Amos Seddon Borough of Enfield H/Essex	72:18
Bill Wright Southampton AAC/Warwicks	73:00

Enfield 40 Sheffield 53 Southend 78
1977 Mar 19 Coventry. Also CAU
Roger Mills Ilford/Essex	72:36
Carl Lawton Belgrave H/Surrey	72:58
John Warhurst Sheffield United H/Yorkshire	73:20
Shaun Lightman Metropolitan WC/Middlesex	73:45
Chris Harvey Lancashire WC/Lancashire	73:51
George Nibre Ilford	74:05

Sheffield 40 Ilford 75 Brighton 82
1978 Mar 18 London (CP)* c.800m short. Also CAU
Olly Flynn Basildon/Essex	67:29
Brian Adams Leicester WC/Leicestershire	68:13
Graham Morris Steyning/Sussex	69:08

Amos Seddon Borough of Enfield H/Essex	69:24
Bill Wright Southampton AAC/Hampshire	69:40
Shaun Lightman Metropolitan WC/Middlesex	70:02
Ilford 58 Leicester 72 Belgrave 77	
1979 Apr 7 York. Also CAU	
Chris Harvey Lancashire WC	71:25
Brian Adams Leicester WC/Leicestershire	71:51
Roger Mills Ilford/Essex	72:14
Graham Morris Steyning/Sussex	72:39
Shaun Lightman Metropolitan WC/Middlesex	73:03
Mike Holmes York Postal RWC/ Yorkshire	73:12
Leicester 61 Steyning 62 York Postal 65	
1980 Mar 15 Leicester 55m short. Also CAU	
Roger Mills Ilford/Essex	68:45
Mike Parker Brighton & Hove/Sussex	69:24
Mick Greasley Sheffield United H	69:28
Ian McCombie Cambridge H	69:37
Graham Morris Steyning/Sussex	70:23
Steve Barry Roath Labour WC	70:56
York Postal 57 Sheffield 73 Belgrave 85	
1981 Mar 21 Exeter. Also CAU	
Mike Parker Brighton & Hove/Sussex	73:37
Graham Morris Steyning/Sussex	74:52
David Jarman Surrey WC/Kent	75:03
Phil Vesty Leicester WC/Leicestershire	75:30
Ian McCombie Cambridge H	75:42
Brian Adams Leicester WC/Leicestershire	75:46
Leicester 31 Surrey WC 56 York Postal 59	
1982 Mar 27 Dronfield. Also CAU	
Steve Barry Roath Labour WC	68:01
Mike Parker Brighton & Hove/Sussex	70:23
Paul Blagg Belgrave H/Kent	70:37
Gordon Vale Surrey WC/Surrey	72:30
Allan King Leicester WC/Leicestershire	72:56
Adrian James Borough of Enfield H/Middlesex	73:03
Belgrave 38 Sheffield 59 York Postal 68	
1983 Mar 26 Kenilworth. Also CAU	
Steve Barry Roath Labour WC	66:41
Phil Vesty Leicester WC/Leicestershire	69:18
Ian McCombie Cambridge H	69:47
Roger Mills Ilford/Essex	71:59
Allan King Leicester WC/Leicestershire	72:26
Dave Jarman Surrey WC/Kent	72:48
Leicester 35 York Postal 56 Sheffield 75	
1984 Mar 24 Southend. Also CAU	
Ian McCombie Cambridge H/Kent	67:32
Phil Vesty Leicester WC/Leicestershire	68:09
Dan O'Connor USA	69:31
Roger Mills Ilford/Essex	70:33
Richard Dorman Belgrave H/Surrey	71:21
Roy Sheppard Anglia Striders/Essex	71:40
Belgrave 55 Leicester 60 Sheffield 73	
1985 Mar 23 York short course?. Also CAU	
Ian McCombie Cambridge H/Kent	66:32
Phil Vesty Leicester WC/Leicestershire	68:04
Roger Mills Ilford/Essex	71:37
Paul Blagg Cambridge H/Kent	72:04
Les Morton Sheffield United H/Yorkshire	72:28
Steve Partington Boundary H	72:32
Leicester 39 Sheffield 39 Coventry 70	
1986 Mar 22 Redditch. Also CAU	
Ian McCombie Cambridge H/Kent	66:35
Chris Maddocks Dawlish & SD/Devon	67:11
Martin Rush Lakeland AAC	68:56
Les Morton Sheffield United H/Yorkshire	70:33
Allan King Leicester WC/Leicestershire	70:42

Mike Parker Brighton & Hove/Sussex	72:11
Coventry 58 Splot 76 Leicester 81	
1987 Mar 14 Ham, Richmond. Also CAU	
Ian McCombie Cambridge H/Kent	67:36
Andi Drake Coventry RWC/Warwicks	69:03
Francisco Reis Ilford/POR	69:12
Andy Penn Coventry RWC/Warwicks	69:49
Darrell Stone Steyning/Sussex	70:00
Jimmy Ball Southampton & E/Hampshire	70:14
Coventry 54 Leicester 77 Steyning 85	
1988 Mar 12 Dronfield. Also CAU	
Ian McCombie Cambridge H/Kent	67:22
Les Morton Sheffield United RWC/Yorkshire	70:20
Martin Bell Splott Conservative	70:53
Sean Martindale York Postal RWC/Yorkshire	70:54
Steve Partington Boundary H/Lancashire	70:59
Andy Penn Coventry RWC/Warwicks	71:28
Splot 51 Sheffield 72 Coventry 88	
1989 Mar 11 Cardiff * 63m short.	
Ian McCombie Cambridge H/Kent	65:39
Sean Martindale York Postal RWC/Yorkshire	67:25
Martin Bell Splott Conservative/Glamorgan	67:55
Steve Johnson Splott Cons./Glamorgan	68:08
Andy Penn Coventry RWC/Warwicks	70:40
Darren Thorn Coventry RWC/Warwicks	71:12
Splot 26 Coventry 50 Leicester 59	
1990 Mar 17 Southend	
Ian McCombie Cambridge H/Yorkshire	68:36
Paul Blagg Cambridge H/Kent	71:43
Darren Thorn Coventry RWC/Warwicks	73:22
Jimmy Ball Southampton & E/Hampshire	75:13
Stuart Phillips Ilford/Essex	75:14
Gareth Holloway Splott Cons./Glamorgan	76:29
Cam 40 Coventry 45 Steyning 76	
1991 May 11 London (VP). Also CAU	
Ian McCombie Cambridge H/Yorkshire	68:17
Mark Easton Surrey WC/Surrey	68:36
Darrell Stone Steyning/Sussex	69:39
Les Morton Sheffield Utd/Yorkshire	71:08
Martin Bell Splott Cons/W.Scotland	71:32
Sean Sullivan Surrey WC	74:57
Steyning 33 Splot 60 Coventry 69	
1992 Mar 21 Birmingham. Also CAU	
Ian McCombie Cambridge H/Yorkshire	69:42
Martin Bell Splott Conservative/W.Scotland	71:00
Gareth Holloway Splott Cons/Glamorgan	72:10
Stuart Phillips Ilford/Essex	73:57
Brian Dowrick Splott Cons/Glamorgan	74:03
Jimmy Ball Steyning/Hampshire	75:25
Splot 20 Leicester 47 Coventry 70	
1993 May 9 Sheffield. Also CAU	
Les Morton Sheffield United RW/Yorkshire	73:16
Sean Martindale York Postal RW/Yorkshire	74:31
Dennis Jackson York Postal RW/Yorkshire	76:47
Karl Atton Leicester WC/Leicestershire	77:05
Kieron Butler Somerset AC/Avon	78:03
Chris Cheeseman Surrey WC/Surrey	78:20
Leicester 34 Sheffield 71 Ilford 74	
1994 July 9 London (VP). Also CAU	
Chris Cheeseman Surrey WC/Surrey	73:17
Mark Easton Surrey WC/Surrey	74:29
Andy O'Rawe Southend on Sea/Essex	76:12
Karl Atton Leicester WC/Leicestershire	78:33
Jimmy Ball Steyning	80:46
Jamie O'Rawe Southend on Sea/Essex	81:12
Leicester 44 Surrey WC 58 Steyning 64	

1995 July 22 Sutton Coldfield. Also CAU
Chris Maddocks Plymouth City W/Devon   69:11
Andy Penn Coventry RWC/Warwicks   70:10
Les Morton Sheffield United RWC/Yorkshire   70:47
Phil King Coventry RWC/Warwicks   71:56
Martin Young Road Hoggs/Leicestershire   72:34
Chris Cheeseman Surrey WC/Surrey   73:18
Coventry 35 Sheffield 51 Leicester 65
1996 Mar 23 Sutton Coldfield. Also CAU
Andy Penn Coventry RWC/Warwicks   71:14
Steve Hollier Wolverhampton & B/Staffs   72:27
Chris Cheeseman Surrey WC/Surrey   73:14
Richard Oldale Sheffield Utd RWC/Yorkshire   73:23
Gareth Brown Steyning/Sussex   73:59
Jamie O'Rawe Southend on Sea/Essex   74:27
Coventry 46 Steyning 69 Sheffield 81
1997 May 17 London (VP). Also CAU
Steve Partington Manx H/Lancashire   75:34
Jamie O'Rawe Road Hoggs/Essex   76:55
Andy O'Rawe Road Hoggs/Essex   77:22
Allan King Road Hoggs/Leicestershire   78:19
Richard Oldale Sheffield Utd RWC/Yorkshire   79:48
Brian Adams Leicester WC/Leicestershire   80:39
RH 28 Leicester 48 Steyning 53
1998 May 16 Leicester. Also CAU
Andi Drake Coventry RWC/Warwicks   71:14
Chris Cheeseman Surrey WC/Surrey   72:59
Les Morton Sheffield United RWC/Yorkshire   75:09
Darrell Stone Steyning/Sussex   76:22
Gareth Brown Steyning/Sussex   76:30
Allan King Road Hoggs/Leicestershire   76:38
Road Hoggs 34 Steyning 35 Leicester 68
2008 Feb 16 London (LV)
Darrell Stone Steyning   73:41
Scott Davis Ilford   76:01
Mark Williams Tamworth   76:39
Nick Silvester Aldershot, Farnham & D   76:34
Jim Ball Steyning   79:45
Philip Barnard Castle Point   81:46
Steyning 287 Ilford 266 Belgrave 244
2009 Feb 21 London (LV)
Ben Wears Redcar   70:22
Luke Finch Colchester H   71:34
Michael Doyle IRL   75:05
Mark O'Kane Coventry   75:16
Scott Davis Ilford   76:15
Carl Thomson Sarnia WC   78:30
Steyning 276 Redcar 274 Sarnia 269
2010 Feb 20 London LV
Darrell Stone Steyning   73:49
Scott Davis Ilford   74:10
Tommy Taylor Birchfield   75:08
Luke Finch Colchester   75:20
Paul Evenett Redcar   78:00
Antonio Cirillo Swansea   82:23
Steyning 285 Ilford 275 Birchfield 266
2011 Mar 6 Coventry
Alex Wright Belgrave H   70:46
Daniel King Colchester   72:34
Mark O'Kane Coventry G   72:59
Paul Evenett Redcar   78:07
Antonio Cirillo Swansea   83:58
Jonathon Hobbs Ashford   85:09
1. Yorkshire, 2. Redcar, 3. Surrey
2012 Mar 4 Coventry
Tom Bosworth Tonbridge   70:07

Stuart Kellmorgan Belgrave/AUS   80:08
Francisco Reis Ilford/POR   81:59
Jonathan Hobbs Ashford   85:17
Steve Uttley Ilford   88:08
Richard Spenceley Yorks RW   90:58
1. Ilford, 2. Belgrave, 3. Enfield & Haringey
2013 Mar 10 London (VP)
Michael Doyle IRL   71:31
Daniel King Colchester   72:54
Dominic King Colchester   75:05
Jonathan Hobbs Ashford   84:51
Steve Uttley Ilford   89:11
Christopher Hobbs Medway & Maidstone   93:42
1. Ashford 290, 2. Ilford 270, 3. Surrey WC 259
2014 Mar 9 London (VP)
Dominic King Colchester   78:17
Daniel King Colchester   79:04
Ian Richards Steyning   89:30
Christopher Hobbs Medway & Maidstone   91:08
Steve Allen Barnet   92:14
Steve Uttley Ilford   93:29
1. Surrey WC, 2. Colchester, 3. Leicester

RWA 20 KILOMETRES CHAMPIONSHIP
1965 May 8 Cardiff
Paul Nihill Surrey WC   1:33:33
Peter Fullager Surrey WC   1:35:15
John Edgington Coventry Godiva   1:35:24
Ron Wallwork Lancashire WC   1:35:33
Peter McCullagh Metropolitan WC   1:37:01
Maurice Fullager Surrey WC   1:37:15
Surrey WC 19 Metropolitan 42 Belgrave 59
1966 May 14 Sheffield
Paul Nihill Surrey WC   1:33:45
Ron Wallwork Lancashire WC   1:34:35
John Webb Basildon   1:35:51
Norman Read Steyning   1:36:21
Peter Fullager Surrey WC   1:36:30
Peter McCullagh Metropolitan WC   1:37:36
Surrey WC 29 Metropolitan 62 Steyning 66
1967 May 13 Ewell East
Ron Wallwork Lancashire WC   1:37:21
Arthur Jones Brighton & Hove   1:38:01
Ray Middleton Belgrave H   1:39:27
Roy Lodge R.Sutton Coldfield   1:40:02
Bryan Eley Trowbridge   1:40:42
Don Thompson Metropolitan WC   1:41:29
Trowbridge 37 Lancashire WC 60 Metropolitan 75
1968 May 11 Coventry
Paul Nihill Surrey WC   1:31:19
John Webb Basildon   1:32:13
Peter Fullager Surrey WC   1:32:38
John Warhurst Sheffield United H   1:33:25
Shaun Lightman Metropolitan WC   1:34:00
Ray Middleton Belgrave H   1:34:06
Belgrave 60 Sheffield 69 Metropolitan 73
1969 May 10 Gomersal
Paul Nihill Surrey WC   1:30:07
Peter Fullager Surrey WC   1:30:58
John Webb Basildon   1:31:42
Shaun Lightman Metropolitan WC   1:33:27
Bill Sutherland Highgate H   1:33:35
John Warhurst Sheffield United H   1:34:25
Belgrave 57 Lancashire WC 76 Basildon 85
1970 May 9 London (CP)
Wilford Wesch Belgrave H/FRG   1:31:47
Ron Wallwork Lancashire WC   1:32:12

Peter Fullager Basildon	1:33:13
Shaun Lightman Metropolitan WC	1:34:58
Roger Mills Ilford	1:35:22
Roy Lodge Bromsgrove & Redditch	1:35:46
Lancashire WC 38 Belgrave 39 Basildon 77	
1971 May 8 Luton	
Paul Nihill Surrey WC	1:32:06
Shaun Lightman Metropolitan WC	1:34:14
Ron Wallwork Lancashire WC	1:34:27
Bill Sutherland Highgate H	1:35:36
Ian Brooks Surrey WC	1:35:45
Carl Lawton Belgrave H	1:37:21
Surrey WC 46 Basildon 48 Lancashire WC 74	
1972 May 13 Redditch	
Paul Nihill Surrey WC	1:28:45
John Warhurst Sheffield United H	1:33:32
Bill Sutherland Highgate H	1:33:37
Peter Marlow Southend on Sea	1:33:50
Roger Mills Ilford	1:34:51
George Chaplin Coventry Godiva	1:36:01
Sheffield 49 Surrey WC 54 Belgrave 56	
1973 May 12 London (VP)	
Roger Mills Ilford	1:31:13
John Warhurst Sheffield United H	1:31:21
Bob Dobson Basildon	1:31:23
Shaun Lightman Metropolitan WC	1:32:50
Roy Thorpe Sheffield United H	1:32:58
John Webb Basildon	1:33:10
Belgrave 44 Sheffield 51 Southend 96	
1974 May 11 Sheffield	
Olly Flynn Basildon	1:32:06
Peter Marlow Southend on Sea	1:32:32
Roger Mills Ilford	1:33:06
Amos Seddon Borough of Enfield H	1:33:46
Mike Holmes Yorkshire RWC	1:33:58
John Warhurst Sheffield United H	1:34:21
Southend 37 Brighton 51 Sheffield 80	
1975 May 10 Coventry	
Olly Flynn Basildon	1:28:58
Roger Mills Ilford	1:29:28
Brian Adams Leicester WC	1:31:54
Amos Seddon Borough of Enfield H	1:33:02
Bob Dobson Southend on Sea	1:33:39
Alan Smallwood Halesowen AC	1:34:05
Southend 36 Sheffield 53 Belgrave 101	
1976 May 15 Southend	
Olly Flynn Basildon	1:30:00
Godfried De Jonckheere BEL	1:31:33
Paul Nihill Surrey WC	1:31:38
Brian Adams Leicester WC	1:31:58
Carl Lawton Belgrave H	1:32:15
Piet Meyer RSA	1:32:50
Sheffield 31 Southend 52 Leicester 86	
1977 May 16 Manchester	
Olly Flynn Basildon	1:28:42
Roger Mills Ilford	1:28:50
Brian Adams Leicester WC	1:31:07
Shaun Lightman Metropolitan WC	1:32:18
Carl Lawton Belgrave H	1:32:36
Mick Greasley Sheffield United H	1:32:39
Sheffield 50 Leicester 84 Belgrave 87	
1978 May 13 Coventry	
Olly Flynn Basildon	1:28:44
Brian Adams Leicester WC	1:29:47
Roger Mills Ilford	1:30:42
Amos Seddon Borough of Enfield H	1:31:45
Steve Gower Ilford	1:31:49
Carl Lawton Belgrave H	1:32:37
Steyning 55 Sheffield 57 Ilford 60	
1979 May 12 London (VP)	
Carl Lawton Belgrave H	1:32:25
Allan King Leicester WC	1:34:31
Shaun Lightman Metropolitan WC	1:35:53
John Warhurst Sheffield United H	1:36:31
Bob Dobson Ilford	1:37:27
Dennis Jackson York Postal RWC	1:37:34
Belgrave 42 Sheffield 53 Leicester 62	
1980 May 10 Southport	
Mike Parker Brighton & Hove	1:29:20
Amos Seddon Borough of Enfield H	1:29:41
Adrian James Borough of Enfield H	1:31:40
Chris Harvey York Postal RWC	1:31:55
Allan King Leicester WC	1:32:00
Mike Holmes York Postal RWC	1:32:08
York Postal 38 Leicester 38 Surrey WC 51	
1981 May 9 Kenilworth	
Mike Parker Brighton & Hove	1:31:08
Dennis Jackson York Postal RWC	1:32:28
Amos Seddon Borough of Enfield H	1:32:36
Murray Lambden Boundary H	1:32:44
Phil Vesty Leicester WC	1:33:04
Brian Adams Leicester WC	1:33:52
Leicester 30 York Postal 48 Sheffield 51	
1982 May 15 Enfield	
Steve Barry Roath Labour WC	1:28:51
Phil Vesty Leicester WC	1:31:25
Roger Mills Ilford	1:32:10
Murray Lambden Boundary H	1:33:30
Dave Jarman Surrey WC	1:34:47
Barry Graham York Postal RWC	1:35:18
York Postal 42 Leicester 58 Sheffield 64	
1983 May 14 Southport	
Steve Barry Roath Labour WC	1:23:15
Ian McCombie Cambridge H	1:27:30
Phil Vesty Leicester WC	1:28:13
Graham White York Postal RWC	1:32:08
Murray Lambden Boundary H	1:33:25
Dave Staniforth Sheffield United H	1:33:36
Leicester 27 Sheffield 48 Coventry 98	
1984 May 12 Redditch	
Ian McCombie Cambridge H	1:25:34
Chris Maddocks Dawlish & SD	1:26:51
Tim Berrett Tonbridge AC	1:30:18
Richard Dorman Belgrave H	1:31:32
Roger Mills Ilford	1:32:01
Adrian James Borough of Enfield H	1:32:14
Sheffield 48 Belgrave 60 Coventry 84	
1985 May 11 Thamesmead	
Ian McCombie Cambridge H	1:22:37
Phil Vesty Leicester WC	1:26:22
Mark Easton Surrey WC	1:28:15
Allan King Leicester WC	1:28:30
Chris Smith Leicester WC	1:28:34
Steve Partington Boundary H	1:29:01
Leicester 21 Coventry 70 Belgrave 75	
1986 May 10 York	
Ian McCombie Cambridge H	1:27:14
Dennis Jackson York Postal RWC	1:29:42
Jimmy Ball Southampton & E	1:30:23
Mike Parker Brighton & Hove	1:30:38
Dave Staniforth Sheffield United H	1:31:51
Darrell Stone Steyning	1:33:03

Steyning 75 Sheffield 89 Coventry 100	
1987 Apr 18 Birmingham	
Les Morton Sheffield United H	1:31:17
Dennis Jackson York Postal RWC	1:33:50
Chris Smith Leicester WC	1:33:51
Steve Johnson Splott Conservative	1:34:05
Steve Partington Boundary H	1:35:03
Dave Staniforth Sheffield United H	1:35:04
Leicester 51 Steyning 61 Sheffield 72	
1988 May 21 Hoddesdon	
Ian McCombie Cambridge H	1:23:31
Darrell Stone Steyning	1:27:02
Andy Penn Coventry RWC	1:28:17
Sean Martindale York Postal RWC	1:29:41
Gordon Vale Boundary H	1:30:53
Steve Johnson Splott Conservative	1:31:03
Leicester 66 Splot 73 Ilford 79	
1989 May 13 Doncaster	
Andi Drake Coventry RWC	1:26:55
Sean Martindale York Postal RWC	1:28:15
Les Morton Sheffield United RWC	1:29:53
Gareth Brown Steyning	1:30:15
Martin Bell Splott Conservative	1:31:06
Jimmy Ball Southampton & E	1:31:31
Coventry 45 Steyning 47 Sheffield 63	
1990 May 12 Leicester	
Sean Martindale York Postal RWC	1:27:37
Querubin Moreno Splott Conservative/COL	1:28:33
Jimmy Ball Southampton & E	1:30:44
Gareth Brown Steyning	1:32:15
Noel Carmody Cambridge H	1:34:38
Gareth Holloway Splott Conservative	1:34:52
Splot 31 Coventry 59 Steyning 65	
1991 Mar 17 Sheffield	
Mark Easton Surrey WC	1:25:36
Martin Rush Lakeland AAC	1:26:01
Andy Penn Coventry RWC	1:26:18
Les Morton Sheffield United RWC	1:28:05
Chris Maddocks Plymouth City W	1:29:23
Jimmy Ball Steyning	1:31:21
Coventry 44 Steyning 61 Boundary H 66	
1992 May 9 Leicester	
Chris Maddocks Plymouth City W	1:23:38
Andy Penn Coventry RWC	1:24:27
Martin Bell Splott Conservative	1:25:42
Les Morton Sheffield United RWC	1:29:20
Martin Young Leicester WC	1:32:53
Carl Walmsley Coventry RWC	1:36:31
Coventry 45 Manx 63 Sheffield 91	
1993 Mar 14 Cardiff also BAF	
Andy Penn Coventry RWC	1:25:57
Darrell Stone Steyning	1:26:59
Martin Rush Lakeland AAC	1:28:54
Steve Partington Manx H	1:29:00
Allan King Leicester WC	1:32:00
Gareth Holloway Splott Conservative	1:33:56
Leicester 43 Manx 48 Coventry 51	
1994 May 21 Birmingham	
Chris Cheeseman Surrey WC	1:29:11
Steve Partington Manx H	1:29:11
Phil King Coventry RWC	1:29:49
Graham White Brighton & Hove	1:34:11
Karl Atton Leicester WC	1:34:28
Noel Carmody Cambridge H	1:36:12
Leicester 38 Coventry 62 Surrey WC 69	
1995 Mar 25 Horsham also BAF	

Darrell Stone Steyning	1:27:44
Chris Cheeseman Surrey WC	1:29:55
Andy Penn Coventry RWC	1:30:30
Chris Maddocks Plymouth City W	1:33:00
Les Morton Sheffield United H	1:33:37
Martin Bell Splott Conservative	1:35:40
Steyning 31 Leicester 78 Surrey WC 94	
1996 Apr 21 Cardiff also BAF	
Darrell Stone Steyning	1:26:44
Steve Partington Manx H	1:29:00
Andy Penn Coventry RWC	1:32:37
Richard Oldale Sheffield United	1:33:17
Kevin Walmsley Manx H	1:33:30
Steve Taylor Manx H	1:34:27
Manx 25 Coventry 54 Leicester 75	
1997 Mar 15 Stoneleigh also BAF	
Andy Penn Coventry RWC	1:28:41
Mark Easton Surrey WC	1:30:40
Chris Cheeseman Surrey WC	1:31:12
Graham White Brighton & Hove	1:32:32
Jamie O'Rawe Road Hoggs	1:32:48
Steve Partington Manx H	1:34:11
Road Hoggs 34 Coventry 54 Manx 86	
1998 Mar 21 Leicester also BAF	
Martin Bell Cardiff AAC (u?)	1:27:22
Andi Drake Coventry RWC	1:30:25
Chris Cheeseman Surrey WC	1:31:58
Don Bearman Steyning	1:34:56
Graham White Brighton & Hove	1:35:11
Allan King Road Hoggs	1:35:13
Leicester 46 Coventry 51 Manx 59	
1999 Mar 20 Leamington Spa	
Chris Maddocks Plymouth City W	1:26:22
Chris Cheeseman Surrey WC	1:26:53
Andi Drake Coventry RWC	1:27:42
Mark Easton Surrey WC	1:28:28
Jamie O'Rawe Road Hoggs	1:28:46
Matthew Hales Steyning	1:30:38
Road Hoggs 38 Coventry 59 Surrey WC 60	
2000 Mar 11 Nottingham	
Darrell Stone Steyning	1:27:08
Andy Penn Coventry RWC	1:28:47
Matthew Hales Steyning	1:31:50
Don Bearman Steyning	1:32:38
Gareth Brown Steyning	1:32:43
Andy O'Rawe Road Hoggs	1:37:19
Steyning 13 Coventry 37 Leicester 70	
2001 July 7 Sheffield	
Andy Penn Nuneaton H	1:31:09
Steve Hollier Wolverhampton & Bilston	1:32:56
Steve Partington Manx H	1:33:30
Mark Easton Surrey WC	1:33:54
Chris Cheeseman Surrey WC	1:34:11
Andy O'Rawe Road Hoggs	1:39:48
Road Hoggs 273 Surrey WC 268 Coventry 264	
2002 Mar 3 East Molesey	
Andi Drake Coventry Godiva H	1:24:43
Andy Penn Nuneaton H	1:26:04
Don Bearman Steyning	1:30:09
Gareth Brown Steyning	1:32:08
Chris Cheeseman Surrey WC	1:34:06
Daniel King Colchester H	1:37:50
Steyning 285 Sheffield 265 Surrey WC 261	
2003 July 5 Sheriff Hutton,Yorkshire	
Andy Penn Nuneaton H	1:28:52
Nathan Adams City of Sheffield	1:40:31

Mike Smith Coventry Godiva H	1:45:22	Steve Arnold Nuneaton	1:51:11
Chris Berwick Leicester WC	1:48:22	Steve Uttley Ilford	1:52:14
Steve Arnold Coventry Godiva H	1:52:23	**2012** Apr 14 Redbridge	
John Paddick Yorkshire RWC	1:59:49	Ben Wears Redcar RWC	1:29:33
Nun 282 Yorks 271 Coventry 192		Tom Bosworth Tonbridge	1:29:52
2004 Mar 20 Leamington Spa		Stuart Kollmorgen Belgrave H/AUS	1:33:54
Jirí Malysa CZE (guest)	1:30:43	Andrew Miller Wolverhampton & Bilston	1:47:50
Daniel King Colchester H	1:31:01	Jonathan Hobbs Ashford	1:48:00
Dominic King Colchester H	1:33:17	Jock Waddington Manx H	1:50:58
Steve Partington Manx H	1:35:13	1. Ilford, 2, Belgrave, 3. Surrey WC	
Peter Kaneen Manx H	1:37:36	**2013** Apr 28 Coventry	
Matthew Hales Steyning	1:39:04	Tom Bosworth Tonbridge	1:27:49
Chris Cheeseman Surrey WC	1:39:55	Dominic King Colchester H	1:32:36
Manx 285 Steyning 271 Sheffield 262		Jock Waddington Manx H	1:49:53
2005 Sep 4 Earls Colne, Essex		Steve Uttley Ilford	1:52:32
Daniel King Colchester H	1:32:55	Richard Wild Manx H	1:55:20
Andy Penn Nuneaton H	1:33:35	Steve Allen Barnet & District	1:55:43
Matt Hales Steyning	1:44:31	1. Surrey WC, 2. Leicester, 3. Isle of Man	
Trevor Jones Hillingdon AC	1:49:27	**2014** Apr 5 Sheffield	
Terry Morris Nuneaton H	2:17:37	Ben Wears Redcar RWC	1:33:33
Uli Fullerman Nuneaton H	2:35:37	Fabian Bernabe ESP	1:35:34
Nuneaton 287		Richard Gerrard Isle of Man	1:48:11
2006 Apr 22 Sheffield		Adam Cowin Manx H	1:49:38
Dominic King Colchester H	1:31:26	Francisco Reis Ilford/POR	1:49:43
Steve Hollier Wolverhampton & Bilston	1:36:23	Steve Allen Barnet & District	1:54:50
Luke Finch Colchester H	1:37:12	**RWA 20 MILES CHAMPIONSHIP**	
Mark Williams Tamworth	1:40:54	**1912** Apr 27 Uxbridge	
Paul Evenett York CIU	1:41:20	Harold Ross Middlesex WC	2:51:21.4
Trevor Jones Hillingdon AC	1:46:20	Edgar Horton Surrey WC	2:54:15.4
Leicester 277, 2. Redcar, 3. Nuneaton		Will Ovens Herne Hill H	2:56:23
2007 Apr 14 Coventry		A.Bunce Surrey WC	3:01:31
Andy Penn Nuneaton H	1:35:24	F.Roberts Woodford Green	3:03:25
Peter Kaneen Manx H	1:40:46	Sidney Schofield Surrey WC	3:03:28
Steve Hollier Wolverhampton & Bilston	1:42:29	Surrey WC 20 Middlesex 42 Herne Hill H 59	
Scott Davis Ilford	1:43:03	**1913** Mar 24 Aylesbury	
Steve Arnold Nuneaton	1:49:48	Harold Ross Uxbridge & W Middlesex	2:49:53.4
Phil Williams Enfield & H	1:54:17	Edgar Horton Surrey WC	2:56:07
1. Nuneaton, 2. Ilford, 3. Birchfield		Sidney Schofield Surrey WC	2:57:41
2008 Apr 6 Earls Colne		Alred Pateman Herne Hill H	3:00:02
Brendan Boyce IRL	1:37:26	William Hehir Herne Hill H	3:00:26
Scott Davis Ilford	1:38:22	E.Hollingsworth Surrey WC	3:00:35
Trevor Jones Steyning	1:46:32	Surrey WC 19 Herne Hill H 30 Surrey WC 62	
Richard Emsley Steyning	1:47:10	**1914** May 16 St. Albans	
Ian Richards Steyning	1:48:29	Harold Ross Uxbridge & W Middlesex	2:50:37.4
Arthur Thomson	1:52:47	B.C.Brown Surrey WC	2:51:17.4
Steyning 284 Ilford 271 Belgrave 181 (+UKA)		William Hehir Surrey WC	2:54:10.8
2009 Apr 12 Shrewsbury		Edgar Horton Surrey WC	2:54:48.4
Luke Finch Colchester H	1:28:31	J.Dowse Uxbridge & W Middlesex	2:55:28.6
Carl Thomson Sarnia	1:39:51	Sidney Schofield Surrey WC	2:55:37.2
Paul Evenett York CIU	1:40:57	Surrey WC 18 Herne Hill H 30 Herne Hill H 44	
Trevor Jones Steyning	1:45:39	**1920** May 15 North Wembley	
Stephen Crane Surrey WC	1:50:47	Harold Ross Herne Hill H	2:51:59.6
Steve Arnold Nuneaton	1:56:08	William Hehir Surrey WC	3:01:39
1. Ilford, 2. Birchfield, 3. Enfield & Haringey		Godwin Withers Herne Hill H	3:02:54
2010 Apr 11 London (Victoria Park)		Edgar Horton Surrey WC	3:05:46
Tom Bosworth Tonbridge	1:31:06	H.Bentham Herne Hill H	3:06:24
Daniel King Colchester H	1:32:52	F.Burbidge Highgate H	3:11:41
Luke Finch Colchester H	1:33:38	**1921** Apr 16 Chislehurst	
Dominic King Colchester H	1:33:48	William Hehir Surrey WC	2:58:56.4
Tommy Taylor Birchfield H	1:34:52	B.C.Brown Surrey WC	2:59:28.8
Colchester 291 Ilford 265 Birchfield 246		Reg Goodwin Surrey WC	3:00:25
2011 May 1 Hainault		Harold Ross Herne Hill H	3:01:12
Tom Bosworth Tonbridge	1:30:13	Alred Pateman Herne Hill H	3:02:13
Dominic King Colchester H	1:35:28	Edgar Horton Surrey WC	3:03:26
Paul Evenett Redcar	1:38:27	Herne Hill H 26 Surrey AC 32 Surrey WC 43	
Antonio Cirillo Swansea H	1:44:09		

1922 Apr 22 Richmond Park, Surrey
William Hehir Surrey WC	2:50:12
Reg Goodwin Surrey WC	2:50:54
Harold Ross Herne Hill H	2:51:32
Edgar Horton Surrey WC	2:55:06
E.Cooper Surrey AC	2:55:10
A.Greening Surrey AC	2:55:17

Surrey WC 26 Surrey AC 30 Belgrave 52

1923 Apr 21 Leicester
Fred Poynton Leicester WC	2:51:35
Reg Goodwin Surrey WC	2:56:04
Lloyd Johnson Leicester WC	2:56:33
Wilf Cowley Surrey AC	2:59:49
Edgar Horton Surrey WC	3:01:02
E.Cooper Surrey AC	3:02:15

Surrey WC 27 Belgrave 46 Leicester H 46

1924 Apr 26 Windsor Great Park
Fred Poynton Leicester WC	2:47:17.5
Reg Goodwin Surrey WC	2:56:04
Lloyd Johnson Leicester WC	2:54:17
E.Cooper Belgrave H	2:56:36
Wilf Cowley Surrey AC	2:58:28
Dave McMullen Belgrave H	2:59:51

Belgrave 32 Surrey WC 41 Surrey AC 49

1925 May 9 Derby
Fred Poynton Derby WC	2:48:17.4
Lloyd Johnson Leicester WC	2:54:31
Reg Goodwin Surrey WC	2:56:16
Frank Rickards Belgrave H	2:56:36
E.Cooper Belgrave H	2:57:22
Billy Baker Queens Park H	2:57:49

Belgrave 28 Surrey WC 29 Queens Park H 69

1926 Not held due to General Strike

1927 May 14 St. Albans
Lloyd Johnson Surrey AC	2:55:53
G.Booker Surrey WC	2:56:20
L.Sandy Surrey AC	2:58:09
Tommy Green Belgrave H	2:58:44
Billy Baker Queens Park H	3:01:22
Walter Batson Surrey AC	3:03:10

Surrey AC 20 Surrey WC 47 Sheffield 62

1928 May 12 Leicester
L.Stewart London Vidarians WC	2:50:20.6
Lloyd Johnson Leicester WC	2:50:39
Fred Smith Birmingham WC	2:57:11
Dave McMullen Belgrave H	2:58:08
H.Glover Ashcombe AC	2:58:57
Walter Batson Surrey AC	2:59:22

Belgrave 33 Sheffield 53 Birmingham 57

1929 May 11 Hayes, Kent
Albert Plumb North London H	2:50:18.4
L.Sandy Surrey AC	2:50:50.6
John Reddish Herne Hill H	2:56:10
James Medlicott Birmingham WC	2:58:32
Fred Smith Birmingham WC	2:58:32
Tommy Green Belgrave H	3:01:59

Belgrave 51 Surrey AC 65 Surrey WC 71

1930 May 10 Derby
Albert Plumb North London H	2:46:30.4
Lloyd Johnson Leicester WC	2:47:22
Tommy Green Belgrave H	2:48:39
Frank Rickards Belgrave H	2:51:49
Dick Edge Derby WC	2:52:16
Fernando Pretti ITA	2:53:00

Birmingham 49 Derby 53 Belgrave 60

1931 May 9 Enfield
Lloyd Johnson Leicester WC	2:52:41.6
Albert Plumb North London H	2:52:43
James Medlicott Birmingham WC	2:55:28
Alf Pope Woodford Green	2:56:12
Harry Taylor Derby WC	2:56:33
J.Ludlow Derby WC	2:56:45

Derby 31 Sheffield 56 Birmingham 58

1932 May 7 Birmingham
Albert Plumb North London H	2:43:38.6
Tommy Green Belgrave H	2:48:34.6
William Archibald Surrey WC	2:49:10
Frank Rickards Belgrave H	2:49:21
Stan Fletcher Derby WC	2:50:26
J.Ludlow Derby WC	2:51:01

Derby 37 Sheffield 45 Surrey WC 51

1933 May 13 London (CP)
Alf Pope Woodford Green	2:48:38.4
Tommy Green Belgrave H	2:49:56
William Archibald Surrey WC	2:50:51
Harold Whitlock Metropolitan WC	2:51:54
John Wilson Sheffield United H	2:52:06
James Medlicott Birmingham WC	2:52:31

Surrey WC 36 Belgrave 47 Sheffield 61

1934 May 12 Sheffield
Lloyd Johnson Leicester WC	2:49:58
Frank Rickards Belgrave H	2:52:00
Albert Plumb Enfield AC	2:53:09
Harold Whitlock Metropolitan WC	2:54:32
William Archibald Surrey WC	2:56:48
A.Bullock Sheffield United H	2:57:49

Surrey WC 40 Belgrave 42 Leicester 56

1935 May 11 Chingford
James Medlicott Birmingham WC	2:47:46
Lloyd Johnson Leicester WC	2:49:06
Harold Whitlock Metropolitan WC	2:50:01
Tommy Green Belgrave H	2:50:06
William Archibald Surrey WC	2:52:06
Frank Bentley Belgrave H	2:52:36

Surrey WC 40 Belgrave 41 Birmingham 56

1936 May 9 Leicester
Henry Hake Surrey WC	2:47:23
Harold Whitlock Metropolitan WC	2:48:11
Stan Fletcher Derbyshire SC	2:49:53
Lloyd Johnson Leicester WC	2:51:31
Frank Rickards Belgrave H	2:51:43
Joe Hopkins Lancashire WC	2:52:04

Surrey WC 35 Leicester 52 Belgrave 53

1937 May 8 Epsom
Stan Fletcher Derbyshire SC	2:47:54.6
Harold Whitlock Metropolitan WC	2:49:19
David Christie-Murray Surrey WC	2:53:54
Albert Staines Leicester WC	2:54:04
John Wilson Sheffield United H	2:55:37
Tommy Richardson Woodford Green	2:56:20

Surrey WC & Leicester 40 Belgrave 56

1938 May 14 Birmingham
Joe Hopkins Lancashire WC	2:49:10
Frank Bentley Belgrave H	2:50:44
Lloyd Johnson Leicester WC	2:51:55
Colin Sutton Belgrave H	2:54:12
Tommy Richardson Woodford Green	2:54:33
Percy Reading Polytechnic H	2:54:44

Belgrave 23 Leicester 34 Surrey WC 55

1939 May 13 London (Hendon)
Harold Whitlock Metropolitan WC	2:51:03

David Christie-Murray Surrey WC	2:52:46	Frank Bailey Polytechnic H		2:56:21
Tommy Richardson Woodford Green	2:53:03	Stan Mantor Enfield AC		2:57:33
Frank Bentley Belgrave H	2:53:38	Alf Cotton Woodford Green		3:00:37
Stan Fletcher Leicester WC	2:54:16	Woodford Green 27 Belgrave 41 Polytechnic 55		
Lloyd Johnson Leicester WC	2:55:54	**1954** May 8 Birmingham		
Belgrave 32 Metropolitan 34 Leicester 60		Lol Allen Sheffield United H		2:47:48
1946 May 11 Coventry		Frank Bailey Polytechnic H		2:52:28
Harry Forbes Birmingham WC	2:50:43	Charlie Colman Yorkshire WC		2:52:43
Rex Whitlock Metropolitan WC	2:53:39	Albert Johnson Sheffield United H		2:53:42
Lloyd Johnson Leicester WC	2:55:22	High McGreechan Belgrave H		2:55:18
David Christie-Murray Surrey WC	2:58:29	Don Thompson Metropolitan WC		2:56:56
Charlie Churcher Belgrave H	2:58:40	Belgrave 42 Metropolitan 53 Sheffield 56		
Charlie Megnin Highgate H	2:59:11	**1955** May 14 Wimbledon		
Leicester 39 Metropolitan 57 Belgrave 57		George Coleman Highgate H		2:40:08
1947 May 10 Hendon		Albert Johnson Sheffield United H		2:43:06
Harry Forbes Birmingham WC	2:47:40	Eric Hall Belgrave H		2:45:47
Alf Pope Woodford Green	2:50:09	Alf Poole Worcester H		2:46:28
Johnny Henderson Sussex WC	2:52:01	Joe Barraclough Lancashire WC		2:47:33
Charlie Megnin Highgate H	2:52:43	Don Thompson Metropolitan WC		2:48:19
Rex Whitlock Metropolitan WC	2:52:48	Belgrave 45 Woodford Green 56 Sheffield 87		
Charlie Churcher Belgrave H	2:55:23	**1956** May 12 Sheffield		
Surrey WC 46 Woodford Green 47 Belgrave 72		Roland Hardy Sheffield United H		2:38:27
1948 May 8 Sudbury Hill		Albert Johnson Sheffield United H		2:43:31
Rex Whitlock Metropolitan WC	2:52:07	Bob Goodall Woodford Green		2:44:46
Bert Martineau Surrey WC	2:52:30	Don Thompson Metropolitan WC		2:47:05
Charlie Megnin Highgate H	2:54:56	Lol Allen Sheffield United H		2:47:55
Alf Cotton Woodford Green	2:55:34	Alf Poole Worcester H		2:51:37
David Christie-Murray Surrey WC	2:56:42	Sheffield 18 Metropolitan 55 Belgrave 59		
Lloyd Johnson Leicester WC	2:57:31	**1957** May 11 Hendon		
Surrey WC 56 Belgrave 78 Woodford Green 80		Eric Hall Belgrave H		2:45:12
1949 May 14 Manchester		George Chaplin Coventry Godiva		2:46:24
Lol Allen Sheffield United H	2:51:18	Albert Johnson Sheffield United H		2:47:12
Alf Cotton Woodford Green	2:51:33	Bob Goodall Woodford Green		2:47:44
Charlie Churcher Belgrave H	2:54:14	Don Thompson Metropolitan WC		2:48:09
John Proctor Sheffield United H	2:54:43	Tom Misson Metropolitan WC		2:49:10
Fred Barrett Cambridge H	2:55:40	Belgrave 33 Woodford Green 51 Metropolitan 68.5		
Harry Forbes Birmingham WC	2:56:22	**1958** May 10 Birmingham		
Sheffield 28 Belgrave 55 Woodford Green 61		Lol Allen Sheffield United H		2:43:21
1950 May 13 Bellingham		Tom Misson Metropolitan WC		2:45:18
Lol Allen Sheffield United H	2:52:16	Joe Barraclough Lancashire WC		2:46:22
John Proctor Sheffield United H	2:54:00	Albert Johnson Sheffield United H		2:47:04
Lloyd Johnson Leicester WC	2:58:07	Eric Hall Belgrave H		2:47:35
Bert Clayton Belgrave H	3:00:05	Don Thompson Metropolitan WC		2:49:18
Alf Cotton Woodford Green	3:01:46	Metropolitan 32 Belgrave 56 Sheffield 59		
Ron Pantling London Vidarians	3:02:14	**1959** May 9 East Molesey		
Woodford Green 47 Belgrave 50 Sheffield 79		Tom Misson Metropolitan WC		2:45:19
1951 May 12 Coventry		Don Thompson Metropolitan WC		2:48:34
Lol Allen Sheffield United H	2:51:52	Lol Allen Sheffield United H		2:54:20
Lloyd Johnson Leicester WC	2:57:21	Ron Davies Woodford Green		2:55:46
Alf Cotton Woodford Green	2:58:57	George Williams Belgrave H		2:59:17
Don Tunbridge Highgate H	2:59:27	Dickie Green Surrey WC		2:59:42
Percy Wright Belgrave H	2:59:59	Metropoliotan 23 Belgrave 42 Woodford Green 62		
Bob Goodall Woodford Green	3:01:09	**1960** May 14 Gomersal		
Woodford Green 40 Belgrave 46 Leicester 66		Stan Vickers Belgrave H		2:41:41
1952 May 10 Enfield		Don Thompson Metropolitan WC		2:42:39
John Proctor Sheffield United H	2:52:07	Tom Misson Metropolitan WC		2:43:44
Don Tunbridge Highgate H	2:53:44	Eric Hall Belgrave H		2:45:08
Rex Whitlock Metropolitan WC	2:53:58	Albert Johnson Sheffield United H		2:56:19
Frank Bailey Polytechnic H	3:00:39	Ray Hall Belgrave H		2:58:10
Hugh McGreechan Belgrave H	3:01:17	Belgrave 22 Metropolitan 32 Sheffield 46		
Harry Forbes Birmingham WC	3:01:37	**1961** May 13 London (Chiswick)		
Belgrave 49 Sheffield 64 Surrey WC 69		Don Thompson Metropolitan WC		2:44:49
1953 May 9 Derby		John Edgington Coventry Godiva		2:48:58
Bob Goodall Woodford Green	2:50:40	Ray Middleton Belgrave H		2:51:12
Lol Allen Sheffield United H	2:54:40	Charlie Fogg Enfield AC		2:52:18
Hugh McGreechan Belgrave H	2:55:49	Bob Clark Polytechnic H		2:53:46

Eric Hall Belgrave H	2:54:21
Sheffield 57 Belgrave 58 Leicester 64	
1962 May 12 Birmingham	
Ken Matthews R.Sutton Coldfield	2:38:39
Don Thompson Metropolitan WC	2:42:42
Paul Nihill Surrey WC	2:46:13
Bob Clark Polytechnic H	2:46:27
Ray Middleton Belgrave H	2:47:05
Colin Young Essex Beagles	2:48:13
Surrey WC 49 Sheffield 56 Belgrave 69	
1963 May 11 Ewell East	
Paul Nihill Surrey WC	2:39:43
Charlie Fogg Enfield AC	2:42:58
Ray Middleton Belgrave H	2:44:21
Ron Wallwork Lancashire WC	2:46:28
Denis Vale Surrey WC	2:47:12
Jim Stancer Sheffield United H	2:48:32
Surrey WC 24 Belgrave 40 Sheffield 63	
1964 May 9 Sheffield	
Paul Nihill Surrey WC	2:40:13
Peter McCullagh Metropolitan WC	2:41:50
Ray Middleton Belgrave H	2:42:06
John Paddick R.Sutton Coldfield	2:43:21
Ron Wallwork Lancashire WC	2:44:51
George Chaplin Coventry Godiva	2:47:06
Surrey WC 37 Belgrave 59 Metropolitan 67	
1965 June 12 Ewell East	
Paul Nihill Surrey WC	2:44:03
Ray Middleton Belgrave H	2:44:46
John Paddick R.Sutton Coldfield	2:45:20
Charlie Fogg Enfield AC	2:48:49
Maurice Fullager Surrey WC	2:50:48
Don Thompson Metropolitan WC	2:53:23
Surrey WC 23 Sheffield 38 Metropolitan 43	
1966 June 11 Hinckley	
Norman Read Steyning	2:39:33
Ray Middleton Belgrave H	2:40:08
Ron Wallwork Lancashire WC	2:40:22
Peter McCullagh Metropolitan WC	2:41:16
Don Thompson Metropolitan WC	2:41:24
Charlie Fogg Enfield AC	2:45:14
Metropolitan 33 Leicester 59 Surrey WC 65	
1967 June 10 Swindon	
Roy Lodge R.Sutton Coldfield WC	2:42:43
Don Thompson Metropolitan WC	2:43:17
Ron Wallwork Lancashire WC	2:44:28
Charlie Fogg Enfield AC	2:45:23
Ray Middleton Belgrave H	2:45:52
Bill Sutherland Highgate H	2:48:53
Trowbridge 52 Lancashire WC 52 Leicester 71	
1968 June 8 Sheffield	
Paul Nihill Surrey WC	2:35:07
Larry Young USA	2:37:04
Shaun Lightman Metropolitan WC	2:39:39
Dave DeNoon USA	2:39:50
John Warhurst Sheffield United H	2:41:57
Phil Thorn Trowbridge	2:43:52
Metropolitan 41 Belgrave 44 Trowbridge 50	
1969 June 14 South Croydon	
Paul Nihill Surrey WC	2:44:51
Bryan Eley Bristol WC	2:46:24
Bill Sutherland Highgate H	2:48:45
Shaun Lightman Metropolitan WC	2:51:10
Ray Middleton Belgrave H	2:51:40
Ron Wallwork Lancashire WC	2:54:42
Belgrave 33 Wakefield 58 Coventry 93	

1970 June 13 Redditch	
Wllford Wesch Belgrave H/FRG	2:38:15
Ron Wallwork Lancashire WC	2:40:27
Bob Dobson Basildon	2:41:36
Shaun Lightman Metropolitan WC	2:41:59
Peter Fullager Basildon	2:42:35
Ray Middleton Belgrave H	2:43:15
Belgrave 31 Lancashire WC 83 Sheffield 97	
1971 June 12 Sheffield	
Paul Nihill Surrey WC	2:30:35
Ron Wallwork Lancashire WC	2:35:18
Ian Brooks Surrey WC	2:35:54
Bill Sutherland Highgate H	2:37:11
Bob Dobson Basildon	2:40:13
Wllford Wesch Belgrave H/FRG	2:41:08
Surrey WC 23 R.Sutton Coldfield 49 Belgrave 60	
1972 June 10 Manchester	
John Warhurst Sheffield United H	2:35:19
Shaun Lightman Metropolitan WC	2:36:54
George Chaplin Coventry Godiva	2:39:41
Ray Middleton Belgrave H	2:40:53
Howard Timms Surrey WC	2:41:12
Carl Lawton Belgrave H	2:42:36
Sheffield 34 Belgrave 39 Leicester 42	
1973 June 16 Ewell East	
Bob Dobson Basildon	2:40:07
John Warhurst Sheffield United H	2:44:03
Roy Thorpe Sheffield United H	2:47:04
Carl Lawton Belgrave H	2:50:26
John Moullin Belgrave H	2:50:39
Peter Selby Surrey WC	2:50:45
Sheffield 30 Belgrave 32 Surrey WC 81	
1974 June 15 Redditch	
Roy Thorpe Sheffield United H	2:39:47
Bob Dobson Southend on Sea	2:42:45
John Warhurst Sheffield United H	2:44:54
Brian Adams Leicester WC	2:48:30
Charlie Fogg Enfield H	2:48:45
Ray Middleton Belgrave H	2:49:41
Southend 46 Sheffield 48 Surrey WC 61	
1975 June 14 Castletown IOM	
Bob Dobson Southend on Sea	2:36:26
Roy Thorpe Sheffield United H	2:37:09
John Warhurst Sheffield United H	2:38:21
Alec Banyard Southend on Sea	2:39:31
Amos Seddon Enfield H	2:39:57
Peter Selby Surrey WC	2:44:48
Sheffield 28 Southend 47 Brighton 66	
1976 June 19 Stevenage	
Roger Mills Ilford	2:32:13
Bob Dobson Southend on Sea	2:33:30
Roy Thorpe Sheffield United H	2:36:53
Carl Lawton Belgrave H	2:37:30
Paul Nihill Croydon H	2:37:37
Stuart Elms Brighton & Hove	2:37:50
Sheffield 44 Southend 49 Brighton 62	
1977 June 18 Sutton Coldfield	
Amos Seddon Enfield H	2:35:15
Mick Greasley Sheffield United H	2:36:15
David Cotton Holloway Polytechnic	2:37:21
George Nibre Ilford	2:38:57
Denis Holly Brighton & Hove	2:39:40
Shaun Lightman Metropolitan WC	2:41:20
Sheffield 30 Enfield 59 Belgrave 79	

RWA 30 KILOMETRES CHAMPIONSHIP
1978 June 17 Chapeltown, S Yorks
Olly Flynn Basildon	2:21:54
Brian Adams Leicester WC	2:22:26
Amos Seddon Enfield H	2:25:26
Roger Mills Ilford	2:27:11
Shaun Lightman Metropolitan WC	2:27:37
Bob Dobson Southend on Sea	2:28:54

Sheffield 29 Steyning 48 York Postal 49

RWA 35 KILOMETRES CHAMPIONSHIP
1979 June 16 Leicester
Roger Mills Ilford	2:52:08
Bob Dobson Ilford	2:52:44
Adrian James Enfield H	2:54:07
Carl Lawton Belgrave H	2:56:47
Dennis Jackson York Postal WC	2:56:51
Peter Ryan Sheffield United H	2:57:35

Sheffield 29 Ilford 36 York Postal 49

1980 June 21 London (VP)
Amos Seddon Enfield H	2:40:04
Tim Erickson AUS	2:42:55
Adrian James Enfield H	2:43:07
Dennis Jackson York Postal WC	2:45:50
George Nibre Ilford	2:48:10
Allan King Leicester WC	2:49:13

Leicester 57 York Postal 73 Steyning 78

1981 June 20 York
Bob Dobson Ilford	2:48:30
Mick Greasley Sheffield United H	2:49:28
Barry Graham York Postal WC	2:52:00
Adrian James Enfield H	2:54:46
John Warhurst Sheffield United H	2:55:52
Rob Elliott York Postal WC	2:57:36

Sheffield 18 York Postal 38 Leicester 53

1982 June 19 Kenilworth
Dave Jarman Surrey WC	2:48:41
Allan King Leicester WC	2:50:26
Bob Dobson Ilford	2:50:30
Murray Lambden Boundary H	2:51:03
Carl Lawton Belgrave H	2:51:51
Amos Seddon Enfield H	2:53:59

Leicester 31 Belgrave 37 Sheffield 40

1983 June 18 Colchester
Carl Lawton Belgrave H	2:58:44
Reg Gardner Bromsgrove & Redditch	2:59:52
Brian Adams Leicester WC	3:00:14
Dennis Jackson York Postal WC	3:02:08
Neale Smith Coventry Godiva H	3:05:12
Barry Graham York Postal WC	3:05:29

Leicester 42 Coventry 48 Sheffield 51

1984 June 16 Beighton, South Yorkshire
Paul Blagg Cambridge H	3:03:54
Les Morton Sheffield United H	3:06:03
Amos Seddon Enfield H	3:07:33
Barry Graham York Postal WC	3:09:01
Reg Gardner Bromsgrove & Redditch	3:11:49
Andy Trigg Leicester WC	3:12:12

Sheffield 42 Belgrave 63 Coventry 73

1985 June 15 Leicester
Dennis Jackson York Postal WC	2:41:03
Les Morton Sheffield United H	2:42:47
Murray Day Belgrave H	2:43:35
Barry Graham York Postal WC	2:48:59
Mick Greasley Sheffield United H	2:50:25
Adrian James Enfield H	2:51:57

Sheffield 25 Belgrave 56 Coventry 67

1986 June 22 Plymouth
Chris Maddocks Dawlish & SD	2:47:54
Mike Smith Coventry Godiva H	2:48:50
Darren Thorn Coventry Godiva H	2:49:08
Allan King Leicester WC	2:50:57
Dave Ratcliffe Coventry Godiva H	2:54:24
Steve Johnson Splott Conservative	2:57:27

Coventry 26 Dawlish 73 Surrey WC 120

1987 June 6 York
Chris Berwick Leicester WC	2:56:28
Adrian James Enfield H	2:57:04
Ian Harvey Coventry RWC	2:59:26
Steve Partington Boundary H	3:00:27
Allan King Leicester WC	3:01:04
Ed Shillabeer Plymouth City W	3:02:05

Leicester 30 Sheffield 65 Steyning 69

1988 June 11 Leicester
Chris Maddocks Plymouth City W	2:45:09
Darrell Stone Steyning	2:51:27
Chris Berwick Leicester WC	2:58:21
Adrian James Enfield H	3:00:37
Ray Hankin Sheffield United RWC	3:01:37
Reg Gardner Bromsgrove & Redditch	3:02:02

Leicester 27

1989 June 10 Colchester
Darrell Stone Steyning	2:50:49
Mike Smith Coventry RWC	2:56:28
Bob Dobson Ilford	3:04:35
Ian Harvey Coventry RWC	3:06:19
Chris Berwick Leicester WC	3:06:42
Gareth Brown Steyning	3:09:15

Steyning 42 Coventry 52 Sheffield 59

1990 June 9 York
Les Morton Sheffield United RWC	2:50:50
Gareth Brown Steyning	2:58:35
Stuart Phillips Ilford	2:58:58
Chris Berwick Leicester WC	3:02:29
Dave Staniforth Sheffield Utd	3:03:14
Ian Harvey Coventry RWC	3:03:40

Sheffield 35 Steyning 49 Leicester 53

1991 June 8 Sutton Coldfield
Stuart Phillips Ilford	2:55:21
Darren Thorn Coventry RWC	2:56:48
Mike Smith Coventry RWC	2:59:00
Chris Berwick Leicester WC	2:59:39
Ian Harvey Coventry RWC	3:00:58
Allan King Leicester WC	3:02:36

Coventry 19 Leicester 39 Steyning 56

1992 June 13 Colchester (over distance)
Les Morton Sheffield United RWC	2:59:38
Steve Partington Manx H	3:08:54
Mark Easton Surrey WC	3:12:14
Sean Martindale York Postal WC	3:16:20
Chris Berwick Leicester WC	3:16:42
Dave Ratcliffe Coventry RWC	3:23:32

York Postal 29 Ilford 45 Sheffield 45

1993 July 10 Sutton Coldfield **20 MILES**
Sean Martindale York Postal WC	2:33:58
Darren Thorn Coventry RWC	2:36:18
Noel Carmody Cambridge H	2:40:57
Chris Berwick Leicester WC	2:48:33
Amos Seddon Enfield H	2:58:12
Denis Holly Brighton & Hove	2:56:15

Coventry 21 Leicester 30 Surrey WC 36

1994 Apr 16 Horsham **30 KILOMETRES**
Chris Maddocks Plymouth City W	2:22:45

Graham White Brighton & Hove	2:26:27	Chris Berwick Leicester WC	3:18:24
Chris Cheeseman Surrey WC	2:27:11	Steve Arnold Coventry Godiva H	3:22:23
Karl Atton Leicester WC	2:33:08	Richard Emsley Steyning	3:22:30
Phil King Coventry RWC	2:33:08	Coventry G C of Sheffield Surrey WC	
Carl Thomson Sarnia WC	2:37:34	**2003** June 14 Sutton Coldfield	
Leicester 22 Surrey WC 41 Sheffield 48		Andi Drake Covnetry Godiva H	2:54:36
1995 June 3 Enfield **20 MILES**		Chris Cheeseman Surrey WC	3:10:06
Gareth Brown Steyning	2:41:36	Mike Smith Coventry Godiva H	3:17:50
Darrell Stone Steyning	2:41:37	Chris Berwick Leicester WC	3:23:49
Scott Davis Ilford	2:51:27	Tim Watt Steyning	3:33:56
Chris Berwick Leicester WC	2:52:39	Colin Bradley Surrey WC	3:37:55
Bob Dobson Ilford	3:01:31	Coventry 290 Steyning 278 Surrey WC 192	
Martin Young Road Hoggs	3:02:41	**2004** June 12 Sutton Coldfield	
Steyning 13 Leicester 31 Belgrave 40		Nathan Adams City of Sheffield	3:06:25
1996 July 6 Stockport **20 MILES**		Matthew Hales Steyning	3:13:30
Chris Cheeseman Surrey WC	2:35:15	Peter Ryan City of Sheffield	3:19:11
Andy Penn Coventry RWC	2:40:31	Richard Emsley Steyning	3:26:57
John Cocker York CIU	2:45:36	Chris Berwick Leicester WC	3:27:09
Richard Oldale Sheffield Utd RWC	2:51:17	Tim Watt Steyning	3:39:08
Scott Davis Ilford	2:51:57	Steyning 288 Sheffield 287 Leicester 186	
Darren Thorn Coventry RWC	2:52:45		

RWA 50 KILOMETRES CHAMPIONSHIP

1930 July 12 South Croydon

Coventry 13 Sheffield 35 Leicester 38	
1997 June 7 Leicester **20 MILES**	
Tommy Green Belgrave H	4:35:36.8
Chris Cheeseman Surrey WC	2:34:04
Francesco Pretti FZ Roma/ITA	4:43:25.6
Graham White Brighton & Hove	2:34:41
J.Ludlow Derby WC	4:48:31
Darrell Stone Steyning	2:38:16
H.Porter Woodford Green	4:56:29
Allan King Road Hoggs	2:43:39
H.Kemp Derby WC	5:00:20
Gareth Brown Steyning	2:49:44
C.Kirkland & Harry Taylor Derby WC	5:02:21
Chris Berwick Leicester WC	2:56:19
1931 May 25 Bradford	
Steyning 15 Road Hoggs 23 Surrey WC 28	
Lloyd Johnson Leicester WC	4:55:48
1998 June 6 Hove **20 MILES**	
Harold Whitlock Metropolitan WC	4:55:48
Les Morton Sheffield Utd RWC	2:43:01
J.Ludlow Derby WC	4:59:58
Allan King Road Hoggs	2:46:57
Held with Bradford Whit Monday walk with intermediate time taken at 50km for 1st 3 only. No team race.	
Don Bearman Steyning	2:49:19
Karl Atton Road Hoggs	2:49:56
1932 June 25 Leicester	
Gareth Brown Steyning	2:50:58
Francesco Pretti ITA	4:41:54.4
Mike Smith Coventry RWC	2:55:07
Lloyd Johnson Leicester WC	4:43:34.2
Coventry 23 Steyning 28 Leicester 56	
Ettore Rivolta ITA	4:46:57.6
1999 June 5 Stockport **Back at 35km**	
Tommy Payne South Shields	4:48:30
Darrell Stone Steyning	2:49:45
J.Ludlow Derby WC	4:50:38
Chris Cheeseman Surrey WC	2:53:59
James Medlicott Birmingham WC	4:55:20
Tim Watt Steyning	2:54:39
Birmingham 12 Derby 16 Leicester 20	
Steve Hollier Wolverhampton & Bilston	2:56:21
1933 June 17 Birmingham	
Mike Smith Coventry RWC	3:07:34
Harold Whitlock Metropolitan WC	4:39:17
Don Bearman Steyning	3:11:21
Frank Rickards Belgrave H	4:41:11
Steyning 10 Coventry 23 Surrey WC 34	
Lloyd Johnson Leicester WC	4:44:47
2000 May 6 Dartford	
James Medlicott Birmingham WC	4:47:45
Chris Cheeseman Surrey WC	2:51:20
Harry Forbes Birmingham WC	4:49:57
Don Bearman Steyning	2:53:10
Fred Smith Birmingham WC	4:54:34
Gareth Brown Steyning	2:55:59
Birmingham 12 Belgrave 16 Derby 33	
Mike Smith Coventry RWC	3:11:00
1934 June 23 Croydon	
Chris Berwick Leicester WC	3:14:41
Lloyd Johnson Leicester WC	4:36:30
Dave Ratcliffe Coventry RWC	3:24:43
Harold Whitlock Metropolitan WC	4:38:08
Steyning 19 Coventry 20 Leicester 26	
Frank Rickards Belgrave H	4:38:39
2001 May 5 Birmingham	
James Medlicott Birmingham WC	4:46:50
Mark Easton Surrey WC	2:55:00
Frank Bentley Belgrave H	4:48:50
Darrell Stone Steyning	2:58:19
Harry Forbes Birmingham WC	4:49:00
Mike Smith Coventry Godiva H	2:58:35
Belgrave 13 Birmingham 20 Surrey WC 27	
Gareth Brown Steyning	3:04:15
1935 June 10 Bradford	
Peter Ryan City of Sheffield	3:14:08
Harold Whitlock Metropolitan WC	4:39:08
Chris Berwick Leicester WC	3:14:54
Tommy Green Belgrave H	4:39:47
Coventry 281 Steyning 194 Sheffield 181	
Lloyd Johnson Leicester WC	4:45:48
2002 July 6 Sutton Coldfield	
James Medlicott Birmingham WC	4:49:07
Martin Young Road Hoggs	3:04:39
H.Charles Birmingham WC	4:53:28
Nathan Adams City of Sheffield	3:09:44
Herbert Cashmore Leicester WC	4:54:26
Mike Smith Coventry Godiva H	3:11:25
Belgrave 17 Birmingham 18 Leicester 20	

1936 July 4 Derby
Harold Whitlock Metropolitan WC	4:30:38
Joe Hopkins Lancashire WC	4:31:01
Frank Bentley Belgrave H	4:33:32
Tommy Green Belgrave H	4:36:02
Henry Hake Surrey WC	4:39:41
Frank Rickards Belgrave H	4:42:33

Belgrave 13 Surrey WC 22 Lancashire WC 35

1937 July 24 New Southgate
Harold Whitlock Metropolitan WC	4:38:43
David Christie-Murray Surrey WC	4:44:30
Rex Whitlock Metropolitan WC	4:46:15
Tommy Richardson Woodford Green	4:47:30
Alf Pope Woodford Green	4:51:22
Johnny Henderson Sussex WC	4:54:12

Metropolitan 15 Belgrave 21 Woodford Green 35

1938 June 6 Bradford
Harold Whitlock Metropolitan WC	4:43:01.5
Frank Bentley Belgrave H	4:43:25
Lloyd Johnson Leicester WC	4:45:30
Joe Hopkins Lancashire WC	4:45:51
Colin Sutton Belgrave H	4:46:38
Frank Rickards Belgrave H	4:55:35

Belgrave 13 Leicester 26 Lancashire WC 33

1939 July 22 New Southgate
Harold Whitlock Metropolitan WC	4:40:43
Rex Whitlock Metropolitan WC	4:41:25
Johnny Henderson Sussex WC	4:43:29
Frank Rickards Belgrave H	4:46:54
Stanley Abel Essex Beagles	4:49:17
David Christie-Murray Surrey WC	4:49:45

Metropolitan 11 Belgrave 20 Essex B 30

1946 June 10 Bradford
Charlie Megnin Highgate H	4:53:25.6
Harry Forbes Birmingham WC	4:57:21
Albert Staines Leicester WC	4:58:35
Lloyd Johnson Leicester WC	4:59:34
Rex Whitlock Metropolitan WC	5:00:24
Stan Mantor Enfield AC	5:02:24

Leicester 18 Metropolitan 22 Belgrave 29

1947 July 12 Eastleigh
Harry Forbes Birmingham WC	4:40:06
Rex Whitlock Metropolitan WC	4:48:59
David Christie-Murray Surrey WC	4:49:52
John Henderson Sussex W&AC	4:52:54
Bert Martineau Surrey WC	4:54:47
Albert Staines Leicester WC	4:55:41

Surrey WC 23 Leicester 29 Woodford Green 36

1948 June 19 Birmingham
Rex Whitlock Metropolitan WC	4:35:35
Lloyd Johnson Leicester WC	4:36:02
Bert Martineau Surrey WC	4:39:40
Harry Forbes Birmingham WC	4:45:20
Stan Mantor Enfield AC	4:45:39
Charlie Megnin Highgate H	4:45:44

Surrey WC 44 Leicester 48 Enfield 71

1949 June 18 Chigwell
Lloyd Johnson Leicester WC	4:51:50
Les Barrett Enfield AC	4:53:52
Ron Pantling London Vidarians	4:55:21
Tommy Richardson Woodford Green	4:57:21
David Christie-Murray Surrey WC	5:03:44
Charlie Megnin Highgate H	5:03:51

Surrey WC 35 Enfield 38 Woodford Green 70

1950 June 17 Sheffield
John Proctor Sheffield United H	4:43:04
Alf Cotton Woodford Green	4:46:38
Bert Clayton Belgrave H	4:47:55
Percy Price Polytechnic H	4:49:31
David Christie-Murray Surrey WC	4:56:31
Percy Reading Polytechnic H	4:57:00

Woodford Green 35 Belgrave 53 Enfield 69

1951 June 16 Brighton
Don Tunbridge Highgate H	4:45:34
Bert Clayton Belgrave H	4:52:06
Percy Reading Polytechnic H	4:52:57
Bill Allen Sheffield United H	4:55:50
Lloyd Johnson Leicester WC	4:59:56
Hugh McGreechan Belgrave H	5:02:00

Belgrave 29 Polytechnic 44 Surrey WC 63

1952 June 14 Leicester
Rex Whitlock Metropolitan WC	4:38:02
Don Tunbridge Highgate H	4:38:02
Harold Whitlock Metropolitan WC	4:47:33
Frank Bailey Polytechnic H	4:48:11
Charles Colman Yorkshire WC	4:49:28
Robert Goodall Woodford Green	4:51:57

Woodford Green 29 Polytechnic 44 Belgrave 75

1953 June 20 Shirley, Croydon
Frank Bailey Polytechnic H	4:46:10
Jim Culver Essex Beagles	4:50:50
Victor Stone Polytechnic H	4:51:38
Tommy Richardson Woodford G	4:55:38
Phil Everard Essex Beagles	4:56:14
Hugh McGreechan Belgrave H	4:58:22

Polytechnic 29 Woodford Green 35 Belgrave 53

1954 June 19 Sheffield
John Ljunggren SWE	4:32:47
Albert Johnson Sheffield United H	4:34:34
Åke Söderlund SWE	4:37:43
Verner Ljunggren SWE	4:40:03
Frank Bailey Polytechnic H	4:42:19
Hugh McGreechan Belgrave H	4:45:14

Belgrave 30 Polytechnic 40 Woodford Green 50

1955 June 11 Coventry
Albert Johnson Sheffield United H	4:31:32
Don Thompson Metropolitan WC	4:34:39
Erik Söderlund SWE	4:39:06
Åke Söderlund SWE	4:39:21
Frank Bailey Polytechnic H	4:39:51
Alex MacFarlane Polytechnic H	4:47:52

Polytechnic 25 Belgrave 35 Leicester 59

1956 June 16 Enfield
Don Thompson Metropolitan WC	4:24:39
Eric Hall Belgrave H	4:31:41
George Chaplin Coventry Godiva	4:35:12
Albert Johnson Metropolitan WC	4:36:43
George Checkley Belgrave H	4:38:28
Ron Davies Woodford Green	4:44:49

Belgrave 17 Woodford Green 53 Surrey WC 54

1957 June 15 Leyland
Don Thompson Metropolitan WC	4:41:48
George Chaplin Coventry Godiva	4:48:10
George Checkley Belgrave H	4:50:28
George Beecham Belgrave H	5:00:19
Harry Taylor Sheffield United H	5:01:47
Hugh McGreechan Belgrave H	5:04:16

Belgrave 16 Sheffield 51 Essex B 80

1958 June 21 Wimbledon
Don Thompson Metropolitan WC	4:21:50
Tom Misson Metropolitan WC	4:25:29
Eric Hall Belgrave H	4:37:04

Nigel Thompson Metropolitan WC	4:40:40	Roy Thorpe Wakefield H		4:59:35
Albert Johnson Sheffield United H	4:43:44	Belgrave 19 Surrey WC 32 Leicester 72		
John Edgington Coventry Godiva	4:47:07	**1967** July 22 Redditch		
Belgrave 32 Metropolitan 48 Sheffield 59		Shaun Lightman Metropolitan WC		4:26:56
1959 June 20 Baddesley		Ray Middleton Belgrave H		4:33:28
Don Thompson Metropolitan WC	4:12:19	Don Thompson Metropolitan WC		4:34:16
Tom Misson Metropolitan WC	4:14:03	Bryan Eley Trowbridge		4:39:33
Nigel Thompson Metropolitan WC	4:38:00	Charlie Fogg Enfield AC		4:47:35
Albert Staines Leicester WC	4:40:17	John Paddick R.Sutton Coldfield		4:48:57
George Checkley Belgrave H	4:42:35	Belgrave 54 Trowbridge 59 Wakefield 59		
Dickie Green Surrey WC	4:43:34	**1968** July 20 Ewell East		
Metropolitan 22 Belgrave 41 Leicester 51		Paul Nihill Surrey WC		4:18:59
1960 June 18 Chigwell Row		Bryan Eley Bristol WC		4:22:16
Don Thompson Metropolitan WC	4:32:55	Shaun Lightman Metropolitan WC		4:23:17
Tom Misson Metropolitan WC	4:39:28	Ray Middleton Belgrave H		4:31:11
Albert Johnson Sheffield United H	4:52:27	Phil Thorn Trowbridge		4:33:25
Dickie Green Surrey WC	4:57:49	Don Thompson Metropolitan WC		4:38:23
Frank O'Reilly Lozells H	4:58:40	Belgrave 30 Metropolitan 41 Wakefield 56		
George Beecham Belgrave H	5:03:33	**1969** July 19 Redditch		
Belgrave 40 Metropolitan 43 Woodford Green 54		Bryan Eley Bristol WC		4:19:13
1961 June 17 Sheffield		Shaun Lightman Metropolitan WC		4:24:58
Don Thompson Metropolitan WC	4:22:51	Goetz Klopfer USA (Guest)		4:25:04
Ray Middleton Belgrave H	4:29:47	Ray Middleton Belgrave H		4:25:46
Nigel Thompson Metropolitan WC	4:39:14	George Chaplin Coventry Godiva		4:30:30
Charlie Fogg Enfield AC	4:42:05	John Warhurst Sheffield United H		4:31:14
Charlie Colman Lancashire WC	4:45:28	Charlie Fogg Enfield H		4:34:24
Colin Young Essex Beagles	4:46:02	Belgrave 29 Wakefield 63 Bristol 68		
Belgrave 36 Lancashire WC 55 Leicester 59		**1970** Aug 15 Ewell East		
1962 June 23 Luton		Bob Dobson Basildon		4:20:22
Don Thompson Metropolitan WC	4:27:26	Ray Middleton Belgrave H		4:21:22
Ray Middleton Belgrave H	4:30:59	Ron Wallwork Lancashire WC		4:25:16
Ray Hall Belgrave H	4:42:25	John Warhurst Sheffield United H		4:26:46
Colin Young Essex Beagles	4:44:36	Don Thompson Metropolitan WC		4:30:18
Jin Stancer Sheffield United H	4:46:41	Ken Harding R.Sutton Coldfield		4:30:47
Ken Mason Surrey WC	4:47:01	Belgrave 26 Surrey WC 48 Lancashire WC 58		
Surrey WC 23 Belgrave 25 Sheffield 25		**1971** July 17 Redditch		
1963 June 15 Baddesley		Paul Nihill Surrey WC		4:15:05
Ray Middleton Belgrave H	4:16:43.2	Bob Dobson Basildon		4:17:44
Don Thompson Metropolitan WC	4:21:43	Carl Lawton Belgrave H		4:19:00
Charlie Fogg Enfield AC	4:22:52	Ron Wallwork Lancashire WC		4:21:02
Paul Nihill Surrey WC	4:26:06	Ray Middleton Belgrave H		4:26:46
Ron Wallwork Lancashire WC	4:28:00	John Warhurst Sheffield United H		4:28:36
Ken Mason Surrey WC	4:28:44	Surrey WC 29 Belgrave 32 R Sutton C 71		
Surrey WC 23 Belgrave 27 Metropolitan 61		**1972** July 15 Badminton		
1964 June 20 Enfield		John Warhurst Sheffield United H		4:18:31
Paul Nihill Surrey WC	4:17:10	Howard Timms Surrey WC		4:24:02
Ray Middleton Belgrave H	4:21:14	Bob Dobson Basildon		4:25:36
Don Thompson Metropolitan WC	4:21:58	Ray Middleton Belgrave H		4:25:52
Ron Wallwork Lancashire WC	4:27:02	Roy Thorpe Sheffield United H		4:30:42
John Paddick R.Sutton Coldfield	4:29:07	George Chaplin Coventry Godiva		4:34:31
Guy Goodair Wakefield H	4:30:57	Sheffield 38 Surrey WC 39 Belgrave 55		
Belgrave 32 Surrey WC 42 Metropolitan 44		**1973** Aug 4 Redditch		
1965 July 24 Bolton		Bob Dobson Basildon		4:14:29
Ray Middleton Belgrave H	4:17:23	Shaun Lightman Metropolitan WC		4:17:45
Don Thompson Metropolitan WC	4:18:31	Mike Holmes Yorkshire WC		4:19:55
Charlie Fogg Enfield AC	4:22:45	Ray Middleton Belgrave H		4:23:47
John Paddick R.Sutton Coldfield	4:25:50	Roy Thorpe Sheffield United H		4:30:42
Paul Nihill Surrey WC	4:26:32	Alec Banyard Southend on Sea		4:27:29
Guy Goodair Wakefield H	4:37:53	Sheffield 54 Metropolitan 54 Yorks 84		
Surrey WC 26 Sheffield 51 Belgrave 54		**1974** July 20 Hendon		
1966 July 23 Chigwell Row		Bob Dobson Southend on Sea		4:16:58
Don Thompson Metropolitan WC	4:28:26	John Warhurst Sheffield United H		4:18:58
Ray Middleton Belgrave H	4:32:18	Roy Thorpe Sheffield United H		4:24:08
Charlie Fogg Enfield AC	4:36:13	Alec Banyard Southend on Sea		4:27:21
Guy Goodair Wakefield H	4:54:37	Brian Adams Leicester WC		4:31:51
Ray Hall Belgrave H	4:57:40	John Nye Surrey WC		4:35:19

Sheffield 43 Belgrave 63 Leicester 74		Barry Graham York Postal RWC	4:24:18
1975 July 19 Leicester		Bob Dobson Ilford AC	4:28:59
John Warhurst Sheffield United H	4:20:32	Murray Lambden Boundary H	4:34:18
John Lees Brighton & Hove	4:26:13	Adrian James Borough of Enfield H	4:36:53
Charlie Fogg Borough of Enfield H	4:27:44	Steve Marshall Belgrave H	4:41:56
Roy Thorpe Sheffield United H	4:28:34	Brian Adams Leicester WC	4:44:50
Alec Banyard Southend on Sea	4:28:41	Leicester 50 Sheffield 65 Belgrave 80	
Bob Dobson Southend on Sea	4:30:31	**1984** July 14 Kendal	
Sheffield 43 Southend 50 Belgrave 71		Paul Blagg Cambridge H	4:20:31
1976 July 17 Birmingham		Gordon Vale Surrey WC	4:23:00
Roy Thorpe Sheffield United H	4:23:43	Barry Graham York Postal RWC	4:24:16
Carl Lawton Belgrave H	4:26:01	Dennis Jackson York Postal RWC	4:30:15
Bob Dobson Southend on Sea	4:26:27	Les Morton Sheffield United H	4:32:11
Peter Selby Surrey WC	4:27:48	Bob Dobson Ilford	4:33:00
Charlie Fogg Borough of Enfield H	4:29:20	York Postal 39 Sheffield 60 Leicester 69	
Peter Hodkinson Cambridge H	4:32:12	**1985** July 13 Corby	
Sheffield 38 Belgrave 79 Surrey WC 85		Les Morton Sheffield United H	4:19:09
1977 July 23 Milton Keynes		Barry Graham York Postal RWC	4:24:52
Brian Adams Leicester WC	4:25:28	Chris Berwick Leicester WC	4:27:29
John Warhurst Sheffield United H	4:27:33	Reg Gardner Bromsgrove & Redditch	4:28:15
Peter Hodkinson Cambridge H	4:36:27	Bob Dobson Ilford	4:33:38
Peter Selby Surrey WC	4:38:07	Adrian James Borough of Enfield H	4:35:39
Graham Young Boundary H	4:42:46	Leicester 35 Coventry 50 Sheffield 58	
Derek Harrison Boundary H	4:46:50	**1986** July 12 Enfield	
Sheffield 47 Boundary H 56 Leicester 58		Godfried De Jonckheere BEL	4:10:21
1978 July 15 Manchester		Chris Berwick Leicester WC	4:23:22
David Cotton Holloway Polytechnic	4:14:25	Andy Trigg Leicester WC	4:25:29
Ian Richards Coventry Godiva H	4:18:32	Reg Gardner Bromsgrove & Redditch	4:26:53
Brian Adams Leicester WC	4:19:22	Bob Dobson Ilford	4:28:59
Adrian James Borough of Enfield H	4:20:24	Mike Smith Coventry Godiva H	4:30:55
Bob Dobson Southend on Sea	4:24:57	Leicester 28 Coventry 62 R.SC 77	
Shaun Lightman Metropolitan WC	4:25:42	**1987** July 11 Beighton	
Sheffield 30 Steyning 68 Coventry 75		Les Morton Sheffield United H	4:23:40
1979 July 21 Coventry		Chris Berwick Leicester WC	4:34:02
Mike Parker Brighton & Hove	4:14:26	Ian Harvey Coventry RWC	4:41:04
Adrian James Borough of Enfield H	4:14:30	Adrian James Borough of Enfield H	4:41:58
Chris Maddocks Dawlish & S.Devon	4:22:08	Bob Dobson Ilford	4:43:02
George Nibre Ilford	4:23:08	Mel McCann Yorkshire RWC	4:46:07
Peter Hodkinson Cambridge H	4:23:12	Sheffield 30 Leicester 34	
Ian Richards Coventry Godiva H	4:25:46	**1988** July 10 York	
Sheffield 39 Leicester 47 Belgrave 64		Les Morton Sheffield United H	4:17:05
1980 July 19 Basildon		Gordon Vale Boundary H	4:24:54
Tim Erickson AUS	4:10:33	Chris Berwick Leicester WC	4:30:06
Dennis Jackson York Postal RWC	4:16:25	Bob Dobson Ilford	4:34:12
Brian Adams Leicester WC	4:23:01	Barry Graham York Postal RWC	4:37:42
Murray Lambden Boundary H	4:24:57	Adrian James Borough of Enfield H	4:39:42
Tony Geal Steyning	4:30:53	Sheffield 32 York Postal 56	
Paul Blagg Belgrave H	4:31:55	**1989** July 8 Hove	
Leicester 34 Sheffield 43 York Postal 49		Les Morton Sheffield United H	4:21:19
1981 July 18 Sleaford		Mike Smith Coventry RWC	4:27:19
Barry Graham York Postal RWC	4:10:46	Chris Berwick Leicester WC	4:32:04
Bob Dobson Ilford	4:14:01	Bob Dobson Ilford	4:33:41
Ian Richards Coventry Godiva H	4:15:45	Ed Shillabeer Plymouth City W	4:43:36
Adrian James Enfield H	4:16:30	Ian Harvey Coventry RWC	4:55:41
Paul Jarman Surrey WC	4:23:50	Sheffield 42 Steyning 52 Coventry 58	
John Warhurst Sheffield United H	4:24:59	**1990** July 14 Sutton Coldfield	
Sheffield 25 Leicester 38 York Postal 68		Chris Berwick Leicester WC	4:33:23
1982 July 10 Leicester		Carl Thomson Sarnia WC	4:40:56
Adrian James Borough of Enfield H	4:14:11	Bob Dobson Ilford	4:41:31
Brian Adams Leicester WC	4:29:05	Gareth Brown Steyning	4:51:10
John Warhurst Sheffield United H	4:31:14	Geoff Tranter Birchfield	4:53:18
Carl Lawton Belgrave H	4:36:32	Ian Harvey Coventry RWC	4:55:41
John Newnham Belgrave H	4:37:58	Sheffield 49 Birchfield 54 Leicester 60	
Alan Worth Leicester WC	4:40:40	**1991** July 13 Basildon	
Leicester 34 Sheffield 36 Belgrave 52		Les Morton Sheffield United RWC	4:15:28
1983 July 8 Enfield		Chris Berwick Leicester WC	4:30:53

Mike Smith Coventry RWC	4:32:17	Brian Adams Leicester WC		4:57:42
Ian Harvey Coventry RWC	4:40:40	Steve Arnold Coventry RWC		5:33:35
Bob Dobson Ilford	4:43:08	Mark Byrne Sheffield United RWC		5:58:26
Stuart Phillips Ilford	4:49:17	Coventry 14 Leicester 15		
Coventry 29 Ilford 38 Sheffield 41		**2000** Sep 9 Victoria Park, Hackney		
1992 Apr 18 Redditch		Darrell Stone Steyning		4:21:23
Chris Maddocks Plymouth City W	4:13:25	Gareth Brown Steyning		4:27:23
Allan King Road Hoggs	4:22:53	Don Bearman Steyning		4:32:42
Chris Berwick Leicester WC	4:25:51	Peter Kaneen Manx H		4:50:47
Derek Stancliffe Sheffield Utd	4:54:10	Mike Smith Coventry RWC		4:51:31
Andy Trigg Leicester WC	4:57:48	Chris Berwick Leicester WC		4:52:15
Geoff Tranter Birchfield H	5:00:53	Steyning 6 Coventry 26 Sheffield 30		
Trowbridge 23 Surrey WC 28 Broimsgrive & R 38		**2001** Mar 25 Victoria Park, Hackney		
1993 Oct 16 Horsham		Mike Smith Coventry Godiva H		4:33:17
Les Morton Sheffield United RWC	4:03:55	Chris Cheeseman Surrey WC		4:41:44
Sean Martindale York Postal RWC	4:12:00	Peter Kaneen Manx H		4:43:14
Pat Murphy IRL (guest?)	4:30:03	Peter Ryan City of Sheffield		4:52:22
Steve Johnson Splott Conservative	4:34:16	Colin Bradley Surrey WC		4:54:38
Chris Berwick Leicester WC	4:42:42	Chris Berwick Leicester WC		4:54:54
Ed Shillabeer Plymouth City W	4:53:25	Surrey WC 285 Coventry 283 Colchester 250		
Colin Bradley Trowbridge	4:54:10	**2002** Sep 8 Colchester		
Leicester 22 Sheffield 24 Surrey WC 40		Mike Smith Coventry Godiva H		4:42:58
1994 Sep 3 Holmewood		Chris Berwick Leicester WC		4:56:13
Les Morton Sheffield United RWC	4:32:25	Steve Arnold Coventry Godiva H		5:09:50
Tim Watt Steyning	4:36:35	Bob Dobson Ilford		5:24:57
Chris Berwick Leicester WC	4:40:41	Dave Ratcliffe Coventry Godiva H		5:25:57
Graham White Brighton & Hove	4:46:13	Paul King Belgrave H		5:39:45
Steve Brennan Manx H	4:48:32	Coventry 293 Ilford 280		
Brian Adams Leicester WC	5:02:17	**2003** Aug 9 Stockport		
Sheffield 23 Leicester 26 Surrey WC 30		Mike Smith Coventry Godiva H		5:00:41
1995 July 1 Stockport also BAF		Chris Berwick Leicester		5:05:46
Les Morton Sheffield United RWC	4:01:36	Steve Arnold Coventry Godiva H		5:32:00
Tim Watt Steyning	4:28:14	Bob Dobson Ilford		5:40:44
Gareth Brown Steyning	4:28:44	Mark Byrne City of Sheffield		5:48:24
John Cocker York CIU	4:33:01	Keith French City of Sheffield		6:13:02
Chris Berwick Leicester WC	4:39:27	Coventry 197 Sheffield 189		
Colin Bradley Trowbridge	4:51:57	**2004** Sep 26 Earls Colne UK/RWA		
Sheffield 22 Leicester 26		Steve Partington Manx H		4:30:08
1996 Sep 7 Horsham also BAF		Mike Smith Coventry Godiva H		4:59:47
Chris Cheeseman Surrey WC	4:22:42	Chris Berwick Leicester WC		5:06:17
Graham White Brighton & Hove	4:24:01	Alf Short Lancashire WC		5:26:08
Dennis Jackson York CIU	4:27:04	Paul King Belgrave H		5:28:59
Steve Partington Manx H	4:32:25	John Stubbs Isle of Man Veterans		5:35:19
Karl Atton Road Hoggs	4:35:48	Lancashire WC 186		
Allan King Road Hoggs	4:39:01	**2005** Sep 4 Earls Colne		
York CIU 21 Leicester 34 Belgrave 43		Scott Davis Ilford		4:47:34
1997 Aug 30 Stockport also BAF		Chris Berwick Leicester WC		5:16:05
Mark Easton Surrey WC	4:07:45	Dwane Butterly Leicester WC		5:29:26
Les Morton Sheffield United RWC	4:08:17	Paul King Belgrave H		5:38:28
Sean Martindale York CIU	4:22:06	Mark Byrne York CIU		5:44:48
Tim Watt Steyning	4:37:32	David Jones Redcar RWC		5:45:02
Chris Berwick Leicester WC	4:42:51	Leicester 284 Ilford 193 Belgrave 187		
Bob Dobson Ilford	4:46:54	**2006** Sep 10 Earls Colne		
York CIU 21 Sheffield 25 Leicester 26		Scott Davis Ilford		4:52:51
1998 Aug 29 Holmewood also BAF		Steve Arnold Nuneaton		5:26:17
Tim Watt Steyning	4:32:00	Ed Shillabeer London Vidarians		5:45:36
Mike Smith Coventry RWC	4:49:40	John Constandinou Birchfield H		6:07:35
Chris Berwick Leicester WC	4:58:08	Dave Fall Birchfield H		6:08:59
Brian Adams Leicester WC	5:11:11	John Borgars Loughton	less 1 lap	6:00:12
Bob Dobson Ilford	5:15:43	Birchfield 191		
Steve Arnold Coventry RWC	5:38:20	**2007** Jul 28 London (BP)		
Leicester 14 Coventry 16		Scott Davis Ilford		4:35:39
1999 Sep 11 Leamington Spa		Steve Arnold Nuneaton		5:20:40
Chris Cheeseman Surrey WC	4:31:08	Marcelino Sobczak NED (guest)		5:27:13
Mike Smith Coventry RWC	4:44:33	Dave Jones Redcar RWC		5:37:01
Chris Berwick Leicester WC	4:52:18	Marcel Dekker NED (guest)		5:37:53

Ian Statter Surrey WC	5:52:42	**1981** Sep 25 Stoke Mandeville	
Andrew Titley Isle of Man Vets	6:01:31	Graham Young Boundary H	9:36:23
Kevin Perry Southend on Sea	6:03:10	Murray Lambden Boundary H	9:38:38
1. Surrey WC, 2. Ilford, 3. Birchfield		Chris Berwick Leicester WC	9:54:22
2008 Apr 26 Stockton-on-Tees		Ed Shillabeer Dawlish & S.Devon	10:21:45
Scott Davis Ilford	4:29:25	Geoff Tranter R.Sutton & Birmingham	10:23:34
Michael George Manx H	5:06:45	Chris Bent Leicester WC	10:33:33
Ian Richards Steyning	5:07:49	Boundary H 14 Leicester 18 Belgrave 30	
Steve Arnold Nuneaton	5:14:16	**1982** Sep 25 Corby	
Stephen Crane Surrey	5:23:19	Chris Berwick Leicester WC	10:02:03
John Constantinou Birchfield	5:27:52	Ed Shillabeer Dawlish & S.Devon	10:26:13
Belgrave 268 Redcar 262 Birchfield 258		John Eddershaw Sheffield Utd H	10:26:52
2009 Apr 26 Stockton-on-Tees		Chris Bent Leicester WC	10:38:53
Scott Davis Ilford	4:30:28	John Sturgess Leicester WC	10:42:03
Christopher Svensson SWE	4:47:28	Martin Jones Dawlish & S.Devon	10:45:03
Paul Evenett York CIU	4:51:39	Leicester 10 Dawlish 16 Sheffield 24	
Trevor Jones Steyning	5:03:04	**1983** Sep 24 Chelmsford	
John Hall Belgrave H	5:39:22	Brian Adams Leicester WC	10:13:16
Martin Fisher Yorkshire RWC	5:40:22	Ed Shillabeer Dawlish & S.Devon	10:35:50
Redcar 287 Belgrave 189		Geoff Tranter Birmingham WC	10:36:13
2010 Oct 17 Northampton		Nolan Simmons Surrey WC	10:42:34
Scott Davis Ilford	4:28:29	Leicester 16	
Paul Evenett Redcar RWC	4:44:23	**1985** Sep 14 Colchester (track)	
Ian Richards Steyning	4:58:05	Ed Shillabeer Dawlish & S.Devon	9:41:54
Steve Arnold Nuneaton	5:17:22	Bob Dobson Ilford	9:56:34
Ed Shillabeer Ilford	5:34:10	Charlie Weston Highgate H	11:10:05
Steve Allen Barnet	5:45:19	Glyn Davies Dawlish & S.Devon	11:14:10
Ilford 288 Leicester 280 Enfield & Haringey 179		John Hedgethorne Colchester H	11:55:51
2011 Oct 2 Northampton		Peter Worth Borough of Enfield H	12:17:15
Scott Davis Ilford	4:45:22	York Postal 34	
Richard Spenceley Yorkshire WC	5:32:53		
Adrian Edwards Lancashire WC	5:37:27	**RWA 100 MILES**	
Martin Fisher Redcar RWC	5:50:52	**1987** Ewhurst	
Ed Shillabeer Ilford	5:53:21	John Cannell Boundary H	17:55:10
Bob Dobson Ilford	5:55:31	Dave Boxall Brighton & Hove	18:16:56
1. Ilford, 2. Surrey WC		Geoff Tranter R.Sutton & Birmingham	18:22:00
2012 Sep 22 Colchester		Gordon Beattie Medway WC	19:41:38
Steve Allen Barnet	5:35:01	Nolan Simmons Surrey WC	20:14:34
Arthur Thomson Enfield & Haringey	5:42:47	Paddy Dowling Sheffield	20:23:00
Colin Vesty Leicester	6:03:24	Boundary H 25	
Sean Pender Enfield & Haringey	6:25:46	**1988** July 29-30 Leicester	
Alan O'Rawe Ilford	6:24:25	Richard Brown Surrey WC	17:00:35
Enfield & Haringey		John Cannell Boundary H	17:10:15
2013 Jul 27 Coventry		Willie Corkill Boundary H	18:34:56
Julian Iglesias Madrid/ESP guest	5:05:58	Tony Collins R.Sutton & Birmingham	18:42:18
Adrian Edwards DASH/Lancashire WC	5:40:16	Dave Boxall Brighton & Hove	18:49:50
Richard Brown Surrey WC	5:55:18	Gordon Beattie Medway WC	18:55:25
Bob Dobson Ilford	6:04:19	Boundary H 17 R.Sutton & Birmingham 28	
Paul King Belgrave H	6:08:59	**1989** July 28-29 Colindale	
		Ed Shillabeer Plymouth City W	18:11:08
RWA 100 KILOMETRES CHAMPS		Gordon Beattie Medway WC	18:46:16
1979 Sep 29 Sutton Coldfield		John Cannell Boundary H	19:28:05
Peter Hodkinson Metropolitan Police	9:46:36	Bob Watts London Vidarians WC	19:46:34
Tony Collins Holloway Polytechnic H	9:52:49	Peter Hodkinson Cambridge H	19:48:00
Chris Berwick Leicester WC	9:57:36	Geoff Tranter R.Sutton & Birmingham	20:04:23
John Eddershaw Sheffield Utd H	10:02:37	Medwat 22 London Vidarians 46 Cambridge H 34	
Ken Harding R.Sutton C & Birmingham	10:08:58	**1990** July 26–27 Hungarton,Leics	
Peter Worth Borough of Enfield H	10:16:32	Richard Brown Surrey WC	17:54:28
Leicester 15 RSC & Birmingham 19 Sheffield 20		Don Thompson Metropolitan WC	19:58:29
1980 Sep 27 Sutton Coldfield		Geoff Tranter Birchfield H	20:16:41
Ian Richards Coventry Godiva H	9:45:48	Tony Collins Birchfield H	21:02:13
Chris Berwick Leicester WC	9:54:00	Glyn Davies Plymouth City W	21:06:23
John Eddershaw Sheffield Utd H	10:02:20	Paddy Dowling Sheffield Utd RWC	21:22:46
Keith Halstead Coventry Godiva H	10:08:52	Birchfield 35	
Geoff Tranter R.Sutton & Birmingham	10:14:08	**1991** June 28-29 Ewhurst,Surrey	
Peter Worth Enfield H	10:36:52	Richard Brown Surrey WC	17:52:47
Leicester 11 Sheffield 14 Lancashire WC 33		2= Bob Watts London Vidarians WC	19:46:18

2= Ken Watts London Vidarians WC	19:46:18	**2002** Aug 10-11 Blackpool (track) in 24 Hours (qv)	
John Sturgess Leicester WC	19:49:45	Kevin Perry Southend on Sea	20:41:17
Dave Baker Birchfield H	20:31:03	Ian Statter Surrey WC	21:07:15
Dave Watson Surrey WC	21:17:26	Martin Fisher York CIU	21:28:09
Surrey WC 15 London Vidarians 15		Chris Flint London Vidarians WC	21:39:22
1992 July 31-Aug 1 Hungarton, Leics No teams		Joe Hardy Lancashire WC	22:00:20
Richard Brown Surrey WC	18:50:29	Ken Watts London Vidarians WC	22:17:26
John Sturgess Leicester WC	19:06:22	London Vidarians 282	
Tony Collins Birchfield H	20:13:28	**2003** July 26–27 Newmarket	
Don Thompson Folkestone AC	20:49:41	Peter Ryan City of Sheffield	19:57:35
Dave Staniforth Sheffield Utd	21:52:42	Ian Statter Surrey WC	20:29:30
Ken Watts London Vidarians WC	22:19:37	Chris Flint London Vidarians WC	20:50:26
1993 Aug 21-22 London (BP) No teams		Paul King Belgrave H	20:59:44
Chris Berwick Leicester WC	17:57:07	Martin Fisher Yorkshire RWC	21:27:46
Richard Brown Surrey WC	17:58.17	Don Cox Colchester H	21:35:06
Tony Collins Birchfield H	20:20:54	London Vidarians 269 Yorkshire 188 Surrey WC 181	
Dave Watson Surrey WC	21:00:01	**2004** Aug 25-26 Colchester	
Pat Duncan Belgrave H	21:22:43	Ian Statter Surrey WC	20:10:31
Kevin Perry Southend on Sea	22:02:32	David Jones Redcar RWC	20:57:58
1994 July 30 Hungarton, Leics		Kevin Marshall Ilford	21:01:27
Richard Brown Surrey WC	18:39:42	Don Cox Colchester H	21:50:45
Brian Ashworth Leicester WC	20:31:54	Ray Pitts Isle of Man VeteransAC	21:53:20
Tony Collins Birchfield H	20:56:19	Isle of Man Vets 185 London Vidarians 182	
Chris Flint London Vidarians WC	22:23:28	**2005** July 30–31 Kings Lynn	
Martin Fisher York Postal RWC	22:26:54	Sean Hands Manx H	19:02:57
Bob Watts London Vidarians WC	23:07:45	Ian Statter Surrey WC	19:52:51
London Vidarians 31		Richard Brown Surrey WC	20:33:00
1995 Aug 5-6 London ((BP))		David Jones Redcar RWC	20:37:42
Richard Brown Surrey WC	19:23:16	Kevin Marshall Ilford	21:09:49
Chris Flint London Vidarians WC	21:24:32	Chris Flint London Vidarians WC	21:13:05
Kevin Perry Southend on Sea	21:41:37	Surrey WC 282 Birchfield 268 London Vidarians 184	
Boyd Millen Kendal AC	22:28:35	**2006** Aug 19/20 Douglas IOM	
Paminder Bhatti Birchfield H	22:28:58	Sean Hands Manx H	19:16:03
Dave Staniforth Sheffield Utd	22:36:56	Kevin Marshall Ilford	20:29:14
Surrey WC 40		Michael George	20:34:01
1996 Aug 3-4 Colchester		Eamon Harkin	20:34:11
Richard Brown Surrey WC	18:12:04	Jack Waddington	20:57:35
Kevin Perry Southend on Sea	20:37:46	Andy Gosnell	21:21:09
Tony Collins Birchfield H	20:47:07	**2007** Aug 28/29 London (BP)	
Chris Flint London Vidarians WC	22:01:20	Chris Flint London Vidarians WC	21:14:40
Boyd Millen unattached	22:05:32	Andrew Titley IOM Veterans AC	21:34:46
Paminder Bhatti Birchfield H	22:23:42	David Hawkins Milton Keynes AC	21:57:13
Birchfield 35		Olly Browne Ilford	22:11:41
1997 July 19-20 Ware (track)		Martin Fisher Yorkshire RWC	22:49:20
Chris Flint London Vidarians WC	20:21:41	Tony Collins Birchfield H	22:58:13
Kevin Perry Southend on Sea	21:14:12	**2008** Aug 16/17 Milton Keynes (track)	
David Watson Surrey WC	21:32:11	Ian Richards Steyning	19:37:11
London Vidarians		Alf Short Lancashire WC	20:58:10
1998 Not held		Dave Jones Redcar RWC	21:55:19
1999 Aug 14-15 London ((BP))		Chris Flint London Vidarians WC	22:43:02
Richard Brown Surrey WC	19:08:16	Olly Browne Ilford	22:45:21
Kevin Perry Southend on Sea	20:27:32	Martin Fisher Redcar RWC	22:57:05
Chris Flint London Vidarians WC	20:28:54	**2009** July 11/12 Newmarket	
Ken Watts London Vidarians WC	21:38:28	Richard Brown Surrey WC	20:12:44
Martin Fisher York CIU	21:43:53	Mark Wall Leicester WC	21:08:39
Derek Appleton Folkestone AC	21:45:05	Kevin Marshall Ilford	22:00:38
London Vidarians 17 Southend 19		Martin Fisher Redcar RWC	23:09:03
2000 Not held – see 24 Hours		Chris Flint London Vidarians	23:14:05
2001 Aug 4-5 Colchester		Steve Kemp unattached	23:21:20
Bob Dobson Ilford	19:46:11	**2010** Aug 7/8 Colchester	
Richard Brown Surrey WC	19:50:39	Richard Spenceley Yorkshire RWC	22:56:03
Chris Flint London Vidarians WC	21:32:39	Chris Flint London Vidarians WC	23:22:01
Charles Arosanyan Surrey WC	21:40:44	Martin Fisher Redcar RWC	23:30:39
Martin Fisher York CIU	21:59:38	Sean Pender Enfield & H	23:28:50
Paul King Belgrave H	22:30:37	Sailash Shah Lancashire WC 94mls 46 yds	23:44:37
London Vidarians 282 Surrey WC 284 Ilford 191		Tony Hill Long Distance WA 88mls 22yds	23:35:88

2011 July 2/3 Lingfield Park
Ian Statter Surrey WC 21:12:25
Kevin Marshall Ilford 21:25:20
Roger Michell Surrey WC 21:36:17
Dave Jones Redcar RWC 21:38:13
Ken Falconer Long Distance Walkers Ass. 22:54:23
Andrew Titley Isle of Man Veterans 27:55:07
2012 Colchester 22/23 Sep
Dominic King Colchester H 18:13:11
Guido Vermeer NED 20:24:24
Daniel King Colchester H 20:51:59

RWA 24 HOURS
2000 Newmarket
Ian Statter Surrey WC 193.114k
Don Cox Colchester H 177.021k
Kevin Perry Southend on Sea 170.584k
Martin Fisher York CIU 104 miles 23:36:16
Chris Flint London Vidarians WC 102 miles 23:30:25
Bob Watts London Vidarians WC 102 miles 23:54:49
London Vidarians
2002 Blackpool
Kevin Perry Southend on Sea 182.591k
Ian Statter Surrey WC 179.764k
Martin Fisher Yorkshire RWC 177.227k
Chris Flint London Vidarians WC 171.627k
Ken Watts London Vidarians WC 170.214k
Parminder Bhatti Birchfield H 166.808k
London Vidarians

BRITISH WALKS CHAMPS (BAF/UKA)
20 KILOMETRES ROAD
1994 Mar 19 Stoneleigh,Warwickshire
Darrell Stone Steyning 1:27:24
Martin Bell Splott Conservative 1:31:08
Chris Cheeseman Surrey WC 1:31:46
Steve Taylor Manx H 1:36:43
Steve Brennan Manx H 1:37:11
Tim Watt Steyning 1:38:15
Steyning 38 Manx 42 Leicester 56
2001 Apr 21 Leamington Spa
Matthew Hales Steyning 1:28:40
Mark Easton Surrey WC 1:29:40
Chris Cheeseman Surrey WC 1:30:32
Steve Partington Manx H 1:33:00
Don Bearman Steyning 1:34:05
Andrew Goudie Belgrave H 1:24:40
2002 Apr 21 Salford
Andy Penn Nuneaton H 1:27:06
Dominic King Colchester H 1:32:23
Matt Hales Steyning 1:33:11
Steve Partington Manx H 1:33:23
Don Bearman Steyning 1:35:13
Nathan Adams City of Sheffield 1:36:08
2003 Apr 26 Leamington Spa
Andi Drake Coventry Godiva H 1:30:13
Dominic King Colchester H 1:31:36
Daniel King Colchester H 1:31:49
Mark Easton Surrey WC 1:32:46
Nathan Adams City of Sheffield 1:35:29
Peter Kaneen Manx H 1:36:50
2004 See RWA
2005 Apr 16 Leamington Spa
Dominic King Colchester H 1:29:21
Frank Buytaert BEL 1:35:59
Mark Williams Tamworth 1:37:19
Andrew Goudie Belgrave H 1:42:05

Trevor Jones Hillingdon AC 1:42:43
Les Brown Isle of Man Veterans 1:54:12

50 KILOMETRES ROAD
1993 May 2 Burrator, Devon
Brian Dowrick Splott Conservative 4:26:10
Les Morton Sheffield Utd RWC 4:31:17
Colin Bradley Trowbridge 4:42:13
Ed Shillabeer Plymouth City W 4:46:42
Bob Dobson Ilford 4:47:17
Gordon Beattie Medway WC 4:59:16
1994 May 1 Burrator, Devon
Ed Shillabeer Plymouth City W 4:54:32
Colin Bradley Trowbridge 5:04:17
Mike Lewis Trowbridge 5:29:45
Keith Batten Trowbridge 5:34:51
W Kingston Basingstoke AC 5:38:54
J Harris St.John Basingstoke AC 5:40:57
2002 Apr 21 Salford
Mark Easton Surrey WC 4:11:36
Steve Hollier Wolverhampton & Bilston 4:14:33
Gareth Brown Steyning 4:16:45
Chris Cheeseman Surrey WC 4:18:49
Karl Atton Road Hoggs 4:23:05
Peter Kaneen Manx H 4:35:31
2003 Mar 1 Douglas IOM
Steve Arnold Coventry Godiva H 5:09:16
Mark Byrne City of Sheffield 5:25:17
Simon Cox Isle of Man Veterans 5:55:52
2004 See RWA

WOMEN'S CHAMPIONSHIPS
UK 10 KILOMETRES ROAD
1994 Mar 19 Stoneleigh,Warwickshire
Lisa Langford Wolverhampton & Bilston 47:07
Sylvia Black Birchfield H 48:41
Cal Partington Manx H 48:46
Karen Smith Coventry RWC 48:54
Elaine Callinan Solihull & Small Heath 49:17
Melanie Brookes Nuneaton H 49:30
Manx 24 Birchfield 37 Dudley 52
See RWA/UKA

UK 20 KILOMETRES ROAD
2001 Apr 21 Leamington Spa
Niobe Menendez Steyning 1:45:19
Sharon Tonks Bromsgrove & Redditch 1:46:15
Sara Jane Cattermole Dartford H 1:47:35
Jane Kennaugh Manx H 1:48:55
Jo Hesketh Steyning 1:50:35
2002 Apr 21 Salford
Lisa Kehler Wolverhampton & Bilston 1:39:13
Niobe Menendez Steyning 1:39:59
Estle Viljoen Hercules Wimbledon 1:44:16
Sharon Tonks Bromsgrove & Redditch 1:45:21
Sara Jane Cattermole Dartford H 1:46:04
Karen Ratcliffe Coventry Godiva H 1:46:35
2003 Apr 26 Leamington Spa
Wendy Bennett Worcester H 1:44:30
Sharon Tonks Bromsgrove & Redditch 1:48:17
Nicky Phillips Dartford H 1:49:32
2004 See RWA
2005 Apr 16 Leamington Spa
Olive Loughnane IRL 1:36:57
Niobe Menendez Steyning 1:42:47
Johanna Jackson Redcar RWC 1:43:07
Katherine Horwill Dudley & Stourbridge 1:45:58
Catriona McMahon IRL 1:46:16

Marie Latham Manx H	1:50:56

UK 5000 METRES TRACK CHAMPS
10,000 Metres – As RWA

1980 June 15 London (CP)
Carol Tyson Lakeland AC	23:48.62
Irene Bateman Basildon	24:06.87
Elaine Cox Solihull AC	25:22.32
Elaine Worth Bolehall Swifts WC	25:36.0
Jill Barrett Verlea	26:02.0
Sarah Brown Steyning	26:13.8

1981 May 25 Antrim
Carol Tyson Lakeland AC	24:09.89
Lillian Millen Lakeland AC	24:32.09
Elaine Cox Solihull & Small Heath	25:18.98
Gillian Edgar Lakeland AC	25:37.60
Brenda Lupton Sheffield United H	25:53.82
Sarah Brown Steyning	26:00.42

1983 May 28 Edinburgh
Irene Bateman Basildon	23:42.2
Jill Barrett Verlea	24:08.4
Virginia Birch Brighton & Hove	24:18.6
Brenda Lupton Sheffield United H	24:51.4
Karen Nipper Roath Labour WC	25:17.0
Sarah Brown Steyning	25:58.5

1984 May 27 Cwmbran
Jill Barrett Verlea	23:53.13
Nicky Jackson Trowbridge	24:02.15
Helen Elleker Sheffield United H	24:04.84
Lillian Millen Lakeland AC	24:21.47
Brenda Lupton Sheffield United H	24:36.06
Karen Nipper Roath Labour WC	24:55.71

1985 May 25 Antrim
Virginia Birch Brighton & Hove	23:20.00
Susan Ashforth Sheffield United H	23:55.27
Helen Elleker Sheffield United H	24:07.97
Nicky Jackson Trowbridge	24:39.26
Beverley Allen Brighton & Hove	24:43.23
Karen Nipper Roath Labour WC	24:47.06

1986 May 26 Cwmbran
Lisa Langford Wolverhampton & Bilston	24:38.99
Victoria Lawrence Reading	25:18.37
Julie Drake Brighton & Hove	25:30.25
Angela Hodd Tonbridge AC	25:50.47
Ruth Harper Sparkhill H	26:06.23
Elaine Worth Bromsgrove & Redditch	26:06.59

1987 May 25 Derby
Lisa Langford Wolverhampton & Bilston	22:19.04
Beverley Allen Brighton & Hove	23:15.04
Helen Elleker Sheffield Utd RWC	23:34.64
Nicky Jackson Trowbridge	23:35.54
Julie Drake Brighton & Hove	24:11.32
Victoria Lawrence Reading	24:33.16

1988 June 4 Derby
Betty Sworowski Sheffield Utd	24:03.88
Julie Drake Brighton & Hove	24:17.86
Nicky Jackson Trowbridge	24:19.41
Sarah Brown Steyning	24:29.40
Karen Dunster Aldershot Farnham	25:03.81
Gillian Edgar Lakeland AC	25:31.86

1989 June 4 Jarrow
Lisa Langford Wolverhampton & Bilston	22:39.43
Betty Sworowski Sheffield Utd	23:17.92
Julie Drake Brighton & Hove	23:32.21
Helen Elleker Sheffield Utd RWC	24:10.87
Andrea Crofts Leicester WC	24:24.31
Sarah Brown Steyning	24:58.83

1990 June 2 Cardiff
Betty Sworowski Sheffield Utd	22:31.59
Lisa Langford Wolverhampton & Bilston	22:42.47
Julie Drake Brighton & Hove	23:03.24
Vicky Lupton Sheffield Utd RWC	23:16.67
Sylvia Black Birchfield H	23:54.38
Verity Larby Aldershot, Farnham & D	24:02.03

1991 June 9 Cardiff
Vicky Lupton Sheffield Utd RWC	22:51.38
Helen Elleker Sheffield Utd RWC	23:26.18
Sylvia Black Birchfield H	23:44.88
Karen Smith Coventry RWC	24:43.95
Melanie Brookes Nuneaton H	24:43.95
Andrea Crofts Leicester WC	25:13.70

1997 July 12 Birmingham
Sylvia Black Birchfield H	23:56.72
Catherine Charnock Barrow & Fylde	25:26.25
Lynn Bradley Sheffield Utd RWC	26:47.67
Vicky Lupton Sheffield Utd RWC	27:38.65

2007 July 29 Manchester (SC)
Johanna Jackson Redcar RWC	22:03.65
Sophie Hales Steyning	25:01.21
Estle Viljoen Hercules Wmbledon	25:03.84
Niobe Menéndez Steyning	25:14.91
Verity Snook Aldershot, Farnham & D	25:35.60
Rebecca Mersh City of Sheffield	26:58.13

2008 July 13 Birmingham
Johanna Jackson Redcar RWC	21:30.75
Niobe Menéndez Steyning	25:18.67
Diane Bradley Tonbridge	26:19.45
Chelsea O'Rawe-Hobbs Blackheath & B	27:08.03
Kathryn Granger Sheffield	28:26.81

2009 July 12 Birmingham
Johanna Jackson Redcar RWC	21:21.67
Emma Doherty North Belfast	25:15.23
Diane Bradley Tonbridge	26:30.85
Fiona McGorum Leicester WC	28:16.53

2010 June 27 Birmingham
Johanna Jackson Middlesbrough & C	21:52.95
Lisa Kehler Wolverhampton & Bilston	24:21.92
Fiona McGorum Leicester WC	26:08.99
Lauren Whelan Manx H	26:16.37
Diane Bradley Tonbridge	26:40.47
Heather Lewis Pembroke	26:57.86

2011 July 31 Birmingham
Johanna Jackson Middlesbrough & C	21:42.32
Heather Lewis Pembroke	24:59.66
Tasha Webster Birchfield	26:57.98
Rebecca Collins Medway & Maidstone	28.02.96
Fiona McGorum Leicester WC	29.07.14

2012 June 24 Birmingham
Johanna Jackson Middlesbrough & C	21:45.98
Heather Lewis Pembroke	24:02.13
Bethan Davies Cardiff	24:47.87
Lauren Whelan Manx H	25:34.13
Ellie Dooley Leeds	26:25.07
Fiona McGorum Leicester WC	26:31.80

2013 June 24 Birmingham
Bethan Davies Cardiff	23:21.08
Heather Lewis Pembroke	23:50.59
Ellie Dooley Leeds	24:04.21
Michelle Turner Northern (IOM)	25:06.90
Grazine Narviliene Ealing S&M/LTU	25:30.69
Jasmine Nicholls OWLS	26:01.41

2014 June 29 Birmingham
| Heather Lewis Pembroke | 22:09.87 |

Alana Barber Hyde Park H/NZL	22:11.52
Emma Achurch Leicester WC	24:14.96
Ellie Dooley Leeds	25:06.84
Grazine Narviliene Ealing S&M/LTU	25:17.00
Heather Butcher Cambridge AC	25:38.46

WAAA TRACK CHAMPIONSHIPS

880 YARDS
1923 Aug 18 Bromley
Edith Trickey North British & Merc   4:35.0
Betty Keeling Manor Park
D.Clark London Olympiades
1924 June 28 Woolwich
Edith Trickey London Olympiades   4:17.4
Florence Faulkner Manor Park
Betty Keeling Manor Park
1925 July 11 London (SB)
Florence Faulkner Manor Park   4:15.0
M.Heggarty Manor Park
I.Brown Manor Park
1926 June 19 London (SB)
Daisy Crossley Middlesex LAC   4:06.0
M.Heggarty Manor Park
J.Parsons London Olympiades
1927 July 9 Reading
M.Heggarty London Olympiades   3:54.2
H.Bates London Olympiades
M.Fish unattached

1 MILE
1928 July 14 London (SB)
Lucy Howes Middlesex LAC   8:27.4
Verna Horwood London Olympiades
M.Heggarty London Olympiades
1929 July 13 London (SB)
Lucy Howes Middlesex LAC   8:18.0
Verna Horwood London Olympiades
M.Heggarty London Olympiades
1930 Aug 16 London (SB)
Constance Mason Middlesex LAC   8:14.4
Lucy Howes Middlesex LAC
W.Bell North London
1931 July 11 London (SB)
Constance Mason Middlesex LAC   7:45.6
Lucy Howes Middlesex LAC
E.Gutteridge Middlesex LAC
1932 July 9 London (SB)
Constance Mason Middlesex LAC   7:47.8
Jeanne Probekk Middlesex LAC   8:06.8
Verna Horwood London Olympiades   8:13.4
Jessie Howes Spartan LAC   8:17.8

1600 METRES
1933 July 15 London (WC)
Jeanne Probekk Middlesex LAC   7:51.2
Jessie Howes Spartan LAC
K.Bellamy Airedale H
1934 June 30 Herne Hill
Jeanne Probekk Middlesex LAC   7:38.2
Jessie Howes London Olympiades   7:40.0
V.Tosh London Olympiades
1935 Aug 10 London (WC)
Jessie Howes London Olympiades   7:57.8
P.Barratt Middlesex LAC
Q.Waters London Olympiades
1936 July 18 London (WC)
Jessie Howes London Olympiades   8:14.2
F.Pengelly Paignton AC
Q.Waters London Olympiades
Emily Littlefair London Olympiades
A.Sanders London Olympiades
I.Gardner Middlesex LAC
1937 Aug 7 London (WC)
F.Pengelly Paignton AC   8:36.5
Doris Harris Birchfield H
I.Gardner Middlesex LAC
M.Gilbert Paignton AC
D.Toms Spartan LAC
G.Scorah Polytechnic LAC
1938 July 2 London (WC)
Evelyn Webb Suffolk RWA   8:39.0
Mary Harrington Birchfield H
D.Cooper London Olympiades
1939 July 22 London (WC)
F.Pengelly Paignton AC   8:19.9
Mary Harrington Birchfield H   8:21.4
Betty Jones West Bromwich AC   8:34.2
Evelyn Webb Hercules
Doris Hart Birmingham LAC
Phyllis Archer Small Heath

1 MILE
1945 Aug 18 Tooting Bec
Diana Riddington London Transport   8:42.8
Doris Hart Birchfield H
Joyce Heath Small Heath H

1600 METRES
1946 July 13 London (WC)
Doris Hart Birchfield H   8:38.6
Beryl Day Birmingham Atalanta
Betty Sankey Dudley H
Margaret Brittain Birmingham Atalanta
1947 Aug 2 Polytechnic Stadium,Chiswick
Diana Riddington Cambridge H   8:36.4
Margaret Brittain Birmingham Atalanta   8:37.7
Beryl Day Birmingham Atalanta   8:40.0
Gwen Thorne Birmingham Atalanta
S.Jones Birmingham Atalanta
DorothyTurner Birmingham Atalanta
1948 June 26 Polytechnic Stadium,Chiswick
Joyce Heath Small Heath H   8:17.8
Beryl Day Birmingham Atalanta   8:18.0
Gwen Thorne Birmingham Atalanta   8:20.0
Jean Lloyd Birchfield H
Margaret Brittain Birmingham Atalanta
Muriel Havill London Olympiades
1949 July 9 London (WC)
Joyce Heath Small Heath H   8:25.0
Angela Douglas Cambridge H   8:32.0
Beryl Day Birmingham Atalanta   8:37.6
Jessie Ashton Birchfield H
Margaret Brittain Birmingham Atalanta
Jean Coley Harborne H
1950 July 8 London (WC)
Joyce Heath Small Heath H   8:17.0
Angela Douglas Cambridge H
Margaret Brittain Birmingham Atalanta
Marie Verbinnen London Olympiades
Jessie Ashton Birchfield H
Mary Lightfoot Leigh H
1951 July 7 London (WC)
Joyce Heath Small Heath H   7:50.0
Leila Deas London Olympiades   7:59.0
Brenda Stevenson Birchfield H
Beryl Day Birmingham Atalanta

Jessie Ashton Birchfield H			Margaret Billingsley Harborne H	13:21.6
Beryl Riggott Sheffield United H			**1961** July 8 London (WC)	
1 MILE			Sheila Jennings London Olympiades	12:18.4
1952 June 14 London (WC)			Judy Woodsford Trowbridge	12:29.6
Beryl Day Birchfield H	7:58.2		Maureen Eyre Birchfield H	12:30.8
Sheila Martin London Olympiades	8:05.7		Audrey Hackett Harborne H	12:32.6
Joyce Heath Small Heath H	8:26.0		Dorothy Wallwork Bolton Utd H	12:56.8
Margaret Brittain Birmingham Atalanta	8:38.6		Margaret Billingsley Harborne H	13:15.4
Irene McCormack Cambridge H			**1962** July 7 London (WC)	
Pat Hatt Ilford			Judy Farr Trowbridge	12:20.0
1953 July 4 London (WC)			Sheila Jennings London Olympiades	12:33.8
Beryl Randle Birchfield H	7:48.2		Maureen Eyre Birchfield H	12:50.2
Sheila Jennings London Olympiades	7:49.8		Joyce Heath Birchfield H	12:51.8
Sheila Irwin London Olympiades	8:16.8		Margaret Billingsley Harborne H	13:17.4
Irene McCormack Cambridge H	8:18.2		Dorothy Wallwork Bolton Utd H	13:18.2
Patricia Grant London Olympiades	8:34.6		**1963** July 6 London (WC)	
Pauline Williams Bletchley AC	8:44.4		Judy Farr Trowbridge	12:26.4
1954 June 19 London (WC)			Sheila Jennings London Olympiades	12:46.2
Beryl Randle Birchfield H	7:38.4		Joyce Heath Birchfield H	13:01.0
Patricia Grant London Olympiades	8:07.2		Margaret Lewis Harborne H	13:09.4
Rita Phillips Birchfield H	8:18.0		Dorothy Wallwork Bolton Utd H	13:14.4
June Yarnold London Olympiades	8:21.2		Joyce Montgomery Harborne H	13:34.6
Mary Rogers London Olympiades	8:29.0		**1964** July 4 London (WC)	
Norma Blaine Birchfield H	8:31.4		Judy Farr Trowbridge	12:06.8
1955 July 2 London (WC)			Joyce Heath Birchfield H	12:49.2
Beryl Randle Birchfield H	7:59.4		Margaret Lewis Harborne H	13:14.0
Sheila Jennings London Olympiades	8:06.6		Norma Blaine Birchfield H	13:39.0
Roma Phillips Smethwick H	8:13.2		Gwen Powell Harborne H	14:02.8
Mary Rogers London Olympiades	8:15.2		Jennifer Keen Croydon H	14:13.0
Norma Blaine Birchfield H	8:17.0		**1965** July 3 London (WC)	
Patricia Grant London Olympiades	8:18.8		Judy Farr Trowbridge	12:14.2
1956 Aug 11 London (WC)			Margaret Lewis Harborne H	12:33.8
Dilys Williams Birchfield H	7:46.7		Joan Wallis Harborne H	12:38.8
Beryl Randle Birchfield H	7:58.2		Betty Jenkins Birchfield H	13:23.8
Rita Phillips Birchfield H	8:13.4		Joyce Heath Birchfield H	13:29.2
Nellie Loines Small Heath H	8:21.6		Susan Dyer Crawley AC	13:36.2
Gillian Williams London Olympiades	8:24.4		**1966** July 2 London (WC)	
Mary Rogers London Olympiades	8:25.4		Judy Farr Trowbridge	12:09.2
1957 July 6 London (WC)			Sheila Jennings London Olympiades	12:16.8
Dilys Williams Birchfield H	8:08.4		Audrey Hackett Harborne H	12:53.0
Helen Vincent London Olympiades	8:08.8		Joan Wallis Harborne H	12:55.0
Betty Franklin Birchfield H	8:23.0		Betty Jenkins Birchfield H	13:09.8
Mary Rogers London Olympiades	8:24.2		Margaret Lewis Birchfield H	13:23.4
Roma Joyce (Phillips) Smethwick H	8:48.2		**1967** July 1 London (WC)	
Janet Stafford London Olympiades	8:59.7		Judy Farr Trowbridge	12:09.2
1958 June 7 Motspur Park, Surrey			Betty Jenkins Birchfield H	12:40.2
Betty Franklin Birchfield H	8:09.4		Sheila Jennings London Olympiades	12:56.8
Helen Vincent London Olympiades	8:17.4		Margaret Lewis Harborne H	13:12.0
Beryl Randle Birchfield H	8:22.8		Barbara Fisk Redhill & Reigate AC	13:24.6
Joan Wallis Harborne H	8:26.8		Sue Tulloh London Olympiades	14:04.0
Jean Pearson Portsmouth Atalanta	8:38.2		**1968** July 20 London (CP)	
Mary Rogers London Olympiades	8:41.8		Judy Farr Trowbridge	12:39.0
1.5 MILES			Betty Jenkins Birchfield H	12:44.2
1959 July 4 Motspur Park, Surrey			Barbara Fisk Redhill & Reigate AC	12:54.6
Betty Franklin Birchfield H	12:56.4		Audrey Hackett Harborne H	13:13.8
Joyce Heath Small Heath H	13:03.6		Margaret Lewis Birchfield H	13:20.2
Nellie Loines Small Heath H	13:15.0		Jennifer Peck Selsonia LAC	14:48.4
Kay Field Small Heath H	13:56.8		**2500 METRES**	
Margaret Billingsley Smethwick H	14:16.8		**1969** July 19 London (CP)	
Pam Horwill Stourbridge AC	14:36.6		Judy Farr Trowbridge	12:45.8
1960 July 2 London (WC)			Betty Jenkins Birchfield H	12:53.4
Judy Woodsford Trowbridge	12:31.2		Barbara Fisk Redhill & Reigate AC	13:02.4
Joan Wallis Harborne H	12:32.0		Margaret Lewis Birchfield H	13:13.2
Sheila Jennings London Olympiafdes	12:38.6		Jennifer Peck Selsonia LAC	13:36.8
Joyce Heath Small Heath H	12:56.2		Heather Profitt Warrington AC	14:31.0
Brenda Cook Bilston	13:04.2			

1970 June 20 London (CP)
Judy Farr Trowbridge	12:34.0
Betty Jenkins Birchfield H	13:04.0
Margaret Lewis Birchfield H	13:09.2
Jennifer Peck Selsonia LAC	13:21.4
Mo Graham Birchfield H	13:25.4
Barbara Brown Croydon H	14:07.0

1971 July 17 London (CP)
Brenda Cook Wolverhampton & Bilston	12:39.8
Margaret Lewis Birchfield H	12:55.4
Mo Graham Birchfield H	12:23.0
Jennifer Peck Selsonia LAC	13:44.0
Cathryn Daniels Warrington AC	13:46.0
Ann Johnstone Houghton H	14:06.6

1972 July 8 London (CP)
Betty Jenkins Birchfield H	12:31.2
Brenda Cook Wolverhampton & Bilston	12:49.0
Virginia Lovell Solihull AC	12:58.8
Margaret Lewis Birchfield H	13:02.4
Marion Adamson North Shields Poly	13:21.4
Mo Graham Birchfield H	13:24.2

3000 METRES

1973 July 21 London (CP)
Betty Jenkins Birchfield H	14:59.4
Marion Fawkes North Shields Poly	15:04.6
Christine Coleman Highgate H	15:10.0
Barbara Cook Redhill & Reigate	15:28.0
Virginia Lovell Birchfield H	15:28.0
Mary Brown Birchfield H	16:31.2

1974 July 20 London (CP)
Marion Fawkes North Shields Poly	14:33.50
Betty Jenkins Birchfield H	15:07.32
Sally Wish Solihull AC	15:21.92
Pam Branson Harborne H	15:48.38
Judy Farr Trowbridge	16:04.94
Joan Mulvenna North Shields Poly	16:18.99

5000 METRES

1975 July 19 London (CP)
Virginia Lovell Birchfield H	25:02.8
Marion Fawkes North Shields Poly	25:14.8
Judy Farr Trowbridge	25:44.4
Sylvia Saunders Nomads WC	26:11.2
Pam Branson Harborne H	26:36.0
Christine Coleman Highgate H	26:38.8

1976 Aug 21 London (CP)
Marion Fawkes North Shields Poly	24:10.0
Carol Tyson Lakeland AAC	24:47.8
Judy Farr Trowbridge	25:05.8
Sylvia Saunders Birchfield H	27:02.4
Irene Bateman Basildon	27:22.2
Pam Reynolds Clonliffe H/IRL	28:31.2

1977 July 23 Wolverhampton
Marion Fawkes North Shields Poly	24:50.6
Judy Farr Trowbridge	25:04.6
Pam Branson Harborne H	26:13.0
Sylvia Saunders Birchfield H	26:29.8
Virginia Lovell Birchfield H	26:30.2
Elaine Cox Solihull AC	26:45.8

1978 Aug 5 Birmingham
Carol Tyson Lakeland AC	24:08.2
Virginia Lovell Birchfield H	25:06.4
Karen Eden Solihull AC	25:46.6
Elaine Cox Solihull AC	27:44.8
Pam Reynolds Clonliffe H/IRL	28:48.0
Carolyn Gee Lakeland AC	29:43.0

1979 June 16 Birmingham
Marion Fawkes North Shields Poly	23:31.5
Carol Tyson Lakeland AC	23:57.0
Irene Bateman Basildon	24:21.9
Judy Farr Trowbridge	25:03.1
Elaine Cox Solihull AC	25:15.5
Karen Eden Solihull AC	25:38.2

1980 Aug 16 London (CP)
Irene Bateman Basildon	24:09.0
Siv Gustavsson SWE	24:47.6
Britt Holmquist SWE	24:49.6
Eva Gustavsson SWE	25:00.5
Jill Barrett Verlea	25:18.5
Elaine Worth Bolehall Swifts WC	26:26.2

1981 July 25 London (CP)
Carol Tyson Lakeland AC	23:12.55
Irene Bateman Basildon	23:48.10
Ann Peel CAN	23:50.85
Lillian Millen Lakeland AC	24:14.72
Jill Barrett Verlea	24:32.69
Elaine Cox Solihull & Small Heath	25:08.81

1982 July 31 London (CP)
Sue Cook AUS	23:05.52
Irene Bateman Havering AC	24:34.02
Rachel Thompson AUS	24:54.03
Frances Toohey AUS	25:16.28
Rosanne Smith AUS	25:28.30
Brenda Lupton Sheffield Utd H	25:31.12

1983 July 30 London (CP)
Ann Peel CAN	24:26.04
Jill Barrett Verlea	25:20.73
Helen Elleker Sheffield United H	25:54.62
Lillian Millen Lakeland AC	26:21.96
Beveley Allen Brighton & Hove	27:45.62
Elaine Allen Sheffield United H	27:57.33

1984 June 15 London (CP)
Jill Barrett Verlea	23:51.63
Virginia Birch Brighton & Hove	24:09.96
Helen Elleker Sheffield United H	24:28.76
Lillian Millen Cumberland AC	24:34.05
Brenda Lupton Sheffield Utd H	24:49.63
Lisa Langford Wolverhampton & Bilston	25:07.88

1985 July 27 Birmingham
Virginia Birch Brighton & Hove	23:53.47
Helen Elleker Sheffield United H	24:25.81
Lisa Langford Wolverhampton & Bilston	24:53.04
Beverley Allen Brighton & Hove	25:02.63
Karen Nipper Roath Labour WC	25:13.45
Sarah Brown Steyning	25:22.62

1986 June 7 Birmingham
Helen Elleker Sheffield United H	24:27.17
Lisa Langford Wolverhampton & Bilston	24:55.01
Sarah Brown Steyning	25:03.83
Angela Hodd Tonbridge AC	25:19.48
Kim Macadam Coventry RWC	25:47.22
Ruth Harper Sparkhill H	26:15.60

1987 May 25 Birmingham
Lisa Langford Wolverhampton & Bilston	22:35.04
Nicky Jackson Trowbridge	23:57.32
Sarah Brown Steyning	24:15.59
Helen Elleker Sheffield Utd RWC	24:20.26
Victoria Lawrence Reading	24:46.82
Julie Drake Brighton & Hove	25:23.39

1988 Aug 6 Birmingham
Betty Sworowski Sheffield United	24:24.32
Karen Dunster Aldershot, Farnham & D	25:28.56

Vicky Lupton Sheffield Utd RWC	25:42.70	**1998** July 26 Birmingham	
Sarah Brown Steyning	26 66.84	Gillian O'Sullivan IRL	21:52.68
Brenda Lupton Sheffield Utd RWC	26:11.45	Lisa Kehler Wolverhampton & Bilston	22:01.53
Tracey Devlin Sheffield Utd RWC	26:55.06	Vicky Lupton Sheffield Utd RWC	23:32.48
1989 Aug 13 Birmingham		Catherine Charnock Barrow & Fylde	23:50.96
Betty Sworowski Sheffield United	22:30.59	Sharon Tonks Bromsgrove & Redditch	24:20.07
Lisa Langford Wolverhampton & Bilston	23:40.68	Debbie Wallen Aldershot, Farnham & D	24:28.60
Sarah Brown Steyning	24:05.68	**1999** July 25 Birmingham	
Julie Drake Brighton & Hove	24:26.94	Vicky Lupton Sheffield Utd RWC	23:37.47
Vicky Lupton Sheffield Utd RWC	24:55.42	Catherine Charnock Barrow & Fylde	23:42 92
Verity Larby Aldershot, Farnham & D	25:05.29	Lisa Crump Sheffield United RWC	24:26.41
1990 Aug 4 Birmingham		Katherine Horwill Dudley & Stourbridge	25:08.24
Betty Sworowski Sheffield United	22:23.35	Amy Hales Steyning	25:22.14
Helen Elleker Sheffield Utd RWC	23:26.86	Nikki Huckerby Birchfield H	25:46.82
Verity Larby Aldershot, Farnham & D	23:46.68	**2001** July 14 Birmingham	
Sarah Brown Steyning	24:36.43	Niobe Menendez Steyning	23:46.30
Sylvia Black Birchfield H	24:56.60	Sharon Tonks Bromsgrove & Redditch	24:20.46
Jane Saville AUS	25:15.42	Wendy Bennett Worcester H	24:35.85
1991 July 21 Birmingham		Estle Viljoen Hercules Wimbledon	24:53.02
Betty Sworowski Sheffield United	22:29.04	Miranda Heathcote Tonbridge AC	25:36.56
Helen Elleker Sheffield Utd RWC	23:27.70	Karen Ratcliffe Covent Godiva H	25:59.47
Melanie Brookes Nuneaton H	24:38.90	**2002** July 13 Birmingham	
Sylvia Black Birchfield H	24:53.14	Lisa Kehler Wolverhampton & Bilston	21:42.51
Karen Smith Coventry RWC	24:57.48	Sharon Tonks Bromsgrove & Redditch	24:05.49
Sarah Brown Steyning	25:47.86	Estle Viljoen Hercules Wimbledon	24:26.11
1992 June 28 Birmingham		**2003** July 26 Birmingham	
Vicky Lupton Sheffield Utd RWC	22:12.21	Lisa Kehler Wolverhampton & Bilston	23:10.15
Verity Larby Aldershot, Farnham & D	23:41.17	Estle Viljoen Hercules Wimbledon	24:15.04
Sylvia Black Birchfield H	23:50.54	Katie Stones Kingston upon Hull	24:24.47
Melanie Brookes Nuneaton H	24:23.24	Sophie Hales Steyning	25:11.42
Karen Smith Coventry RWC	24:39.05	Verity Snook Aldershot, Farnham & D	25:13.34
Carolyn Brown Manx H	24:39.41	Jenny Gagg Kingston upon Hull	25:36.37
1993 July 17 Birmingham		**2004** July 11 Manchester (SC)	
Vicky Lupton Sheffield Utd RWC	22:34.50	Niobe Menendez Steyning	23:53.75
Julie Drake Brighton & Hove	22:37.47	Sophie Hales Steyning	24:37.37
Jane Saville AUS	23:17.06	Rebecca Mersh City of Sheffield	24:44.31
Linda Coffee AUS	23:26.91	Kath Horwill Dudley & Stourbridge	24:54.88
Sylvia Black Birchfield H	23:48.77	Johanna Jackson Redcar RWC	25:10.69
Melanie Brookes Nuneaton H	24:07.02	Sharon Tonks Bromsgrove & Redditch	25:24.49
1994 June 19 Horsham		**2005** July 10 Manchester (SC)	
Verity Larby Aldershot, Farnham & D	23:22.52	Johanna Jackson Redcar RWC	23:34.12
Vicky Lupton Sheffield Utd RWC	23:24.50	Niobe Menendez Steyning	24:00.37
Jane Barbour AUS	23:43.23	Katie Stones Kingston upon Hull	24:03.61
Melanie Wright Nuneaton H	24:06.27	Estle Viljoen Hercules Wimbledon	24:19.82
Karen Smith Coventry RWC	24:18.79	Sharon Tonks Bromsgrove & Redditch	25:09.89
Sian Spacey CAN	24:50.09	Kath Horwill Dudley & Stourbridge	25:29.04
1995 July 16 Birmingham		**2006** July 10 Manchester (SC)	
Lisa Langford Wolverhampton & Bilston	22:20.03	Ann Loughnane IRL	22:54.97
Vicky Lupton Sheffield Utd RWC	22:23.80	Johanna Jackson Redcar RWC	23:27.56
Cal Partington Manx H	22:40.19	Fiona McGorum Leicester WC	28:42.19
Perry Williams London Irish	23:58.84		
Verity Snook Aldershot, Farnham & D	24:04.57	**WAAA 10,000 METRES TRACK**	
Melanie Wright Nuneaton H	24:09.66	**1978** Mar 25 London (WL)	
1996 June 15 Birmingham		Carol Tyson Lakeland AC	49:59.0
Vicky Lupton Sheffield Utd RWC	23:04.57	Marion Fawkes North Shields Poly	50:31.0
Melanie Wright Nuneaton H	24:36.65	Judy Farr Trowbridge	50:46.0
Catherine Charnock Barrow & Fylde	25:00.22	Virginia Lovell Birchfield H	52:16.0
Brenda Lupton Sheffield Utd RWC	25:28.26	Christine Coleman Lowestoft AC	52:59.0
Liz Corran Manx H	25:52.99	Irene Bateman Basildon	53:51.0
1997 Aug 25 Birmingham		**1979** Mar 31 Hornchurch Stadium, Upminster	
Olive Loughnane IRL	24:09.18	Marion Fawkes North Shields Poly	48:37.6
Catherine Charnock Barrow & Fylde	25:00.22	Irene Bateman Basildon	49:05.0
Nikki Huckerby Birchfield H	25:41.85	Judy Farr Trowbridge	51:18.0
Sally Warren Steyning	26:28.10	Beverley Francis Brighton & Hove	51:35.0
Lyn Bradley Sheffield Utd RWC	27:44.79	Carol Tyson Lakeland AC	52:27.0
Helen Ford-Dunn Steyning	28:53.47	Virginia Birch Enfield H	52:41.0
		1980 Mar 29 London (PH)	

Carol Tyson Lakeland AC	49:30.4	Helen Elleker Sheffield Utd RWC	49:07
Irene Bateman Basildon	50:38.8	Sarah Brown Steyning	49:22
Karen Eden Solihull AC	53:46.8	Lisa Simpson Mitcham & Sutton	51:34
Elaine Worth Bolehall Swifts WC	55:00.6	**1990** Sep 1 London (He)	
Julie Robery Havering AC	56:30.4	Vicky Lupton Sheffield Utd RWC	48:12.2
Christine Coleman Highgate H	56:54.0	Helen Elleker Sheffield Utd RWC	48:58.9
1981 Mar 28 London (PH)		Verity Larby Aldershot Farnham & D	51:56.0
Irene Bateman Basildon	49:54.3	Brenda Lupton Sheffield Utd RWC	55:12.1
Lillian Millen Lakeland AC	52:58.3	Melanie Brookes Nuneaton H	55:37.6
Jill Barrett Verlea	53:11.4	Philippa Savage Steyning	57:32.3
Elaine Cox Solihull AC	53:25.1	**1991** Aug 4 Stoke-on-Trent	
Sandra Hogg Lakeland AC	55:38.6	Betty Sworowski Sheffield Utd	46:23.08
Virginia Biirch Brighton & Hove	55:43.8	Melanie Brookes Nuneaton H	50:10.85
1982 Mar 20 London (WC)		**1993** June 20 Horsham	
Irene Bateman Havering AC	48:57.6	Verity Larby Aldershot Farnham	47:10.07
Lillian Millen Lakeland AC	51:06.1	Vicky Lupton Sheffield Utd RWC	47:37.32
Sarah Brown Steyning	52:10.4	Cal Partington Manx H	50:43.87
Virginia Birch Brighton & Hove	52:29.8	Elaine Callinan Solihull AC	51:58.80
Brenda Lupton Sheffield United H	53:50.1	Sandra Brown Surrey WC	52:43.71
Liz Gaffer Leicester WC	54:09.0	Cath Reader Colchester W	52:50.57
1983 Mar 19 Kirkby		**1994** May 7 Bolton	
Irene Bateman Havering AC	48:52.5	Verity Larby Aldershot, Farnham & D	48:05.0
Jill Barrett Verlea	50:11.2	Cal Partington Manx H	48:20.0
Brenda Lupton Sheffield United H	51:13.1	Melanie Wright Nuneaton H	49:16.0
Karen Nipper Roath Labour WC	53:14.7	Vicky Lupton Sheffield Utd RWC	50:11.0
Sarah Brown Steyning	53:49.0	Karen Kneale Manx H	51:22.0
Helen Ringshaw Steyning	54:14.0	Nicky Jackson Trowbridge	52:37.0
1984 Mar 17 Birmingham		**1995** Sep 2 Watford	
Helen Elleker Sheffield United H	49:52.3	Vicky Lupton Sheffield Utd RWC	45:18.8
Brenda Lupton Sheffield United H	50:10.2	Melanie Wright Nuneaton H	48:35.8
Helen Ringshaw Steyning	51:31.2	Sylvia Black Birchfield H	52:40.9
Karen Nipper Roath Labour WC	52:31.5	Brenda Lupton Sheffield Utd RWC	53:05.6
Lillian Millen Cumberland AC	54:13.5	Gill Watson Sheffield Utd RWC	54:06.6
Liz Ryan Epsom & Ewell H	54:37.6	Nina Howley Sheffield Utd RWC	54:18.7
1985 June 29 London (He)		**1996** Aug 31 Enfield	
Helen Elleker Sheffield United H	51:22.3	Vicky Lupton Sheffield Utd RWC	49:15.0
Lisa Langford Wolverhampton & Bilston	52:02.9	Kim Braznell Dudley & Stourbridge	50:52.3
Karen Nipper Roath Labour WC	52:57.4	Liz Corran Manx H	51:17.1
Lisa Simpson Mitcham & Sutton	54:02.8	Claire Walker Coventry RWC	52:43.3
Sarah Brown Steyning	55:19.5	Kath Horwill Dudley & Stourbridge	53:38.3
Gill Trower Steyning	55:36.2	Brenda Lupton Sheffield Utd RWC	54:24.2
1986 May 31 London (He)		**1997** Sep 7 Worcester	
Helen Elleker Sheffield United H	49:21.8	Catherine Charnock Barrow & Fylde	54:33.6
Sarah Brown Steyning	52:25.0	Sally Warren Steyning	56:21.4
Brenda Lupton Sheffield United H	52:59.6	Sally Hall Birchfield H	57:34.5
Elaine Worth Bromsgrove & Redditch	54:49.5	**1998** Sep 26 Basildon	
Karen Dunster Aldershot Farnham	55:59.0	Pam Phillips Ilford	64:08.9
Suzanne Kew Belgrave H	56:45.4	Pam Ficken Surrey WC	67:32.8?
1987 Sep 5 Middlesbrough		**2000** Aug 13 Birmingham	
Sarah Brown Steyning	51:48.7	Lisa Kehler Wolverhampton & Bilston	45:09.57
Susan Gibson Sheffield Utd RWC	53:05.1	Nikki Huckerby Birchfield H	54:53.35
Betty Sworowski Sheffield Utd	53:31.6	Kath Horwill Dudley & Stourbrige	55:59.54
Vicky Lupton Sheffield Utd RWC	53:34.1	Jo Hesketh Steyning	56:34.13
Lillian Millen Cumberland AC	54:27.6		
Gill Trower Steyning	54:50.4	**WOMEN'S ROAD CHAMPIONSHIPS**	
1988 Sep 10 London (He)		**3 MILES**	
Betty Sworowski Sheffield Utd	50:12.0	**1933** Mar 18 Southgate	
Sarah Brown Steyning	54:47.2	Jeanne Probekk Middlesex LAC	25:56.4
Vicky Lupton Sheffield Utd RWC	55:04.9	Jessie Howes Spartan LAC	26:18
Brenda Lupton Sheffield Utd RWC	55:23.0	H.Pugh London Olympiades AC	27:03
Gill Trower Steyning	56:44.2	R.Browne Middlesex LAC	27:17
Melanie Brookes Nuneaton H	56:53.0	A.Sanders London Olympiades	27:23
1989 Sep 3 Leeds (Road)		L.Landsell Polytechnic H	27:36
1= Lisa Langford Wolverhampton & Bilston	47:15	London Olympiades 21 MLAC 24 Polytechnic 35	
1= Betty Sworowski Sheffield Utd	47:15	**1934** Feb 17 Wimbledon	
Julie Drake Brighton & Hove	48:55	Jessie Howes London Olympiades AC	22:47
		E.Parsons Mitcham AC	23:29

A.Sanders London Olympiades	23:36
L.Murray Middlesex LAC	23:51
W.Savage London Olympiades	24:23
L.Landsell Polytechnic H & M.Pugh London Ol	24:44
London Olympiades 11 MLAC - Polytechnic 28	

1935 Jan 19 Epsom

Jessie Howes London Olympiades AC	26:22
V.Tosh London Olympiades AC	27:28
L.Murray Middlesex LAC	27:57
Emily Littlefair London Olympiades	27:58
E.Parsons Mitcham AC	27:59
D.Cooper London Olympiades	28:56
London Olympiades 18 MLAC 37 Mitcham 40	

1936 Mar 7 Ilford

Emily Littlefair London Olympiades	27:15
E.Pugh London Olympiades	28:08
J.Waters London Olympiades	26:18
London Olympiades -	

1937 venue?

Doris Harris Birchfield LAC	29:00
Mary Pritchard Small Heath H	29:07
Hettie Beeson Small Heath H	29:17
Small Heath H 18 Birchfield 19	

1938 Apr 9 Bristol

Doris Harris Birchfield H	25:48
Dorothy Onions Small Heath H	26:00
Mary Harrington Birchfield H	26:34
? Small Heath H	
? London Olympiades	
? Small Heath H	
Small Heath 22 London Oly 29 Birchfield 31	

1939 May 13 Wembley - distance unknown

F.Pengelly Paignton	33:32
Evelyn Webb Hercules AC	33:40
Mary Harrington Birchfield H	33:52
Betty Jones West Bromwich	33:59
Doris Harris Birchfield H	34:09
Phyllis Archer Small Heath H	34:15
Birchfield 26 Small Heath 30 Birchfield 'B' 39	

2.5 MILES

1946 Apr 22 Birmingham

Doris Hart Birchfield H	22:28
Joan Riddington London Transport	23:04
Gwen Thorne Birmingham Atalanta	23:15
Margaret Brittan Birmingham Atalanta	23:19
Betty Harris Birchfield H	23:31
Beryl Day Birmingham Atalanta	23:53
Birmingham At 13 Birchfield 14 London Tr 33	

1947 Apr 5 Birmingham

Joyce Heath Small Heath H	21:29
Gwen Thorne Birmingham Atalanta	21:30
Margaret Brittan Birmingham Atalanta	21:47
Doris Mann Birchfield H	22:19
Beryl Day Birmingham Atalanta	22:56
Nellie Batson Small Heath H	23:23
Birmingham At 10 Small Heath 17 Birchfield 21	

1948 Mar 28 Birmingham

Joyce Heath Small Heath H	20:49
Gwen Thorne Birmingham Atalanta	20:54
Jean Lloyd Birchfield H	21:12
Margaret Brittan Birmingham Atalanta	21:19
Beryl Day Birmingham Atalanta	21:28
Zoe White Birchfield H	22:01
Birmingham At 11 Small Heath 14 Harborne 35	

1949 Mar 19 Epsom

Joyce Heath Small Heath H	22:42.4
Gwen Thorne Birmingham Atalanta	22:57
Margaret Brittan Birmingham Atalanta	23:11
Jessie Ashton Birchfield H	23:22
Gwen Thomas Birmingham Atalanta	23:33
Zoe White Birchfield H	23:36
Birmingham At 10 Birchfield 18 Small Heath 24	

1949 Dec 3 Birmingham

Joyce Heath Small Heath H	22:03
Margaret Brittan Birmingham Atalanta	22:26
Zoe White Birchfield H	22:42
Jessie Ashton Birchfield H	22:48
Iris Flower Birchfield H	22:53
Joyce Perry Birchfield H	23:12
Birchfield 12 Birmingham At 19 Birchfield B 25	

1950 Dec 9 Chigwell Row

Joyce Heath Small Heath H	23:04.8
Iris Williams Birchfield H	23:32
Jessie Ashton Birchfield H	23:41
Nellie Batson Small Heath H	23:53
Marion O'Riordan Birchfield H	24:05
Brenda Harris Birchfield H	24:17
Birchfield 10 Small Heath 14 Harborne 35	

1951 Dec 8 Newcastle

Leila Deas London Olympiades	21:06.6
Sheila Martin London Olympiades	21:07
Joyce Heath Small Heath H	21:46
Margaret Brittan Birmingham Atalanta	21:55
Sheila Cottrell Harborne H	21:59
Brenda Stevenson Birchfield H	22:00
Birchfield 15 London Oly 25 Small Heath 25	

From 1953 onwards the distance varies

1953 Jan 24 Stockport

Dilys Williams Birchfield H	17:09
Beryl Randle Birmingham Atalanta	17:25
Margaret Babington Birmingham Atalanta	18:11
J.Barber Stockport H	18:12
Brenda Stevenson Birchfield H	18:14
Heather Cawston Birchfield H	18:18
Birchfield 12 Birmingham At 14 London Oly 25	

1954 Jan 16 Alperton

Dilys Williams Birchfield H	20:59
Beryl Randle Birchfield H	21:10
Joyce Heath Small Heath H	21:57
Mary Nusser Birchfield H	22:19
Helen Vincent London Olympiades	22:24
Rita Phillips Birchfield H	22:47
Birchfield 7 London Oly 20 Small Heath 22	

1955 Dec 4 Birmingham

Dilys Williams Birchfield H	17:49
Beryl Randle Birchfield H	18:31
Joyce Heath Small Heath H	18:47
Nellie Loines Small Heath H	18:49
Barbara Hamilton Birchfield H	19:20
Karen Field Small Heath H	19:37
Birchfield 8 Small Heath 13 London Oly 26	

1956 Feb 11 Ruislip

Dilys Williams Birchfield H	20:42
Nellie Loines Small Heath H	21:42
Joyce Heath Small Heath H	21:50
Helen Vincent London Olympiades	22:13
Rita Phillips Birchfield H	22:27
Beryl Randle Birchfield H	22:31
Birchfield 12 Small Heath 12 London Oly 22	

1956 Dec 15 Birmingham

Dilys Williams Birchfield H	18:39
Pat Myatt Smethwick H	19:16

Joyce Heath Small Heath H	19:59	Joyce Heath Birchfield H	37:16
Gillian Williams London Olympiades	20:07	Margaret Lewis Harborne H	38:27
Betty Franklin Birchfield H	20:39	Gwen Powell Harborne H	39:25
Nellie Loines Small Heath H	20:46	Harborne 13 Birchfield 14 N.Shields P 36	
Birchfield 14 Small Heath 18 London Oly 21		**1965** Dec 4 Birchfield	
1957 Dec 11 Sudbury Hill		Judy Farr Trowbridge	33:35
Gillian Williams London Olympiades	23:58	Sheila Jennings London Olympiades	34:25
Joan Wallis Harborne H	25:38	Betty Jenkins Birchfield H	36:58
Betty Franklin Birchfield H	25:43	Audrey Hackett Harborne H	38:15
V.Reynolds Small Heath H	25:54	Margaret Lewis Harborne H	38:25
Helen Vincent London Olympiades	26:06	Mo Graham Birchfield H	38:54
Norma Blaine Birchfield H	27:06	Birchfield 16	
London Oly 13 Small Heath 25		**1966** Dec 3 Birmingham	
1958 Dec 13 Birmingham		Sheila Jerninngs London Olympiades	28:15
Pat Myatt Smethwick H	34:55	Betty Jenkins Birchfield H	28:30
Betty Franklin Birchfield H	36:16	Joan Wallis Harborne H	29:21
Joyce Heath Small Heath H	36:33	Diane Cotterill South Shields H	29:21
Sandra Smith Birchfield H	36:51	Margaret Lewis Harborne H	29:55
Nellie Loines Small Heath H	37:05	Maureen Armstrong North Shields Poly	30:37
Joan Wallis Harborne H	37:43	Harborne 15	
Birchfield 13 Small Heath 18 Birmingham At 32		**1967** Dec 2 Sheffield	
1959 Dec 12 Eltham 4 Miles		Betty Jenkins Birchfield H	35:21
Beryl Randle Birchfield H	35:48	Diane Cotterill South Shields H	37:01
Nellie Loines Small Heath H	36:57	Audrey Hackett Harborne H	37:10
Sandra Smith Birchfield H	37:07	Doris Froome Harborne H	37:29
Sheila Jennings London Olympiades	37:16	Barbara Fisk Redhill & Reigate	37:30
Helen Milne London Olympiades	37:27	Joan Wallis Harborne H	37:37
Norma Ashby Birchfield H	37:36	Harborne 13 Birchfield 18 North Shields P 40	
Birchfield 10 Small Heath 26 London Oly 28		**1968** Dec 14 Enfield	
1960 Dec 10 Birmingham		Judy Farr Trowbridge	34:05
Sheila Jennings London Olym	36:01	Betty Jenkins Birchfield H	34:10
Judy Woodsford Trowbridge	36:09	Margaret Lewis Harborne H	35:00
Joan Wallis Harborne H	36:30	Barbara Fisk Redhill & Reigate	35:51
Maureen Eyre Birchfield H	37:27	Audrey Hackett Harborne H	36:06
Val Simpson Stourbridge H	38:07	Doris Froome Harborne H	36:30
Pam Horwill Stourbridge H	38:19	Birchfield 19	
Harborne 24 London Oly 26 Birchfield 27		**1969** Dec 7 Holloway, Derbyshire	
1961 Dec 9 Croydon		Betty Jenkins Birchfield H	32:57
Sheila Jennings London Olympiades	34:30	Barbara Fisk Redhill & Reigate	33:35
Mo Eyre Birchfield H	34:46	Margaret Lewis Birchfield H	34:11
Audrey Hackett Harborne H	34:49	Barbara Brown Croydon H	34:20
Joan Wallis Harborne H	35:04	Joan Wallis Harborne H	34:33
Joyce Heath Birchfield H	35:09	Mo Graham Birchfield H	34:40
Heather Sargent Harborne H	36:21	Birchfield 10 Harborne 30 Warrington 42	
Harborne 13 Birchfield 16 Small Heath 42		**6500 METRES**	
1962 Dec 8 Bradford 3.5 Miles		**1970** Dec 5 Birmingham	
Judy Farr Trowbridge	32:55	Judy Farr Trowbridge	34:02
Joyce Heath Birchfield H	33:20	Betty Jenkins Birchfield H	34:30
Margaret Lewis Harborne H	34:05	Margaret Lewis Birchfield H	35:49
Jennifer Keen Croydon H	34:22	Marian Hindley Birchfield H	36:16
Gwen Powell Harborne H	35:00	Cathryn Daniels Warrington AC	36:36
Pam Horwill Stourbridge H	35:12	Mo Graham Birchfield H	37:24
Harborne 17 Harborne 'B' 33		Birchfield 9 Dudley 29	
1963 Dec 14 Birmingham 4.25 Miles		**1971** Dec 4 Wombourne, Staffs	
Judy Farr Trowbridge	39:33	Betty Jenkins Birchfield H	33:50
Sheila Jennings London Olympiades	40:49	Judy Farr Trowbridge	34:18
Audrey Hackett Harborne H	40:55	Margaret Lewis Birchfield H	34:28
Joan Wallis Harborne H	41:18	Christine Coleman Highgate H	35:15
Joyce Heath Birchfield H	41:34	Mo Graham Birchfield H	35:50
Margaret Lewis Harborne H	42:17	Marian Hindley Birchfield H	36:18
Harborne 13 Birchfield 20 Harborne 'B' 33		Birchfield 9	
4 MILES		**1972** Dec 2 Bromsgrove	
1964 Dec 5 Stourbridge		Betty Jenkins Birchfield H	33:51
Judy Farr Trowbridge	35:51	Barbara Cook Redhill & Reigate	34:07
Audrey Hackett Harborne H	36:18	Virginia Lovell Solihull AC	34:32
Betty Jenkins Birchfield H	36:55	Christine Coleman Highgate H	34:47

Marion Fawkes North Shields Poly	36:42	Wendy Toach Leicester WC		26:30
Kim Braznell Warley AC	37:37	Lakeland 10 Trowbridge 20 Bolton 27		
Birchfield		**1981** Mar 21 Exeter		
1973 Dec 1 Bolton 5000 Metres		Irene Bateman Havering AC		25:00
Marion Fawkes North Shields Poly	31:55	Jill Barrett Verlea		25:45
Pam Branson Harborne H	32:21	Gillian Edgar Lakeland AAC		26:09
Christine Coleman Highgate H	32:32	Lillian Millen Lakeland AAC		26:19
Sally Wish Solihull AC	33:44	Sarah Brown Steyning		26:57
Sylvia Saunders Harborne H	34:26	Liz Gaffer Leicester WC		27:22
Mary Brown Birchfield H	34:53	Lakeland 8 Havering 30 Bolehall 37		
Harborne 22. Snow and ice		**1982** May 15 Enfield		
1974 Dec 7 Birmingham 5300 Metres		Irene Bateman Havering AC		24:09
Marion Fawkes North Shields Poly	27:25	Brenda Lupton Sheffield United H		25:20
Pam Branson Harborne H	28:14	Helen Ringshaw Steyning		25:40
Virginia Lovell Birchfield H	28:41	Sarah Brown Steyning		25:54
Christine Coleman Highgate H	28:55	Lisa Langford Wolverhampton		26:08
Susan Booth Bolton United H	29:00	Virginia Birch Brighton & Hove		26:26
Sylvia Saunders Harborne H	29:29	Steyning 6 Bolehall 28 Southend 30		
Harborne 25		**1983** May 14 Southport		
1975 Dec 6 Uxbridge 6500 Metres		Irene Bateman Havering AC		23:28
Judy Farr Trowbridge	32:12	Jill Barrett Verlea		23:46
Marion Fawkes North Shields Poly	32:24	Lillian Millen Lakeland AAC		23:51
Christine Coleman Highgate H	32:48	Virginia Birch Brighton & Hove		24:05
Sylvia Saunders Nomads WC	33:51	Brenda Lupton Sheffield United H		24:22
Sally Wish Solihull AC	34:10	Helen Elleker Sheffield United H		24:55
Joan Mulvenna North Shields Poly	34:57	Sheffield 19 Steyning 37 Bromsgrive 53		
N.Shields P 23 City of Stoke 36 Harborne 60		**1984** May 12 Redditch		
1976 Dec 11 Whitley Bay 6000 Metres		Jill Barrett Verlea		23:38
Judy Farr Trowbridge	29:24	Virginia Birch Brighton & Hove		23:41
Carol Tyson Lakeland AAC	29:47	Nicky Jackson Trowbridge		23:44
Marion Fawkes North Shields Poly	30:25	Helen Elleker Sheffield United H		24:06
Sylvia Saunders Birchfield H	31:11	Lillian Millen Cumberland AC		24:14
Elaine Cox Solihull AC	33:41	Helen Ringshaw Steyning		24:53
Susan Booth Bolton United H	34:24	Brighton & Hove 22		
N.Shields Poly 19		**1985** May 11 Thamesmead		
5 KILOMETRES		Janice McCaffrey CAN		23:12
1977 Dec 10 Birmingham		Virginia Birch Brighton & Hove		23:21
Carol Tyson Lakeland AAC	24:02	Helen Elleker Sheffield United H		24:06
Judy Farr Trowbridge AAC	24:24.3	Susan Ashforth Sheffield United H		24:17
Sylvia Saunders Birchfield	25:05	Lisa Langford Wolverhampton		24:23
Marion Fawkes North Shields Poly	25:15	Karen Nipper Roath Labour WC		24:25
Virginia Lovell Birchfield H	25:27	Sheffield 26 Steyning 35 Bromsgrove 56		
Elaine Cox Solihull AC	25:40	**1986** May 10 York		
Birchfield 18		Beverley Allen Brighton & Hove		23:29
1978 Dec 5 Melksham		Lisa Langford Wolverhampton		24:10
Carol Tyson Lakeland AAC	24:08	Nicky Jackson Trowbridge		24:44
Karen Eden Solihull AC	24:20	Kim McAdam Coventry Godiva H		24:55
Irene Bateman Basildon	24:27	Julie Drake Brighton & Hove		25:06
Judy Farr Trowbridge	24:29	Sarah Brown Steyning		25:18
Beverley Francis Brighton & Hove	25:54	Steyning 31 Leicester 36 Bromsgrove 40		
Susan Till Brighton & Hove	26:26	**1987** Apr 18 Birmingham		
Brighton & Hove 24		Lisa Langford Wolverhampton		23:07
1979 Dec 8 Birmingham c. 500m short		Sarah Brown Steyning		23:57
Elaine Cox Solihull AC	22:30	Helen Elleker Sheffield Utd RWC		24:05
Virginia Lovell Enfield	22:43	Victoria Lawrence Reading		25:16
Judy Farr Trowbridge	23:39	Julie Drake Brighton & Hove		25:44
Karen Eden Solihull AC	23:42	Susan Gibson Sheffield Utd RWC		25:51
Elaine Worth Bolehall Swifts WC	23:46	Steyning 25 Brighton 28 Sheffield 28		
Susan Howard Bolton United H	25:39	**1988** June 11 Leicester		
Solihull 13		Betty Sworowski Sheffield Utd		23:43
1980 Dec 6 London (BP)		Sarah Brown Steyning		24:46
Carol Tyson Lakeland AAC	23:05	Tracey Devlin Sheffield Utd RWC		25:29
Lillian Millen Lakeland AAC	25:24	Andrea Crofts Leicester WC		25:47
Judy Farr Trowbridge	25:47	Brenda Lupton Sheffield Utd RWC		26:02
Brenda Lupton Sheffield United H	25:51	Suzie Pratt Leicester WC		26:08
Sheila Jennings Trowbridge	26:28	Sheffield 9 Steyning 28 Leicester 34		

1989 June 10 Colchester
Julie Drake Brighton & Hove	24:04
Nicky Jackson Trowbridge	24:25
Helen Elleker Sheffield Utd RWC	24:32
Sarah Brown Steyning	24:40
Sylvia Black Birchfield H	24:50
Andrea Crofts Leicester WC	25:53

Sheffield 28 Steyning 30 Brighton 31

1990 June 9 York
Lisa Langford Wolverhampton	22:24
Helen Elleker Sheffield Utd RWC	23:05
Vicky Lupton Sheffield Utd RWC	23:11
Sylvia Black Birchfield H	23:55
Verity Larby Aldershot, Farnham & D	24:03
Andrea Crofts Leicester WC	24:15

Leicester 34 AFD 36 Sheffield 36

1991 July 13 Basildon
Vicky Lupton Sheffield Utd RWC	22:50
Betty Sworowski Sheffield Utd	22:56
Sylvia Black Birchfield H	23:48
Helen Elleker Sheffield Utd RWC	23:48
Karen Smith Coventry RWC	24:10
Sarah Brown Steyning	24:39

Sheffield 7 Steyning 33 Dudley 35

1992 June 13 Colchester (over distance)
Sylvia Black Birchfield H	25:18
Andrea Crofts Leicester WC	26:50
Karen Smith Coventry RWC	26:59
Sarah Brown Steyning	27:30
Katherine Horwill Dudley & Stourbridge	28:04
Gill Trower Steyning	28:18

Steyning 20 Dudley 26 Sheffield 37

1993 July 10 Sutton Coldfield
Joanne Pope Brighton & Hove	25:13
Gill Watson Sheffield United RWC	25:33
Elaine Callinan Solihull AC	25:59
Sandra Brown Surrey WC	26:03
Helen Ford-Dunn Steyning	26:34
Katherine Horwill Dudley & Stourbridge	26:51

Sheffield 29 Steyning 30 Birchfield 30

1994 May 21 Birmingham
Melanie Wright Nuneaton H	24:27
Kim Baird Dudley & Stourbridge	25:36
Katherine Horwill Dudley & Stourbridge	25:38
Nicky Jackson Trowbridge	26:12
Catherine Charnock Barrow AC	26:18
Claire Walker Coventry RWC	26:28

Dudley 20 Birchfield 32 Sheffield 41

1995 June 3 Enfield. Also CAU
Lisa Langford Wolverhampton/Worcs	23:00
Vicky Lupton Sheffield Utd RWC/Sussex?	23:12
Perry Williams London Irish/Middlesex	24:00
Sylvia Black Birchfield H	24:10
Katherine Horwill Dudley & Stourbridge	25:00
Sarah Brown Steyning	25:31

Sheffield 17 Steyning 31 Dudley 35

1996 July 6 Stockport
Vicky Lupton Sheffield Utd RWC	23:05
Melanie Wright Nuneaton H	24:13
Karen Kneale Manx H	24:22
Sylvia Black Birchfield H	24:26
Katherine Horwill Dudley & Stourbridge	24:44
Lisa Crump Sheffield Utd RWC	25:27

Sheffield 14 Birchfield 23 Sheffield B 43

1997 June 7 Leicester – also CAU
Lisa Kehler Wolverhampton & B/Staffs	23:30
Karen Kneale Manx H/Lancashire	24:36
Catherine Charnock Barrow/Cumbria	24:52
Sara-Jane Cattermole Edinburgh/guest	26:57
Lynn Bradley Sheffield Utd RWC/Yorkshire	27:03
Sally Warren Steyning/Sussex	27:09
Brenda Lupton Sheffield Utd RWC/Yorkshire	27:32

Steyning 20 Sheffield 25 Birchfield 33

1998 June 6 Hove – also CAU
Kim Braznell Dudley & S/Warwicks	24:35
Debbie Wallen Aldershott, Farnham & D/Bucks	25:24
Amy Hales Steyning/Sussex	25:52
Sally Warren Steyning/Sussex	25:57
Nikki Huckerby Birchfield H/Warwicks	26:16
Sarah Bennett Birchfield H/Warwicks	26:23

Birchfield 15 Steyning 25 AFD

1999 June 5 Stockport
Catherine Charnock Barrow AC	23:09
Vicky Lupton Sheffield Utd RWC	23:23
Niobe Menendez Steyning	23:47
Lisa Crump Sheffield Utd RWC	24:28
Katherine Horwill Dudley & Stourbridge	24:37
Sharon Tonks Bromsgrove & Redditch	24:52

Sheffield 13 Dartford 29 Steyning 30

2000 Sep 9 London (VP)
Niobe Menendez Steyning	24:19
Sharon Tonks Bromsgrove & Redditch	24:59
Lisa Crump City of Sheffield	26:01
Nikki Huckerby Birchfield H	26:28
Jo Hesketh Steyning	27:05
Vicky White City of Sheffield	27:32

Sheffield 16 Steyning 16 Sheffield B 29

2001 Mar 25 Victoria Park, Hackney
Sharon Tonks Bromsgrove & Redditch	24:51
Estle Viljoen Hercules Wimbledon	25:10
Sophie Hales Steyning	25:46
Jo Hesketh Steyning	26:11
Nicky Phillips Cambridge H	27:18
Claire Reeves Dartford H	28:26

Dartford 281 Dartford B 261 Tonbridge 183

2002 July 6 Sutton Coldfield
Lisa Kehler Wolverhampton & Bilston	22:20
Sharon Tonks Bromsgrove & Redditch	23:53
Karen Ratcliffe Coventry Godiva H	25:27
Jo Hesketh Steyning	26:11
Ann Wheeler Nuneaton H	28:28

Nuneaton Dudley & Stourbridge

2003 Aug 9 Stockport
Katie Stones Kingston upon Hull	26:49
Katherine Horwill Dudley & Stourbridge	28:13
Ann Wheeler Nuneaton H	29:31
Julie Bellfield Dudley & Stourbridge	31:48
Carolyn Dyall Nuneaton H	32:45
Laura Malkin Nuneaton H	35:38

Dudley & Stourbridge 287 Nuneaton 314

2004 Apr 24 Sheffield
Rebecca Mersh City of Sheffield	26:09
Katherine Horwill Dudley & Stourbridge	26:17
Sharon Tonks Bromsgrove & Redditch	26:21
Lynn Bradley City of Sheffield	28:47
Helen Elleker City of Sheffield	29:38
Sheila Owen Tamworth	29:51

Sheffield 291 Dudley & Stourbridge 278

RWA 10 KILOMETRES ROAD CHAMPS
1981 June 20 York
Irene Bateman Havering AC	48:47
Elaine Cox Solihull AC	49:12
Jill Barrett Verlea	50:54
Gillian Edgar Lakeland AAC	53:02
Brenda Lupton Sheffield United H	53:04
Dawn Birbeck Leicester WC	53:26

Sheffield 7 Steyning 17 Epsom 28
1982 July 10 Leicester
Irene Bateman Havering AC	51:18
Brenda Lupton Sheffield United H	52:11
Virginia Birch Brighton & Hove	52:51
Helen Ringshaw Steyning	53:53
Gill Trower Steyning	54:22
Sarah Brown Steyning	56:17

Steyning 9 Sheffield 18 Bolehall 25
1983 June 18 Colchester
Virginia Birch Brighton & Hove	51:48
Brenda Lupton Sheffield United H	53:28
Helen Ringshaw Steyning	54:55
Beverley Allen Brighton & Hove	55:06
Liz Ryan Epsom & Ewell	55:19
Irene Corlett Boundary H	55:58

Sheffield 19 Boundary 25 Brighton & Hove 26
1984 July 14 Kendal
Virginia Birch Brighton & Hove	50:25
Lillian Millen Cumberland AC	50:51
Brenda Lupton Sheffield United H	51:29
Helen Elleker Sheffield United H	52:19
Lisa Langford Wolverhampton	52:51
Sarah Brown Steyning	54:44

Sheffield 20 Steyning 40 Dudley 48
1985 July 13 Corby
Susan Ashforth Sheffield United H	53:08
Beverley Allen Brighton & Hove	53:44
Lisa Simpson Mitcham AC	53:58
Sarah Brown Steyning	55:15
Brenda Lupton Sheffield United H	55:29
Lillian Millen Cumberland AC	55:59

Sheffield 21 Steyning 29 Bromsgrove 31
1986 July 12 Enfield
Helen Elleker Sheffield United H	49:27
Sarah Brown Steyning	50:27
Lisa Langford Wolverhampton	51:07
Betty Sworowski Sheffield Utd H	51:34
Virginia Birch Brighton & Hove	51:43
Brenda Lupton Sheffield United H	53:29

Sheffield 11 Steyning 18 Bromsgrove 41
1987 Mar 14 Ham, Richmond
Lisa Langford Wolverhampton	46:37
Nicky Jackson Trowbridge	48:33
Helen Elleker Sheffield Utd RWC	49:02
Victoria Lawrence Reading	49:10
Lisa Simpson Mitcham & Sutton	49:33
Sarah Brown Steyning	49:57

Sheffield 19 Steyning 39 AFD 70
1988 May 21 Hoddesdon
Julie Drake Brighton & Hove	49:26
Betty Sworowski Sheffield Utd RWC	49:39
Sian Spacey Belgrave H	52:27
Andrea Crofts Leicester WC	53:42
Sue Wilson Brighton & Hove	53:53
Brenda Lupton Sheffield Utd RWC	53:55

Brighton 17 Sheffield 24 Boundary 25

1989 Mar 11 Cardiff (31m short)
Betty Sworowski Sheffield Utd RWC	45:30
Lisa Langford Wolverhampton	45:55
Helen Elleker Sheffield Utd RWC	48:23
Sarah Brown Steyning	49:55
Andrea Crofts Leicester WC	51:29
Sue Wilson Brighton & Hove	51:43

Sheffield 16 Leicester 29 Steyning 40
1990 Mar 17 Southend
Betty Sworowski Sheffield Utd RWC	46:40
Helen Elleker Sheffield Utd RWC	49:24
Sylvia Black Birchfield H	50:27
Vicky Lupton Sheffield Utd RWC	51:12
Melanie Brookes Nuneaton H	51:46
Verity Larby Aldershot, Farnham & D	53:32

Sheffield 7 Leicester 32 AFD 39
1991 Mar 17 Sheffield
Betty Sworowski Sheffield Utd RWC	47:23
Helen Elleker Sheffield Utd RWC	47:26
Vicky Lupton Sheffield Utd RWC	47:30
Julie Drake Brighton & Hove	48:42
Verity Larby Aldershot, Farnham & D	49:27
Sylvia Black Birchfield H	49:35

Sheffield 6 Steyning 50 Belgrave 56
1992 May 9 Lancaster
Vicky Lupton Sheffield Utd RWC	46:04
Melanie Brookes Nuneaton H	48:18
Verity Larby Aldershot, Farnham & D	49:24
Karen Smith Coventry RWC	50:12
Carolyn Brown Manx H	51:10
Andrea Crofts Leicester WC	51:54

Dudley 32 Sheffield 32 Manx 36
1993 Mar 14 Cardiff also BAF
Verity Larby Aldershot, Farnham & D	47:51
Sylvia Black Birchfield H	49:47
Melanie Brookes Nuneaton H	50:52
Kim Baird Dudley & Stourbridge	51:46
Elaine Callinan Solihull AC	51:51
Sandra Brown Surrey WC	52:15

Dudley & St 25 Sheffield 48 Steyning 49
1994 Apr 16 Horsham
Karen Smith Coventry RWC	48:30
Melanie Brookes Nuneaton H	49:03
Elaine Callinan Solihull AC	51:16
Nicky Jackson Trowbridge	52:42
Sarah Brown Steyning	53:11
Sandra Brown Surrey WC	53:25

Steyning 40 Surrey WC 40
1995 Mar 25 Horsham also BAF
Vicky Lupton Sheffield Utd RWC	47:44
Lisa Langford Wolverhampton	48:04
Melanie Wright Nuneaton H	48:44
Elaine Callinan Solihull AC	50:05
Karen Kneale Manx H	51:23
Sylvia Black Birchfield H	51:31

Manx 25 Sheffield 25 Steyning 34
1996 Apr 21 Cardiff also BAF
Vicky Lupton Sheffield Utd RWC	47:48
Lisa Langford Wolverhampton	48:27
Melanie Wright Nuneaton H	50:24
Kim Baird Dudley & Stourbridge	50:45
Karen Kneale Manx H	50:50
Brenda Lupton Sheffield Utd RWC	52:57

Sheffield 18 Manx 27 Dudley & St 29
1997 Mar 15 Stoneleigh, Warwickshire also BAF
Sylvia Black Birchfield H	49:39

Vicky Lupton Sheffield Utd RWC	50:20	Fiona McGorum Leicester WC	58:32
Verity Snook Aldershot, Farnham & D	50:48	Ann Wheeler Nuneaton H	61:06
Lisa Crump Sheffield Utd RWC	51:39	Julie Bellfield Dudley & Stourbridge	63:38
Nikki Huckerby Birchfield H	52:28	Nuneaton 279 Leicester 278	
Liz Corran Manx H	52:38	**2006** Sep 10 Earls Colne	
Sheffield 14 Birchfield 17 Steyning 39		Johanna Jackson Redcar	51:24
1998 Mar 21 Leicester also BAF		Sophie Hales Steyning	55:00
Lisa Kehler Wolverhampton	47:10	Fiona McGorum Leicester WC	57:19
Vicky Lupton Sheffield Utd RWC	48:38	Fiona Bishop Aldershot, Farnham & D	64:41
Kim Braznell Dudley & Stourbridge	49:27	Karen Davies Birchfield H	65:50
Lisa Crump Sheffield Utd RWC	50:31	Jill Eve Leicester WC	66:53
Nikki Huckerby Birchfield H	51:07	Leicester 282	
Karen Kneale Manx H	51:25	**2007** Sep 9 Earls Colne	
Sheffield 20 Birchfield 28 Manx 37		Johanna Jackson Redcar	47:49
1999 Sep 5 Leicester		Lisa Kehler Wolverhampton & Bilston	48:15
Catherine Charnock Dudley & Stourbridge	47:51	Anne Loughnane IRL	50:54
Katherine Horwill Dudley & Stourbridge	53:06	Estle Viljoen Hercules Wimbledon	52:03
Nikki Huckerby Birchfield H	53:30	Fiona McGorum Leicester WC	56:01
Sally Warren Birchfield H	53:55	Diane Bradley Tonbridge	57:56
Jo Hesketh Steyning	57:15	Leicester	
Cath Reader Ryston Runners	61:11	**2008** Sep 6 London (LV) RWA/UK	
Dudley & Stourbridge 11		Johanna Jackson Redcar	46:20
2000 May 6 Dartford		Chelsea O'Rawe-Hobbs Blackheath & B	56:32
Sharon Tonks Bromsgrove & Redditch	52:00	Diane Bradley Tonbridge	56:34
Sally Warren Steyning	52:37	Helen Middleton Leicester	58:33
Nikki Huckerby Birchfield H	54:15	Anne Belchambers Hillingdon	62:51
Katherine Horwill Dudley & Stourbridge	54:25	Jacqueline Cox Loughton	65:41
Lisa Crump City of Sheffield	54:56	Leicester	
Jo Hesketh Steyning	55:42	**2009** Sep 5 Leicester RWA/UK	
Steyning 27 Sheffield 28		Johanna Jackson Redcar	46:23
2001 May 5 Birmingham		Estle Viljoen Hercules Wimbledon	54:11
Niobe Menendez Steyning	49:19	Diane Bradley Tonbridge	54:58
Sara Jane Cattermole Dartford H	50:42	Fiona McGorum Leicester WC	55:25
Wendy Bennett Worcester H	50:45	Kelsey Howard Tonbridge	55:57
Estle Viljoen Hercules Wimbledon	51:41	Ann Wheeler Nuneaton	58:45
Catherine Charnock Dudley & Stourbridge	52:48	Tonbridge Leicester Redcar	
Miranda Heathcote Tonbridge AC	53:11	**2010** Sep 11 Coventry RWA/UK	
Steyning 285 Dudley 272 Dartford 189		Johanna Jackson Middlesbrough & C	45:31
2002 Aug 31 Leicester		Lisa Kehler Wolverhampton & B	48:24
Estle Viljoen Hercules Wimbledon	49:06	Fiona McGorum Leicester	53:23
Sharon Tonks Bromsgrove & Redditch	52:07	Emma Doherty North Belfast H	53:55
Kim Braznell Dudley & Stourbridge	53:18	Heather Lewis Pembroke	54:34
Sophie Hales Steyning	53:59	Lauren Whelan Manx H	54:44
Katherine Horwill Dudley & Stourbridge	54:01	Redcar Tonbridge Leicester	
Jo Hesketh Steyning	54:54	**2011** Sep 11 London (Victoria Park) RWA/UK & CAU	
Steyning		Johanna Jackson Middlesbrough & C /N.East	44:59
2003 June 14 Sutton Coldfield		Nerinda Aidietyte Ilford/LTU /Essex	46:29
Lisa Kehler Wolverhampton	49:44	Fiona McGorum Leicester /Leicestershire	58:42
Estle Viljoen Hercules Wimbledon	50:46	Helen Middleton Enfield & Ha/Bedfordshire	59:24
Wendy Bennett Worcester H	52:25	Enfield & Haringey	
Jo Hesketh Steyning	53:50	**2012** Sep 2 Hillingdon RWA/UK	
Sally Warren Steyning	57:26	Johanna Jackson Middlesbrough & C	46:52
Jenny Gagg Kingston upon Hull	57:50	Heather Lewis Pembroke	50:25
Dudley 270 Steyning 191		Grazina Narviliene Ealing S&M/LTU	55:20
2004 June 12 Sutton Coldfield		Gemma Bridge Radley	55:35
Sophie Hales Steyning	54:37	Fiona McGorum Leicester	55:35
Katherine Horwill Dudley & Stourbridge	55:00	Alana Barber NZL	56:46
Jo Hesketh Steyning	55:15	Leicester RWC Enfield & Haringey	
Johanna Jackson Redcar RWC	56:25	**2013** Jul 20 Hayes RWA/UK	
Helen Elleker City of Sheffield	61:05	Michelle Turner Northern (IoM)	50:40
Julie Bellfield Dudley & Stourbridge	64:41	Heather Lewis Pembroke	51:46
Dudley 285 Steyning 197		Alana Barber Hyde Park H/NZL	55:08
2005 June 4 Sheffield		Jasmine Nicholls OwlsAC Leicester	55:54
Johanna Jackson Redcar RWC	48:37	Lauren Whelan Manx H	56:47
Katie Stones Kingston upon Hull	51:41	Brenda Gannon Hyde Park H	58:55
Rebecca Mersh City of Sheffield	53:11	Hyde Park H Belgrave	

RWA 15 KILOMETRES ROAD
1987 July 11 Beighton, Sheffield
Helen Elleker Sheffield Utd RWC	1:17:29
Sarah Brown Steyning	1:17:35
Susan Gibson Sheffield Utd RWC	1:22:58
Gill Trower Steyning	1:24:06
Brenda Lupton Sheffield Utd RWC	1:24:59
Gillian Brackpool Woking AC	1:28:38

Sheffield 9 Steyning 15 Dudley 45
1988 Mar 12 Dronfield, Derbyshire
Betty Sworowski Sheffield Utd	1:19:03
Helen Elleker Sheffield Utd RWC	1:22:37
Sue Wilson Brighton & Hove	1:23:12
Melanie Brookes Nuneaton H	1:24:18
Gillian Brackpool Belgrave H	1:25:12
Brenda Lupton Sheffield Utd RWC	1:25:21

Sheffield 9 Brighton & H 18 Steyning 39
1989 May 13 Doncaster
Vicky Lupton Sheffield Utd RWC	1:22:00
Sian Spacey Belgrave H/CAN	1:22:14
Brenda Lupton Sheffield Utd RWC	1:22:39
Gill Trower Steyning	1:23:51
Melanie Brookes Nuneaton H	1:24:42
Karen Smith Coventry RWC	1:26:27

Sheffield 19 Steyning 21 Belgrave 24
1990 May 12 Leicester
Betty Sworowski Sheffield Utd	1:12:36
Helen Elleker Sheffield Utd RWC	1:18:01
Vicky Lupton Sheffield Utd RWC	1:18:02
Sarah Brown Steyning	1:18:37
Melanie Brookes Nuneaton H	1:19:38
Gill Trower Steyning	1:21:51

Sheffield 6 Steyning 22 Dudley 35
1991 May 11 London (VP)
1= Vicky Lupton Sheffield Utd RWC	1:12:32
1= Betty Sworowski Sheffield Utd	1:12:32
Helen Elleker Sheffield Utd RWC	1:15:17
Sarah Brown Steyning	1:17:56
Melanie Brookes Nuneaton H	1:20:13
Andrea Crofts Leicester WC	1:21:24

Sheffield 6 Steyning 22 Leicester 41
1992 Mar 21 Birmingham
Melanie Brookes Nuneaton H	1:16:17
Sandra Brown Surrey WC	1:20:24
Kim Baird Dudley & Stourbridge	1:22:35
Katherine Horwill Dudley & Stourbridge	1:25:07
Helen Sharratt Southend on Sea	1:25:15
Gill Trower Steyning	1:25:49

Dudley 16

RWA 10 MILES ROAD
1993 May 9 Sheffield
Vicky Lupton Sheffield Utd RWC	1:21:19
Melanie Brookes Nuneaton H	1:24:14
Kim Baird Dudley & Stourbridge	1:27:31
Brenda Lupton Sheffield Utd RWC	1:31:20
Helen Sharratt Southend on Sea	1:31:21
Katherine Horwill Dudley & Stourbridge	1:33:36

Sheffield 13 Dudley 18 Manx 29
1994 July 9 London (VP)
Cath Reader Ryston Runners	1:30:37
Helen Sharratt Southend on Sea	1:33:13
Jeanette Bleach Steyning	1:43:32
Mary Worth Steyning	1:47:50
Pam Phillips Ilford	1:47:50
M.Parker Road Hoggs	1:48:02

Steyning 16

1995 July 22 Sutton Coldfield
Vicky Lupton Sheffield Utd RWC	1:21:23
Sylvia Black Birchfield H	1:26:23
Brenda Lupton Sheffield Utd RWC	1:30:14
Gill Watson Sheffield Utd RWC	1:31:05
Claire Childs Coventry RWC	1:31:54
Lynn Bradley Sheffield Utd RWC	1:35:01

Sheffield 8
1996 Mar 23 Sutton Coldfield
Vicky Lupton Sheffield Utd RWC	1:22:11
Elaine Callinan Solihull & Small Heath	1:25:27
Claire Childs Coventry RWC	1:29:36
Brenda Lupton Sheffield Utd RWC	1:30:41
Nina Howley Sheffield Utd RWC	1:31:31
Lisa Crump Sheffield Utd RWC	1:41:24

Sheffield 10
1997 May 17 London (VP)
Vicky Lupton Sheffield Utd RWC	1:25:11
Lynn Bradley Sheffield Utd RWC	1:35:35
Cath Reader Ryston Runners	1:37:53
Brenda Lupton Sheffield Utd RWC	1:40:16
Ann Lewis Aldershot, Farnham & D	1:41:11
Gill Trower Steyning	1:43:40

Sheffield 7 Steyning 22
1998 May 16 Leicester
Vicky Lupton Sheffield Utd RWC	1:21:15
Lisa Crump Sheffield Utd RWC	1:26:21
Catherine Charnock Barrow	1:29:55
Melanie Wright Nuneaton H	1:34:32
Karen Ratcliffe Coventry RWC	1:35:08
Kirsty Coleman Steyning	1:37:24

Sheffield 11 Steyning 25
2008 Feb 16 London (LV)
Anne Belchambers Hillingdon	1:37:37
Helen Middleton Leicester	1:37:51
Maureen Noel Belgrave H	1:38:31
Fiona Bishop Aldershot F&D	1:46:06
Susan Rey Leicester	1:48:10
Diana Braverman Enfield & Haringey	1:52:40

1. Leicester, 2. Enfield & Haringey
2009 Feb 21 London (LV)
Lisa Kehler Wolverhampton & Bilston	1:22:27
Fiona McGorum Leicester WC	1:28:37
Diane Bradley Tonbridge	1:30:04
Helen Middleton Enfield & Haringey	1:35:23
Chelsea O'Rawe-Hobbs Blackheath & Br	1:37:41
Angela-Maria Paddick Redcar	1:38:54

1. Redcar, 2. Leicester, 3. Enfield & Haringey
2010 Feb 20 London LV
Lisa Kehler Wolverhampton & Bilston	1:23:14
Diane Bradley Tonbridge	1:31:58
Helen Middleton Enfield & Haringey	1:33:33
Karen Wears Redcar	1:35:50
Angela-Marie Paddick Redcar	1:41:02
Stephanie Rukin Tonbridge	1:41:39

1. Redcar, 2. Tonbridge, 3. Leicester
2011 Mar 6 Coventry
Neringa Aidietyte Ilford/LTU	1:16:19
Diane Bradley Tonbridge	1:29:38
Fiona McGorum Leicester WC	1:34:20
Karen Wears Redcar	1:34:54
Ann Wheeler Leicester WC	1:39:52

1. Leicester, 2. Redcar
2012 Mar 4 Coventry
Heather Lewis Pembroke	1:25:03
Rebecca Collins Medway & Maidstone	1:32:44

Diane Bradley Tonbridge	1:34:48	Mary Wallen Aldershot, Farnham & D	2:04:10
Helen Middleton Enfield & Haringey	1:37:28	Jo Hesketh Steyning	2:06:48
Maureen Noel Belgrave H	1:40:07	Gill Trower Steyning	2:10:27
Judy Howard Abingdon	1:41:41	Jeanette Bleach Steyning	2:17:53

1. Enfield & Haringey, 2. Abingdon
Steyning 15
2013 Mar 10 London (VP)   **1999** Mar 20 Leamington Spa

Neringa Aidietyte Ilford/LTU	1:19:43	Niobe Menendez Steyning	1:40:12
Lauren Whelan Manx	1:28:06	Kim Braznell Dudley & Stourbridge	1:44:29
Rebecca Collins Medway & Maidstone	1:31:42	Lisa Crump Sheffield Utd RWC	1:47:47
Fiona McGorum Leicester WC	1:39:30	Vicky Lupton Sheffield Utd RWC	1:47:57
Suzanne Beardsmore Abingdon	1:42:16	Elaine Callinan Solihull & Small Heath	1:48:50
Geraldine Legon Bexley	1:58:39	Nikki Huckerby Birchfield H	1:50:51

2014 Mar 9 London (VP)
Sheffield 21 Steyning 22

Grazina Narvileine Ealing S & M/LTU	1:32:28	**2000** Mar 11 Nottingham	
Fiona McGorum Leicester WC	1:33:38	Lisa Kehler Wolverhampton & Bilston	1:39:28
Sandra Brown Surrey WC	1:38:19	Niobe Menendez Steyning	1:44:55
Penelope Cummings Aldershot F & D	1:44:23	Kim Braznell Dudley & Stourbridge	1:48:14
Maureen Noel Belgrave H	1:48:10	Sharon Tonks Bromsgrove & Redditch	1:49:51

1. Belgrave H
Sally Warren Birchfield H   1:53:17

RWA 20 KILOMETRES ROAD
Katherine Horwill Dudley & Stourbridge   1:54:46
1985 Apr 14 Bournemouth
Dudley 23 Steyning 24 Manx 25

Lillian Millen Lakeland	1:46:32	**2001** July 7 Sheffield	
Beverley Allen Brighton & Hove	1:59:35	Sheila Bull Midland Veterans AC	2:18:53

1993 Oct 16 Horsham   **2002** Mar 3 East Molesey

Elaine Callinan Solihull AC	1:45:11	Lisa Kehler Wolverhampton & Bilston	1:43:08
Vicky Lupton Sheffield Utd RWC	1:47:11	Sharon Tonks Bromsgrove & Redditch	1:43:29
Julie Drake Brighton & Hove	1:48:46	Kim Braznell Dudley & Stourbridge	1:49:44
Helen Sharratt Southend on Sea	1:49:18	Karen Ratcliffe Coventry Godiva H	1:56:27
Kim Baird Dudley & Stourbridge	1:51:55	Marie Latham Manx H	2:01:24
Brenda Lupton Sheffield Utd RWC	2:00:56	Dudley & Stourbridge 284	

Sheffield 15 Dudley 26 Steyning 51
2003 July 5 Sheriff Hutton, Yorkshire
1994 Sep 3 Holmewood, Derbyshire
Jo Hesketh Steyning   1:47:50

Vicky Lupton Sheffield Utd RWC	1:44:48	**2004** Mar 20 Leamington Spa	
Kim Baird Dudley & Stourbridge	1:50:21	Niobe Menendez Steyning	1:50:59
Sarah Brown Steyning	1:51:38	Jo Hesketh Steyning	1:51:36
Sandra Brown Surrey WC	1:52:04	Marie Latham Manx H	1:55:12
Brenda Lupton Sheffield Utd RWC	2:02:28	Fiona Bishop Aldershot, Farnham & D	2:01:57
Helen Battle Bolton United H	2:12:57	Steyning	

Sheffield 14
2005 Sep 4 Earls Colne,Essex
1995 July 1 Stockport also BAF
Lyn Ventris AUS (guest)   1:45:23

Vicky Lupton Sheffield Utd RWC	1:42:47	1. Katie Stones Kingston upon Hull	1:46:48
Elaine Callinan Solihull & Small Heath	1:46:31	Estle Viljoen Belgrave H	1:47:20
Brenda Lupton Sheffield Utd RWC	1:53:14	Johanna Jackson Redcar RWC	1:48:41
Liz Corran Manx H	1:55:10	Lisa Kehler Wolverhampton & Bilston	1:52:33
Sarah Brown Steyning	1:57:07	Niobe Menendez Steyning	1:56:01
Helen Battle Bolton United H	2:07:42	**2006** Sep 10 Earls Colne	

Sheffield 11 Steyning 22
Johanna Jackson Redcar RWC   1:43:37
1996 Sep 7 Horsham also BAF
Karen Davies Birchfield   2:13:56

Vicky Lupton Sheffield Utd RWC	1:46:43	Susan Rey Leicester	2:24:42
Sandra Brown Surrey WC	1:48:46	**2007** Apr 11 Coventry	
Verity Snook Aldershot, Farnham & D	1:54:15	Johanna Jackson Redcar RWC	1:38:34
Brenda Lupton Sheffield Utd RWC	1:54:33	Anne Belchambers Steyning	2:12:54
Lynn Bradley Sheffield Utd RWC	1:55:00	Julie Bellfield Dudley & Stourbridge	2:18:59
Jill Green London Vidarians WC	2:07:12	Sue Ray Leicester WC	2:24:42

Sheffield 10 Surrey WC 23 Steyning 26
2008 Apr 6 Earls Colne
1997 Aug 30 Stockport also BAF
Diane Bradley Tonbridge   1:57:18

Sylvia Black Birchfield	1:45:48	Fiona McGorum Leicester WC	1:58:53
Kim Braznell Dudley & Stourbridge	1:46:02	Maureen Noel Belgrave H	2:05:20
Cal Partington Manx H	1:48:46	Anne Belchambers Hillingdon	2:09:16
Lynn Bradley Sheffield Utd RWC	1:55:31	Helen Middleton Leicester	2:10:10
Brenda Lupton Sheffield Utd RWC	2:00:50	Fiona Bishop Aldershot	2:17:58
Gill Trower Steyning	2:03:41	Leicester	

Steyning 21
2009 Apr 12 Shrewsbury
1998 Aug 29 Holmewood, Derbyshire also BAF
Johanna Jackson Redcar RWC   1:35:57

Vicky Lupton Sheffield Utd RWC	1:44:35	Lisa Kehler Wolverhampton & Bilston	1:44:18
Catherine Charnock Barrow & Fylde	1:45:24	Diane Bradley Tonbridge	1:53:39

Helen Middleton Enfield & Haringey	2:05:31
Anne Belchambers Steyning	2:11:49
Fiona Bishop Woking	2:16:07
Leicester	
2010 Apr 11 London (VP)	
Johanna Jackson Middlesbrough & C	1:39:14
Niobe Menendez Steyning	1:45:45
Fiona McGorum Leicester WC	1:53:06
Diane Bradley Tonbridge AC	1:54:51
Helen Middleton Enfield & Haringey	2:00:06
Maureen Noel Belgrave H	2:05:11
Steyning 191 Leicester 187	
2011 May 1 Hainault	
Neringa Aidietyte Ilford/LTU (guest)	1:34:26
1. Jo Hesketh Steyning	1:53:37
Julie Drake Arena 80	1:55:51
Diane Bradley Tonbridge AC	1:56:13
Karen Wears Redcar	1:58:43
Maureen Noel Belgrave H	2:04:27
2012 Apr 14 Redbridge	
Neringa Aidietyte Ilford/LTU	1:38:21
Rebecca Collins Medway & Maidstone	1:57:34
Sandra Brown Surrey WC	1:59:37
Helen Middleton Enfield & H	2:04:47
Maureen Noel Belgrave H	2:07:03
Cath Duhig Colchester H	2:09:22
Enfield & Haringey	
2013 Apr 28 Coventry	
Bethan Davies Cardiff	1:44:15
Heather Lewis Pembroke	1:47:51
Grazina Narviliene Ealing S&M/LTU	1:50:41
Michelle Turner Northern (IOM)	1:51:26
Rebecca Collins Medway & Maidstone	1:54:49
Brenda Gannon Hyde Park H	2:00:17
Aldershot, Farnham & D	
2014 Apr 6 Sheffield	
Michelle Turner Northern (IOM)	1:50:37
Alana Barber Hyde Park H/NZL	1:55:21
Sandra Brown Surrey WC	1:59:36
Angela Martin Paddock Wood	2:22:34
Sandra Campbell Surrey WC	2:38:30

RWA 50 KILOMETRES ROAD

2004 Sep 26 Earls Colne UKA	
Kim Howard Southend	5:59.22
2005 Sep 4 Earls Colne UKA	
Maureen Noel Belgrave H	6:02:53
Kim Howard Southend	6:10:00
2006 Sep 10 Earls Colne	
Cath Duhig Loughton	6:09:38
2007 Jul 28 London (BP)	
Maureen Noel Belgrave H	5:52:02
Cath Duhig Loughton	6:29:40
Susan Rey Leicester	6:32:17
Karen Davies Birchfield H	6:59:17
2008 Apr 27 Stockton-on-Tees	
Marie Jackson Manx H	5:27:32
Maureen Noel Belgrave H	5:44:08
Cath Duhig Loughton	6:02:08
Susan Rey Leicester	6:13:08
Karen Davies Birchfield	45.32km in 6 12 27
2009 Apr 26 Stockton	
Maureen Noel Belgrave H	6:07:26
Sue Rey Leicester WC	45.7k in 6:09:13
2010 Oct 17 Northampton	
Maureen Noel Belgrave H	5:49:55
Helen Starling Redcar	6:05:10

2011 Oct 2 Northampton	
Maureen Noel Belgrave H	5:55:31
2012 Sep 22 Colchester	
Maureen Noel Belgrave H	6:01:12
Angie Alstrachen Enfield & Haringey	6:22:17
Karen Davies Birchfield H	6:43:25
2013 Jul 27 Coventry	
Sandra Brown Surrey WC	5:29:04
Maureen Noel Belgrave H	5:59:44

RWA 100 MILES

1992 July 31-Aug 1 Hungarton, Leics	
Sandra Brown Surrey WC	18:50:29
1993 Aug 21/22 London (BP)	
Sandra Brown Surrey WC	20:09:05
Lillian Millen Lakeland AC	20:13:15
Jill Green London Vidarians WC	22:59:40
Christine Gray Surrey WC	23:36:34
1994 July 30 Hungarton, Leics	
Sandra Brown Surrey WC	19:09:17
1995 Aug 5/6 London (BP)	
Sandra Brown Surrey WC	21:37:21
Jill Green London Vidarians	22:32:35
Kathy Crilley Surrey WC	23:05:21
Pam Ficken Surrey WC	23:09:53
Maureen Cox Manx H	23:36:43
Christine Gray London Vidarians WC	23:44:53
Surrey 8	
1996 Aug 3/4 Colchester	
Sandra Brown Surrey WC	19:42.53
Kathy Crilley Surrey WC	23:31:43
Pam Ficken Surrey WC	90 miles 22:47:00
1997 Jul 19/20 Ware (track)	
Sandra Brown Surrey WC	19:27:15
Jill Green London Vidarians	22:17:07
1998 not held	
1999 Aug 15 London (BP)	
Sandra Brown Surrey WC	20:01:49
Jill Green London Vidarians	23:02:25
Sue Clements London Vidarians	23:39:38
2001 Aug 4/5 Colchester	
Sandra Brown Surrey WC	20:36:45
Kathy Crilley Surrey WC	88mls 450y 23:05:21
Surrey 198	
2003 July 26/27 Newmarket	
Sandra Brown Surrey WC	20:23:25
Cath Duhig Loughton AC	21:27:43
Hazel Fairhurst Lancashire WC	22:57:18
Wendy Watson Long Distance Walkers Ass.	23:50:11
2004 Aug 21/22 Colchester	
Sandra Brown Surrey WC	19:17:28
Sharon Gayter Redcar RWC	22:41:08
Sue Clements London Vidarians 98mls 15y	23:37:11
Sereena Queeney unattached 77mls 87y	23:26:27
2005 July 30/31 King's Lynn	
Sandra Brown Surrey WC	19:25:07
Cath Duhig Loughton AC	22:09:40
Kim Howard Southend on Sea	22:23:39
Hazel Fairhurst Lancashire WC	22:35:37
Sereena Queeney Enfield & H 88 miles	23:31:28
2006 Aug 19/20 Douglas IOM	
Sandra Brown Surrey WC	19:28:38
Sue Biggart Isle of Man	20:08:10
Catherine Lowey	20:50:26
Anne Oates	23:15:02
Jackie Campbell	23:19:26
Terri Salmon	23:19:26

2007 Aug 28/29 London (BP)
Cath Duhig Loughton AC   23:28:11
Jill Green London Vidarians WC   23:49:42
2008 Aug 16/17 Milton Keynes (track)
Sandra Brown Surrey WC   19:59:29
2009 July 11/12 Newmarket
Sandra Brown Surrey WC   19:57:24
2010 Aug 7/8 Colchester
Sandra Brown Surrey WC   20:23:30
Bernie Ball Manx H   22:56:03
Sereena Queeney Enfield & H   92mls 61y   23:33:50
2011 July 2/3 Lingfield Park
Sandra Brown Surrey WC   20:18:23
Wendy Thurrell LD Walkers Assoc   21:33:35
Tara Williams LD Walkers Assoc   21:33:35
Sarah Lightman Leicester WC   22:55:58
Suzanne Beardsmore unattached   23:23:43

Angie Alstrachen Enfield & Haringey   23:42:48
Kim Howard Southend   22:23:39
2012 Sep 22/23 Colchester
Sandra Brown Surrey WC   20:45:03
Susan Beardsmore Abingdon Amblers   21:15:43
Caroline Mestdagh NED   21:37:44

RWA 24 HOURS

2000 Aug 12/13 Newmarket
Sandra Brown Surrey WC   183.458k
Jill Green London Vidarians   167.365k
Marie Latham Manx H   160.928k
2002 Aug 10/11 Blackpool (track)
Sandra Brown Surrey WC   186.324k
Jill Green London Vidarians   165.830k
Sue Clements London Vidarians   164.012k
London Vidarians

INTER COUNTIES (CAU) CHAMPIONSHIPS

3 MILES TEAM TRACK
1925 Aug 22 London (SB)
Reg Goodwin Surrey   21:48.4
Wilf Cowley Middlesex
C.W.Cater Essex
Essex 13 Surrey 17 Middlesex 18
1926 July 17 London (SB)
Alf Pope Essex   22:35.4
Wilf Cowley Middlesex   22:45.0
E.Sharman Sussex   22:58.4
dq Lloyd Johnson Leics   (22:46.2)
1927 Aug 13 London (SB)
Albert Fletcher Surrey   22:11.4
Alf Pope Essex
Wilf Cowley Middlesex
Essex 12 Middlesex & Kent 26
1928 ?
1929 Aug 17 London (SB)
Cecil Hyde Middlesex   21:53.6
Essex 13

3 MILES TRACK
1930 Aug 23 London (SB)
Albert Cooper Essex   21:54.6
Alf Pope Essex   22:08.6
Cecil Hyde Middlesex   22:19.0

2 MILES TRACK
1932 July 16 London (WC)
Bert Cooper & Alf Pope
  Essex   14:04.8
Essex 11 Surrey 12 Kent 28
1933 ----
1934 Sept 1 Loughborough
Johnny Johnson Middx   14:57.4
L.Hancock Surrey
T.Wiseman Devon
1935 Aug 31 Loughborough
Bert Cooper Essex   14:44.6
1936?
Fred Redman Middlesex
Harry Churcher Surrey
Albert Staines Leics
T.Wiseman Devon
C.North Bedfordshire
1936 June 27 Plymouth
Bert Cooper Essex   13:53.9
Alf Harley Middlesex
T.Wiseman Devon

1937 May 17 London (WC)
Bert Cooper Essex   13:51.6
Harry Churcher Surrey
Fred Redman Middlesex
1938 June 6 London (WC)
Don Brown Surrey   14 15.6
Bert Cooper Essex
Leslie Dickinson Lancs
W.Thompson Hampshire
E.Upton Sussex
Dai Richards Glamorgan & Mon
1939 London (WC)
Harry Churcher Surrey   14 11.0
Bert Cooper Essex
Eddie Staker Middlesex
Leslie Dickinson Lancashire
Gwyn Rees Warwicks
A.J.Slater Sussex
1947 Aug 4 London (WC)
Bill Wilson Bedfordshire   14:34.8
Bill Leveridge Essex   14:37.0
Allan Furniss Yorkshire   14:43.0
Dave McMullen Surrey
Charlie Brown Middlesex
T.Owens Lancashire
1948 May 17 London (WC)
Jim Morris Middlesex   14:27.0
Ron West Kent
Joe Coleman Surrey
Frederick Howarch Bucks
D.Cox Northumb. & Durham
John Copperwheat Bedfordshire
1949 July 2 London (WC)
Jim Morris Middlesex   14:05.4
Allan Furniss Yorkshire   14:49.0
Harry Churcher Surrey   14:53.0
1950 May 29 London (WC)
Harry Churcher Surrey   14:21.0
John Proctor Yorkshire   14:40.6
John Copperwheat Beds   14:48.6
A.Jackson N&D
Bill Leveridge Essex   14:52.7
James McCormick Cheshire
1951 May 14 London (WC)
George Coleman Beds   14:16.2
Harry Churcher Surrey   14:20.2
Gerald Gregory Somerset   14:26.2

Donald Warren Cheshire   14:52.6
Dan Dumican Dorset   15:15.6
Henry Harwood Lancs   15:18.0
1952 June 2 London (WC)
Bob Goodall Essex   15:02.4
Brian Shepherd Surrey   15:08.8
Reg Harrold Wiltshire   15:09.2
Terry Whitlock Middlesex
Ken Smith Kent
Henry Harwood Lancashire
1953 May 25 London (WC)
Roland Hardy Derby   14:27.2
Bob Richards Kent   14:42.8
Reg Harrold Wiltshire   15:04.2
Bob Goodall Essex
Gerald Warr Huntingdonshire
F.Ellis Leicestershire
1954 June 7 London (WC)
George Coleman Beds   14:05.2
Alf Poole Worcs
George Williams Surrey
1955 May 30 London (WC)
Joseph Barraclough Lancs   14:19.6
Alf Poole Worcs   14:27.6
Gareth Howell Glamorgan   14:38.0
George Coleman Beds   14:52.2
Bob Goodall Essex   14:56.8
Alec Mash Middlesex   14:59.4
1956 May 21 London (WC)
Gareth Howell Glamorgan   14:12.0
Alf Poole Worcs   14:23.0
George Williams Surrey   14:51.6
Charles Colman Lancs   15:00.2
Ron Davies Essex   15:04.2
Ron West Kent   15:05.8
1957 June 10 London (WC)
Stan Vickers Kent   14:08.4
Colin Williams Essex   14:15.4
George Williams Surrey   14:42.4
Alf Poole Worcs   14:45.6
Ted Smith Middlesex   15:04.6
Ken Harding Staffs   15:08.2
1958 May 26 London (WC)
Stan Vickers Kent   13:48.0
Ken Matthews Warwicks   13:54.6
Colin Williams Essex   14:22.0
George Williams Surrey   14:45.8

80

Alf Poole Worcs	14:47.8
Abe Rozentals Notts	14:49.8

1959 May 18 London (WC)

Ken Matthews Warwicks	13:37.2
Stan Vickers Kent	14:01.0
George Williams Surrey	14:17.4
Robert Goodall Essex	14:34.2
John Northcott Middlesex	14:38.6
Alf Poole Worcs	14:53.0

1960 June 6 London (WC)

Ken Matthews Warwicks	13:46.2
Robert Goodall Essex	14:11.4
George Williams Surrey	14:15.0
Arthur Thomson Middlesex	14:37.8
Douglas Greasley Derby	15:10.0

1961 May 22 London (WC)

Ken Matthews Warwicks	13:33.8
Colin Williams Essex	14:12.4
Ray Middleton Surrey	14:32.0
John Godbeer Kent	14:34.0
John Northcott Middlesex	14:45.0
Ron Wallwork Lancashire	14:47.0

1962 June 11 London (WC)

Ken Matthews Warwicks	13:35.0
Colin Williams Essex	13:53.4
George Williams Surrey	13:57.6
Bob Clark Kent	14:17.6
Arthur Thomson Middx	14:18.2
John Paddick Staffs	14:18.6

1963 June 3 London (WC)

Ken Matthews Warwicks	13:35.6
Paul Nihill Surrey	13:50.0
Colin Williams Essex	14:09.4
John Paddick Staffs	14:22.8
Eric Hall Cheshire	14:24.8
Arthur Thomson Middx	14:24.8

1964 May 18 London (WC)

Ken Matthews Warwicks	13:36.2
Paul Nihill Surrey	13:45.2
John Paddick Staffs	14:15.6
Malcolm Tolley Yorkshire	14:27.0
Shaun Lightman Middx	14:36.2
Eric Hall Cheshire	14:41.4

1965 June 7 London (WC)

Paul Nihill Surrey	13:24.0
Roy Hart Glamorgan	14:13.0
Malcolm Tolley Yorkshire	14:15.0
George Chaplin Warwicks	14:22.6
Neil Munro Hampshire	14:24.8
Ken Easlea Middlesex	14:25.6

1966 May 30 London (WC)

Malcolm Tolley Yorkshire	13:45.8
Ron Wallwork Lancashire	13:50.0
Paul Nihill Surrey	14:01.0
John Webb Essex	14:08.0
Norman Read Sussex	14:24.8
Roy Hart Glamorgan	14:29.0

1967 May 29 London (WC)

Arthur Jones Sussex	13:47.0
Ron Wallwork Lancashire	13:49.6
Bob Hughes Worcs	14:07.6
Geoff Toone Leics	14:08.0
Malcom Tolley Yorkshire	14:17.0
Ken Easlea Middlesex	14:18.8

1968 June 3 London (CP)

Bob Hughes Worcs	13:44.4
Arthur Jones Sussex	13:51.0
Ron Wallwork Lancashire	14:06.6
Ken Easlea Middlesex	14:26.6
Ken Bobbett Glamorgan	14:35.2
Geoff Toone Leics	14:35.8

3000 METRES TRACK

1969 May 26 London (WC)

Bob Hughes Worcs	12:46.6
Roger Mills Essex	13:02.0
Alex Ross Middlesex	13:14.6
Bob Clark Kent	13:19.4
Roy Thorpe Yorkshire	13:22.0
Len Duquemin Hampshire	13:23.6

1970 May 25 Leicester

Bob Hughes Worcs	12:25.2
Olly Caviglioli Essex	12:27.4
Wilf Wesch Surrey/FRG	12:38.2
Shaun Lightman Middx	13:00.4
Geoff Toone Leics	13:03.6
Tony Taylor Lancashire	13:21.0

1971 May 30 Leicester

Bob Hughes Worcs	12:15.6
Geoff Toone Leics	12:30.2
Wilf Wesch Surrey/FRG	12:33.4
Ron Wallwork Lancashire	13:03.6
Guy Goodair Yorkshire	13:35.6
Alan Buchanan Sussex	13:35.6

1972 May 29 Leicester

Paul Nihill Surrey	12:13.4
Don Cox Essex	12:48.2
Geoff Toone Leics	12:50.8
Ron Wallwork Lancashire	12:58.4
Bob Hughes Worcs	13:12.0
Mike Holmes Yorkshire	13:20.2

1973 May 28 Warley

Roger Mills Essex	12:35.0
Alan Smallwood Worc/Glos	12:56.8
Brian Adams E.Mids	13:01.8
Mike Holmes Yorkshire	13:12.2
Peter Selby Surrey	13:45.8
Ken Harding Cheshire	13:46.4

1974 May 27 London (CP)

Brian Adams E.Mids	12:29.14
Paul Nihill Surrey	12:34.08
Shaun Lightman Middx	12:55.2
Ken Carter Kent	12:57.6
Tony Taylor Lancashire	13:14.0
Dave Stevens Hants & Sx	13:18.0

1975 May 26 London (CP)

Shaun Lightman Middx	12:47.8
Don Cox Essex	12:50.4
Barry Lines Yorkshire	13:13.2
Dave Stevens Hants & Sx	13:13.8
Carl Lawton Surrey	13:24.8
Roger Michel Kent	13:27.0

1976 May 31 London (CP)

Brian Adams E.Mids	12:09.75
Roger Mills Essex	12:18.28
Shaun Lightman Middx	12:37.72
Carl Lawton Surrey	12:41.70
Chris Harvey Cheshire	13:11.10
Barry Lines Yorks	13:11.52

1977 June 6 Leicester

Roger Mills Essex	12:14.6
Brian Adams E.Mids	12:18.0

Carl Lawton Surrey	13:02.8
Graham Morris Hants & Sx	13:05.8
Chris Harvey Cheshire	13:08.0
Barry Lines Yorkshire	13:22.8

1978 May 29 Cwmbran

Brian Adams Leics	12:27.04
Shaun Lightman Middx	12:47.64
Amos Seddon Essex	12:48.34
John Hall Sussex	12:57.26
Mike Holmes Yorkshire	12:58.41
Carl Lawton Surrey	13:03.92

1979 May 28 Cwmbran

Mike Holmes Yorkshire	12:55.4
Shaun Lightman Middx	12:55.4
Gordon Vale Surrey	13:01.3
Amos Seddon Essex	13:13.5
Allan King Leicestershire	13:18.8
John Hall Sussex	13:26.1

1980 May 26 Birmingham

Roger Mills Essex	12:05.04
Mike Parker Sussex	12:15.64
Mick Greasley Derby	12:23.82
George Nibre N.East	12:32.50
Allan King Leicestershire	12 35.2
Mike Holmes Yorkshire	12 43.0

1981 Aug 22 Birmingham

Steve Barry Glamorgan	12:09.33
Ian McCombie N.East	12:27.53
Phil Vesty Leicestershire	12:36.27
Adrian James Middlesex	12:46.26
Amos Seddon Essex	12:52.24
Ray Hankin Yorkshire	12:58.59

1982 Aug 21 Birmingham

Steve Barry Glamorgan	11:53.46
Phil Vesty Leicestershire	12:20.78
Chris Harvey Cheshire	12:39.30
Richard Dorman Surrey	12:42.52
Adrian James Middlesex	12:43.91
Roy Sheppard Essex	12:49.45

1983 July 10 Leicester

Chris Maddocks Devon	12:06.4
Tim Berrett Kent	12:30.7
Chris Smith Leicestershire	12:46.6
Richard Dorman Surrey	12:48.1
Chris Harvey Cheshire	13:02.4
Kevin Baker Dorset	13:24.8

1984 July 1 Birmingham

Martin Rush Cumbria	11:49.48
Tim Berrett Kent	12:26.94
Graham Seatter Surrey	12:33.28
Ken Carter Essex	12:35.23
Dave Henley Worcs	12:37.34
Jimmy Ball Hampshire	12:53.66

1985 July 28 Thurrock

Chris Maddocks Devon	12:24.2
Murray Day Middlesex	12:29.4
Chris Smith Leicestershire	12:37.0
Dave Staniforth Yorkshire	12:37.6
Ken Carter Essex	12:56.4
Dave Henley Worcs	12:58.6

1986 July 5 Corby

Phil Vesty Leicestershire	11:55.3
Martin Rush Cumbria	12:05.6
Mike Smith Warwicks	12:57.5
Ray Hankin Yorkshire	13:09.5
Ed Shillabeer Devon	13:12.5

Kevin Baker Dorset	13:27.2	
1987 May 31 Corby		
Andi Drake Warwicks	12:03.3	
Roger Mills Essex	12:16.5	
Dave Staniforth Yorkshire	12:19.0	
Tim Berrett Kent	12:42.3	
Chris Smith Leics	12:43.3	
Paul Warburton Middlesex	13:42.3	
1988 July 10 Corby		
Chris Maddock S.Devon	12:01.4	
Paul Blagg Kent	12:16.2	
Graham White W.Scotland	12:26.1	
Jon Vincent Leics	12:57.2	
Dave Henley Worcs	13:05.1	
Stuart Phillips Essex	13:30.5	
1989 May 29 Corby		
Sean Martindale Yorkshire	12:01.5	
Martin Bell W.Scotland	12:20.2	
Stuart Phillips Essex	12:54.4	
Bob Care Worcs	13:11.2	
Peter Hannell Surrey	13:47.7	
Shaun Lightman Middx	14:07.4	
1990 May 28 Corby		
Sean Martindale Yorkshire	12:07.6	
Andy Penn Warwicks	12:19.8	
Martin Rush Cumbria	12:25.4	
Noel Carmody Kent	12:27.6	
Stuart Phillips Essex	12:51.6	
Bob Care Worcs	12:54.4	
1991 May 27 Corby		
Martin Bell W.Scotland	12:16.7	
Stuart Phillips Essex	12:47.9	
Bob Care Worcs	12:59.6	
Karl Atton Leicestershire	13:15.2	
Andrew Thacker Humber	14:00.9	
Shaun Lightman Middx	14:03.6	
1992 May 25 Corby		
Martin Bell W.Scotland	12:25.79	
Stuart Phillips Essex	12:31.11	
Sean Martindale Yorks	13:03.75	
Jimmy Ball Hampshire	13:08.39	
Bob Care Worcs	13:14.00	
Noel Carmody Kent	13:18.56	
1993 May 31 Corby		
Kieron Butler Avon	12:40.85	
Gary Witton Sussex	12:45.92	
Scott Davis Essex	12:59.73	
Steve Brennan Lancs	13:22.13	
Karl Orchard Leics	13:50.61	
Peter Hannell Surrey	14:18.71	
Shaun Lightman Middx	14:27.46	
1994 May 30 Corby		
Martin Bell W.Scotland	12:23.50	
Gary Witton Sussex	12:59.63	
Scott Davis Essex	13:01.88	
Chris Smith Leics	13:14.30	
Peter Hannell Surrey	14:18.71	
Shaun Lightman Middx	14:27.46	
1995 May 29 Bedford		
Philip King Sussex	11:49.64	
Steve Partington Lancs	12:04.13	
Andy Penn Warwicks	12:12.36	
Martin Young Leics	12:33.58	
Les Morton Yorkshire	12:43.57	
Stuart Monk Essex	12:59.35	
1996 May 27 Bedford		

Andy Penn Warwicks	12:13.26	
Richard Oldale Yorkshire	12:21.22	
Martin Young Leics	12:26.61	
Gary Witton Sussex	12:35.02	
Derek Cross Herts	13:16.79	
Karl Atton Gt Manchester	13:18.68	
1997 May 26 Bedford		
Martin Bell W .Scotland	12:31.93	
Andy O'Rawe Essex	12:49.41	
Martin Young Leics	13:12.69	
Derek Cross Herts	13:28.53	
Sean Martindale Yorks	14:14.24	
Dave Ratcliffe Warwicks	14:43.59	
1998 May 25 Bedford		
Martin Bell W.Scotland	11:59.46	
Jamie O'Rawe Essex	12:47.72	
Richard Oldale Yorkshire	13:03.36	
Martin Young Leics	13:16.23	
Matt Hales Sussex	13:26.58	
Nigel Whorlow Kent	14:07.20	
1999 May 31 Bedford		
Matt Hales Sussex	12:56.59	
Andrew Goudie Kent	13:20.95	
Dominic King Essex	13:35.95	
Derek Cross Herts	13:52.71	
John Hall Middlesex	14:04.31	
Ian Richards Warwicks	14:10.03	
2000 May 29 Bedford		
Andi Drake Warwicks	11:59.96	
Matt Hales Sussex	12:13.84	
Dominic King Essex	13:12.60	
Andrew Goudie Kent	13:25.25	
James Davis Hampshire	13:47.69	
Nathan Adams Yorkshire	13:53.95	
2001 May 29 Bedford		
Lloyd Finch Leics	12:33.90	
Andy Penn Warwicks	12:39.30	
Andrew Goudie Kent	13:07.00	
James Davis Hampshire	13:48.60	
Nathan Adams Yorkshire	13:53.35	
Mark Williams Staffs	13:57.90	
2002 May 26 Bedford		
Daniel King Essex	12:20.46	
Lloyd Finch Leics	12:40.96	
Nathan Adams Yorkshire	12:56.23	
Andrew Goudie Kent	13:21.05	
Mark Williams Staffs	13:31.05	
Tim Watt Surrey	14:27.92	
2003 Not held		
2004 May 31 Bedford		
Andi Drake Warwicks	11:48.72	
Daniel King Essex	11:51.37	
Luke Finch Leics	12:12.03	
Nathan Adams Yorkshire	12:35.06	
Nick Ball Hampshire	12:54.28	
Peter Kaneen Lancashire	13:01.19	
2005 May 30 Bedford		
Daniel King Essex n/s	11:34.82	
Dominic King Essex	11:54.38	
Nick Ball Hampshire	12:25.96	
Matt Hales Sussex	12:32.44	
Andi Drake Warwicks	12:46.02	
Mark Williams Staffs	13:02:31	
Robbie Bain Kent	13:22.16	
2006 May 29 Bedford		
Nick Ball Hampshire	11:50.55	

Dominic King Essex	11:51.44	
Luke Finch Leicestershire	12:34.62	
Steve Hollier Staffs	12:42.89	
Ben Wears N.East	12:45.38	
Paul Evenett Yorkshire	13:30.44	
2007 May 28 Bedford		
Daniel King Essex	11:58.50	
Dominic King Essex n/s	12:26.14	
Mark Williams Staffs	12:46.45	
Ben Wears N.East	13:08.83	
Nick Silvester Hampshire	13:59.51	
Antonio Cirillo W.Wales	13:59.76	
Mark O'Kane Warwicks	14:19.52	
2008 May 26 Bedford		
Daniel King Essex	12:28.18	
Mark Williams Staffs	12:49.35	
Mark O'Kane Warwicks	13:07.46	
Alex Wright Surrey	14:07.85	
Tim Bosworth Kent	14:14.30	
Trevor Jones Middlesex	14:19.27	
2009 May 25 Bedford		
Brendan Boyce Wks/IRL	12:25.37	
Alex Wright Surrey	13:08.80	
Steve Davis Essex	13:21.35	
Mark Williams Staffs	14:03.85	
John Hall Middlesex	15:03.12	
Mark Wall Northants	15:04.37	
2010 May 31 Bedford		
Alex Wright Surrey	11:38.16	
Tom Bosworth Kent	11:43 44	
Brendan Boyce Wks/IRL	11:49 93	
Luke Finch South Wales	11:50.26	
Mark O'Kan e Warwicks	13:03.46	
Antonio Cirillo W.Wales	13:34.40	
2011 May 29 Bedford		
Daniel King Essex	12:34.03	
Dominic King Essex	12:49.77	
Alex Eaton Lancashire	13:53.85	
Mark Williams Staffs	14:05.38	
Francisco Reis Mx/POR	14:23.54	
2012 Aug 25 Bedford		
Alex Wright Surrey	11:49.41	
Tom Bosworth Kent	12:13.47	
Dominic King Essex	12:49.90	
Mark Williams Staffs	14:10.32	
Ian Richards Sussex	14:25.85	
2013 not held		

7 MILES TRACK

1947 Aug 4 London (WC)		
Harry Churcher Surrey		53:04.6
James Morris Middlesex		54:28.8
Bill Burgess Kent		58:08.0
Arthur Leveridge Essex		
W.Malone Northumb & Durham		
W.Ashworth Lancashire		
1948 May 17 London (WC)		
Harry Churcher Surrey		54:46.4
Bill Wilson Bedfordshire		56:56.0
Allan Furniss Yorkshire		57:36.0
Gordon Dick Middlesex		
Gwyn Rees Warwickshire		
James McCormick Cheshire		
1949 July 2 London (WC)		
Harry Churcher Surrey		52:15.0
Lawrence Allen Yorkshire		53:19.6
Bill Wilson Bedfordshire		55:38.0

10,000 METRES TRACK

1950 May 27 London (WC)
Lawrence Allen Yorkshire 51:21.0
A.E.Jackson N&D 56:22.0
Bert Clayton Hampshire 56:43.0
1951 May 12 London (WC)
George Rushton Yorkshire 54:18.0
Bryan Hawkins Middlesex 54:35.0
George Coleman Beds 55:10.0
Henry Harwood Lancashire
Maurice Long Kent
Ian Paul Hertfordshire
1952 May 31 London (WC)
Roland Hardy Derby 49:28.6
Lawrence Allen Yorkshire 50:46.6
George Coleman Beds 50:51.6
Bryan Hawkins Middlesex
A.McGregor Somerset
Fred Barrett Kent
1953 May 23 London (WC)
Bryan Hawkins Middlesex 54:02.2
George Coleman Beds 54:54.8
Fred Barrett Kent 55:00.0
Bill Leveridge Essex
Brian Shepherd Surrey
Alf Poole Worcestershire
1954 June 5 London (WC)
Roland Hardy Derby 53:41.4
Bryan Hawkins Middlesex 54:25.2
Joe Barraclough Lancs 55:09.0
George Coleman Beds 55:25
Alf Poole Worcestershire
John Hubball Hertfordshire
1955 May 28 London (WC)
Roland Hardy Derby 51:52.6
George Coleman Beds 52:15.4
Bryan Hawkins Middlesex 52:45.6
Joe Barraclough Lancs 53:47.0
Alf Poole Worcestershire 53:47.0
Bob Goodall Essex 56:14.8
1956 May 19 London (WC)
George Coleman Beds 51:08.4
Roland Hardy Derby 51:37.6
Bob Goodall Essex 52:11.0
Stan Vickers Kent 52:19.4
Alf Poole Worcs 53:05.6
George Chaplin Warwicks 53:15.6
1957 June 8 London (WC)
Stan Vickers Kent 51:52.4
George Coleman Beds 52:55.0
Eric Hall Surrey 53:15.0
Bryan Hawkins Middlesex 54:05.8
Bob Goodall Essex 54:16.0
Gareth Howell Glamorgan 54:27.8
1958 May 26 London (WC)
Stan Vickers Kent 51:11.0
Ken Matthews Warwicks 51:42.0
Eric Hall Surrey 52:47.8
Bob Goodall Essex 53:01.0
Ken Camp Derby 54:09.6
Abe Rozentals Notts 54:55.0
1959 May 16 London (WC)
Ken Matthews Warwicks 49:47.4
Stan Vickers Kent 50:52.4
George Coleman Beds 52:58.8
Tom Misson Middlesex 53:48.8
Colin Williams Essex 54:57.4

Ken Harding Staffs 55:28.6
1960 June 4 London (WC)
Ken Matthews Warwicks 50:24.4
Eric Hall Surrey 53:11.4
Tom Misson Middlesex 53:35.2
Stan Vickers Kent 54:01.6
Doug Greasley Derby 56:57.4
J.Secker Wiltshire 59:53.0
1961 May 20 London (WC)
Ken Matthews Warwicks 48:24.0
Colin Williams Essex 51:47.8
Bob Clark Kent 53:07.8
Eric Hall Surrey 53:39.6
Ron Wallwork Lancashire 54:00.8
Don Thompson Middlesex 54:06.2
1962 June 9 London (WC)
Ken Matthews Warwicks 53:24.4
Don Thompson Middlesex 54:04.0
John Godbeer Kent 54:28.0
Ray Middleton Surrey 54:55.0
Bryan Hawkins Sussex 56:05.2
John Paddick Staffs 57:18.8
1963 June 1 London (WC)
Ken Matthews Warwicks 51:40.6
Vaughan Thomas Surrey 54:22.0
Ron Wallwork Lancashire 54:38.6
John Paddick Staffs 54:49.4
Arthur Thomson Middx 54:52.6
John Godbeer Kent 55:27.2
1964 May 16 London (WC)
Ken Matthews Warwicks 50:02.2
Paul Nihill Surrey 52:32.4
Bob Clark Kent 53:34.2
Roy Hart Glamorgan 53:48.0
Arthur Thomson Middx 54:31.4
Ron Wallwork Lancashire 54:32.0
1965 June 5 London (WC)
Paul Nihill Surrey 50:23.4
Malcolm Tolley Yorkshire 52:33.4
Peter McCullagh Oxford 52:43.6
Roy Hart Glamorgan 52:59.4
Peter Fullager Kent 53:18.4
John Edgington Warwicks 54:37.0
1966 May 28 London (WC)
Peter Fullager Kent 50:16.2
Ron Wallwork Lancashire 50:29.6
Malcolm Tolley Yorkshire 52:15.0
John Webb Essex 52:54.8
Bill Sutherland Middlesex 53:19.2
Bryan Hawkins Sussex 54:05.0
1967 May 27 London (WC)
Ron Wallwork Lancashire 51:38.2
Arthur Jones Sussex 52:53.2
Ray Middleton Surrey 53:33.0
Ken Easlea Middlesex 53:52.0
Dave Smyth Somerset 53:58.6
Bob Hughes Worcs 54:13.4
1968 June 2 London (CP)
John Webb Essex 51:36.8
Arthur Thomson Middx 51:49.2
Phil Thorn Wiltshire 52:08.2
Arthur Jones Sussex 52:47.4
Len Duquemin Hampshire 52:59.2
Roy Thorpe Yorkshire 53:38.4

1969 May 25 London (WC)
Paul Nihill Surrey 43:49.6
Phil Embleton Essex 44:47.0
Bob Hughes Worcs 45:15.8
Ron Wallwork Lancashire 45:28.4
Bill Sutherland Middlesex 45:42.2
Malcolm Tolley Leics 46:34.2
1970 May 24 Leicester
Wilf Wesch Surrey/FRG 45:42.4
Bill Sutherland Middlesex 46:18.2
Phil Embleton Essex 47:31.4
Chris Eyre Cumberland 47:42.6
Tony Taylor Lancashire 48:41.0
Phil Thorn Wiltshire 48:48.8
1971 May 30 Leicester
Phil Embleton Essex 42:24.0
Ron Wallwork Lancashire 43:57.0
Bob Hughes Worcs 44:26.2
Wilf Wesch Surrey/FRG 45:02.2
Roy Hart Glamorgan 46:49.0
Eric Taylor Leicestershire 47:14.0
1972 May 28 Leicester
Paul Nihill Surrey 42:34.6
Ron Wallwork Lancashire 45:33.0
Olly Flynn Essex 45:48.6
Geoff Toone Leics 45:56.8
Shaun Lightman Middx 46:09.0
Bob Hughes Worcs 46:19.0
1973 May 28 Warley
John Warhurst Yorkshire 44:07.4
Olly Flynn Essex 45:27.6
Geoff Toone E.Mids 45:28.2
Shaun Lightman Middx 45:59.4
Ron Wallwork Lancashire 46:20.4
Ken Carter Kent 46:37.0
1974 May 27 London (CP)
Carl Lawton Surrey 46:07.8
Ron Wallwork Lancashire 46:24.2
Shaun Lightman Middx 45:58.0
Geoff Toone E.Mids 47:27.0
Charlie Fogg South West 48:58.8
Alan Buchanan Sussex 49:50.0
1975 May 25 London (CP)
Shaun Lightman Middx 45:07.87
John Warhurst Yorkshire 45:10.97
Bob Dobson Essex 45:30.39
Carl Lawton Surrey 46:08.59
Alan Buchanan Sussex 46:11.81
Ted Ardley Kent 46:22.75
1976 May 30 London (CP)
Roger Mills Essex 43:52.00
Brian Adams E.Mids 44:33.73
Carl Lawton Surrey 44:50.00
John Warhurst Yorkshire 45:55.45
Bill Wright Hampshire 46:11.97
George Nibre N.East 46:36.77
1977 June 5 Leicester
Brian Adams E.Mids 43:57.2
Roger Mills Essex 44:16.8
Carl Lawton Surrey 45:48.6
Chris Harvey Cheshire 46:16.4
Graham Morris Sussex 46:30.6
John Warhurst Yorkshire 46:36.4
1978 May 28 Cwmbran
John Warhurst Yorkshire 45:02.78

Amos Seddon Essex	45:32.10	Martin Bell W.Scotland	46:05.4	1969 Essex 46 Middx 54 Surrey 76			
Mick Greasley Derby	46:04.83	Stuart Phillips Essex	46:35.0	1970 Essex 34 Surrey 49 Lancs 54			
Brian Adams Leics	46:44.11	Russell Rawlings Worcs	47:16.3	1971 Essex 24 Surrey 38 Lancs 57			
John Hall Sussex	47:35.37	**1989** May 29 Corby		1972 Essex 21 Surrey 40 Middx 59			
Steve Barry Glamorgan	47:46.62	Sean Martindale Yorkshire	42:50.9	1973 Essex 15 Yorks 40 Leics 72			
1979 May 27 Cwmbran		Martin Bell W.Scotland	44:07.4	1974 Essex 22 Lancs 44 Leics 62			
Gordon Vale Surrey	44:45.2	Steve Uttley Essex	49:16.6	1975 Essex 16 Sussex 67 Yks 68			
Mike Holmes Yorkshire	44:55.0	Dave Henley Worcs	49:49.8	1976 Essex 22 Middx 52 Yorks 54			
Adrian James Middlesex	45:03.8	? Surrey	52:13.0	1977 Yks 31 Sussex 50 Essex 52			
Amos Seddon Essex	45:19.8	**1990** May 28 Corby		1978 Essex 19 Sussex 45 Yks 49			
Steve Barry Glamorgan	46:38.6	Sean Martindale Yorkshire	42:49.4	1979 Yorks 39 Leics 62 Essex 67			
Chris Maddocks Devon	46:48.4	Martin Rush Cumbria	43:09.8	1980 Yks 30 Essex 40 Sussex 44			
1980 May 25 Birmingham		Darren Thorn Warwicks	44:18.2	1981 Leics 29 Sussex 36 Yks 41			
Mick Greasley Derby	42:41.6	Stuart Phillips Essex	45:20.9	1982 Sy 43 Essex 57 Sussex 69			
Roger Mills Essex	42:54.6	Brian Adams Leics	46:36.9	1983 Leics 29 Yorks 45 Essex 58			
Chris Harvey Cheshire	43:19.4	Martin Bell W.Scotland	47:20.2	1984 Essex 38 Leics 47 Yorks 62			
Allan King Leicestershire	43:37.9	**1991** May 27 Corby		1985 Yorks 31 Leics 36 Kent 63			
Adrian James Middlesex	43:43.9	Martin Bell W.Scotland	43:15.3	1986 Yorks 33 Sussex 47 Wks 55			
George Nibre N.East	44:42.0	Stuart Phillips Essex	45:52.6	1987 Yorks 46 WarWks 46 Kent 63			
1981 Aug 23 Birmingham		Brian Adams Leics	47:51.8	1988 Yorks 30 Wks 54 Kent 104			
Adrian James Middlesex	44:14.24	John Hall Middlesex	48:38.2	1989 Glam 37 Wks 50 Sussex 75			
Ian McCombie N.East	44:41.71	Carl Lawton Surrey	49:56.2	1990 Kent 40 Wks 44 Sussex 63			
Amos Seddon Essex	44:50.59	Andrew Thacker Humber	50:55.8	1991 Sussex 52 Wks 69 Leics 78			
Ray Hankin Yorkshire	46:06.43	**1992** May 25 Corby		1992 Glam 33 Leics 47 Essex 48			
Jimmy Ball Hampshire	46:25.55	Martin Bell W.Scotland	43:09.0	1993 Yorks 26 Leics 34 Essex 40			
Ian Richards Warwicks	46:43.21	Jimmy Ball Hampshire	45:08.7	1994 Essex 37 Leics 44 Surrey 52			
1982 Aug 22 Birmingham		Stuart Phillips Essex	45:47.2	1995 Yorks 38 Leics 40 Herts 61			
Phil Vesty Leicestershire	43:59.34	Sean Martindale Yorkshire	47:28.0	1996 Essex 39 Leics 59 Yorks 64			
Adrian James Middlesex	44:06.25	Nole Carmody Kent	47:45.7	1997 Essex 26 Leics 33 Sussex 51			
Roy Sheppard Essex	44:53.38	Brian Adams Leics	48:22.6	1998 Sussex 35 Leics 45 Essex 56			
Chris Harvey Cheshire	45:34.17	**1993** May 31 Corby		**10 KILOMETRES ROAD**			
Richard Dorman Surrey	45:46.72	Steve Partington Lancs	42:15.86	**1999** Apr 24 Sheffield			
Martin Rush Cumbria	45:50.31	Chris Cheeseman Surrey	44:52.20	Martin Bell W.Scotland	41:28		
1983 not held		Jamie O'Rawe Essex	45:44.63	Martin Young Leicestershire	46:49		
1984 July 1 Birmingham		John Hall Middlesex	47:47.99	Lloyd Finch Leicestershire	46:53		
Roger Mills Essex	44:03.40	Martin Bell W.Scotland	48:22.80	Brian Adams Leicestershire	48:12		
Jimmy Ball Hampshire	44:14.90	**1994** May 30 Corby		Tim Watt Sussex	49:10		
Andi Drake Warwicks	45:04.28	Martin Bell W.Scotland	42:32.3	Les Morton Yorkshire	49:31		
Adrian James Middlesex	45:17.36	Kieron Butler Avon	45:50.3	1. Leics, 2. Yorkshire			
Richard Dorman Surrey	46:27.85	Brian Adams Leics	47:06.6	**2000** Apr 15 Sheffield			
Les Morton Yorkshire	46:56.91	Scott Davis Essex	47:54.1	Thomas Taylor Leics	47:44		
1985 July 28 Thurrock		John Hall Middlesex	48:52.1	Noel Carmody Kent	49:40		
Martin Rush Cumbria	43:27.6	Denis Holly Surrey	51:41.4	Brian Adams Leicestershire	50:33		
Les Morton Yorkshire	44:08.3	**10 MILES ROAD**		Graham Jackson Yorkshire	50:41		
Roger Mills Essex	44:29.9	1948-1998 With RWA (qv)		Dennis Jackson Yorkshire	51:37		
Chris Smith Leics	45:01.1	1948 Surrey & Middx 18 Essex 61		Sean Martindale Yorkshire	51:58		
Jimmy Ball Hampshire	45:04.1	1949 Middx 22 Yorks 31 Kent 46		**5 KILOMETRES ROAD**			
Steve Partington Lancs	45:17.3	1950 Middx 39 Surrey 51 Essex 52		**2001** Apr 28 Sheffield			
1986 July 5 Corby		1951 Yorks 18 Surrey 26 Middx 44		Andy Penn Warwicks	22:01		
Martin Rush Cumbria	41:24.7	1952 Surrey 29 Middx 36 Yorks 60		Luke Finch Leicestershire	22:06		
Chris Maddocks Devon	41:36.8	1953 Middx 22 Surrey 47 Kent 62		Mark Williams Staffs	23:40		
Phil Vesty Leicestershire	43:05.4	1954 Middx 36 Yorks 37 Essex 57		Nathan Adams Yorkshire	24:20		
Andi Drake Warwicks	44:28.4	1955 Middx 36 Yorks 44 Wks 83		Alan Ellam Essex	24:47		
Steve Partington Lancs	44:29.3	1956 Middx 30 Yorks 57 Surrey 61		Brian Adams Leicestershire	24:55		
Les Morton Yorkshire	45:38.8	1957 Essex 39 Middx 52 Yorks 60		1. Warwicks, 2. Yorkshire, 3. Leics			
1987 May 31 Corby		1958 Essex 36 Middx 47 Yorks 60		**5000 METRES TRACK**			
Les Morton Yorkshire	43:44.2	1959 Middx 29 Surrey 41 Kent 61		**2002** Mar 16 Dartford			
Gordon Vale Surrey	44:06.3	1960 Middx 37 Surrey 38 Essex 49		Matt Hales Sussex	21:40.3		
Chris Smith Leicestershire	44:51.7	1961 Middx 44 Kent 46 Essex 56		Nathan Adams Leics	22:08.6		
John Hall Middlesex	47:05.2	1962 Wks 42 Middx 44 Essex 47		Andrew Goudie Kent	23:22.6		
Steve Uttley Essex	47:06.3	1963 Surrey 30 Wks 60 Essex 69		Mark Williams Staffs	23:34.4		
Russell Rawlings Worcs	47:19.3	1964 WarWks 26 Sy 36 Yorks 36		Steve Arnold Warwicks	24:30.6		
1988 July 10 Corby		1965 Surrey 32 Middx 52 Yorks 76		Noel Carmody Kent	24:49.2		
Chris Maddock Devon	41:16.4	1966 Middx 44 Yorks 61 Essex 71		**10 KILOMETRES ROAD**			
Sean Martindale Yorkshire	43:32.3	1967 Middx 26 Yorks 64 Lancs 68		**2003** Mar 15 Leamington Spa			
Jimmy Ball Hampshire	44:13.4	1968 Middx 35 Essex 56 Surrey 71					

Dominic King Essex	43:12	
Daniel King Essex	43:42	
Luke Finch Leicestershire	44:03	
Nathan Adams Yorkshire	45:25	
Mark Easton Surrey	45:52	
Darrell Stone Sussex	46:49	

2004 Mar 6 Leamington Spa
Daniel King Essex	42:39
Chris Cheeseman Surrey	44:24
Matt Hales Sussex	44:59
Nathan Adams Yorkshire	45:07
Darrell Stone Sussex	46:35
Nick Ball Hampshire	47:23

1. Sussex

2005 Mar 12 Coventry
Dominic King Essex	44:18
Daniel King Essex	44:41
Nick Ball Hampshire	46:56
Matt Hales Sussex	47:29
Mark Williams Staffs	48:14
Robbie Bain Kent	49:04

1. Essex, 2. Sussex, 3. Leics

2006 Mar 12 Coventry
Nick Ball Hampshire	43:38
Steve Hollier Staffs	44:50
Ben Wears N.East	46:07
Andi Drake Warwicks	46:08
Mark Williams Staffs	46:44
Scott Davis Essex	47:13

2007 Mar 17 Coventry
Ben Wears N.East	44:16
Mark Williams Staffs	47:53
Paul Evenett Yorkshire	49:13
Steve Arnold Warwicks	51:03
Chris Hobbs Kent	53:49
Nick Silvester Hampshire	54:40

2008 Mar 8 Leamington Spa
Nick Silvester Hampshire	47:45
Mark Williams Staffs	48:49
Mark O'Kane Warwicks	49:05
Antonio Cirillo W.Wales	49:36
Chris Barnard Essex	50:05
Richard Emsley Sussex	51:04

2009 Coventry Apr 4
Luke Finch Leicestershire	41:51
Ben Wears Yorkshire	41:57
Brendan Boyce Wks/IRL	43:21
Steve Davis Essex	45:31
Philip Barnard Essex	48:51
Jimmy Ball Hampshire	49:06

1. Essex

2010 Mar 6 Coventry
Brendan Boyce Wks/IRL	41:50
Alex Wright Surrey	43:31
Michael Doyle Bedfordshire	43:37
Tom Bosworth Kent	43:39
Daniel King Essex	44:22
Scott Davis Essex	44:44

1. Essex, 2. Warwicks, 3. Sussex
2011 Sep 11 London (VP) RWA qv
1. Essex, 2. Middlesex, 3. Surrey

WOMEN'S 3,000 METRES TRACK
1995 May 29 Bedford
Vicky Lupton Yorkshire	13:17.68
Cal Partington Lancs	13:19.29

Perry Williams Middlesex	13:25.99
Verity Snook E.Scotland	13:38.19
Catherine Charnock Cum	14:28.25
Ann Lewis Hampshire	16:13.25

1996 May 27 Bedford
Vicky Lupton Yorkshire	13:06.27
Verity Snook Hampshire	13:16.23
Melanie Wright Warwicks	14:04.72
Catherine Charnock Cum	14:23.15
Sharon Tonks Worcs	14:59.09
Cressida Van Doorn Sy	16:23.72

1997 May 26 Bedford
Verity Snook Hampshire	14:08.53
Catherine Charnock Cum	14:53.92
Lynn Bradley Yorkshire	15:49.10
Karen Ratcliffe Warwicks	16:08.20
Helen Ford-Dunn Sussex	16:36.01
Cressida Van Doorn Sy	16:54.92

1998 May 25 Bedford
Vicky Lupton Yorkshire	13:42.73
Catherine Charnock Cum	14:21.55
Ann Lewis Hampshire	15:59.68
Mary Wallen Bucks	16:11.94
Cressida Van Doorn Sy	16:56.60

1999 May 31 Bedford
Lisa Crump Yorkshire	14:25.09
Claire Reeves Kent	16:30.32
Ann Lewis Hampshire	16:33.19

2000 May 29 Bedford
Ann Lewis Hampshire	16:17.70
Fiona Bishop Surrey	18:38.44

2001 May 29 Bedford
Estle Viljoen Surrey	14:52.7
Miranda Heathcote Kent	15:16.7
Katie Stones Humberside	16:09.4
Ann Lewis Hampshire	16:39.2

2002 May 26 Bedford
Estle Viljoen Surrey	14:09.99
Sarah Chetwynd Wks	16:20.37

1. Humber, 2. Kent, 3. Warwicks
2003 not held
2004 May 31 Bedford
Sophie Hales Sussex	13:49.64
Rebecca Mersh Yorks	13:50.52
Jenny Gagg Humberside	14:52.80
Fiona McGorum Leics	15:48.78
Johanna Jackson N.East	15:52.58
Anne Belchambers Mx	17:12.89

2005 May 30 Bedford
Jo Jackson N.East	13:22.23
Sharon Tonks Worcs	13:53.79
Estle Viljoen Surrey	14:06.15
Sophie Hales Sussex	14:28.28
Rebecca Mersh Yorks	14:33.77
Maureen Noel Middlesex	17:33.00

2006 May 29 Bedford
Jo Jackson N.East	13:39.83
Rebecca Mersh Yorks	13:55.81
Sophie Hales Sussex	14:41.17
Sarah Foster Kent	15:00.40
Chelsea O'Rawe-Hobbs Essex	15:11.56
Ann Wheeler Warwicks	16:46.54

2007 May 28 Bedford
Jo Jackson N.East	13:22.72
Sophie Hales Sussex	13:57.45

Rebecca Mersh Yorks	14:53.21
Verity Snook Hampshire	15:24.71
Chelsea O'Rawe-Hobbs Essex	
	15:57.93
Fiona McGorum Leics	16:00.91

2008 May 26 Bedford
Jo Jackson N.East	12:40.98
Rebecca Mersh Yorks	15:34.04
Chelsea O'Rawe-Hobbs Essex	
	15:40.39
Diane Bradley Kent	15:41.45
Ann Wheeler Warwicks	16:34.41
Clare Grace Hampshire	16:52.01

2009 May 25 Bedford
Verity Snook Hampshire	15:13.02
Diane Bradley Kent	15:23.77
Fiona McGorum Leics	15:50.78
Ann Wheeler Warwicks	17:16.49
Helen Middleton Beds	17:21.47
Vicky Morgan Staffs	17:31.27

2010 May 31 Bedford
Johanna Jackson N.East	12:57.08
Lauren Whelan Lancs	15:05.98
Heather Lewis W.Wales	15:25.58
Diane Bradley Kent	15:31.84
Fiona McGorum Leics	15:42.96
Ann Wheeler Warwicks	16:02.42

2011 May 29 Bedford
Johanna Jackson N.East	13:15.54
Ann Wheeler Warwicks	16:42.16
Helen Middleton Beds	17:27.58

2012 Aug 25 Bedford
Johanna Jackson N.East	12:57.20
Heather Lewis W.Wales	14:00.98
Bethan Davies S.Wales	14:04.27
Lauren Whelan Lancs	15:37.35
Grazina Narviliene Mx/LTU	15:28.39
Jasmine Nicholls Leics	15:58.62

2013 not held

5 KILOMETRES ROAD
1995-8 With RWA (qv)
1995 Yorks 17, Worcs 23, Sx 31
1997 1. Sussex, 2. Yorks, 3. Staffs
1998 Sx 17, Wks 19, Worcs 16
1999 Apr 24 Sheffield
Vicky Lupton Yorkshire	23:52
Lisa Crump Yorkshire	24:51
Sarah Bennett Warwicks	25:10
Katie Ford Yorkshire	25:32
Nicky Phillips Kent	25:35
Sian Woodcock Yorkshire	26:52

1. Yorkshire, 2. Warwicks, 3. Kent
2000 Apr 15 Sheffield
Wendy Bennett Worcs	25:47
Nikki Huckerby Warwicks	25:53
Lisa Crump Yorkshire	25:57
Nicky Phillips Kent	25:59
Liz Corran Lancashire	26:11
Katie Ford Yorkshire	26:29

2001 Apr 28 Sheffield
Niobe Menendez Sussex	24:53
Sophie Hales Sussex	26:05
Bryna Chrismas Humberside	27:32
Natalie Geens Warwicks	27:40
Katie Ford Yorkshire	28:18
Nicky Reynolds Warwicks	28:35

1. Yorks, 2. Wks, 3. Merseyside
2002 Mar 16 Dartford (Track)
Sophie Hales Sussex 25:28.5
Jo Hesketh Sussex 26:00.4
Nicky Phillips Kent 26:45.5
Natalie Geens Warwicks 27:06.2
Claire Reeves Kent 27:19.3
Sarah Chetwynd Wks 28:16.3
2003 Mar 15 Leamington Spa
Estle Viljoen Surrey 23:33
Sophie Hales Sussex 23:47
Katie Stones Humberside 23:58
Bryna Chrismas Humberside 25:18
Jenny Gagg Humberside 25:25
Jo Hesketh Sussex 25:33
2004 Mar 6 Leamington Spa
Jenny Gagg Humberside 24:27
Sarah Foster Kent 25:09
Kath Horwill Worcs 25:46
Sharon Tonks Worcs 26:12
Rachael Wooolley Leics 29:08
Ann Wheeler Warwicks 29:37

2005 Mar 12 Coventry
Sharon Tonks Worcs 25:07
Jenny Gagg Humberside 25:30
Debbie Wallen Hampshire 25:42
Rachael Woolley Leics 29:16
Holly Williams Kent 29:26
Carley Tomlin Kent 29:49
1. Kent, 2. Worcs, 3. Warwicks
2006 Mar 12 Coventry
Sarah Foster Kent 25:32
Sharon Tonks Worcs 25:50
Chelsea O'Rawe-Hobbs Kent 26:18
Kathryn Granger Yorkshire 27:01
Holly Smith Warwicks 28:16
Ann Wheeler Warwicks 29:38
2007 Mar 17 Coventry
Lisa Kehler Staffs 24:33
Verity Snook Hampshire 26:33
Chelsea O'Rawe-Hobbs Kent 27:03
Jenny Gagg Humberside 27:56
Rachael Woolley Leics 28:01
Diane Bradley Kent 29:39
2008 Mar 8 Leamington Spa
Verity Snook Hampshire 26:24

Rebecca Mersh Yorkshire 26:54
Sharon Tonks Worcs 26:57
Diane Bradley Kent 27:21
Holly Smith Warwicks 27:24
Fiona McGorum Leics 28:00
2009 Apr 4 Coventry
Lisa Kehler Staffs 23:48
Kelsey Howard Kent 26:03
Diane Bradley Kent 26:15
Vicky Morgan Staffs 28:29
Heather Lewis Wales 29:29
Rebecca Collins Kent 29:39
1. Kent, 2. Warwicks, 3. Leics
2010 Mar 6 Coventry
Lisa Kehler Staffs 23 58
Diane Bradley Kent 26 37
Helen Middleton Beds 27 32
Ann Wheeler Warwicks 29 34
Mizzie Marshall Staffs 31 23
Julie Bellfield Worcs 32 04

10 KILOMETRES ROAD
2011 Sep 11 London (VP) RWA qv
1. Cleveland, 2. Middx, 3. Leics

SCOTTISH CHAMPIONSHIPS
3000 METRES TRACK
1976 Mike Dunion (Essex Police) 13:03.4
1977 Mike Parker (Brighton/NZL) 13:12.2
1988 Martin Bell (Splott) 12:17.33
1989 Martin Bell (Splott) 12:32.96
1990 Martin Bell (Splott) 12:20.98
1991 Steve Beecroft AUS 11:47.44
3 MILES TRACK
1883 John Harvie (Queens Park FC) 24:10
1884 John Harvie (Queens Park FC) 23:16
1885 James Caw (St Georges FC) 24:54
1886 James Caw (St Georges FC) 24:03.2
1887 A.Brown (Airdrieonians) 24:32.2
1888 A.Brown (Airdrieonians) 24 26.4
1889 W.Miller (Clydesdale H) 23:50.2
1890 J.Urquhart (Edinburgh H) 24:49.4
1891 James Caw (St Georges FC) 25:20.8
1892 J.Dickison (Edinburgh H) 24:17.0
1893 J.Dickison (Edinburgh H) 29:10.6
1904 Richard Quinn (Motherwell H) 24:57.8
1905 Richard Quinn (Motherwell H) 24:27.6
1906 Richard Quinn (Motherwell H) 23:01.4
1907 Richard Quinn (Bellahouston H) 22:31.6
1908 Richard Quinn (Bellahouston H) 22:41.4
1909 Richard Quinn (Bellahouston H) 23:22.0
1910 Richard Quinn (Bellahouston H) 22:10.6
1911 D.Trotter (Ashcombe AC) 22:41.8
1912 D.Trotter(Ashcombe AC) 22:19.6
1913 Alex Justice (Clydesdale H) 23:01.0
1914 Alex Justice (Clydesdale H) 23:45.2
1919 Colin McLellan (Shettleston H) 23:22.6
1920 Colin McLellan (Shettleston H) 23:22.6
1921 Colin McLellan (Shettleston H) 22:38.2
1922 Colin McLellan (Shettleston H) 22:41.8
1923 Colin McLellan (Shettleston H) 23:13.2
1924 Edward McLeod (Shettleston H) 22:49.4
1925 Colin McLellan (Shettleston H) 22:15.4
1926 John Jordan (Shettleston H) 23:14.2
1927 John Jordan (Shettleston H) 23:24.6
1928 George Galloway (Dundee Hawkhill) 22:55.6
1929 George Galloway (Dundee Hawkhill) 22:47.6
1930 George Galloway (Dundee Hawkhill)
1931 C.Scott Daly 24:10.0
1932 J.Creegan (Dundee Hawkhill H) 21:53.0
1933 George Galloway (Surrey WC) 21:43.4
1934 Andrew Galloway (Edinburgh H) 22:07.2
1935 W.Thomson (Edinburgh H) 23:05.4
1936 Alex Jamieson (Dundee Hawkhill H) 21:46.4
1937 Alex Jamieson (Dundee Hawkhill H) 22:23.4
1938 Alex Jamieson (Dundee Hawkhill H) 22:13.8
1939 Alex Jamieson (Dundee Hawkhill H) 22:12.8
1946 Alex Jamieson (Dundee Hawkhill H) 24:07.4
1947 Alex Jamieson (Dundee Hawkhill H) 23:37.0
1948 Alex Jamieson (Dundee Hawkhill H) 23:46.0
7 MILES TRACK
1923 Colin McLellan (Shettleston) 57:25:0
1924 Colin McLellan (Shettleston H) 56:57.4
1925 Colin McLellan (Shettleston H) 51:42.4
1926 T.McAllister (Irvine YMCA) 56:34.0
1927 George Galloway (Dundee Hawkhill) 57:31.2
1928 George Galloway (Dundee Hawkhill) 56:07.0
1929 George Galloway (Dundee Hawkhill) 56:53.6
1930 Andrew Galloway (Dundee Hawkhill) 63:19.8
1931 --
1932 George Galloway (Dundee Hawkhill) 51:57.0
7 MILES ROAD
1967 Bill Sutherland (Highgate H) 52:25.0
1968 Bill Sutherland (Highgate H) 51:45.6
1969 Bill Sutherland (Highgate H) 49:57.6
10,000 METRES TRACK
1971 Les Dick (Highgate H) 47:29.8
1972 Bill Sutherland (Highgate H) 45:27.8
1973 Roy Thorpe (Sheffield) 44:52.2
1974 Roy Thorpe (Sheffield) 46:51.2
1975 Alan Buchanan (Brighton) 46:36.6
20 KILOMETRES ROAD
1980 Mike Dunion (Essex Police) 1:38:29
1981 Barry Graham (York Postal) 1:38:23
1983 Graham White (York Postal) 1:31:02
1984 Graham White (York Postal) 1:35:04
1985 Graham White (York Postal) 1:38:58

1987 Martin Rush (Cumberland) 1:30:06
30 KILOMETRES ROAD
1978 David Howie (Stirling) 2:42:29
1979 Alan Buchanan (Brighton) 2:52:00
1982 Barry Graham (York Postal) 2:27:08
1986 Ian McCombie (Cambridge H/ENG) 2:07:56
WOMEN 1 MILE TRACK
1935 V Murray (Dundee HH) 8:43.8
Note: No walking events have been held in Scotland since 1991, although a few Scots have competed in England and abroad.

WELSH CHAMPIONSHIPS
1 MILE TRACK
1904 Norman Moses (Newport H) 7:27.6
2 MILES TRACK
1905 Alf Yeoumans (Swansea) 14:23.8
1906 W.Sullivan (Swansea) 14:57.0
1907 Alf Yeoumans (Swansea) 14:46.8
1908 Alf Yeoumans (Swansea) 14:44.4
1909 Alf Yeoumans (Swansea) 14:30.4
1910 Edward Frankham (Abersychn) 15:09.0
1911 Edward Frankham (Abersychn) 15:52.8
1912 Edward Frankham (Abersychn) 15:18.0
1913 John Evans (Uxbridge) 14:35.6
1914 John Evans (Uxbridge) 14:58.0
1920 Will Ovens (Newport H) 14:40.0
1921 John Evans (Metropolitan Police) 15:28.0
1922 Will Ovens (Newport H) 16:04.6
1923 George Eaton (Cwmavon) 16:28.2
1924 Will Ovens (Newport H) 16:44.8
1925 Will Ovens (Newport H) 17:48.0 (1 lap long)
1926 Will Ovens (Glamorgan WC) 15:11.4
1927 Harry Lewis (Glamorgan WC) 15:59.4
1928 Rees Richards (Penarth H) 14:27.2
1929 Jim Edwards (Newport H) 15:38.4
1930 Jim Edwards (Newport H) 14:45.0
1931 Harry Lewis (Cardiff City WC) 15:42.0
1932 Jeremiah Keohane (Glamorgan WC) 15:30.4
1933 Harry Lewis (Cardiff City) 15:00.0
1934 Arthur Pearcey (Newport H) 14:52.2
1935 Arthur Pearcey (Newport H) 15:07.4
1936 Arthur Pearcey (Newport H) 14:30.4
1937 Dai Richards (Newport H) 14:31.0
1938 Dai Richards (Newport H) 15:17.4 (14:24.4?)
1946 Dai Richards (Newport H) 15:35.0
1947 Dai Richards (Newport H) 16:09.0
1948 T.Owens (Manchester) 15:38.9
1949 Gwyn Rees (Coventry) 15:05.6
1950 Gwyn Rees (Coventry) 15:05.6
1951 Maurice Bingham (Roath) 15:21.2
1952 David Barry (Roath) 14:47.8
1953 Gareth Lewis (Roath) 14:38.6
1954 Gareth Howell (Highgate H) 14:49.5
1955 Gareth Howell (Highgate H) 14:25.6
1956 Gareth Howell (Highgate H) 14:47.4
1957 Mike Shannon (Newport H) 14:53.0
1958 John Lowther (Newport H) 14:48.6
1959 Mike Shannon (Newport H) 15:07.2
1960 Mel Pope (Newport H) 15:23.4
1961 Mike Shannon (Newport H) 15:20.8
1962 Mike Shannon (Highgate) 14:58.0
1963 Roy Hart (Roath Labour) 14:43.6
1964 Roy Hart (Roath Labour) 14:02.6
1965 Les Haines (Roath Labour) 15:15.6
1966 Roy Hart (Roath Labour) 13:54.6

1967 Ken Bobbett (Roath Labour) 14:50.2
1968 Ken Bobbett (Roath Labour) 15:05.8
3000 METRES TRACK
1969 Roy Hart (Roath Labour) 13:33.0
1970 Dave Rosser (Southend) 13:54.2
1971 Roy Hart (Roath Labour) 14:13.0
1973 Jack Thomas (Woodford Green) 14:26.8
1974 Nye Tanner (Surrey WC) 14:28.4
1975 John Eddershaw (Sheffield) 13:48.0
1976 Jack Thomas (Woodford Green) 13:59.2
1977 John Eddershaw (Sheffield) 13:54.0
1978 Steve Barry (Roath Labour) 13:23.6
1979 Steve Barry (Roath Labour) 13:29.6
1980 Steve Barry (Roath Labour) 12:26.33
1981 Bob Dobson (Ilford) 12:59.6
1982 Steve Barry (Roath Labour) 12:11.56
1983 Reg Gardner (Hales) 13:33.1
1984 Steve Johnson (Splott Cons) 12:17.9
1985 Steve Johnson (Splott Cons) 12:31.75
1986 Steve Johnson (Splott) 12:34.34
1987 Steve Johnson (Splott) 11:45.77
1988 Steve Johnson (Splott) 12:10.4
1989 Martin Bell (Splott) 12:11.4
1990 Martin Bell (Splott) 12:44.9
1991 Martin Bell (Splott) 12:19.41
1992 Gareth Holloway (Splott) 12:12.36
2000 Mark Williams (Tamworth) 14:21.7
2001 Cameron Smith (Cardiff) 13:23.5
2002 Mark Williams (Tamworth) 13:37.28
2004 Mark Williams (Tamworth) 13:17.0
2010 Stephen Walker (Wrexham) 18:27.38
2013 Ken Bobbett (Hillingdon) 17:44.60
5000 METRES TRACK
1999 Colin Bradley (Surrey WC) 25:09.22
7 MILES TRACK
1952 John King (Roath Y) 56:51.0
1953 not held
1954 David Barry (Roath Y) 57:37.8
1955 Gareth Howell (Highgate H) 54:10.3
1956 Terry Simons (Worcester) 59:31.0
1957 David Davies (St. Julians) 57:03.8
1958 Mike Shannon (Newport H) 57:38.8
1959 Mel Pope (Newport H) 56:17.0
1960 Mel Pope (Newport H) 55:57.0
1961 Mike Shannon (Newport H) 56:00.6
1962 Mike Shannon (Highgate) 54:43.6
1963 Les Haines (Roath Labour) 58:09.2
1964 Roy Hart (Roath Labour) 57:23.6
1965 Les Haines (Roath Labour) 56:33.6
1966 Roy Hart (Roath Labour) 52:02.4
1967 Ken Bobbett (Roath Labour)
1968 Ken Bobbett (Roath Labour) 53:42.8
10,000 METRES TRACK
1969 Dave Rosser (Southend) 47:49.0
1970 Trevor Morgan (Roath Labour) 58:08.4
1971 Roy Hart (Bromsgrove) 46:56.0
1974 Dave Rosser (Southend) 50:52.4
1975 John Eddershaw (Sheffield) 49:28.4
1976 Bill Wright (Coventry) 51:29.0
1977 John Eddershaw (Sheffield) 49:04.2
1978 Steve Barry (Roath Labour) 47:13.8
1979 Steve Barry (Roath Labour) 47:56.8
1980 Steve Barry (Roath Labour) 43:34.02
1981 Bob Dobson (Ilford) 45:50.2
1982 Steve Barry (Roath Labour) 42:44.13

1983	Bob Dobson (Ilford) 48:05.6		1933	Maurice Bingham (Glamorgan WC) 2:20:19
1984	Steve Barry (Roath Labour) 42:08.99		1934	Arthur Pearcey (Newport H) 2:12:2
1985	Steve Johnson (Splott) 44:26.2		1935	Maurice Bingham (Glamorgan WC) 2:21:07
1986	Steve Johnson (Splott) 45:35.21		1936	Dai Richards (Newport H) 2:05:10
1987	Steve Johnson (Splott) 43:03.15		1937	Dai Richards (Newport H) 2:09:19
1988	Steve Johnson (Splott) 43:16.0		1938	Dai Richards (Newport H) 2:05:08
1989	Kirk Taylor (Splott) 46:00.7		1939	Maurice Bingham (Roath) 2:08:12
1990	Gareth Holloway (Splott) 46:13.54			

20 MILES ROAD

1991	Martin Bell (Splott) 43:23.0
1992	Martin Bell (Splott) 42:12.88
1993	Gareth Holloway (Splott) 45:02.2
1994	Colin Bradley (Lliswerry) 48:48.3
1996	Colin Bradley (Lliswerry) 48:21.67
1997	Martin Bell (Splott) 43:53.07
1998	Martin Bell (Splott) 43:47.6

1951	David Barry (Roath Y) 3:10:35
1952	David Barry (Roath Y) 3:09:50
1954	David Barry (Roath Y) 2:53:03
1955	David Barry (Roath Y) 3:09:12
1963	Roy Hart (Roath Labour) 3:13:02
1966	Roy Hart (Roath Labour) 2:40:53

30 KILOMETRES ROAD

7 MILES ROAD

1957	David Davies (Newport H) 55:17
1958	Mel Pope (Newport H) 53:34
1960	Mel Pope (Newport H) 49:51
1961	Mel Pope (Newport H) 53:52
1962	Vaughan Thomas (Belgrave H) 52:20
1963	Roy Hart (Roath Labour) 55:20
1965	Roy Hart (Roath Labour) 51:40
1966	Roy Hart (Roath Labour) 51:32
1967	Ken Bobbett (Roath Labour) 49:50

1991	Gareth Holloway (Splott) 2:25:15
1992	Brian Dowrick (Splott) 2:21:10
1993	Dave Ratcliffe (Coventry) 2:33:16
1994	Martin Bell (Splott) 2:22:21
1995	Colin Bradley (Trowbridge) 2:41:55

WOMEN'S 3000 METRES TRACK

1974	C Bourne (Swansea) 19:36.4
1975	S Morgan (Bridgend Y) 19:18.6
1976	S Morgan (Bridgend Y) 17:44.6
1980	Karen Nipper (Barry) 17:03.3
1981	Karen Nipper (Barry) 15:32.1
1983	Karen Nipper (Roath W) 16:14.2
1984	Karen Nipper (Roath W) 15:43.31
1990	Lisa Simpson (Splott) 15:16.0
2001	Keirina Rowland 18:37.3
2010	Heather Lewis (Pembrokeshire) 15:06.12
2013	Bethan Davies (Cardiff) 14:18.0

10 MILES ROAD

1945	Dai Richards (Newport H) 82:14
1946	Dai Richards (Newport H) 87:45
1947	Dai Richards (Newport H) 83:02
1948	Dai Richards (Newport H) 88:25
1949	Gwyn Rees (Coventry Godiva) 92:20
1950	Gwyn Rees (Coventry Godiva) 86:29
1951	Ken Smith (Cambridge H) 81:08
1952	Ken Smith (Cambridge H) 81:50
1953	David Barry (Roath Y) 82:33
1954	David Barry (Roath Y) 84:43
1955	Gareth Howell (Highgate H) 83:40
1956	Terry Simons (Bromsgrove) 83:35
1957	David Davies (Newport H) 82:10
1958	Mel Pope (Newport H) 78:21
1959	Mel Pope (Newport H) 77:14
1960	Mel Pope (Newport H) 84:26
1961	Mel Pope (Newport H) 82:06
1962	Vaughan Thomas (Belgrave H) 76:16
1963	Roy Hart (Roath Labour) 80:10
1964	Roy Hart (Roath Labour) 77:45
1965	Ken Bobbett (Roath Labour) 76:24
1966	Ken Bobbett (Roath Labour) 76:44
1967	Ken Bobbett (Roath Labour) 74:39

WOMEN'S 5000 METRES TRACK

1996	Sian Woodcock (Bingley) 28:39.16,
1997	Hayley Morgans (Road Hoggs) 29:58.73
1999	Philippa Reilly (Lliswerry) 27:10.42
2000	Philippa Reilly (Lliswerry) 26:37.2

WOMEN'S 10 KILOMETRES ROAD

1991	Karen Dunster (AFD) 52:52

AREA CHAMPIONSHIPS
MIDLAND CHAMPIONSHIPS

2 MILES TRACK

20 KILOMETRES ROAD

1958	Mel Pope (Newport H) 1:40:34
1959	Mel Pope (Newport H) 1:50:29
1960	Mel Pope (Newport H) 1:44:53
1961	Mel Pope (Newport H) 1:37:45
1963	Vaughan Thomas (Belgrave) 1:38:18
1964	Roy Hart (Roath Labour) 1:37:04
1965	Les Haines (Roath Labour) 1:44:14
1966	Ken Bobbett (Roath Labour) 1:40:04
1967	Ken Bobbett (Roath Labour) 1:42:04
1968	Les Haines (Roath Labour) 1:44:52

1911	H.Morris (Birmingham WC) 14:50.0
1920	E.Rogers (Birmingham WC) 15:00.0
1921	W.Hobbis (Birmingham WC) 15:43.8
1922	Lloyd Johnson (Leicester WC) 15:01.4
1923	Fred Smith (Birmingham WC) 14:59.6
1924	Lloyd Johnson (Leicester WC) 15:12.6
1925	Lloyd Johnson (Leicester WC) 14:50.8
1926	G.Edge (North Staffs) 15:10.0
1927	Dick Edge (North Staffs) 14:49.4
1928	Dick Edge (North Staffs) 14:43.4
1929	Dick Edge (Derby WC) 14:42.4
1930	Dick Edge (Derby WC) 14:40.0
1931	Dick Edge (Derby WC) 14:25.0
1932	Dick Edge (Derby WC) 14:23.8
1933	Dick Edge (Birmingham WC) 14:14.8
1934	Dick Edge (Birmingham WC) 14:24.8
1935	Dick Edge (Birmingham WC) 14:42.0
1936	Dick Edge (Birmingham WC) 14:46.0
1937	Ernie Warwick (Birmingham WC) 14:17.4
1938	Dick Edge (Coventry Godiva H) 15:27.8
1939	Dick Edge (Coventry Godiva H) 14:48.2
1946	Dick Edge (Coventry) 14:43.8

15 MILES ROAD

1929	Jim Edwards (Newport H) 2:19:42
1930	Maurice Bingham (Glamorgan WC) 2:21:52
1931	F.Gibbon (Newport H) 2:22:05
1932	F.Gibbon (Newport H) 2:16:26

1947	Bill Wilson (Highgate H) 15:01.0	
1948	Gwyn Rees (Coventry Godiva H) 15:42.0	
1949	Gwyn Rees (Coventry Godiva H) 15:48.0	
1950	John Copperwheat (Highgate H) 14:39.4	
1954	George Coleman (Highgate H) 13:48.2	
1955	George Coleman (Highgate H) 14:04.02	
1956	Alf Poole (Worcester) 14:52.0	
1957	Ken Matthews (R.Sutton C) 14:25.6	
1958	Ken Matthews (R.Sutton C) 13:51.0	
1959	Ken Matthews (R.Sutton C) 13:43.6	
1960	Ken Matthews (R.Sutton C) 13:30.6	
1961	Ken Matthews (R.Sutton C) 13:41.6	
1962	Ken Matthews (R.Sutton C) 13:36.2	
1963	Ken Matthews (R.Sutton C) 13:27.0	
1964	Ken Matthews (R.Sutton C) 13:21.8	
1965	George Chaplin (Coventry) 14:26.0	
1966	Barry Thomas (Birmingham) 14:19.6	
1968	Bob Hughes (R.Sutton C) 14:04.0	

3000 METRES TRACK

1969	Geoff Toone (Leicester) 12:40.2	
1970	Bob Hughes (R.Sutton C) 12:50.6	
1971	Alan Smallwood (Harborne) 13:13.6	

7 MILES TRACK

1924	Fred Smith (Birchfield) 58:35.0	
1925	Lloyd Johnson (Surrey AC) 57:45.0	
1928	Dick Edge (North Staffs) 56:05.6	
1933	Dick Edge (Birmingham) 56:44.0	
1934	Dick Edge (Birmingham) 54:45.6	
1946	Dick Edge (Coventry) 56:35.0	
1947	Gwyn Rees (Coventry) 56:50.0	
1948	Harry Forbes (Birmingham) 56:30.0	
1949	F.Clare (Birmingham) 62:29.4	
1950	John Copperwheat (Highgate) 57:14.6	
1951	George Coleman (Highgate) 53:41.4	
1952	George Coleman (Highgate) 51:23.4	
1953	Alf Poole (Worcester) 58:03.4	
1954	George Coleman (Highgate) 54:01.0	
1955	Alf Poole (Worcester) 54:18.08	
1956	George Coleman (Highgate) 52:51.4	
1957	Ken Matthews (R.Sutton C) 51:13.4	
1959	Ken Matthews (R.Sutton C) 50:16.6	
1960	Ken Matthews (R.Sutton C) 50:50	
1961	Ken Matthews (R.Sutton C) 49:07.2	
1962	Ken Matthews (R.Sutton C) 52:40.0	
1963	Ken Matthews (R.Sutton C) 49:58.8	
1964	Ken Matthews (R.Sutton C) 49:49.0	
1965	John Edgington (Coventry) 53:50.4	
1966	John Paddick (R.Sutton C) 53:26.2	
1967	Bob Hughes (R.Sutton C) 53:16.2	
1968	Bob Hughes (R.Sutton C) 51:14.8	

10,000 METRES TRACK

1969	Geoff Toone (Leicester) 45:58.8	
1970	Geoff Toone (Leicester) 45:29.6	
1971	Brian Adams (Leicester) 47:05.0	
1972	Geoff Toone (Leicester) 45:11.0	
1975	Brian Adams (Leicester) 43:45.0	
1976	George Chaplin (Coventry) 45:59	
1977	Brian Adams (Leicester) 44:07.0	
1978	Brian Adams (Leicester) 43:46.0	
1979	Brian Adams (Leicester) 44:57.0	
1980	John Paddick (Leicester) 47:21.0	
1981	Allan King (Leicester) 44:21.0	
1982	Allan King (Leicester) 46:08.8	
1983	Chris Smith (Leicester) 45:44.35	
1984	Allan King (Leicester) 44:39.6	
1985	Andi Drake (Coventry) 45:38.0	
1986	Andi Drake (Coventry) 44:06.0	
1987	Andi Drake (Coventry) 44:52.0	
1988	Andy Penn (Coventry) 45:22.0	
1989	Andi Drake (Coventry) 42:07.82	
1990	Darren Thorn (Coventry) 43:31.0	
1992	Carl Walmsley (Coventry) 46:51.0	
1993	Darren Thorn (Coventry) 44:55.9	
1994	Karl Orchard (Leicester) 48:40.9	
1995	Martin Young (Road Hoggs) 44:30.0	
1996	Chris Smith (Leicester) 51:20.7	
1998	Martin Young (Road Hoggs) 46:40.79	
1999	D.Bentley 52:46.10	
2000	Brian Adams (Leicester) 51:31.05	
2001	Andi Drake (Coventry) 43:21.0	
2002	Steve Arnold (Coventry) 51:38.14	
2003	Chris Berwick (Leicester) 53:23.90	
2004	Luke Finch (Leicester) 44:42.01	
2005	Steve Hollier (Wolverhampton & B) 46:28.5	
2006	Mark Williams (Tamworth) 46 11.42	
2010	Tommy Taylor (Birchfield) 46 15.0	
2013	Mark Williams (Tamworth) 52:45.6	

10 KILOMETRES ROAD

2000	Lloyd Finch (Leicester) 46:36	
2001	Lloyd Finch (Leicester) 46:35	
2002	Lloyd Finch (Leicester) 44:53	
2003	Andrew Parker (Wolverhampton & B) 49:22	
2004	Luke Finch (Leicester) 46:28	
2005	Mark Williams (Tamworth) 50:49	
2008	Mark Williams (Tamworth) 46:46	
2010	Tommy Taylor (Birchfield) 46 43	
2011	Mark Williams (Tamworth) 50:56	

10 MILES ROAD

1934	Lloyd Johnson (Leicester) 79:40	
1935	Dick Edge (Birmingham) 79:24	
1936	Syd Smith (Birmingham) 86:03	
1937	Syd Smith (Birmingham) 81:43	
1938	Albert Staines (Leicester) 83:25	
1939	Albert Staines (Leicester) 81:23	
1947	Albert Staines (Leicester) 83:35	
1948	Lloyd Johnson (Leicester) 82:04	
1949	Albert Staines (Leicester) 81:40	
1950	George Coleman (Highgate) 82:50	
1951	George Coleman (Highgate H) 81:59	
1952	George Coleman (Highgate H) 79:18	
1953	George Coleman (Highgate H) 82:43	
1954	George Coleman (Highgate H) 81:03	
1955	George Coleman (Highgate H) 79:13	
1956	Alf Poole (Worcester) 79:46	
1957	Alf Poole (Worcester) 69:19	
1958	Ken Matthews (R.Sutton C) 77:08	
1959	Ken Matthews (R.Sutton C) 69:25	
1960	Ken Matthews (R.Sutton C) 73:47	
1961	Ken Matthews (R.Sutton C) 75:36	
1962	Ken Harding (R.Sutton C) 79:28	
1963	Ken Matthews (R.Sutton C) 74:55	
1964	Ken Matthews (R.Sutton C) 70:21	
1965	John Edgington (R.Sutton C) 77:38	
1966	John Paddick (R.Sutton C) 76:06	
1967	Bob Hughes (R.Sutton C) 74:30	
1968	Bob Hughes (R.Sutton C) 74:55	
1969	Geoff Toone (Leicester) 74:58	
1970	Geoff Toone (Leicester) 76:47	
1971	Eric Taylor (Bromsgrove & R) 76:05	
1972	Geoff Toone (Leicester) 73:31	
1973	Geoff Toone (Leicester) 74:55	
1974	Eric Taylor (Nomads) 76:12	

1975	Brian Adams (Leicester) 73:53		1952	Harry Forbes (Birmingham) 2:56:54
1977	Brian Adams (Leicester) 73:50		1953	Albert Staines (Leicester) 3:02:52
1978	Brian Adams (Leicester) 73:36		1954	Albert Staines (Leicester) 3:02:25
1979	Brian Adams (Leicester) 75:05		1955	Alf Poole (Worcester) 2:51:32
1980	Brian Adams (Leicester) 76:22		1956	Alf Poole (Worcester) 2:52:43
1981	Steve Barry (Roath) 69:28		1957	George Chaplin (Coventry) 2:46:39
1982	Steve Barry (Roath) 67:59		1958	George Chaplin (Coventry) 2:50:25
1983	Allan King (Leicester) 71:41		1959	Ken Matthews (R.Sutton C) 2:46:40
1984	Allan King (Leicester) 71:28		1960	John Edgington (Coventry) 3:01:48
1986	Chris Smith (Leicester) 69:59		1961	John Edgington (Coventry) 2:46:38
1987	Mike Smith (Coventry) 72:58		1962	John Edgington (Coventry) 2:49:44
1989	Mike Smith (Coventry) 71:52		1963	John Edgington (Coventry) 2:42:43
1990	Mike Smith (Coventry) 73:20		1964	John Edgington (Coventry) 2:48:52
1991	Darren Thorn (Coventry) 77:00		1966	John Paddick (R.Sutton C) 2:56:50
1992	Andy Penn (Coventry) 67:58		1967	Roy Lodge (R.Sutton C) 2:43:56
1993	Allan King (Leicester) 72:36		1968	John Paddick (R.Sutton C) 2:41:27
1994	Kieron Butler (Trowbridge) 74:48		1969	Eric Taylor (Hinckley) 2:41:57
1995	Brian Adams (Leicester) 82:0		1970	Roy Lodge (Bromsgrove) 2:43:12
1996	Martin Young (Road Hoggs) 69:40		1971	Eric Taylor (Bromsgrove) 2:38:39
1997	Allan King (Road Hoggs) 77:13		1972	Malcolm Tolley (Leicester) 2:41:30
1998	Michael Kemp (Leicester) 77:41		1973	Eric Taylor (Nomads) 2:41:10
1999	Andi Drake (Coventry) 78:00		1974	Brian Adams (Leicester) 2:41:50

20 KILOMETRES ROAD

			1975	George Chaplin (Coventry) 2:50:57
1975	Brian Adams (Leicester) 1:33:27		1976	Eric Taylor (Coventry) 2:48:12
1977	Brian Adams (Leicester) 1:36:12		1977	Brian Adams (Leicester) 2:42:06
1978	Brian Adams (Leicester) 1:35:54		1978	Brian Adams (Leicester) 2:37:37
1979	Brian Adams (Leicester) 1:33:05			

35 KILOMETRES ROAD

1980	John Paddick (Leicester) 1:41:00		1981	Mike Smith (Coventry) 2:59:42
1981	Allan King (Leicester) 1:35:16		1982	Allan King (Leicester) 2:54:59
1982	Allan King (Leicester) 1:35:34 track		1983	Chris Smith (Leicester) 2:54:38
1983	Allan King (Leicester) 1:37:15		1984	Allan King (Leicester) 2:50:24
1988	Jon Vincent (Leicester) 1:35:10		1985	Allan King (Leicester) 2:46:11
1990	Darren Thorn (Coventry) 1:31:39		1986	Mike Smith (Coventry) 2:55:35
1992	Chris Smith (Leicester) 1:42:51		1988	Chris Berwick (Leicester) 3:02:08
1993	Chris Smith (Leicester) 1:44:02		1989	Andi Drake (Coventry) 2:38:01
1994	Karl Atton (Leicester) 1:42:12		1990	Ian Harvey (Coventry) 3:02:21

30 KILOMETRES ROAD

1996	Martin Young (Road Hoggs) 1:32:46			
1997	Martin Young (Road Hoggs) 1:35:12		1998	Allan King (Road Hoggs) 2:30:25
1998	Karl Orchard (Leicester) 1:40:23		1999	Allan King (Road Hoggs) 2:21:09
1999	Steve Hollier (Wolverhampton & B) 1:28:34		2000	Mike Smith (Coventry) 2:45:06
2000	Allan King (Leicester) 1:38:21		2001	Steve Hollier (Wolverhampton & B) 2:18:31
2001	Mike Smith (Coventry) 1:41:20		2002	Martin Young (Road Hoggs) 2:26:47
2002	Mark Williams (Tamworth) 1:37:30		2003	Andy Penn (Nuneaton) 2:24:21
2003	Mike Smith (Coventry) 1:44:06		2004	Luke Finch (Leicester) 2:48:47
2004	Chris Berwick (Leicester) 1:49:56		2005	Mark Williams (Tamworth) 2:43:59
2006	Mark Williams (Tamworth) 1:38:45		2006	Andy Penn (Nuneaton) 2:24:18
2007	Mark Williams (Tamworth) 1:36:17		2007	Mark Williams (Tamworth) 2:45:56
2008	Mark Williams (Tamworth) 1:39:29		2008	Mark Williams (Tamworth) 2:38:08
2009	Chris Berwick (Leicester) 1:59:37		2009	Steve Arnold (Nuneaton) 3 03.00
2010	Steve Arnold (Nuneaton) 1 49 58		2010	Tommy Taylor (Birchfield) 2:38:58
2011	Mark Williams (Tamworth) 1:49:03		2011	Daniel King (Colchester) 2:24:50
2013	Mark Williams (Tamworth) 1:56:09		2013	Chris Berwick (Leicester) 3:12:08

20 MILES ROAD

50 KILOMETRES ROAD

1933	Lloyd Johnson (Leicester) 2:40:51		1932	Lloyd. Johnson (Leicester) 4:43:34.2
1934	Dick Edge (Birmingham) 2:50:11		1933	Lloyd Johnson (Leicester) 4:44:47
1935	Lloyd Johnson (Leicester) 2:50:29		1935	Lloyd Johnson (Leicester) 4:39:20
1936	Lloyd Johnson (Leicester) 2:51:54		1936	Harry Forbes (Birmingham) 4:58:59
1937	Albert Staines (Leicester) 2:47:44		1937	Herbert Cashmore (Leicester) 4:49:56
1938	Lloyd Johnson (Leicester) 2:53:12		1950	Lloyd Johnson (Leicester) 4:56:32
1939	Albert Staines (Leicester) 2:57:58		1951	Albert Staines (Leicester) 4:59:35
1946	Harry Forbes (Birmingham) 2:50:43		1952	Harry Forbes (Birmingham) 4:52:55
1947	Harry Forbes (Birmingham) 2:58:14		1956	Wilf Smith (Leicester) 4:54:07
1948	Lloyd Johnson (Leicester) 2:57:47		1957	George Chaplin (Coventry) 4:37:41
1949	Lloyd Johnson (Leicester) 3:02:43		1958	George Chaplin (Coventry) 4:37:15
1950	Lloyd Johnson (Leicester) 2:58:52		1959	Albert Staines (Leicester) 4:40:17
1951	Lloyd Johnson (Leicester) 2:53:56		1960	Frank O'Reilly (Lozells) 4:50:10

1961	Albert Staines (Leicester) 4:47:30	
1962	Albert Staines (Leicester) 5:00:04	
1963	Frank O'Reilly (Lozells) 4:39:10	
1964	John Paddick (R.Sutton C) 4:29:07	
1965	John Paddick (R.Sutton C) 4:25:50	
1966	Albert Staines (Leicester) 5:22:30	
1967	John Paddick (R.Sutton C) 4:48:57	
1968	George Chaplin (Coventry) 4:44:47	
1969	George Chaplin (Coventry) 4:30:30	
1970	Ken Harding (R.Sutton C) 4:30:47	
1971	Ken Harding (R.Sutton C) 4:36:00	
1972	George Chaplin (Coventry) 4:34:31	
1973	Ken Harding (R.Sutton C) 4:30:34	
1974	Brian Adams (Leicester) 4:31:51	
1975	Ken Harding (R.Sutton C) 4:40:35	
1976	Ian Richards (Coventry) 4:43:05	
1977	Brian Adams (Leicester) 4:25:28	
1978	David Cotton (Holloway Poly) 4:14:25	
1979	Ian Richards (Coventry) 4:25:46	
1980	Brian Adams (Leicester) 4:23:01	
1981	Ian Richards (Coventry) 4:15:45	
1982	Brian Adams (Leicester) 4:29:05	
1983	Brian Adams (Leicester) 4:44:50	
1984	Darren Thorn (Coventry) 4:41:56	
1985	Chris Berwick (Leicester) 4:27:29	
1986	Chris Berwick (Leicester) 4:23:22	
1987	Chris Berwick (Leicester) 4:34:02	
1988	Tony Collins (RS& B) 5:07:54	
1989	Mike Smith (Coventry) 4:27:19	
1990	Chris Berwick (Leicester) 4:33:23	
1991	Chris Berwick (Leicester) 4:30:53	
1992	Allan King (Leicester) 4:22:53	
1993	Chris Berwick (Leicester) 4:42:42	
1994	Chris Berwick (Leicester) 4:40:41	
1995	Chris Berwick (Leicester) 4:39:27	
1996	Karl Atton (Road Hoggs) 4:35:48	
1997	Chris Berwick (Leicester) 4:42:51	
1998	Mike Smith (Coventry) 4:49:40	
1999	Mike Smith (Coventry) 4:44:33	
2000	Mike Smith (Coventry) 4:51:31	
2001	Mike Smith (Coventry) 4:33:17	
2002	Mike Smith (Coventry) 4:42:58	
2003	Mike Smith (Coventry) 5:00:41	
2004	Mike Smith (Coventry) 4:59:47	
2005	Chris Berwick (Leicester) 5:16:05	
2006	Steve Arnold (Nuneaton) 5:26:17	
2007	Steve Arnold (Nuneaton) 5:20:40	
2008	Steve Arnold (Nuneaton) 5:14:16	
2009	John Constandinou (Birchfield) 5:58:34	
2010	Steve Arnold (Nuneaton) 5:17:22	
2011	not held	

WOMEN'S 1 MILE TRACK
1934	Edna Duffield (Birchfield) 9:28.0
1935	Hettie Beeson (Small Heath) 8:24.0
1936	Mary Pritchard (Small Heath) 8:49.0
1938	Mary Harrington (Birchfield) 8:45.8
1939	Mary Harrington (Birchfield) 8:30.2
1946	Doris Hart (Birchfield) 8:41.5
1947	Beryl Day (Birmingham Atalanta) 8:40.0
1949	Joyce Heath (Small Heath) 8:20.8
1950	Joyce Heath (Small Heath) 8:21.5
1951	Joyce Heath (Small Heath)
1952	Beryl Day (Birmingham Atalanta) 8:10.2
1953	Beryl Randle (Day) (B'ham Atalanta) 8:15.5
1954	Beryl Randle (Birmingham Atalanta) 7:44.0
1955	Beryl Randle (Birchfield) 7:59.2
1956	Joyce Heath (Small Heath) 7:57.1
1957	Pat Myatt (Smethwick H) 8:10.2
1958	Pat Myatt (Smethwick H) 8:21.4

WOMEN'S 1½ MILES TRACK
1959	Pat Myatt (Smethwick) 12:29.4
1960	Joyce Heath (Small Heath) 12:33.8
1961	Joan Wallis (Harborne) 13:08.2
1962	Maureen Eyre (Birchfield) 13:32.8
1963	Audrey Hackett (Harborne) 12:52.6
1964	Audrey Hackett (Harborne) 12:47.6
1965	Audrey Hackett (Harborne) 12:49.2
1966	Audrey Hackett (Harborne) 12:41.4
1967	Betty Jenkins (Birchfield) 13:15.0
1968	Betty Jenkins (Birchfield) 13:10.4

WOMEN'S 2500 METRES TRACK
1969	Betty Jenkins (Birchfield) 13:14.8
1970	Betty Jenkins (Birchfield) 13:17.0

WOMEN'S 3000 METRES TRACK
1971	Margaret Lewis (Birchfield) 15:36.2
1972	Betty Jenkins (Birchfield) 15:24.4
1973	Betty Jenkins (Birchfield) 15:18.6
1974	Pam Branson (Harborne) 16:04.6
1975	Virginia Lovell (Birchfield) 15:08.6
1976	Pam Branson (Harborne) 14:46.6
1977	Sylvia Saunders (Birchfield) 15:20.4

WOMEN'S 5000 METRES TRACK
1978	Karen Eden (Solihull & SH) 25:09.4
1979	Karen Eden (Solihull & SH) 25:24.0
1980	Elaine Cox (Solihull & SH) 24:43.2
1981	Elaine Cox (Solihull & SH) 25:38.1
1982	Elaine Worth (Bolehall) 27:23.6
1983	Elaine Worth (Bolehall) 27:48.5
1984	Elaine Worth (Bolehall) 26:45.5
1985	Ruth Harper (Birchfield) 26:44.0
1986	Ruth Harper (Sparkhill) 26:24.0
1988	Andrea Crofts (Leicester) 26:02.60
1989	Sylvia Black (Birchfield) 25:41.81
1990	Sylvia Black (Birchfield) 24:22.65
1991	Sylvia Black (Birchfield) 24:25.03
1992	Sylvia Black (Birchfield) 23:34.43
1993	Elaine Callinan (Solihull & SH) 25:38.7
1994	Melanie Wright (Nuneaton) 23:47.0
1995	Sharon Tonks (Bromsgrove & R) 27:06.19
1996	Melanie Wright (Nuneaton) 24:14.7
1999	Kath Horwill (Dudley) 25:38.07
2001	Wendy Bennett (Worcester) 24:24.0
2002	Ann Wheeler (Nuneaton) 28:07.19
2003	Wendy Bennett (Worcester) 25:24.78
2004	Kath Horwill (Dudley) 25:14.0
2005	Sharon Tonks (Bromsgrove & R) 24:17.7
2006	Sharon Tonks (Bromsgrove & R) 27:07.62
2007	Lisa Kehler (Wolverhampton & B) 27:53.0
2010	Fiona McGorum (Leicester) 26 59.0
2011	Ann Wheeler (Leicester) 29:39.4
2012	Fiona McGorum (Leicester) 26:53.7
2013	Ann Wheeler (Leicester) 28:46.00

WOMEN'S 2.5 MILES ROAD
1935	Thelma Winter (Westbury H) 23:46
1937	Doris Harris (Birchfield) 23:10
1938	Doris Harris (Birchfield) 25:35
1939	Mary Harrington (Birchfield)
1945	Doris Hart (Birchfield)
1946	Doris Hart (Birchfield) 21:49
1948-9	Joyce Heath (Small Heath) 22:50
1949	Joyce Heath (Small Heath) 21:05

1950	Joyce Heath (Small Heath) 21:47	1986	Lisa Langford (Wolverhampton & B) 48:34.0
1951	Joyce Heath (Small Heath) 21:13	1987	Elaine Worth (Bromsgrove & R) 54:12.0
1952	Beryl Randle (B'ham Atalanta) 23:02	1988	Melanie Brookes (Nuneaton) 55:22.0
1953	Beryl Randle (B'ham Atalanta) 20:26	1989	Julie Bellfield (Dudley) 60:24.0
1954	Dilys Williams (Birchfield) 21:10	1990	Karen Smith (Coventry) 54:40.0
1955	Dilys Williams (Birchfield) 20:59	1991	Melanie Brookes (Nuneaton) 50:02.0
1956	Dilys Williams (Birchfield) 18:28	1992	Karen Smith (Coventry) 52:55.0
1957	Pat Myatt (Smethwick) 22:58	1993	Karen Smith (Coventry) 52:05.4

WOMEN'S 4 MILES ROAD

2006   Karen Davies (Birchfield) 61:07.62

1958	Pat Myatt (Smethwick) 34 65
1959	Beryl Randle (Birchfield) 32:29
1960	Joan Wallis (Harborne) 36:16
1962	Joyce Heath (Small Heath) 35:02
1963	Audrey Hackett (Harborne) 36:26
1964	Audrey Hackett (Harborne) 34:46
1965	Audrey Hackett (Harborne) 35:33
1966	Betty Jenkins (Birchfield) 34:22
1967	Betty Jenkins (Birchfield) 34:55
1968	Betty Jenkins (Birchfield) 32:45
1969	Betty Jenkins (Birchfield) 35:13

WOMEN'S 10 KILOMETRES ROAD

1988	Andrea Crofts (Leicester) 55:04
1989	Melanie Brookes (Nuneaton) 51:58
1990	Andrea Crofts (Leicester) 52:09
1992	Karen Smith (Coventry) 52:03
1993	Karen Smith (Coventry) 49:43
1999	Kim Braznell (Dudley) 50:34
2000	Nikki Huckerby (Birchfield) 55:24
2001	Sharon Tonks (Bromsgrove & R) 53:04
2002	Kath Horwill (Dudley) 59:45
2003	Ann Wheeler (Nuneaton) 61:56
2004	Sheila Owen (Tamworth) 61:57
2006	Fiona McGorum (Leicester) 56:47
2007	Jill Eve (Leicester) 60:59
2009	Fiona McGorum (Leicester) 56 46

WOMEN'S 6500 METRES ROAD

1970	Betty Jenkins (Birchfield) 32:27
1971	Betty Jenkins (Birchfield)
1972	Betty Jenkins (Birchfield) 33:09
1973	Pam Branson (Harborne) 39:50
1974	Virginia Lovell (Birchfield) 34:43
1975	Virginia Lovell (Birchfield) 33:46
1976	Sylvia Saunders (Birchfield) 32:01
1977	Sylvia Saunders (Birchfield) 33:30
1979	Elaine Cox (Solihull & SH) 33:04

WOMEN'S 20 KILOMETRES ROAD

2000	Sheila Bull (Tamworth) 2:21:22
2001	Sheila Bull (Tamworth) 2:16:46
2002	Kim Braznell (Dudley) 1:45:07
2003	Wendy Bennett (Worcester) 1:48:51
2006	Karen Davies (Birchfield) 2:11:16
2007	Jill Eve (Leicester) 2:15:05
2008	Helen Middleton (Leicester, g) 2:07:34
	Sue Rey (Leicester) 2:19:08
2009	Sarah Lightman (Leicester) 2:21:10
2010	Fiona McGorum (Leicester) 1 54 29
2013	Heather Lewis (Pembrokeshire) 1:45:54

WOMEN'S 5 KILOMETRES ROAD

1980	Elaine Cox (Solihull & SH) 25:39
1983	Karen Nipper (Roath) 26:23
1984	Karen Nipper (Roath) 25:29
1986	Lisa Langford (Wolverhampton & B) 24:14
1987	Lisa Langford (Wolverhampton & B) 23:25
1989	Andrea Crofts (Leicester) 24:38
1990	Sylvia Black (Birchfield) 22:32 (short)
1991	Karen Smith (Coventry) 25:08
1992	Karen Smith (Coventry) 25:01
1993	Sylvia Black (Birchfield) 23:13
1994	Sylvia Black (Birchfield) 23:58
1995	Lisa Langford (Wolverhampton & B) 23:24
1996	Lisa Langford (Wolverhampton & B) 23:13
1997	Sylvia Black (Birchfield) 23:40
1998	Lisa Kehler (Wolverhampton & B) 23:59
1999	Sarah Bennett (Birchfield) 25:56
2000	Lisa Kehler (Wolverhampton & B) 23:31
2001	Sharon Tonks (Bromsgrove & R) 24:58
2002	Karen Ratcliffe (Coventry) 25:36
2003	Sharon Tonks (Bromsgrove & R) 24:47
2004	Sharon Tonks (Bromsgrove & R) 26:43
2005	Fiona McGorum (Leicester) 27:55
2006	Sharon Tonks (Bromsgrove & R) 27:13
2007	Fiona McGorum (Leicester) 27:08
2008	Lisa Kehler (Wolverhampton & B) 24:32
2011	Lisa Kehler (Wolverhampton & B) 24:16

WOMEN'S 30 KILOMETRES ROAD

2006	Karen Davies (Birchfield) 3:36:38
2007	Sarah Lightman (Leicester) 4:04:02

NORTHERN CHAMPIONSHIPS

2 MILES TRACK

1910	Bill Yates (Salford H) 14:19.4
1911	Bobby Bridge (Lancashire WC) 13:48.8
1913	Bobby Bridge (Lancs WC) 13:57.4
1914	Bobby Bridge (Lancs WC) 14:32.4
1920	Bill Yates (Salford H) 14:58.8
1921	Bobby Bridge (Lancs WC) 15:30.4
1922	Bobby Bridge (Lancs WC) 14:46.8
1923	F.Hutchins (Stockport H) 18:15.0
1924	J.Harrop (Makerfield) 14:47.0
1925	R.Marston (Lancs WC) 14:36.0
1926	C.Coulson (Sheffield UH) 14:46.2
1927	C.Coulson (Sheffield UH) 14:51.8
1928	John Wilson (Sheffield UH) 14:27.0,
1929	C.Coulson (Bradford City Police) 14:29.2
1930	Leslie Dickinson (Lancs WC) 13:58.0
1931	Leslie Dickinson (Lancs WC) 14:17.6
1932	Leslie Dickinson (Lancs WC) 14:04.2
1933	Leslie Dickinson (Lancs WC) 14:21.4
1934	Leslie Dickinson (Lancs WC) 14:21.4
1935	W.Bullock (Sheffield UH) 14:30.4
1936	Leslie Dickinson (Lancs WC) 14:56.6
1937	Leslie Dickinson (Lancs WC) 14:22.8
1938	Leslie Dickinson (Lancs WC) 14:25.4
1939	Leslie Dickinson (Lancs WC) 14:41.6

WOMEN'S 10,000 METRES TRACK

1975	Pam Branson (Harborne) 54:48.6
1977	Sylvia Saunders (Harborne) 54:54
1978	Virginia Lovell (Birchfield) 51:36.0
1979	Karen Eden (Birchfield) 52:12.0
1980	Elaine Cox (Solihull & SH) 51:51.0
1981	Liz Gaffer (Leicester) 54:59.0,
1985	Lisa Langford (Wolverhampton & B) 50:44.0

Year	Winner
1946	T.Owen (Manchester AC) 15:24.4
1947	Allan Furniss (Sheffield UH) 14:38.4
1948	Allan Furniss (Sheffield UH) 14:31
1949	Lol Allen (Sheffield UH) 14:13.4
1950	Roland Hardy (Sheffield) 13:46.2
1951	Roland Hardy (Sheffield) 14:19.6
1952	Roland Hardy (Sheffield) 13:38.0
1953	Richard Holland (Sheffield) 14:38.2
1954	Joe Barraclough (Lancs) 14:09.4
1955	Joe Barraclough (Lancs) 14:10.2
1956	Maurice Greasley (Sheffield) 14:49.6
1957	Maurice Greasley (Sheffield) 15:38.2
1958	Joe Barraclough (Lancs WC) 14:13.2
1959	Douglas Greasley (Sheffield) 14:47.8
1960	Douglas Greasley (Sheffield) 14:44.6
1961	Ron Wallwork (Lancs) 14:45.6
1962	Ron Wallwork (Lancs) 15:14.8
1963	Jim Stancer (Sheffield) 14:37.0
1964	Malcolm Tolley (Sheffield) 14:48.0
1965	Ron Wallwork (Lancs) 14:15.2
1966	Ron Wallwork (Lancs) 13:36.0
1967	Donald Warren (Lancs WC) 16:29.4
1968	Phil Bannan (Boundary H) 14:16.8

3000 METRES TRACK
1969	Ron Wallwork (Lancs WC) 13:24.0
1970	Ron Wallwork (Lancs WC) 12:57.0
1971	Guy Goodair (Wakefield) 13:51.8

5000 METRES TRACK
2006	Ben Wears (Redcar) 22:49.41
2008	Ben Wears (Redcar) 22:38.46

7 MILES TRACK
1913	Bobby Bridge (Lancs WC) 53:34.0
1914	Bobby Bridge (Lancs WC) 52:06.8
1924	J.Harrop (Makerfield) 55:01.4
1947	Allan Furniss (Sheffield) 56:57.0
1952	George Rushton (Sheffield) 56:32.0
1957	Lol Allen (Sheffield) 53:59.0
1958	Albert Johnson (Sheffield) 52:57.0
1959	Maurice Greasley (Sheffield) 55:16.0
1960	Douglas Greasley (Sheffield) 56:07.0
1961	Ron Wallwork (Lancs) 54:41.0
1965	Malcolm Tolley (Sheffield) 51:31.0
1966	Ron Wallwork (Lancs) 49:50.0
1968	Ron Wallwork (Lancs) 51:11.0

10,000 METRES TRACK
1969	Ron Wallwork (Lanc) 45:35.0
1970	Ron Wallwork (Lancs) 44:55.0
1971	Ron Wallwork (Lancs) 44:05.8
1972	Roy Thorpe (Sheffield) 45:18.0
1973	Jake Warhurst (Sheffield) 45:15.0
1974	Roy Thorpe (Sheffield) 46:16.0
1975	Chris Harvey (Lancs) 48:13.0
1976	Chris Harvey (Lancs) 46:39.8
1977	Jake Warhurst (Sheffield) 45:04.0
1978	Jake Warhurst (Sheffield) 45:34.0
1979	Mike Holmes (Yorks) 44:33.0
1980	Mike Holmes (Yorks) 44:26.0
1981	Dennis Jackson (York Postal) 44:17.0
1982	Ray Hankin (Sheffield) 47:36
1983	Dave Staniforth (Sheffield) 45:11.5
1984	Dennis Jackson (York Postal) 45:07.6
1985	Les Morton (Sheffield) 43:41.0
1986	Sean Martindale (York Postal) 50:34.0
1987	Ian McCombie (Cambridge H) 41:40.43
1988	Sean Martindale (York Postal) 45:05.0
1995	Les Morton (Sheffield) 45:27.35
1996	Nick Barrabie 52:04.05
1997	Les Morton (Sheffield) 45:32.66
1999	Nathan Adams (Sheffield) 49:33.50
2004	Dwane Butterly (Leicester) 50:16.65
2005	Dave Turner (Yorks) 52:50.55

10 KILOMETRES ROAD
2002	Steve Partington (Manx) 43:08
2004	Nathan Adams (Sheffield) 48:29
2007	Ben Wears (Redcar) 47:32
2008	Ben Wears (Redcar) 45:50
2010	Ben Wears (Redcar) 44:39
2011	Paul Evenett (Redcar) 42:25

10 MILES ROAD
1949	John Proctor (Sheffield) 76:14
1950	Lol Allen (Sheffield) 75:18
1951	Roland Hardy (Sheffield) 71:43
1952	Roland Hardy (Sheffield) 72:10 (440y short)
1953	Roland Hardy (Sheffield) 76:10
1954	Lol Allen (Sheffield) 72:21
1955	Roland Hardy (Sheffield) 76:22
1956	Roland Hardy (Sheffield) 75:53
1957	Lol Allen (Sheffield) 77:25
1958	Lol Allen (Sheffield) 76:39
1959	Maurice Greasley (Sheffield) 80:23
1960	Douglas Greasley (Sheffield) 81:18
1961	Ray Ibbotson (Sheffield) 78:46
1962	Jim Stancer (Sheffield) 81:48
1963	Ron Wallwork (Lancs) 75:29
1964	Ron Wallwork (Lancs) 76:33
1965	Ron Wallwork (Lancs) 75:59
1966	Ron Wallwork (Lancs) 75:29
1967	Ron Wallwork (Lancs) 75:00
1968	Jake Warhurst (Sheffield) 73:59
1969	Jake Warhurst (Sheffield) 74:20
1970	Jake Warhurst (Sheffield) 75:25
1971	Ron Wallwork (Lancs) 77:33
1972	Jake Warhurst (Sheffield) 74:48
1973	Jake Warhurst (Sheffield) 73:12
1974	Ron Wallwork (Blackburn) 75:48
1975	Jake Warhurst (Sheffield) 77:48
1976	Jake Warhurst (Sheffield) 73:50
1977	Jake Warhurst (Sheffield) 73:21
1978	Jake Warhurst (Sheffield) 74:03
1979	Chris Harvey (Lancs) 73:28
1980	Mick Greasley (Sheffield) 72:08
1981	Mick Greasley (Sheffield) 76:11
1982	Mick Greasley (Sheffield) 74:07
1983	Dennis Jackson (York Postal) 76:29
1984	Dennis Jackson (York Postal) 74:23
1986	Ray Hankin (Sheffield) 72:33
1987	Dave Staniforth (Sheffield) 72:28
1988	Ian McCombie (Cambridge H) 66:25
1989	Ian McCombie (Cambridge H) 68:23
1990	Les Morton (Sheffield) 72:51
1996	Richard Oldale (Sheffield) 74:35
1998	Les Morton (Sheffield) 76:07
2003	Nathan Adams (Sheffield) 77:35
2004	Dave Turner (Yorks) 86:33
2005	Paul Evenett (York CIU) 83:52
2006	Paul Evenett (York CIU) 84:30
2010	Paul Evenett (Redcar) 79 48

20 KILOMETRES ROAD
1975	Jake Warhurst (Sheffield) 1:35:27
1976	Roy Thorpe (Sheffield) 1:33:19
1977	Jake Warhurst (Sheffield) 1:33:31

1978	Chris Harvey (Lancs) 1:35:01		1986	Dave Staniforth (Sheffield) 2:49:05
1979	Mike Holmes (York Postal) 1:32:25		1988	Les Morton (Sheffield) 2:53:19
1980	Mick Greasley (Sheffield) 1:31:21		**50 KILOMETRES ROAD**	
1982	Dennis Jackson (York Postal) 1:32:05		1932	J.Ludlow (Derby) 4:49:47
1983	Graham White (York Postal) 1:32:47		1933	H.Kirkbight (Yorks) 5:05:10
1984	Mick Greasley (Sheffield) 1:35:42		1934	Tommy Payne (South Shields) 4:56:22.8
1985	Dave Staniforth (Sheffield) 1:32:11		1935	L.Richards (Derbyshire) 4:59:33
1986	Les Morton (Sheffield) 1:29:53		1936	Joe Hopkins (Lancs) 4:42:00
1987	Ian McCombie (Cambridge H) 1:26:51		1937	G.Birchall (Lancs) 5:14:55
1989	Les Morton (Sheffield) 1:31:58		1938	Joe Hopkins (Lancs) 4:45:51
1993	Les Morton (Sheffield) 1:35:13		1947	Jim Hackwood (Sheffield)
1996	Richard Oldale (Sheffield) 1:36:57		1948	Norman Hopkinson (Sheffield) 5:18:17
1999	Les Morton (Sheffield) 1:40:05		1949	Les Barrett (Enfield) 5:05:24
2001	Karl Atton (Road Hoggs) 1:35:10		1950	Norman Hopkinson (Sheffield) 5:06:01
2002	Peter Ryan (Sheffield) 1:44:35		1951	Charles Colman (Yorks) 5:03:17
2004	Paul Evenett (York CIU) 1:51:18		1952	Charles Colman (Yorks) 4:51:43
2007	Paul Evenett (York CIU) 1:38:24		1953	James Hartley (Sheffield) 5:01:42
2008	Ben Wears (Redcar) 1:36:27		1954	Albert Johnson (Sheffield) 4:36:36
2009	Paul Evenett (Redcar) 1:40:32		1955	Albert Johnson (Sheffield) 4:51:03
2010	Paul Evenett (Redcar) 1:35:29		1956	Albert Johnson (Sheffield) 4:45:55
20 MILES ROAD			1957	Albert Johnson (Sheffield) 4:43:45
1912	Bobby Bridge (Lancs) 3:06:15		1958	Albert Johnson (Sheffield) 4:26:40
1913	J.Sutton (Lancs) 2:56:04.2		1959	Albert Johnson (Sheffield) 5:01:39
1914	J.Sutton (Lancs) 4:01:07		1960	Albert Johnson (Sheffield) 4:48:55
1933	John Wilson (Sheffield) 2:53:47		1961	Albert Johnson (Sheffield) 4:48:14
1934	A.Bullock (Sheffield) 2:57:49		1962	Ray Ibbotson (Sheffield) 4:45:55
1935	Joe Hopkins (Lancs) 2:39:58		1963	Albert Johnson (Sheffield) 4:48:03
1936	Joe Hopkins (Lancs) 2:59:52.8		1964	Ron Wallwork (Lancs) 4:32:52
1937	Joe Hopkins (Lancs) 3:09:06		1965	Guy Goodair (Wakefield) 4:37:53
1938	Joe Hopkins (Lancs) 2:56:38		1966	Albert Johnson (Sheffield) 4:53:29
1939	Joe Hopkins (Lancs) 3:00:24		1967	George Barras (Wakefield) 4:49:19
1946	Henry Moorhouse (Lancs) 3:02:11		1968	George Barras (Wakefield) 4:49:0
1947	Joe Smith (Lancs) 3:15:08		1969	Jake Warhurst (Sheffield) 4:28:58
1948	Lol Allen (Sheffield) 2:59:05		1970	Jake Warhurst (Sheffield) 4:37:11
1949	Lol Allen (Sheffield) 3:04:10		1971	Ron Wallwork (Lancs) 4:29:20
1950	John Proctor (Sheffield) 2:43:20		1974	Mel McCann (Yorks) 4:44:26
1951	Lol Allen (Sheffield) 2:59:17		1976	Jake Warhurst (Sheffield) 4:32:05
1952	John Proctor (Sheffield) 2:49:28		1977	Jake Warhurst (Sheffield) 4:28:10
1953	Lawrence Allen (Sheffield) 2:57:32		1978	Graham Young (Bound) 4:56:55
1954	Roland Hardy (Sheffield) 2:41:40		1979	Jake Warhurst (Sheffield) 4:31:05
1955	Albert Johnson (Sheffield) 2:55:03		1980	Murray Lambden (Bound) 4:31:40
1956	Roland Hardy (Sheffield) 2:35:58		1981	Murray Lambden (Bound) 4:26:49
1957	Albert Johnson (Sheffield) 2:56:06		1982	Murray Lambden (Bound) 4:37:46
1958	Joe Barraclough (Lancs) 2:46:45		1984	Dennis Jackson (York Postal) 4:27:02
1959	Joe Barraclough (Lancs) 2:52:46		1985	Mel McCann (Yorks) 4:37:34
1960	Albert Johnson (Sheffield) 2:53:50		1986	Mel McCann (Yorks) 4:22:05
1961	Lol Allen (Sheffield) 2:53:21		1987	Les Morton (Sheffield) 4:23:40
1962	Ray Ibbotson (Sheffield) 2:52:10		1988	Les Morton (Sheffield) 4:23:46
1963	Ron Wallwork (Lancs) 2:43:23		1989	Dave Staniforth (Sheffield) 4:35:06
1964	Ron Wallwork (Lancs) 2:48:37		1990	Dave Turner (Yorks) 4:56:14
1965	Malcolm Tolley (Sheffield) 2:47:42		1991	Derek Stancliffe (Sheffield) 4:59:37
1966	Ron Wallwork (Lancs) 2:48:16		1992	Derek Stancliffe (Sheffield) 5:08:17
1967	Ron Wallwork (Lancs) 2:49:04		1993	Dave Turner (Yorks) 5:10:04
1969	Jake Warhurst (Sheffield) 2:39:51		1994	Dave Turner (Yorks) 4:47:12
1970	Jake Warhurst (Sheffield) 2:49:04		1995	John Paddick (Yorks) 5:02:35
1971	Ron Wallwork (Lancs) 2:37:34		1996	John Paddick (Yorks) 5:01:20
1973	Roy Thorpe (Sheffield) 2:42:38		1997	Les Morton (Sheffield) 4:29:27
1974	Jake Warhurst (Sheffield) 2:39:03		1998	Martin Fisher (York CIU) 5:11:02
1975	John Eddershaw (Sheffield) 2:41:15		1999	Dave Turner (Yorks) 5:03:43
1976	Roy Thorpe (Sheffield) 2:47:47		2000	Dave Turner (Yorks) 4:56:59
1979	Jake Warhurst (Sheffield) 2:40:47		2001	Dave Turner (Yorks) 4:55:43
1980	Dennis Jackson (York Postal) 2:32:52		2002	Dave Turner (Yorks) 4:53:31
1981	Dennis Jackson (York Postal) 2:35:04		2003	Martin Fisher (York CIU) 5:15:24
1982	Jake Warhurst (Sheffield) 2:36:21		2004	David Jones (Redcar) 5:48:18
1983	Bary Graham (York Postal) 2:39:53		2005	Martin Fisher (unattached) 5:33:31
1984	Les Morton (Sheffield) 2:36:37		2006	Graham Jackson (York CIU) 5:30:18

2007 Martin Fisher (unatt) 5:32:21
WOMEN'S 1 MILE TRACK
1950 Molly Lightfoot (Leigh H) 9:17.0
1952 Beryl Riggott (Sheffield) 8:35.4
1953 Beryl Riggott (Sheffield) 8:35.6
1954 Beryl Riggott (Sheffield) 8:30.8
1955 Jean Gillyean (Doncaster PW) 8:57.6
1956 Jean Gillyean (Airedale H) 9:15.8
1957 Renee Scott (Winton H) 9:00.0,
1960 Jean Gillyean (Airedale H) 8:57.8
1961 Dorothy Wallwork (Bolton) 8:47.0
1962 Dorothy Wallwork (Bolton) 8:25.8
1963 Dorothy Wallwork (Bolton) 8:49.8
1964 Renee Scott (Winton H) 9:19.8
1965 Maureen Armstrong (N Shields P) 9:23.4
WOMEN'S 1.5 MILES TRACK
1966 Diane Cotterill (S Shields) 13:00.0
1967 Diane Cotterill (S Shields) 12:51.8
1968 Diane Cotterill (S Shields) 12:59.2
1969 Heather Profitt (Warrington) 13:54.8
WOMEN'S 2500 METRES TRACK
1970 Anne Johnstone (Houghton) 14:58.2
1971 Kathryn Daniels (Warr) 13:39.0
1972 Kathryn Daniels (Warr) 13:39.8
WOMEN'S 3000 METRES TRACK
1975 Marion Fawkes (NSP) 14:28.8
1976 Carol Tyson (Lakeland) 14:10.2
1977 Carol Tyson (Lakeland) 14:00.0
1978 Carol Tyson (Lakeland) 13:40.0
1979 Carol Tyson (Lakeland) 13:48.1
1980 Carol Tyson (Lakeland) 14:07.0
1981 Janice Wilkinson (Lakeland) 16:38.9
1982 Gillian Edgar (Lakeland) 16:06.8
2004 Rebecca Mersh (C of Sheffield) 14:29.91
WOMEN'S 5000 METRES TRACK
1983 Lillian Millen (Lakeland) 24:52.0
1985 Helen Elleker (Sheffield) 24:35.8
1986 Betty Sworowski (Sheffield) 25:16.0
1987 Susan Gibson (Sheffield) 25:57.3
1988 Betty Sworowski (Sheffield) 23:29
1989 Louise Spreadborough (AFD) 29:00.3
1990 Anne Irving 28:19.38
1995 Vicky Lupton (Sheffield) 22:38.93
1996 Catherine Charnock (Barrow) 25:01.01
1997 Lynn Bradley (Sheffield) 26:35.33
1998 Cal Partington (Manx) 23:32.03
1999 Catherine Charnock (Barrow) 23:11.7
2005 Johanna Jackson (Redcar) 24:50.38
2006 Johanna Jackson (Redcar) 23:20.05
2011 Johanna Jackson (Middlesbrough) 21:49.
WOMEN'S ROAD
1951 Beryl Riggott (Sheffield) 21:57.1
WOMEN'S 5 KILOMETRES ROAD
1980 Gillian Edgar (Lakeland) 27:26
1981 Carol Tyson (Lakeland) 25:13
1982 Lillian Millen (Lakeland) 25:56
1983 Lillian Millen (Lakeland) 23:42
1984 Brenda Lupton (Sheffield) 24:34
1986 Brenda Lupton (Sheffield) 26:53
1987 Helen Elleker (Sheffield) 24:31
1988 Louise Carr (Sheff Utd) 25:43
1989 Tracey Devlin (Sheffield) 26:32
1990 Betty Sworowski (Sheffield) 22:48
1996 Vicky Lupton (Sheffield) 23:43
1998 Vicky Lupton (Sheffield) 23:54

1999 Catherine Charnock (Barrow) 23:40
2004 Jo Jackson (Redcar) 27:12
2005 Jo Jackson (Redcar) 23:39
2006 Jo Jackson (Redcar) 23:35
2007 Angela Paddick (Redcar) 29:45
WOMEN'S 10 KILOMETRES ROAD
1982 Brenda Lupton (Sheffield) 53:07
1983 Brenda Lupton (Sheffield) 53:07
1984 Lillian Millen (Cumberland) 49:35
1985 Helen Elleker (Sheffield) 50:29
1986 Betty Sworowski (Sheffield) 55:08
1987 Betty Sworowski (Sheffield) 51:26
1993 Vicky Lupton (Sheffield) 49:21
1995 Liz Corran (Manx) 52:50
1996 Lisa Crump (Sheffield) 56:05
1997 Lisa Crump (Sheffield) 55:52
2001 Hazel Fairhurst (Lancs) 62:45
2007 Jo Jackson (Redcar) 49:43
2008 Angela Paddick (Redcar) 58:34
WOMEN'S 20 KILOMETRES ROAD
1999 Lisa Crump (Sheffield) 1:48:57
2002 Cal Partington (Manx) 1:44:54
2011 Karen Wears (Redcar) 2:01:08

SOUTHERN CHAMPIONS
2 MILES TRACK
1923 Gordon Watts (Surrey WC) 14:28.0
1924 Reg Goodwin (Surrey WC) 14:27.2
1925 Reg Goodwin (Surrey WC) 14:09.6
1926 Wilf Cowley (Surrey AC) 14:49.0
1927 Alf Pope (Woodford Green) 14:34.8
1928 Alf Pope (Woodford Green) 14:13.6
1929 Alf Pope (Woodford Green) 14:11.0
1930 Alf Pope (Woodford Green) 13:56.6
1931 Bert Cooper (Woodford Green) 14:12.6
1932 Bert Cooper (Woodford Green) 13:56.4
1933 Johnny Johnson (Enfield) 14:32.4
1934 Bert Cooper (Woodford Green) 13:54.4
1935 Bert Cooper (Woodford Green) 13:54.8
1936 Bert Cooper (Woodford Green) 14.02.0
1937 Bert Cooper (Woodford Green) 14:17.0
1938 Bert Cooper (Woodford Green) 14:18.0
1939 Bert Cooper (Woodford Green) 14:14.8
1946 Eddie Staker (Highgate H) 14:19.2
1947 Harry Churcher (Belgrave H) 14:25.6
1948 Harry Churcher (Belgrave H) 13:53.0
1949 Harry Churcher (Belgrave H) 14:35.0
1950 Harry Churcher (Belgrave H) 14:28.8
1951 William Anderson (Cambridge H) 14:54.2
1952 Gerald Gregory (Belgrave H) 14:12.4
1953 Bryan Hawkins (Metropolitan) 14:11.6
1954 Bryan Hawkins (Metropolitan) 14:18.8
1955 Bob Richards (Cambridge H) 14:29.02
1956 Stan Vickers (Belgrave H) 14:10.2
1957 Stan Vickers (Belgrave H) 13:57.6
1958 Stan Vickers (Belgrave H) 13:49.6
1959 Stan Vickers (Belgrave H) 14:00.2
1960 Stan Vickers (Belgrave H) 13:31.8
1961 Colin Williams (Ilford) 14:17.2
1962 Colin Williams (Ilford) 14:13.6
1963 Paul Nihill (Surrey WC) 13:43.6
1964 Bob Clark (Poly) 14:11.4
1965 Paul Nihill (Surrey WC) 13:26.8
1966 Norman Read (Steyning) 14:09.8
1967 Arthur Jones (Brighton) 14:21.8
1968 Arthur Jones (Brighton) 13:44.2

3000 METRES TRACK
1969 Alan Buchanan (Brighton) 13:40.8
1970 Roger Mills (Ilford) 12:37.8
1971 Ken Easlea (Enfield) 14:25.6
1972 Peter Marlow (Southend) 12:34.6
1973 Peter Marlow (Southend) 12:33.6
1974 Roger Mills (Ilford) 12:18.6
1975 Alan Buchanan (Brighton) 12:52.67
1976 Roger Mills (Ilford) 12:07.4
1977 Shaun Lightman (Metropolitan) 12:40.0
1978 Roger Mills (Ilford) 11:59.10
1979 Roger Mills (Ilford) 12:31.2
1980 Roger Mills (Ilford) 11:59.1
1981 Richard Dorman (Belgrave H) 12:42.2
1982 Adrian James (Enfield) 12:52.2
1983 Paul Warburton (Belgrave H) 13:21.0
1984 Murray Day (Belgrave H) 12:32.0
1985 Tim Berrett (Tonbridge) 13:00.6
1986 Gareth Brown (Steyning) 12:52.6
1987 John Hall (Belgrave H) 13:11.70
1988 Paul Blagg (Cambridge H) 12:37.04
1989 Mark Easton (Surrey WC) 11:45.62
1990 Paul Blagg (Cambridge H) 12:32.60
1991 Mark Easton (Surrey WC) 11:48.39
1992 Mark Easton (Surrey WC) 12:13.0
1993 Mark Easton (Surrey WC) 12:00.76
1994 Mark Easton (Surrey WC) 12:23.80
1995 Mark Easton (Surrey WC) 12:15.45
1996 Gary Witton (Brighton) 12:42.7
1997 Mark Easton (Surrey WC) 12:31.53
1998 Darrell Stone (Steyning) 12:31.50
1999 Noel Carmody (Cambridge H) 13:16.44
2000 Andrew Goudie (Belgrave H) 13:29.0

5000 METRES TRACK
2006 Trevor Jones (Hillingdon) 24:05.51
2010 Tom Bosworth (Tonbridge) 20:57.91
2012 Francisco Reis (Ilford/POR) 24:18.20

7 MILES TRACK
1947 Jack Rutland (Belgrave H) 55:37.0
1949 Fred Barrett (Cambridge H) 60:20.0
1950 Harry Churcher (Belgrave H) 54:16.4
1951 Harry Churcher (Belgrave H) 54:02.2
1952 Bryan Hawkins (Metropolitan) 53:56.8
1953 Bryan Hawkins (Metropolitan) 53:41.8
1954 Bryan Hawkins (Metropolitan) 53:36.0
1955 Bryan Hawkins (Metropolitan) 54:19.2
1956 Bryan Hawkins (Metropolitan) 53:09.4
1957 Stan Vickers (Belgrave H) 52:23.6
1958 Stan Vickers (Belgrave H) 51:51.2
1959 Colin Williams (Ilford) 53:04.0
1960 Colin Williams (Ilford) 52:51.4
1961 Bob Clark (Poly) 52:48.0
1962 Bob Clark (Poly) 53:05.0
1963 Arthur Thomson (Metropolitan) 53:38
1964 Paul Nihill (Surrey WC) 51:44.0
1965 Paul Nihill (Surrey WC) 50:58
1966 John Webb (Basildon) 53:26
1967 Paul Nihill (Surrey WC) 52:10.8
1968 Paul Nihill (Surrey WC) 50:09.0

10,000 METRES TRACK
1969 Paul Nihill (Surrey WC) 44:24.0
1970 Roger Mills (Ilford) 45:03.8
1971 Bob Dobson (Basildon) 46:14.4
1972 Bill Sutherland (Highgate H) 45:14.2
1973 Shaun Lightman (Metropolitan) 46:45.4
1974 Shaun Lightman (Metropolitan) 44:40.4
1975 Roger Mills (Ilford) 44:19.2
1976 Roger Mills (Ilford) 43:36.8
1977 Carl Lawton (Belgrave H) 45:07.8
1978 Roger Mills (Ilford) 44:39.0
1979 Gordon Vale (Surrey WC) 44:41.6
1980 Adrian James (Enfield) 43:47.7
1981 Mike Parker (Brighton) 42:17.9
1982 Adrian James (Enfield) 46:26.9
1983 Roy Sheppard (Anglia) 42:57.2
1984 Adrian James (Enfield) 44:40.1
1985 Jimmy Ball (Southampton) 46:36.0
1986 Graham Seatter (Belgrave H) 44:00.4
1987 Mark Easton (Surrey WC) 41:51.0
1988 Paul Blagg (Cambridge H) 43:30.8
1989 Paul Blagg (Cambridge H) 44:14.1
1991 Mark Easton (Surrey WC) 41:39.8
1992 Mark Easton (Surrey WC) 44:02.9?
1993 Chris Cheeseman (Surrey WC) 43:05.11
1994 Noel Carmody (Cambridge H) 48:41.70
1995 Mabon Dane (Belgrave H) 50:18.0
1996 Derek Cross (Verlea) 49:41.0
1997 Kevin Baker (Weymouth) 49:42.43
1998 Tim Watt (Steyning) 47:39.32
1999 Andrew Goudie (Belgrave H) 52:11.42
2000 Jamie O'Rawe (Road Hoggs) 46:21.75
2001 Mark Easton (Surrey WC) 47:52.86
2002 Richard Elmsley (Steyning) 53:18.50
2003 Richard Elmsley (Steyning) 53:16.50
2004 Richard Elmsley (Steyning) 50:28.81

10 KILOMETRES ROAD
1997 Darrell Stone (Steyning) 41:37
1998 Chris Cheeseman (Surrey WC) 42:28
1999 Darrell Stone (Steyning) 43:41
2000 Chris Cheeseman (Surrey WC) 42:11
2001 Chris Cheeseman (Surrey WC) 43:21
2002 Darrell Stone (Steyning) 42:54
2003 Mark Easton (Surrey WC) 46:25
2004 Dominic King (Colchester) 42:34
2005 Andrew Goudie (Belgrave H) 48:54
2006 Nick Ball (Steyning) 45:39
2007 Daniel King (Colchester) 44:30
2008 Nick Silvester (AFD) 50:07
2009 Darrell Stone (Steyning) 44:57
2010 Phil Barnard (Ilford) 50:24
2011 Dominic King (Colchester) 44:58
2012 Francisco Reis (Ilford/POR) 50:04
2013 Dominic King (Colchester) 45:34
2014 Trevor Jones (Steyning) 53:10

10 MILES ROAD
1983 Ian McCombie (Cambridge H) 69:02
1984 Richard Dorman (Belgrave H) 77:03
1985 Mark Easton (Surrey WC) 69:58
1986 Dave Rowland (Steyning) 76:27
1987 Kevin Baker (Weymouth) 77:05
1988 Noel Carmody (Cambridge H) 75:28
1989 Denys Jones (Weymouth) 73:57
1990 Noel Carmody (Cambridge H) 75:07
1992 Mark Easton (Surrey WC) 72:18
1993 Mark Easton (Surrey WC) 70:53
1994 Chris Cheeseman (Surrey WC) 72:26
2009 Mark Easton (Surrey WC) 81:02

20 KILOMETRES ROAD
1977 Carl Lawton (Belgrave) 1 32 44
1983 Chris Maddocks (Dawlish) 1:29:42
1984 Graham Seatter (Belgrave H) 1:30:46
1985 Kevin Baker (Weymouth) 1:34:42

1986	Mike Parker (Brighton) 1:27:05		1945	Diana Riddington (Cambridge H) w/o
1987	JimmyBall (Southampton) 1:28:46		1946	Diana Riddington (Cambridge H) 8:36.0
1988	Jimmy Ball (Southampton) 1:31:48		1947	Diana Riddington (Cambridge H) 9:32.0
1989	Jimmy Ball (Southampton) 1:35:12		1948	Muriel Havell (London Oly) 9:18.6
1990	Noel Carmody (Cambridge H) 1:38:30		1949	Angela Douglas (Cambridge H) 9:03.6
1991	Stuart Phillips (Ilford) 1:34:00		1950	Angela Douglas (Cambridge H) 9:04.2
1992	Jimmy Ball (Steyning) 1:30:45		1951	Leila Deas (London Oly) 8:20.8
1993	Noel Carmody (Cambridge H) 1:37:16		1952	Sheila Martin (London Oly) 8:17.0
1996	Chris Maddocks (Plymouth) 1:33:38		1954	Patricia Grant (London Oly) 8:05.4
2001	Alan Ellam (Colchester) 1:49:19		1955	Sheila Jennings (London Oly) 8:23.0
2003	Mark Easton (Surrey WC) 1:41:36		1956	Helen Vincent (London Oly) 8:14.4
2004	Andrew Goudie (Belgrave H) 1:42:35		1957	Helen Vincent (London Oly) 8:16.2
2005	Don Bearman (Steyning) 1:38:38		1959	Sheila Jennings (London Oly) 8:26.2
2006	Nick Ball (Steyning) 1:44:22		1960	Sheila Jennings (London Oly) 8:14.2
2007	Nick Silvester (AFD) 1:52:16		1961	Judy Woodsford (Trowbridge) 7:52.8
2008	Ian Richards (Steyning) 1 52 08		1962	Judy Farr (Trowbridge) 7:56.6
2009	Trevor Jones (Steyning) 1 48 34		1964	Jennifer Keen (Croydon H) 8:43.0
2010	Ian Richards (Steyning) 1 44 51		1965	Judy Farr (Trowbridge) 7:36.2
2011	Peter Ryan (Ilford) 1:55:26		1966	Judy Farr (Trowbridge) 7:37.4
2013	Francisco Reis (Ilford/POR) 1:48:47		1967	Judy Farr (Trowbridge) 8:12.8

20 MILES ROAD

1908	Harold Ross (Tooting) 2:56:32		1968	Judy Farr (Trowbridge) 8:22.0

2000 METRES TRACK

1909	Sidney Schofield (Surrey WC) 2:56:48.		1969	Judy Farr (Trowbridge) 9:54.2
1910	Harold Ross (Tooting) 2:53:45.4		1970	Judy Farr (Trowbridge) 10:01.0

| 1911 | Tommy Payne (Middlesex WC) 2:50:30 |

3000 METRES TRACK

1976	Roger Mills (Ilford) 2:32:13		1971	Judy Farr (Trowbridge) 16:01.2
1977	Amos Seddon (Enfield) 2:35:15		1972	Jennifer Finch (Selsonia) 16:43.0
1978	Carl Lawton (Belgrave H) 2:39:32		1973	Barbara Cook (Redhill) 15:03.0
1979	Mike Parker (Brighton) 2:36:28		1974	Judy Farr (Trowbridge) 15:45.4
1980	Bob Dobson (Ilford) 2:33:57		1975	Judy Farr (Trowbridge) 15:20.06
1981	Mike Parker (Brighton) 2:34:07		1976	Judy Farr (Trowbridge) 14:51.8
1982	Mike Parker (Brighton) 2:33:28		1977	Judy Farr (Trowbridge) 15:02.6
1983	Gordon Vale (Surrey WC) 2:40:10		1978	Irene Bateman (Basildon) 14:33.9
1984	Adrian James (Enfield) 2:44:23		1979	Julie Robery (Havering) 15:42.5
1985	Carl Lawton (Belgrave H) 2:46:31		1980	Irene Bateman (Basildon) 14:26.4
1986	Carl Lawton (Belgrave H) 2:45:07		1981	Jill Barrett (Verlea) 14:37.4
1987	Adrian James (Enfield) 2:47:11		1982	Sarah Brown (Steyning) 14:43.9
1988	Stuart Phillips (Ilford) 2:43:23		1983	Helen Ringshaw (Steyning) 15:39.4
1989	Darrell Stone (Steyning) 2:36:24		1984	Jill Barrett (Verlea) 13:57.8
1990	Stuart Phillips (Ilford) 2:46:00		1985	Beverley Allen (Brighton) 14:46.3
1991	Darrell Stone (Steyning) 2:50:14		1986	Beverley Allen (Brighton) 14:15.7
1992	Gareth Brown (Steyning) 2:55:46		1987	Angela Hodd (Tonbridge) 15:10.
1993	Mark Easton (Surrey WC) 2:32:07		1988	Verity Larby (AFD) 15:47.25
1996	Mark Easton (Surrey WC) 2:38:52		1989	Verity Larby (AFD) 14:57.3

30 KILOMETRES ROAD

			1990	Fiona Rose (Cambridge H) 15:11.70
1997	Mabon Dane (Belgrave H) 2:38:58		1991	Philippa Savage (Steyning) 15:34.91

50 KILOMETRES ROAD

			1992	Verity Larby (AFD) 13:49.3
1975	Bob Dobson (Southend) 4:42:22		1993	Nicole Parsons (AFD) 17:22.90
1976	Dave Boxall (Brighton) 4:51:22		1994	Verity Snook (AFD) 13:31.78
1977	Peter Hodkinson (Cambridge H) 4:36:27		1995	Perri Williams (London Irish) 13:27.87
1981	Bob Dobson (Ilford) 4:14:01		1996	Cressida Van Doorn (Mitcham) 16:17.61
1982	Adrian James (Enfield) 4:14:11		1998	Mary Wallen (Chiltern & C) 16:03.33
1984	Roger Mills (Ilford) 4:25:10		1999	Amy Hales (Steyning) 14:55.44
1985	Bob Dobson (Ilford) 4:32:38		2000	Sally Warren (Steyning) 14:49.6

5000 METRES TRACK

1986	Bob Dobson (Ilford) 4:28:59		1989	Sarah Brown (Steyning) 24:23.1
1988	Bob Dobson (Ilford) 4:28:08		1994	Sarah Brown (Steyning) 25:21.38
1992	Noel Carmody (Cambridge H) 4:41:14		1995	Carole Hollett 36:30.0
1993	Bob Dobson (Ilford) 4:53:54		1996	Verity Snook (AFD) 24:16.1
1994	Colin Bradley (Trowbridge) 4:59:07		1997	Jo Hesketh (Steyning) 29:24.40
1995	Gary Smith (Enfield) 5:16:09		1998	Verity Snook (AFD) 26:33.56

WOMEN – 1 MILE TRACK

			1999	Nicola Donnelly (AFD) 29:49.88
1933	Jeanne Probekk (MLAC) 8:04.8)		2000	Sigrun Sangvik (Sevenoaks) 27:08.35
1937	F.Pengelly (Paignton) 8:38.2		2008	Helen Middleton (Leicester WC) 29:35.18
1938	F.Pengelly (Paignton) 8:51.2		2009	Helen Middleton (Enfield & Ha) 29:40.20
1939	E.Webb (Hercules) 9:19.0		2010	Diane Bradley (Tonbridge) 27 03.83

2012 Geraldine Legon (Bexley) 37:22.79
10,000 METRES TRACK
2001 Estle Viljoen (Hercules Wimbledon) 52:18.23
2002 Claire Reeves (Dartford H) 54:47.0
2003 Liz Harris (Dartford H) 72:31.80
2004 Fiona Bishop (Dartford H) 62:18.3
3 MILES ROAD
1937 L.Murray (MLAC) 30:23
1948 Maude Curson (MLAC) 23:15
1949 Jessie Jones (London Oly) 24:27
Distance varies:
1950 2.5 miles Brenda Harris (Met Police) 19:30
1951 3 miles Leila Deas (London Oly) 25:01
1955 2.5 miles Patricia Grant (London Oly) 22:22
1961 Judy Farr (Trowbridge) 34:25
1962 3.5 miles Judy Farr (Trowbridge) 26:30
1965 Judy Farr (Trowbridge) 27:09
5000 METRES ROAD
1966 Barbara Fisk (Redhill & R) 28:54
1970 Judy Farr (Trowbridge) 26:40
1971 Christine Coleman (Highgate H) 29:14
1975 Christine Coleman (Highgate H) 26:19
1976 Judy Farr (Trowbridge) 25:14
1977 Christine Coleman (Luton) 25:45
1978 Judy Farr (Trowbridge) 25:04
1979 Jan Beverley Francis (Brighton) 26:11
1979 Dec Judy Farr (Trowbridge) 25:59
1980 Sarah Brown (Steyning) 23:57
1981 Jill Barrett (Verlea) 24:21
1982 Jill Barrett (Verlea) 25:03
1983 Jill Barrett (Verlea) 27:19
1984 Jill Barrett (Verlea) 23:56
1985 Virginia Birch (Brighton) 23:56
1986 Beverley Allen (Brighton) 23:31
1987 Sarah Brown (Steyning) 24:07
1988 Julie Drake (Brighton) 23:55
1989 Verity Larby (AFD) 25:35
1990 Sian Spacey (Belgrave H) 25:36
1991 Sarah Brown (Steyning) 26:09
1992 Carol Bean (Steyning) 29:10
1994 Cressida Van Doorn (Mitcham) 29:24
1995 Perri Williams (London Irish) 25:17
1997 Debbie Wallen (AFD) 25:53
1998 Helen Ford Dunn (Steyning) 26:08
1999 Verity Snook (AFD) 27:30
2000 C.Watson (Dartford) 29:29
2005 Verity Snook (AFD) 27:09

10 KILOMETRES ROAD
1982 Virginia Birch (Brighton) 53:43
1983 Virginia Birch (Brighton) 51:28
1984 Virginia Birch (Brighton) 50:18
1985 Virginia Birch (Brighton) 50:29
1986 Beverley Allen (Brighton) 47:31
1987 Sian Spacey (Belgrave H) 53:16
1988 Sian Stacey (Belgrave H/CAN) 53:16
1989 Fiona Rose (Cambridge H) 53:39
1990 Sian Spacey (Belgrave H) 55:48
1991 Sarah Brown (Steyning) 49:55
1992 Joanne Pope (Brighton) 52:49
1993 Louise Spreadborough (AFD) 59:19
1997 Perri Williams (London Irish) 48:43
1998 Debbie Wallen (AFD) 47:10
1999 Debbie Wallen (AFD) 52:04
2000 Nicky Phillips (Dartford) 52:20
2001 Estle Viljoen (Hercules Wimb) 52:50
2002 Sophie Hales (Steyning) 53:20
2003 Sophie Hales (Steyning) 53:12
2004 Estle Viljoen (Hercules Wimb) 48:36
2005 Cath Duhig (Colchester) 63:25
2006 Sophie Hales (Steyning) 50:57
2007 Estle Viljoen (Hercules Wimbledon) 52:03
2008 Chelsea O'Rawe-Hobbs (Blackheath) 56 22
2009 Diane Bradley (Tonbridge) 55:04
2010 Diane Bradley (Tonbridge) 54:39
2011 Neringa Aidietyte (Ilford/ITU) 47:27
2012 Diane Bradley (Tonbridge) 57:36
2013 Helen Middleton (Enfield & Ha) 61:59
2014 Sandra Brown (Surrey WC) 58:59
10 MILES ROAD
2009 Helen Middleton (Enfield & Ha) 1:33:27
20 KILOMETRES ROAD
1993 Julie Drake (Brighton) 1:36:58.6 (short)
2001 Sara Jane Cattermole (Dartford) 1:49:07
2004 Verity Snook (AFD) 1:59:51
2005 Maureen Noel (Belgrave H) 2:03:14,
2006 Sarah Foster (Dartford) 1:56:51
2007 Maureen Noel (Belgrave H) 2:06:22
2008 Maureen Noel (Belgrave H) 2:10:27
2009 Cath Duhig (Loughton) 2:14 25
2010 Helen Middleton (Enfield & Ha) 2:02:08
2011 Helen Middleton (Enfield & Ha) 2:06:12
2013 Maureen Noel (Belgrave H) 2:05:12
50 KILOMETRES ROAD
1997 Sandra Brown (Surrey WC) 5:02:48

WINNERS OF OTHER MAJOR RACES IN BRITAIN

BELGRAVE HARRIERS OPEN 7 MILES
1920: William Hehir (RAF) 55:16.8
1921: William Hehir (Surrey AC) 55:22.4
1922: Reg Goodwin (Surrey WC) 54:09
1923: Harold King (Belgrave) 55:15
1924: Reg Goodwin (Surrey WC) 55:52
1925: F.Sharman (Southern Rly) 58:13
1926: Harold King (Belgrave) 56:04
1927: Tommy Green (Belgrave) 55:11
1928: Cecil Hyde (Enfield) 51:02
1929: Alf Pope (Woodford G) 55:12
1930: Alf Fletcher (Belgrave) 54:38.4
1931: Cecil Hyde (Enfield) 54:13
1932: Johnny Johnson (Enfield) 54:58
1933: Johnny Johnson (Enfield) 54:05
1934: Johnny Johnson (Enfield) 52:49
1935: Bert Cooper (Woodford Green) 54:21
1936: Vic Stone (Poly) 53:48.4
1937: Harry Churcher (Belgrave) 54:28
1938: Harry Churcher (Belgrave) 53:05
1942: David Christie-Murray (Highgate) 56:18
1943: Jim Morris (Surrey AC) 53:50
1944: Eddie Staker (Highgate) 53:13
1945: Bill Burgess (Surrey WC) 54:03
1946: Jack Rutland (Belgrave) 54:40
1947: Bill Wilson (Highgate) 54:22
1948: Harry Churcher (Belgrave) 54:46
1949: Harry Churcher (Belgrave) 54:39
1950: George Coleman (Highgate) 54:25
1951: Harry Churcher (Belgrave) 54:41
1952: Fred Barrett (Cambridge H) 54:51
1953: Bob Richards (Cambridge H) 54:18
1954: Len Evans (Highgate) 54:53
1955: Alf Poole (Worcester) 54:10
1956: Ken Matthews (RSC) 53:06
1957: Ken Matthews (RSC) 52:18
1958: Ken Matthews (RSC) 49:29
1959: Ken Matthews (RSC) 51:19
1960: Ken Matthews (RSC) 52:30
1961: Ken Matthews (RSC) 49:51
1962: Paul Nihill (Surrey WC) 53:10
1963: Paul Nihill (Surrey WC) 51:08
1964: Ray Middleton (Belgrave) 52:44
1965: Peter McCullagh (Metropolitan) 51:56
1966: John Webb (Basildon) 51:58
1967: José Pedraza MEX 50:21
1968: Arthur Jones (Brighton) 51:37
1969: Pablo Colin MEX 50:58
1970: Phil Embleton (Metropolitan) 50:21
1971: Phil Embleton (Metropolitan) 50:41
1972: Olly Flynn (Basildon) 51:47
1973: Peter Marlow (Southend) 51:00
1974: Brian Adams (Leicester) 51:37
1975: Carl Lawton (Belgrave) 52:11
1976: Shaun Lightman (Metropolitan) 51:13
1977: Graham Seatter (Belgrave) 51:40
1978: Mike Parker (Brighton) 50:46
1979: George Nibre (Ilford) 52:19
1980: Mike Parker (Brighton) 50:59
1981: Phil Vesty (Leicester) 49:56
1982: Phil Vesty (Leicester) 50:48
1983: Richard Dorman (Belgrave) 52:12
1984: Phil Vesty (Leicester) 51:12
1985: Les Morton (Sheffield) 50:35
1986: Chris Maddocks (Dawlish) 47:54

1987: Jimmy Ball (Southampton) 49:46
1988: Jimmy Ball (Steyning) 51:05
1989: Darrell Stone (Steyning) 49:00
1990: Steve Taylor (Boundary) 50:54
1991: Jimmy Ball (Steyning) 52:11
1992: John Hall (Belgrave) 53:44
1993: Mark Easton (Surrey WC) 48:38
1994: Steve Partington (Manx) 47:57
1995: Darrell Stone (Steyning) 47:24
1996: Darrell Stone (Steyning) 47:42
1997: Mark Easton (Surrey WC) 49:23
1998: Darrell Stone (Steyning) 47:27
1999: Steve Hollier (Wolverhampton) 47:15
2000: Darrell Stone (Steyning) 48:55
'B' races
2001: Chris Cheeseman (Surrey WC) 48:46
2002: Steve Hollier (Wolverhampton) 48:51
2003: Chris Cheeseman (Surrey WC) 51:25
2004: Darrell Stone (Steyning) 49:23
2005: Scott Davis (Ilford) 52:27
2006: Scott Davis (Ilford) 54:51
2007: Jimmy Ball (Steyning) 55:05
2008: Darrell Stone (Steyning) 50:12
2009: Darrell Stone (Steyning) 51:12
2010: Francisco Reis (Ilford/POR) 54:29

BIRMINGHAM OUTER CIRCLE 25 MILES
1929: Tommy Green (Belgrave) 3:50:20
1930: Lloyd Johnson (Leicester) 3:45:08.6
1931: H.Taylor (Derby WC) 3:49:55.8
1932: Tommy Green (Belgrave) 3:44:55.8
1933: Tommy Green (Belgrave) 3:42:35
1934: Lloyd Johnson (Leicester) 3:41:40
1935: Harold Whitlock (Metropolitan) 3:47:19
1936: Lloyd Johnson (Leicester) 3:36:38,
1937: Harold Whitlock (Metropolitan) 3:40:09
1938: Joe Hopkins (Lancs WC) 3:35:47
1939: Dick Edge (Coventry) 3:41:04
1946: Lloyd Johnson (Leicester) 3:49:16
1947: Rex Whitlock (Metropolitan) 3:49:55
1948: Harry Forbes (Birmingham) 3:44:43
1949: Lloyd Johnson (Leicester) 3:55:08
1950: John Proctor (Sheffield) 3:45:08
1951: Bert Clayton (Belgrave) 3:44:00
1952: Frank Bailey (Poly) 3:46:17
1953: Frank Bailey (Poly) 3:45:58
1954: Albert Johnson (Sheffield) 3:41:47
1955: Don Thompson (Metropolitan) 3:40:11
1956: Don Thompson (Metropolitan) 3:32:27
1957: Don Thompson (Metropolitan) 3:33:33
1958: Don Thompson (Metropolitan) 3:34:52
1959: Don Thompson (Metropolitan) 3:29:12
1960: Don Thompson (Metropolitan) 3:26:20
1961: Don Thompson (Metropolitan) 3:32:37
1962: Don Thompson (Metropolitan) 3:31:37
1963: Vaughan Thomas (Belgrave) 3:25:43
1964: Don Thompson (Metropolitan) 3:35:38
1965: Ray Middleton (Belgrave) 3:28:59
1966: Paul Nihill (Surrey WC) 3:23:44
1967: Charlie Fogg (Enfield) 3:35:07
1968: Ken Harding (RSC) 3:52:42
1969: John Warhurst (Sheffield) 3:30:42
1970: Ray Middleton (Belgrave) 3:39:59
1971: Bob Dobson (Basildon) 3:38:52
1972: Shaun Lightman (Metropolitan) 3:35:07

1973: Ken Harding (RSC) 3:46:56
1974: Bob Dobson (Southend) 3:35:40

BIRMINGHAM OPEN 35 KILOMETRES
1975: Ian Brooks (Southend) 3:07:50
1976: David Cotton (Holloway Poly) 3:07:05
1977: David Cotton (Holloway Poly) 3:03:10
1978: David Cotton (Holloway Poly) 2:52:30
1979: Bob Dobson (Ilford) 2:54:44
1980: Barry Graham (York Postal) 2:56:30
1981: Barry Graham (York Post) 2:52:24
1982: Graham Young (Boundary) 3:03:14
1985: Ray Hankin (Sheffield) 2:57:50

BRADFORD OPEN
Held from 1903 it was the oldest continuous annual event in race walking. Originally it was from Bradford to York. Traditionally held every Whit Monday.
40.5 MILES
1906: Tommy Hammond (Surrey WC) 6:45:08
1907: Tommy Hammond (Surrey WC) 6:37:47
1908: Tommy Hammond (Surrey WC) 6:45:43
1909: Tommy Hammond (Surrey WC) 6:49:40
1910: A.Edwards (Lancs WC) 6:53:06
1911: Tommy Payne (Morpeth) 6:56:27
1912: F.Roberts (Woodford Green) 6:44:37
1913: Tommy Hammond (Surrey WC) 6:45:15
1914: F.Roberts (Woodford Green) 6:43:01
32.25 MILES
1915: Edgar Horton (Surrey WC) 5:19:12.8
1916: T.Fox (Yorks WC) 5:23:02.8
1917: Tommy Payne (Morpeth) 5:24:17.2
1918: Tommy Payne (Morpeth) 5:22:05
1919: Tommy Payne (Morpeth) 5:09:45
1920: Tommy Payne (Morpeth) 5:30:11
1921: Tommy Payne (Yorks WC)5:14:11.8
1922: Edgar Horton (Surrey WC) 5:14:49.4
1923: Frank Holt (Yorks WC) 5:07:03
1924: Frank Holt (Yorks WC) 5:12:01
1925: Fred Poynton (Derby WC) 5:01:09.2
1926: Frank Holt (Yorks WC) 5:20:35
1927: Frank Holt (Yorks WC) 5:07:34.6
1928: H.Kirkland (Derby WC) 5:13:34
1929: Frank Holt (Yorks WC) 4:58:37
1930: Tommy Green (Belgrave) 5:04:14
1931: Lloyd Johnson (Leicester) 5:02:27
1932: Tommy Green (Belgrave) 4:49:01.4
1933: Tommy Green (Belgrave) 4:59:20
1934: Lloyd Johnson (Leicester) 4:51:41.6
1935: Harold Whitlock (Metropolitan) 4:45:22.6
1936: Harold Whitlock (Metropolitan) 4:45:35
1937: Harold Whitlock (Metropolitan) 4:50:44
50 KILOMETRES
1938: Harold Whitlock (Metropolitan) 4:43:01.2
1946: Charlie Megnin (Highgate) 4:53:25.6
1947: Albert Staines (Leicester) 5:02:14
1948: Albert Staines (Leicester) 5:14:23
1949: Albert Staines (Leicester) 5:04:30
1950: Harold Whitlock (Metropolitan) 5:05:56
1951: Percy Reading (Poly) 4:58:20
1952: Charles Colman (Yorks WC) 4:51:43
1953: Jim Hartley (Sheffield) 5:01:42
1954: Albert Johnson (Sheffield) 4:36:36
1955: Albert Johnson (Sheffield) 4:51:03
1956: Albert Johnson (Sheffield) 4:45:55
1957: Albert Johnson (Sheffield) 4:43:45
1958: Albert Johnson (Sheffield) 4:26:30

1959: Albert Johnson (Sheffield) 5:01:39
1960: Albert Johnson (Sheffield) 4:48:55
1961: Albert Johnson (Sheffield) 4:48:14
1962: Ray Ibbotson (Sheffield) 4:45:55
1963: Albert Johnson (Sheffield) 4:48:03
1964: Guy Goodair (Wakefield) 4:54:03
1965: Ray Middleton (Belgrave) 4:43:17
1966: Ray Middleton (Belgrave) 4:38:59
1967: Ray Middleton (Belgrave) 4:40:30
1968: Bryan Eley (Bristol) 4:30:39
1969: John Warhurst (Sheffield) 4:32:58
1970: John Warhurst (Sheffield) 4:37:11
1971: Ron Wallwork (Lancs WC) 4:29:20
1972: Shaul Ladany ISR 4:26:29
1973: John Eddershaw (Sheffield) 4:44:00
1974: Ken Harding (RSC) 4:38:51
1975: John Warhurst (Sheffield) 4:31:40
1976: John Warhurst (Sheffield) 4:32:05
1977: John Warhurst (Sheffield) 4:28:10
1978: GrahamYoung (Boundary) 4:56:55
1979: John Warhurst (Sheffield) 4:31:05
1980: Murray Lambden (Boundary) 4:31:40
1981: Murray Lambden (Boundary) 4:26:49
1982: Murray Lambden (Boundary) 4:37:46
1983: Mel McCann (Yorks WC) 4:29:41
1984: Mel McCann (Yorks WC) 4:25:53
1985: Russell Rawlins (Bromsgrove & R) 4:34:02
1986: Ray Hankin (Sheffield) 4:29:31
1987: Mel McCann (Yorks WC) 4:32:16
1988: Ray Hankin (Sheffield) 4:39:47
1989: Mike Lewis (Trowbridge) 5:10:00
1990: Dave Turner (Yorks WC) 4:56:14
1991: Andy Trigg (Leicester) 4:48:42
1992: Derek Stancliffe (Sheffield) 5:08:17
1993: Colin Bradley (Trowbridge) 4:59:20
1994: Dave Turner (Yorks WC) 4:47:12
1995: Colin Bradley (Trowbridge) 4:58:01
1996: John Paddick (Yorks WC) 5:01:20
1997: Les Morton (Sheffield) 4:29:27
1998: Martin Fisher (York CIU) 5:11:02
1999: Dave Turner (Yorks) 5:03:43
2000: Dave Turner (Yorks) 4:56:59
2001: Dave Turner (Yorks) 4:55:43
2002: Dave Turner (Yorks) 4:53:31
2003: Martin Fisher (York CIU) 5:15:24
2004: Dave Jones (Redcar) 5:48:18
2005: Martin Fisher (unattached) 5:33:31
2006: Steve Arnold (Nuneaton) 5:11:59
2007: Steve Arnold (Nuneaton) 5:25:59
Held at shorter distances to 2011

CAMBRIDGE HARRIERS OPEN 10 MILES
1923: Harold King (Erith) 77:54   1924: Handicap
1925: A.Greening (Surrey AC) 84 12
1926: A.Hurst (Cambridge H) 89 23
7 MILES
1927: R.Purves (Walthamstow YMCA) 54:25.6
1928: L.Sandy (Surrey AC) 53:14
1929: L.Sandy (Surrey AC) 53:02
1930: Cecil Hyde (Enfield) 50:24
1931: Alf Fletcher (Belgrave) 51:28
1932: Tommy Green (Belgrave) 52:11
1933: Johnny Johnson (Enfield) 53:18
1946: Jack Rutland (Surrey AC) 54:49
1947: Harry Churcher (Belgrave) 54:31
1948: Harry Churcher (Belgrave) 53:35
1949: Harry Churcher (Belgrave) 54:45

1950: George Coleman (Highgate) 51:35
1951: Paddy Woods (Surrey AC) 55:47
1952: Fred Barrett (Cambridge H) 53:21
1953: George Coleman (Highgate) 51:51
1954: Bryan Hawkins (Metropolitan) 52:09
1955: Bryan Hawkins (Metropolitan) 52:26
1956: Bob Goodall (Woodford Green) 51:51
1957: Stan Vickers (Belgrave) 51:07
1958: Stan Vickers (Belgrave) 51:13
1959: Stan Vickers (Belgrave) 53:05
1960: Bob Clark (Poly) 53:32
1961: Bob Clark (Poly) 53:42
1962: Ken Matthews (RSC) 51:45
1963: Peter McCullagh (Metropolitan) 53:31
1964: Maurice Fullager (Surrey WC) 54:26
1965: Peter McCullagh (Metropolitan) 52:42
1966: John Webb (Basildon) 51:51
1967: José Pedraza (Mexico) 50:13
1968: Paul Nihill (Surrey WC) 50:53
1969: Paul Nihill (Surrey WC) 51:17
1970: Shaun Lightman (Metropolitan) 52:11
1971: Paul Nihill (Surrey WC) 50:43
1972: Shaun Lightman (Metropolitan) 51:37
1973: John Webb (Basildon) 51:55
1974: Shaun Lightman (Metropolitan) 50:37
1975: Amos Seddon (Enfield) 49:53
1976: Shaun Lightman (Metropolitan) 50:31
10 KILOMETRES
1977: Enrique Vera (Mexico) 43 32
1978: Bob Dobson (Ilford) 45:56
1979: Ian McCombie (N Shields Poly) 45:22
1980: Mike Parker (Brighton) 43 27
1982: Jan: Paul Blagg (Belgrave) 44:49
1982: Oct: Ian McCombie (Cambridge H) 43 44
1983: Ian McCombie (Cambridge H) 43 27
1984: Mark Easton (Surrey WC) 45:48
CHIPPENHAM TO CALNE OPEN 6 MILES
1950: Harry Churcher (Belgrave) 45:18
1951: Roland Hardy (Sheffield) 44:18
1952: Roland Hardy (Sheffield) 46:16
1953: Roland Hardy (Sheffield) 45:08
1954: George Coleman (Highgate) 46:46
1955: Roland Hardy (Sheffield) 44:09
1956: George Coleman (Highgate) 44:19
1957: Norman Read (Steyning) 46:33
1958: Stan Vickers (Belgrave) 43:04
1959: Ken Matthews (RSC) 43:04.6
1960: Ken Matthews (RSC) 43:34
1961: Arthur Thomson (Metropolitan) 45:33
1962: Ken Matthews (RSC) 42 47
1963: Bob Clark (Poly) 47:36
1964: Bob Clark (Poly) 45:14
1965: Peter McCullagh (Metropolitan) 44:10
1966: Ron Wallwork (Lancs) 44:44
1967: Dave Smyth (Bristol) 44:08
1968: Peter Fullager (Surrey WC) 44:12
1969: Paul Nihill (Surrey WC) 42:09
1970: Alan Smallwood (Harborne) 43:28
1971: Carl Lawton (Belgrave) 43 12
1972: Shaun Lightman (Metropolitan) 44:03
1973: Peter Marlow (Southend) 42:27
1974: Carl Lawton (Belgrave) 43:29
1975: Carl Lawton (Belgrave) 43:20
1976: Carl Lawton (Belgrave) 44:21
1977: Brian Adams (Leicester) 43:22
1978: Carl Lawton (Belgrave) 43:58

1979: Allan King (Leicester) 44:12
1980: Steve Barry (Roath Labour) 41:22
1981: Phil Vesty (Leicester) 42:14
1982: Phil Vesty (Leicester) 43:22
1983: Chris Maddocks (Dawlish) 40:02
1984: Phil Vesty (Leicester) 40:11
1985: Chris Maddocks (Dawlish) 40:20
1986: Chris Maddocks (Dawlish) 40:04
1987: Andy Penn (Coventry) 41:05
1988: Andy Penn (Coventry) 41:58
1989: Querubin Moreno COL 46:58
1990: Martin Bell (Splott Cons) 42:21
1991: Martin Rush (Lakeland) 39:44
1992: Martin Bell (Splott Cons) 41:25
1993: Phil King (Brighton) 42:18
1994: Andy Penn (Coventry) 42:57
1995: Chris Maddocks (Plymouth) 41 48
1996: Jimmy Ball (Steyning) 45:08
1997: Darrell Stone (Steyning) 40:35
1998: Chris Maddocks (Plymouth) 40:32
1999: Darrell Stone (Steyning) 38:54
In:1967 the race was held from Hilmarton to Calne and between:1968 and:1971 on a course starting and finishing at Calne.

ENFIELD OPEN 7 MILES
1920: C.Bolt (Belgrave) (off 8:30) 55:08
1921: R.Martin (NLH) (8:30) 50:36
1922: A.Webber (Enfield) (8:00) 55:56.6
1923: Billy Simkins (Highgate) (11:00) 55:52
1924: S.Clark (Woodford Green) (8:00) 50:01
1925: A.Richards (Surrey WC) (7:00) 53:52
1928: Cecil Hyde (Enfield) 53:04
1929: Cecil Hyde (Enfield) 52:42.5
1930: Cecil Hyde (Enfield) 53:23.4
1931: Cecil Hyde (Enfield) 52:21
1932: Tommy Green (Belgrave) 52:38
1933: Bert Cooper (Woodford Green) 52:46
1934: Johnny Johnson (Enfield) 52:45
1935: Bert Cooper (Woodford Green) 52:39
1936: Harry Churcher (Belgrave) 53:29
1937: Harry Churcher (Belgrave) 52:39
1938: Harry Churcher (Belgrave) 54:05
1941: David Christie-Murray (Surrey WC) 55:25
1942: David Christie-Murray (Surrey WC) 55:07
1943: Charlie Megnin (Highgate) 56:35
1944: Harold Whitlock (Metropolitan) 55:17
1945: Jim Morris (Surrey AC) 54:17
1946: Harry Churcher & Jack Rutland (Belgrave) 54:34
1947: Ron West (Cambridge H) 55:48
1948: Harry Churcher (Belgrave) 55:13
1949: Harry Churcher (Belgrave) 55:14
1950: Jim Morris (Surrey AC) 52:08
1951: Fred Barrett (Cambridge H) 54:44
1952: George Coleman (Highgate) 53:06
1953: Bob Goodall (Woodford Green) 53:45
1954: Bryan Hawkins (Metropolitan) 53:51
1955: Bryan Hawkins (Metropolitan) 53:19
1956: Bob Goodall (Woodford Green) 53:46
1957: Eric Hall (Belgrave) 51:28
1958: Ken Matthews (RSC) 50:18
1959: John Northcott (Highgate) 53:34
1960: Ken Matthews (RSC) 50:40
1961: Ken Matthews (RSC) 49:09
1962: Bob Clark (Poly) 52:46
1963: Paul Nihill (Surrey WC) 52:37
1964: Bob Clark (Poly) 52:01

1965: Peter McCullagh (Metropolitan) 50:30
1966: John Webb (Basildon) 51:06
1967: Paul Nihill (Surrey WC) 50:48
1968: John Webb (Basildon) 50:20
1969: Shaun Lightman (Metropolitan) 51:09
1970: Wilf Wesch (Belgrave/FRG) 49:59
1971: Ron Laird USA 50:22
1972: Shaun Lightman (Metropolitan) 49:25
1973: Raúl González MEX 50:05.6
1974: Carl Lawton (Belgrave) 50:56
1975: Brian Adams (Leicester) 50:09
1976: Shaun Lightman (Metropolitan) 49:59
1977: Enrique Vera MEX 48:44
1978: Bob Dobson (Unattached) 50:17
1979: Roger Mills (Ilford) 49:20
1980: Allan King (Leicester) 49:05
1981: Phil Vesty (Leicester) 49:10
1982: Roy Sheppard (Anglia) 48:30
1983: Roy Sheppard (Anglia) 49:58
1984: Mick Greasley (Sheffield) 49:37
1985: Les Morton (Sheffield) 49:33
1986: Paul Blagg (Cambridge H) 48:13
1987: Francisco Reis (Ilford/POR) 48:32
1988: Mark Easton (Surrey WC) 48:35
1989: Darrell Stone (Steyning) 48:24
1991: Darrell Stone (Steyning) 48:41
1992: Darrell Stone (Steyning) 48:56
1993: Mark Easton (Surrey WC) 51:12
1994: Tim Watt (Steyning) 54:07
1995: Chris Cheeseman (Surrey WC) 51:02
1998: Mark Easton (Surrey WC) 52:52
1999: Don Bearman (Steyning) 51:17
2000: Dominic King (Colchester) 54:02
2001: Steve Allen (Ilford) 57:44
2002: Peter Ryan (Loughton) 57:06 Now 'B' races
2003: Tim Watt (Steyning) 56:34
2004: Zach.Pollinger USA 55:33
2005: Scott Davis (Ilford) 54:40
2006: Scott Davis (Ilford) 55:21
2007: Scott Davis (Ilford) 55:21
2008: Darrell Stone (Steyning) 51:52
2009: Darrell Stone (Steyning) 52:51
2010: Dan & Dominic King (Colchester) 52:20
2011: Dominic King (Colchester) 49:29
2012: Dominic King (Colchester) 52:52
2013: Callum Wilkinson (Enfield & Ha) 57:46

COLCHESTER TO IPSWICH
1929: H.Moule (Suffolk) 2:40:46
1930: E.Hall (Suffolk) 2:49:10
1938: Colin Sutton (Belgrave) 2:22:03
1939: Colin Sutton (Belgrave) 2:22:38
1949: Stan Mantor (Enfield) 2:33:24
1950: Bob Goodall (Woodford Green) 2:29:07
1951: Bob Goodall (Woodford Green) 2:26:24
1952: Paddy Woods (Surrey AC) 2:39:26
1953: Bob Goodall (Woodford Green) 2:35 43
1954: Bob Goodall (Woodford Green) 2:30:00
1955: Alec Macfarlane (Poly) 2:33:38
1956: Bryan Hawkins (Metropolitan) 2:31:56
1957: Eric Hall (Belgrave) 2:23 49
1958: Tom Misson (Metropolitan) 2:27 43
1959: Tom Misson (Metropolitan) 2:23:08
1961: Don Thompson (Metropolitan) 2:12:59
1962: Don Thompson (Metropolitan) 2:16:34
1963: Don Thompson (Metropolitan) 2:14:58
1964: Don Thompson (Metropolitan) 2:16:45

1965: Don Thompson (Metropolitan) 2:15:52
1966: Peter McCullagh (Metropolitan) 2:07:35,
1967: Shaun Lightman (Metropolitan) 2:12 13,
1968: Alec Banyard (Southend) 2:16:24
1969: Bill Sutherland (Herne Hill) 2:11:57

HASTINGS TO BRIGHTON 38 MILES
1930: Tommy Green (Belgrave) 6:00:35
1931: Tommy Green (Belgrave) 6:06:54
1932: Harold Whitlock (Metropolitan) 5:56:03
1933: Tommy Green (Belgrave) 5:51:25
1934: Harold Whitlock (Metropolitan) 5:46:45
1935: Tommy Richardson (Woodford Green) 5:53:06
1936: Tommy Richardson (Woodford Green) 5:45:29
1937: Tommy Richardson (Woodford Green) 5:55:56.8
1946: Rex Whitlock (Metropolitan) 5:55:28
1947: Johnny Henderson (Sussex WC) 6:22:29
1948: Johnny Henderson (Sussex WC) 6:03:07
1949: Charlie Megnin (Highgate) 6:12:14
1950: Charlie Megnin (Highgate) 6:10:39
1951: Percy Reading (Poly) 6:05:27
1952: Charlie Megnin (Highgate) 6:04:07
1953: Norman Guilmant (Belgrave) 5:55:25.2
1954: Hugh McGreechan (Belgrave) 6:00:37
1955: Hew Neilson (Woodford Green) 5:57:40
1956: George Checkley (Belgrave) 6:01:02
1957: Don Thompson (Metropolitan) 5:45:22
1958: George Beecham (Belgrave) 6:04:11
1959: Nigel Thompson (Metropolitan) 5:56:01
1960: Don Thompson (Metropolitan) 5:25:53
1961: Don Thompson (Metropolitan) 5:31:51
1962: Don Thompson (Metropolitan) 5:32:07
1963: Dennis Read (Steyning) 5:41:00
1964: Ray Middleton (Belgrave) 5:39:29
1965: Don Thompson (Metropolitan) 5:31:07
1966: Bryan Eley (Trowbridge) 5:49:24
1967: Shaun Lightman (Metropolitan) 5:35:10
1968: Don Thompson (Metropolitan) 5:45:00
1969: Shaun Lightman (Metropolitan) 5:47:01
1970: Ray Middleton (Belgrave) 5:41:57
1971: Shaul Ladany ISR 5:33:36
1972: Shaun Lightman (Metropolitan) 6:35:28
1973: Peter Selby (Surrey WC) 5:44:48
1974: Ray Middleton (Belgrave) 5:36:42
1975: Ray Middleton (Belgrave) 5:52:04
1976: Peter Selby (Surrey WC) 5:43:23
1977: Alain Moulinet (US St Denis/FRA) 5:34:54
1978: Alain Moulinet (US St Denis/FRA) 5:38:19
1979: Carl Lawton (Belgrave) 5:34:57
1980: Tim Erickson AUS 5:31:40
1981: Bob Dobson (Ilford) 5:28:18
1982: Bob Dobson (Ilford) 5:33:45
1983: Bob Dobson (Ilford) 5:38:05
1984: Adrian James (Enfield) 5:28:30
1985: Bob Dobson (Ilford) 5:32:54
1986: Bob Dobson (Ilford) 5:46:11
1987: Bob Dobson (Ilford) 5:39:51

HIGHGATE HARRIERS OPEN 7 MILES
1931: Tommy Green (Belgrave) 53:08
1932: Albert Plumb (North London) 50:33
1933: Bert Cooper (Woodford Green) 53:09
1934: Johnny Johnson (Enfield) 53:29
1935: Bert Cooper (Woodford Green) 49:28
1936: Vic Stone (Poly) 51:12
1937: Harry Churcher (Belgrave) 53:08
1938: Harry Churcher (Belgrave) 52:01

1940: Eddie Staker (Highgate) 59:48
1941: David Christie-Murray (Surrey WC) 54:45
1942: David Christie-Murray (Surrey WC) 55:55
1943: Charlie Megnin (Highgate) 54:58
1944: Harold Whitlock (Metropolitan) 55:05
1945: Charlie Megnin (Highgate) 55:17
1946: Harry Churcher (Belgrave) 54:47
1947: Ron West (Cambridge H) 55:08
1948: Jim Morris (Surrey AC) 55:05
1949: Harry Churcher (Belgrave) 54:52
1950: George Coleman (Highgate) 53:48
1951: Fred Barrett (Cambridge H) 54:24
1952: Fred Barrett (Cambridge H) 54:39
1953: George Coleman (Highgate) 53:58
1954: George Coleman (Highgate) 52:42
1955: George Coleman (Highgate) 53:31
1956: George Coleman (Highgate) 51:30
1957: Eric Hall (Belgrave) 51:42
1958: Ken Matthews (RSC) 49:09
1959: Ken Matthews (RSC) 50:36
1960: Bob Clark (Poly) 52:33
1961: Arthur Thomson (Metropolitan) 52:15
1962: Ken Matthews (RSC) 50:36
1963: Ken Matthews (RSC) 49:40
1964: Bob Clark (Poly) 52:25
1965: Ray Middleton (Belgrave) 53:16
1966: Ron Wallwork (Lancs) 49:39
1967: John Webb (Basildon) 51:04
1968: Len Duquemin (Belgrave) 54:03
1969: Roy Lodge (Bromsgrove & R) 50:57

HIGHGATE HARRIERS OPEN 1 HOUR
1942: Eddie Staker (Highgate) 7mls 1103y
1943: Norman Burt (Surrey WC) 7:1085
1944: Norman Burt (Surrey WC) 7:1073
1945: Charlie Megnin (Highgate) 7:1005
1946: Jim Morris (Surrey AC) 7:1090
1947: Jim Morris (Surrey AC) 7:1455
1948: Ron West (Cambridge H) 7:770
1949: Jim Morris (Surrey AC) 8:015
1950: George Coleman (Highgate) 7:1495
1951: Fred Barrett (Cambridge H) 7:1175
1952: Fred Barrett (Cambridge H) 7:1240
1953: George Coleman (Highgate) 7:1210
1954: George Coleman (Highgate) 8:78
1955: Len Evans (Highgate) 7:1474
1956: Stan Vickers (Belgrave) 8:702
1957: Ken Matthews (RSC) 8:9
1958: Stan Vickers (Belgrave) 8:702
1959: Bob Goodall (Woodford Green) 7:1454
1960: Ken Matthews (RSC) 8:1018
1961: Arthur Thomson (Metropolitan) 8:78
1962: John Edgington (Coventry) 8:68
1963: Paul Nihill (Surrey WC) 8:462
1964: Paul Nihill (Surrey WC) 8:670
1965: Peter McCullagh (Metropolitan) 8:184
1966: John Webb (Basildon) 7:1719
1967: Arthur Jones (Brighton) 8:245
1968: Peter Fullager (Basildon) 8:319
1969: Paul Nihill (Surrey WC) 13,671m
1970: Phil Embleton (Metropolitan) 13,368
1971: Bob Dobson (Basildon) 13,327
1972: Shaun Lightman (Metropolitan) 13,142
1973: Olly Flynn (Basildon) 13,084
1974: Roger Mills (Ilford) 13,412
1975: Brian Adams (Leicester) 13,382
1976: Brian Adams (Leicester) 13,184

1977: Marcel Jobin CAN 13,599
1978: Carl Lawton (Belgrave) 12,922
1979: Allan King (Leicester) 13,447
1980: Amos Seddon (Enfield) 13,373
1981: Phil Vesty (Leicester) 13,393
1988: Mark Easton (Surrey WC) 13,597
1989: Michael Lane (Mullingar H) 13,273

LEICESTER MERCURY 20 MILES
1927: Lloyd Johnson (Surrey AC) 3:01:01
1928: Lloyd Johnson (Leicester WC) 2:51:18
1929: Lloyd Johnson (Leicester) 2:53:42
1930: Lloyd Johnson (Leicester) 2:52:27
1931: Stan Smith (Derby WC) 2:57:10
1932: Tommy Green (Belgrave) 2:55:52.6
1933: John Wilson (Sheffield) 2:52:08.8
1934: Lloyd Johnson (Leicester) 2:52:39
1935: Harry Hake (Surrey WC) 2:49:17.2
1936: Lloyd Johnson (Leicester) 2:52:17
1937: Stan Fletcher (Derbyshire) 2:53:03
1938: Stan Fletcher (Derbyshire) 2:46:45
1939: Albert Staines (Leicester) 2:53:48
1947: Harry Forbes (Birmingham) 2:58:14
1948: Lloyd Johnson (Leicester) 3:00:00
1949: Lloyd Johnson (Leicester) 3:00:07
1950: John Proctor (Sheffield) 2:53:24
1951: Lloyd Johnson (Leicester) 2:57:48
1952: John Proctor (Sheffield) 2:59:55
1953: Frank Bailey (Poly) 2:59:41
1954: Roland Hardy (Sheffield) 2:50:06
1955: Albert Johnson (Sheffield) 2:52:36
1956: Albert Johnson (Sheffield) 2:50:01
1957: Eric Hall (Belgrave) 2:51:00
1958: Tom Misson (Metropolitan) 2:46:30
1959: Don Thompson (Metropolitan) 2:49:56
1960: Tom Misson (Metropolitan) 2:46:05
1961: Peter Markham (Leicester) 2:52:25
1962: Don Thompson (Metropolitan) 2:45:58
1963: Vaughan Thomas (Belgrave) 2:54:52
1964: Ray Middleton (Belgrave) 2:51:41
1965: Peter McCullagh (Metropolitan) 2:53:51
1966: Peter McCullagh (Metropolitan) 2:41:22
1967: Roy Lodge (RSC) 2:52:29
1968: Bryan Eley (Bristol) 2:41:22
1969: Bryan Eley (Bristol) 2:42:15
1970: Ron Wallwork (Lancs) 2:37:22
1971: Shaun Lightman (Metropolitan) 2:38:16
1972: Carl Lawton (Belgrave) 2:39:39
1973: John Moullin (Belgrave) 2:45:59
1974: Carl Lawton (Belgrave) 2:35:36
1975: Shaun Lightman (Metropolitan) 2:39:53
1976: Daniel Bautista MEX 2:22:53
1977: Brian Adams (Leicester) 2:34:45
1978: Brian Adams (Leicester) 2:39:44
1979: Brian Adams (Leicester) 2:37:35
1980: Amos Seddon (Enfield) 2:31:33
1981: Allan King (Leicester) 2:39:07
1982: Allan King (Leicester) 2:43:26
1983: Murray Lambden (Boundary) 2:39:41
1984: Graham Seatter (Belgrave) 2:26:56
1985: Murray Day (Belgrave) 2:35:37

LEICESTER OPEN 7 MILES
1950: Roland Hardy (Sheffield) 51:59
1951: Roland Hardy (Sheffield) 51:21
1952: Roland Hardy (Sheffield) 53:31
1953: Roland Hardy (Sheffield) 53:22

1954: Albert Johnson (Sheffield) 53:02
1955: Len Evans (Highgate) 53:11
1956: Roland Hardy (Sheffield) 51:26
1957: Ken Matthews (RSC) 51:39
1958: Stan Vickers (Belgrave) 49:36
1959: Stan Vickers (Belgrave) 51:16
1960: Ken Matthews (RSC) 48:25
1961: Ken Matthews (RSC) 49:41
1962: Ken Matthews (RSC) 51:04
1963: Ken Matthews (RSC) 48:52
1964: George Chaplin (Coventry) 53:29
1965: Peter McCullagh (Metropolitan) 50:34
1966: Malcolm Tolley (Sheffield) 52:03
1967: Ron Wallwork (Lancs) 52:30
1968: Peter Fullager (Surrey WC) 50:52
1969: Paul Nihill (Surrey WC) 48:25
1970: Bob Hughes (RSC) 49:38
1971: John Warhurst (Sheffield) 51:17
1972: Tony Taylor (Leigh H) 51:25
1973: John Warhurst (Sheffield) 50:31
1974: Brian Adams (Leicester) 49:28
1975: Brian Adams (Leicester) 51:06
1976: Graham Seatter (Belgrave) 50:41
1977: Brian Adams (Leicester) 50:12
1978: Allan King (Leicester) 51:32
1979: Graham Seatter (Belgrave) 43:22
1980: Allan King (Leicester) 48:55
1981: Phil Vesty (Leicester) 49:10
1982: Roy Sheppard (Anglia) 49:29
1983: Phil Vesty (Leicester) 49:25
1984: Phil Vesty (Leicester) 47:52
1985: Héctor Moreno COL 46:33
1986: Andy Penn (Coventry) 50:18
1987: Martin Bell (Splott Cons) 47:10
1988: Andy Penn (Coventry) 50:40
1989: Andi Drake (Coventry) 48:14
1990: Martin Bell (Splott Cons) 48:09
1991: Andy Penn (Coventry) 48:17
1992: Martin Bell (Splott Cons) 48:47
1993: Darren Thorn (Coventry) 52:39
1994: Martin Young (Road Hoggs) 52:27
1995: Martin Young (Road Hoggs) 50:25
1996: David Keown (Road Hoggs) 53:21
1997: Richard Oldale (Sheffield) 53:38
1998: Karl Orchard (Road Hoggs) 53:31
1999: Martin Bell (Splott Cons) 53:46
2000: Karl Orchard (Road Hoggs) 55:47
Not under full IAAF definition of walking
2001: Lloyd Finch (Leicester) 52:02
2002: Steve Hollier (Wolverhampton & B) 49:04
In 2003 a handicap was held

LONDON TO BRIGHTON OPEN
1886: J.McIntosh (Compton) 9:25:08
1897: Teddy Knott (South London H) 8:56:44
Times from the Polytechnic Regent Street and Westminster respectively – the only time the race started at the former
1903: Jack Butler (Poly) 8:43:16
1906: Jack Butler (Poly) 8:23:27
1909: Harold Ross (Tooting) 8:11:14
1911: Tommy Payne (Middlesex) 8:20:06
1913: Edgar Horton (Surrey WC) 8:36:08.2
1919: Tommy Payne (North Shields) 8:38:23
1920: Harold Ross (Herne Hill H) 8:15:58
1920: Tommy Payne (North Shields) 8:21:33.4
1921: Donato Pavesi (Molinari/ITA) 8:37:27.6

1922: Edgar Horton (Surrey WC) 8:27:12.4
1923: Fred Poynton (Leicester H) 8:35:37
1924: Billy Baker (QPH) 8:40:51.2
1925: Billy Baker (QPH) 8:16:16.4
1926: Billy Baker (QPH) 8:39:39
1927: C.Giani (Como ITA) 8:18:33
1928: Billy Baker (QPH) 8:32:39
1929: Tommy Green (Belgrave) 8:15:41
1930: Tommy Green (Belgrave) 8:02:55
1931: Tommy Green (Belgrave) 8:05:43
1932: Jack Ludlow (Derby) 8:01:06
1933: Tommy Green (Belgrave) 8:01:19
1934: Harold Whitlock (Metropolitan) 8:17:23
1935: Harold Whitlock (Metropolitan) 7:53:50
1936: Harold Whitlock (Metropolitan) 8:01:25
1937: Harold Whitlock (Metropolitan) 8:02:38
1938: Tommy Richardson (Woodford Green) 8:08:01
1946: Harry Forbes (Birmingham) 8:20:12
1947: Rex Whitlock (Metropolitan) 8:21:54
1948: Rex Whitlock (Metropolitan) 8:14:29
1949: Charlie Megnin (Highgate) 8:34:41
1950: Rex Whitlock (Metropolitan) 8:19:13
1951: Rex Whitlock (Metropolitan) 8:14:36
1952: Vic Stone (Poly) 8:25:25
1953: Bill Cowley (Surrey WC) 8:20:38
1954: Norman Guilmant (Belgrave) 8:20:44
1955: Don Thompson (Metropolitan) 8:06:24
1956: Don Thompson (Metropolitan) 7:45:32
1957: Don Thompson (Metropolitan) 7:35:12
1958: Don Thompson (Metropolitan) 7:49:22
1959: Don Thompson (Metropolitan) 7:35:28
1960: Don Thompson (Metropolitan) 7:37:42
1961: Don Thompson (Metropolitan) 7:39:57
1962: Don Thompson (Metropolitan) 7:49:58
1963: Dennis Read (Steyning) 8:06:58
1964: George Hazle RSA 8:25:20
1965: Abdon Pamich ITA 7:37:42
1966: Ken Mason (Surrey WC) 8:21:39
1967: Don Thompson (Metropolitan) 7:55:12
1968: Bryan Eley (Bristol) 8:00:50
1969: Bryan Eley (Bristol) 8:02:09
1970: Shaul Ladany ISR 7:46:37
1971: Shaul Ladany ISR 7:57:17
1972: Peter Selby (Surrey WC) 8:13:47
1973: Shaul Ladany ISR 7:57:27
1974: Ray Middleton (Belgrave) 8:17:50
1975: Ray Middleton (Belgrave) 8:10:27
1976: Peter Hodkinson (Cambridge H) 8:06:13
1977: John Lees (Brighton) 7:54:32
1978: Shaun Lightman (Metropolitan) 8:06:39
1979: Ian Richards (Coventry) 8:18:22
1980: Peter Selby (Surrey WC) 8:21:35
1981: Carl Lawton (Belgrave) 8:20:51
1982: John Warhurst (Sheffield) 8:24:04
1983: Peter Hodkinson (Cambridge H) 8:28:17
A final Centenary Stock Exchange walk including an open race was held in 2003
2003 Mark Easton (Surrey WC) 8:06:15

LONDON TRAMWAYS 10 MILES
1926: A.Hurst (Cambridge H) 85:45
1927: A.Webb (Poly) 80:19
1928: L.Sandy (Surrey AC) 78:22
1929: Cecil Hyde (Enfield) 78:24
1930: Cecil Hyde (Enfield) 76:08

7 MILES
1931: Alf Fletcher (Belgrave) 54:37.4

1932: Alf Fletcher (Belgrave) 54:54
1933: Alf Fletcher (Belgrave) 54:46
1934: Johnny Johnson (Enfield) 55:16
1935: Fred Redman (Metropolitan) 54:17
1936: Fred Redman (Metropolitan) 55:18
1937: Harry Churcher (Belgrave) 54:43
1938: Harry Churcher (Belgrave) 56:10
1939: Harry Churcher (Belgrave) 56:00
1943: Eddie Staker (Herne Hill) 54:57
1944: Eddie Staker (Herne Hill) 54:18

MANCHESTER TO BLACKPOOL

A 53 mile/83km race (although distance varied slightly) held annually except in the War years. Organised by the Lancashire Walking Club and held in June (with a 6:15 am start). Finishing at the Blackpool Tower.

1908: Tommy Payne (South Shields) 8:20:19
1909: Tommy Payne (South Shields) 7:43:53.8
1910: Tommy Payne (South Shields) 8:37:51
1911: Tommy Payne (Morpeth) 9:08:55
1912: F.Roberts (Woodford Green) 8:00:30
1913: F.Roberts (Woodford Green) 8:05:00
1919: Tommy Payne (Yorks WC) 8:18:07.2
1920: Tommy Payne (Yorks WC) 8:41:17
1921: Ralph Wallwork (Lancs WC) 8:52:37
1922: Donato Pavesi ITA 8:12:44
1923: Fred Poynton (Leicester H) 8:31:47
1924: Frank Holt (Yorks WC) 8:20:40
1925: P.Granville (Hamilton YMCA) 8:06:39
1926: Joe Hopkins (North Manchester) 8:29:01
1927: Arthur Hignett (Lancs WC) 8:28:36
1928: Frank Holt (Yorks WC) 8:00:04
1929: Tommy Green (Belgrave) 7:56:55
1930: Tommy Green (Belgrave) 7:39:30.4
1931: Tommy Green (Belgrave) 7:49:19
1932: Tommy Green (Belgrave) 7:50:57
1933: Tommy Green (Belgrave) 8:14:46
1934: Lloyd Johnson (Leicester) 8:52:16
1950: Percy Reading (Poly) 8:21:14
1951: Percy Reading (Poly) 8:28:05
1952: Percy Reading (Poly) 8:37:05
1953: Vic Stone (Poly) 8:32:55
1954: Norman Guilmant (Belgrave) 8:17:45
1955: Norman Guilmant (Belgrave) 8:16:12
1956: Hew Neilson (Woodford Green) 8:30:54
1957: Karl Abolins (RSC) 8:34:18
1958: Frank O'Reilly (Lozells H) 8:20:00
1959: Frank O'Reilly (Lozells H) 8:16:30
1960: Albert Johnson (Sheffield) 8:23:15
1961: John Edgington (Coventry) 8:25:24
1962: Hew Neilson (Woodford Green) 8:53:22
1963: Frank O'Reilly (Lozells H) 8:14:25
1964: Guy Goodair (Wakefield) 8:16:54
1965: Guy Goodair (Wakefield) 8:29:07
1966: John Paddick (RSC) 8:19:27
1967: Pat Duncan (Belgrave) 7:59:17
1968: Pat Duncan (Belgrave) 7:57:01
1969: George Barras (Wakefield) 8:13:35
1970: Karl Abolins (RSC) 8:14:00
1971: Peter Markham (Leicester) 8:28:08
1972: John Eddershaw (Sheffield) 8:16:10
1973: Guy Goodair (Blackburn) 8:07:45
1974: Ken Harding (RSC) 8:08:51
1975: Ken Harding (RSC) 8:03:44
1976: Ken Harding (RSC) 8:09:33
1977: Ken Harding (RSC) 7:51:52
1978: John Lees (Brighton) 7:46:45

1979: Ken Harding (RSC) 8:01:02
1980: Tony Collins (Holloway P) 8:04:30
1981: John Paddick (Leicester) 8:07:48
1982: Mike Holmes (York Postal) 7:56:59
1983: Tony Collins (Holloway P) 8:15:52
1984: Mike Holmes (York Postal) 8:02:12
1985: John Warhurst (Sheffield) 8:16:05
1986: Richard Brown (Surrey WC) 8:41:03
1987: Dave Turner (Yorks WC) 8:32:08
1988: Allan King (Leicester) 7:51:26
1989: Richard Brown (Surrey WC) 8:08:00
1990: ---------
1991: Andy Trigg (Leicester) 7:50:20
1992: Dave Turner (Yorks WC) 8:17:17
1994: Dave Turner (Yorks WC) 7:51:58
1995: Colin Bradley (Trowbridge) 8:21:17
1996: John Paddick (Yorks WC) 8:39:57
1997: Martin Fisher (York CIU) 8:42:05
1999: Martin Fisher (York CIU) 8:21:08
2000: Martin Fisher (York CIU) 8:28:21

BLACKPOOL OPEN 50 MILES

2003: Martin Fisher (York CIU) 8:53:12
2004: John Paddick (Redcar) 8:58:33
2005: John Paddick (Redcar) 9:03:14
2006: Martin Fisher (Yorks WC) 9:19:47
2007: Martin Fisher (Yorks WC) 9:18:17
2008: Ray Pitts (IOM Vets) 8:58:44

METROPOLITAN POLICE OPEN 7 MILES

1942: David Christie-Murray (Highgate) 53:19
1943: Jim Morris (Surrey AC) 53:25
1944: Bill Burgess (Surrey WC) 53:43
1945: Charlie Megnin (Highgate) 53:54
1946: Jack Rutland (Belgrave) 52:19
1947: Harry Churcher (Belgrave) 53:15
1948: Harry Churcher (Belgrave) 51:43
1949: Harry Churcher (Belgrave) 52:09
1950: Harry Churcher (Belgrave) 51:48
1951: George Coleman (Highgate) 53:10
1952: Paddy Woods (Surrey AC) 53:31
1953: Bryan Hawkins (Metropolitan) 52:02
1954: Bryan Hawkins (Metropolitan) 52:32
1955: George Meadows (Highgate) 55:07
1956: Bryan Hawkins (Metropolitan) 51:52
1957: Stan Vickers (Belgrave) 51:32
1958: Stan Vickers (Belgrave) 50:14
1959: Ken Matthews (RSC) 48:14
1960: Eric Hall & Stan Vickers (Belgrave) 51:20
1961: Ken Matthews (RSC) 48:02
1962: Ken Matthews (RSC) 49:51
1963: Paul Nihill (Surrey WC) 52:08
1964: Ken Matthews (RSC) 48:36
1965: John Paddick (RSC) 51:20
1966: Malcom TolleySheff) 50:34
1967: Ron Wallwork (Lancs) 51:13
1968: John Webb (Basildon) 50:47
1969: Paul Nihill (Surrey WC) 50:46
1970: Paul Nihill (Surrey WC) 49:50
1971: Bob Hughes (RSC) 49:46
1972: Ron Laird USA 50:11
1973: Olly Flynn (Basildon) 50:07
1974: John Webb (Basildon) 51:17
1975: Brian Adams (Leicester) 50:57
1976: Brian Adams (Leicester) 49:49
1977: Shaun Lightman (Metropolitan) 49:27
1978: Shaun Lightman (Metropolitan) 49:07

OPEN 11 KILOMETRES
1979: Shaun Lightman (Metropolitan) 49:21
1980: Mike Parker (Brighton) 48:42
1981: Adrian James (Enfield) 48:14
1982: Paul Blagg (Belgrave) 49:41
1983: Jimmy Ball (Southampton) 48:37
1984: Ian McCombie (Cambridge H) 46:14
1985: Ian McCombie (Cambridge H):45:48
1986: Mike Parker (Brighton) 47:36
1987: Jimmy Ball (Southampton) 47:33
1988: Darrell Stone (Steyning) 47:11
1989: Querubin Moreno COL 45:45
1990: Mark Easton (Surrey WC) 47:40
1991: Chris Cheeseman (Surrey WC) 43:21
1992: Mark Easton (Surrey WC):45:06
1993: Jimmy Ball (Steyning) 50:35
1994: Mark Easton (Surrey WC) 46:47
1995: Chris Cheeseman (Surrey WC) 50:22

OPEN 10 KILOMETRES
1996: Darrell Stone (Steyning) 40:55
1997: Darrell Stone (Steyning) 41:37
1998: Chris Cheeseman (Surrey WC) 42:28
1999: Darrell Stone (Steyning) 43:41
2000: Andi Drake (Coventry) 41:26
2001: Chris Cheeseman (Surrey WC) 43:21
2002: Darrell Stone (Steyning) 42:54
2003: Mark Easton (Surrey WC) 46:25
2004: Dominic King (Colchester) 42:34
2005: Dominic King (Colchester) 42:26
2006: Nick Ball (Steyning):45:39

METROPOLITAN WALKING CLUB OPEN 20 KILOMETRES
1958: Stan Vickers (Belgrave) 1:32:38
1959: Ken Matthews (RSC) 1:30:08
1960: Stan Vickers (Belgrave) 1:32:28
1961: Ken Matthews (RSC) 1:29:11
1962: Ken Matthews (RSC) 1:32:31
1963: Paul Nihill (Surrey WC) 1:32:09
1964: Paul Nihill (Surrey WC) 1:31:39
1965: Peter Fullager (Surrey WC) 1:36:24
1966: Peter McCullagh (Metropolitan) 1:34:07
1967: Shaun Lightman (Metropolitan) 1:35:45
1968: Paul Nihill (Surrey WC) 1:32:53
1969: Peter Fullager (Basildon) 1:33:37
1970: Wilf Wesch (Belgrave/FRG) 1:29:02
1971: Phil Embleton (Metropolitan) 1:27:59
1972: Phil Embleton (Metropolitan) 1:29:19
1973: Bob Dobson (Basildon) 1:32:56
1974: Roy Thorpe (Sheffield) 1:35:24
1975: Peter Selby (Surrey WC) 1:33:56
1976: Roger Mills (Ilford) 1:33:31
1977: Shaun Lightman (Metropolitan) 1:32:29
1978: Graham Morris (Steyning) 1:32:56
1979: George Nibre (Ilford) 1:35:21
1980: -----
1981: Dave Jarman (Surrey WC) 1:29:28
1982: Ian McCombie (Cambridge H) 1:29:15
1983: Richard Dorman (Belgrave) 1:33:25
1984: Steve Barry (Roath Labour) 1:24:37
1985: Kevin Baker (Weymouth) 1:34:42
1986: Mike Parker (Brighton) 1:27:05
1987: Jimmy Ball (Southampton) 1:28:46
1988: ------
1989: Jimmy Ball (Southampton) 1:25 12

NOTTINGHAM TO BIRMINGHAM 55 MILES
1922: Edgar Horton (Surrey WC) 9:32:26.6
1923: Fred Poynton (Leicester H) 8:58:27
1924: Joe Hopkins (North Manchester) 9:10:10
1925: Billy Baker (QPH) 8:53:55
1926: Billy Baker (QPH) 8:52:17
1927: Frank Holt (Yorks WC) 9:36:57
1928: Billy Baker (QPH) 9:05:34.8
1929: Jack Ludlow (Derby WC) 8:57:55
1930: Tommy Green (Belgrave) 8:41:02.6
1931: Tommy Green (Belgrave) 8:59:45
1932: Cecil MacMaster RSA 9:00:35
1933: Tommy Green (Belgrave) 8:39:10.8
1934: Tommy Green (Belgrave) 8:46:06.6
1935: Harold Whitlock (Metropolitan) 8:56:13
1936: Tommy Richardson (Woodford Green) 8:58:35
1937: Tommy Richardson (Woodford Green) 9:19:58

REGENTS PARK OPEN 15 MILES
1940: Harold Whitlock (Metropolitan) 2:00:38
1941: Not held
1942: David Christie-Murray (SurreyWC) 2:06:18
1943: Sid Roberts (Belgrave) 2:11:18
1944: Norman Burt (Surrey WC) 2:05:50
1945: Harold Whitlock (Metropolitan) 2:02:42
1946: Harold Whitlock (Metropolitan) 2:03:51
1947: Charlie Churcher (Belgrave) 2:03 47
1948: Charlie Megnin (Herne Hill) 2:02:46
1949: Fred Barrett (Cambridge H.) 2:06:46
1950: John Proctor (Sheffield) 1:58:39
1951: Lol Allen (Sheffield) 1:57:15
1952: Charlie Churcher (Belgrave) 2:04 49
1953: George Coleman (Herne Hill) 2:01:23.6
1954: Bob Goodall (Woodford Green) 2:00:45
1955: George Coleman (Herne Hill) 1:59:25
1956: Bob Goodall (Woodford Green) 1:56:06
1957: Eric Hall & Stan Vickers (both Belgrave) 1:56:35

SHEFFIELD OPEN 15 MILES
1951: Roland Hardy (Sheffield) 1:55:05
1952: Roland Hardy (Sheffield) 1:54:03
1953: Lol Allen (Sheffield) 2:04:50
1954: Roland Hardy (Sheffield) 1:56:11
1955: Roland Hardy (Sheffield) 2:03:25
1956: -----
1957: Lol Allen (Sheffield) 1:56:21
1958: Lol Allen (Sheffield) 1:56:10
1959: Lol Allen (Sheffield) 1:59:20
1960: Don Thompson (Metropolitan) 1:54:55
1961: John Edgington (Coventry) 1:58:42
1962: Ray Ibbotson (Sheffield) 2:03:26
1963: Ron Wallwork (Lancs) 1:59:54
1964: Ron Wallwork (Lancs) 2:01 43
1965: Don Thompson (Metropolitan) 2:00:27
1966: Peter McCullagh (Metropolitan) 1:51:25
1967: Ron Wallwork (Lancs) 1:58:09
1968: John Warhurst (Sheffield) 1:54:52
1969: John Warhurst (Sheffield) 1:55:16
1970: Ron Wallwork (Lancs) 1:53:24
1971: Ron Wallwork (Lancs) 1:52:58
1972: John Warhurst (Sheffield) 1:53:25
1973: John Warhurst (Sheffield) 1:55:32
1974: Roy Thorpe (Sheffield) 1:54:07
1977: Mick Greasley (Sheffield) 1:54:33
1978: Jim Sullivan (York Postal) 1:59:15

MOST NATIONAL CHAMPIONSHIPS – AAA/WAAA/UK/RWA

Men

Wins	1st 3	Name
27	35	Paul Nihill
24	29	Ian McCombie
17	39	Roger Mills
16	18	Ken Matthews
14	15	Roland Hardy
13	23	Les Morton
11	20	Darrell Stone
11	11	Steve Barry
9	19	Don Thompson
9	12	Richard Brown
9	11	Olly Flynn
8	22	Andy Penn
8	18	Harry Churcher
8	13	Stan Vickers
8	13	Scott Davis
8	10	William Sturgess
7	23	Brian Adams
7	22	Chris Cheeseman
7	20	Bob Dobson
7	19	Domin King
7	16	'Lol' Allen
7	13	Harold Whitlcok
7	13	Chris Maddocks
7	12	Harold Ross
7	12	Tom Bosworth
7	10	Bert Cooper
7	8	Bobby Bridge

Wins	1st 3	Name
6	22	Lloyd Johnson
6	18	Mark Easton
6	11	Alfred Pope
5	13	George Coleman
5	11	Andi Drake
5	7	Ernest Webb
5	7	Harry Curtis
5	7	Alex Wright
4	20	Chris Berwick
4	19	Ron Walwork
4	13	Reg Goodwin
4	13	Steve Partington
4	9	Mike Parker

Others with 10 or more 1st 3 places

3	17	Phil Vesty
3	15	Daniel King
3	15	Mike Smith
3	13	John Warhurst
3	10	Phil Embleton
3	10	William Hehir
2	15	Ray Middleton
2	10	Peter Marlow
2	10	Martin Bell
1	12	Shaun Lightman
1	12	Eric Hall

Women (up to 20k)

23	39	Lisa Langford/Kehler
23	37	Vicky Lupton

Wins	1st 3	Name
18	29	Judy Woodsford/Farr
18	20	Johanna Jackson
15	19	Betty Sworowski
10	17	Irene Bateman
9	20	Joyce Heath
9	12	Carol Tyson
7	14	Niobe Menendez
7	12	Marion Fawkes
7	8	Dilys Williams
6	27	Helen Elleker
6	15	Betty Jenkins
5	14	Beryl Day/Randle
5	13	Virginia Lovell/Birch
4	15	Sheila Martin/Jennings
4	12	Sylvia Black
4	11	Jill Barrett
4	7	Jessie Howes

Others with 10 or more 1st 3 places

2	14	Melanie Brookes/Wright
2	11	Sarah Brown
2	11	Sharon Tonks
2	10	Julie Drake
2	10	Catherine Charnock
1	12	Kim Baird/Braznell

Note:
0   5   Sandra Brown
also won 17 titles at 100 miles and 2 at 24 hours

AGE-GROUP TRACK CHAMPIONS

ENGLAND UNDER-23
10,000 METRES
1999 Robert Heffernan IRL 43:49.80 (3. Matt Hales 45:38.01)
2000-01 not held
2002 Nathan Adams 46:22.2
2003 Dominic King 43:27.93
2004 Daniel King 43:52.86
2005 Daniel King 44:40.35
2006 Luke Finch 47:59.51
2007-11 not held
2012 Tom Bosworth 43:58.54

WOMEN 5000 METRES
1999 Nikki Huckerby 25:30.07
2000-04 not held
2005 Jo Jackson 22:55.89
2006 Jo Jackson 23:22.42
2007 Jo Jackson 22:38.19
2008 Fiona McGorum 29:46.81
2009 Rebecca Mersh 27:05.17

WOMEN 10,000 METRES
2010 Fiona McGorum 54:37.61
2011 Heather Lewis 54:27.48
2012 Bethan Davies 52:32.33
2013 Heather Lewis 50:17.76
2014 Heather Lewis 49:06.83

AAA/ENGLAND JUNIOR CHAMPIONSHIPS
1931-52: Under 19 on the day of competition; 1953-64: Under-19 on 1st April; 1965-72: Under-19 on 1st September (in 1973 this was changed to 31st August);

From 1974: Under-20 on 31st December in the year of competition

ONE MILE
1947 Kenneth Harding 7:30.2
1948 E Sharp 7:22.6
1949 Daniel Bolt 7:06.0
1950 Norman Read 7:04.8
1951 John Lowther 6:59.2
1952 Gareth Lewis 6:53.6
1953 Gareth Howell 6:49.9
1954 Gareth Howell 6:54.0
1955 John Edgington 7:13.4
1956 Michael Shannon 7:07.4
1957 Michael Shannon 6:55.3
1958 Dennis Read 6:51.8
1959 Peter Marlow 7:05.4
1960 Ron Wallwork 6:59.1
1961 Shaun Lightman 6:54.5
1962 Shaun Lightman 6:46.2
1963 Malcolm Tolley 6:57.9
1964 Christopher Trimming 7:12.4
1965 Robert Care 6:58.2
1966 Kevin Smith 7:33.0
1967 Phil Embleton 7:04.9
1968 Olly Flynn 6:58.4

3000 METRES
1969 Richard Evans 14:04.0
1970 David Ward 13:22.4
1971 Brian Laver 13:39.0
1972 John Lord 13:27.8

10,000 METRES
1973 John Lord 45:39.6
1974 John Lord 45:20.0
1975 David Cotton 46:29.6
1976 Michael Dunion 47:24.4
1977 Graham Morris 46:51.0
1978 Michael Miley 47:44.8
1979 Gordon Vale 45:55.2
1980 Gordon Vale 45:06.3
1981 Gordon Vale 42:06.35
1982 Phil Vesty 47:54.38
1983 Tim Berrett 43:21.28
1984 David Hucks 46:11.38
1985 Ian Ashforth 45:04.37
1986 Darrell Stone 45:15.68
1987 Darrell Stone 44:09.29
1988 Jonathan Vincent 45:19.11
1989 Carl Walmsley 51:26.82
1990 Guy Jackson 46:50.69
1991 Philip King 45:40.64
1992 David Cullinane IRL 44:13.91
    (2. Scott Davis 45:30.02)
1993 Philip King 46:07.60
1994 Dion Russell AUS 43:26.22
1995 Jamie Costin IRL 44:12.51
1996 Jamie Costin IRL 44:55.20
    (3. Matt Hales 50:17.25)
1997 Thomas Taylor 48:44.42
1998 Thomas Taylor 45:56.16
1999 Lloyd Finch 45:52.39
2000 Colin Griffin IRL 46:45.31
    (2. Daniel King 48:25.61)
2001 Lloyd Finch 44:29.4
2002 Dominic King 42:49.8
2003 Nick Ball 49:38.49
2004 Luke Finch 46:48.40
2005 Nick Ball 45:36.24
2006 Nick Ball 43:50.94

2007	not held	
2008	Mark O'Kane (5k)	24:10.10
2009	Alex Wright	48:18.98
2010	Mark O'Kane	47:04.42
2011	Jamie Higgins	48:39.62
2012	Ben Parsons	52:53.29
2013	Jamie Higgins	42:58.11
2014	Callum Wilkinson	46:09.84

WOMEN 5000 METRES

1986	Karen Dunster	27:43.33
1987	Louise Carr	26:26.22
1988	Julie Drake	24:07.22
1989	Vicky Lupton	25:06.27
1990	Vicky Lupton	23:41.5
1991	Carla Jarvis	25:13.8
1992	Theresa Ashman	25:32.95
1993	Katherine Horwill	26:49.41
1994	Natalie Saville AUS	23:12.03
	(3. Kate Horwill 25:31.47)	
1995	Nikki Huckerby	26:03.46
1996	Rosaleigh Comerford IRL	
	24:40.2 (2. Nina Howley 24:48.1)	
1997	Nikki Huckerby	25:01.55
1998	Katie Ford	25:30.29
1999	Amy Hales	24:35.55
2000	Serena O'Keeffe IRL	25:07.32
2001	Sophie Hales	26:29.35
2002	Sophie Hales	25:18.56
2003	Sophie Hales	25:16.90
2004	Sophie Hales	24:54.62
2005	Rebecca Mersh	25:32.85
2006	Chelsea O'Rawe-Hobbs	26:22.51
2007	Rebecca Mersh	27:26.11
2008	Rebecca Mersh	27:33.43
2009	Rebecca Mersh	27:05.17

WOMEN 10,000 METRES

2010	Emma Doherty IRL	52:15.26
	(4. Lauren Whelan 52:54.26)	
2011	Heather Lewis	54:27.48
2012	Heather Lewis	51:57.20
2013	Ellie Dooley	52:07.36
2014	Emma Achurch	51:16.81

UNDER-17 CHAMPS
(Event instituted for Intermediates in 1968 at 1 Mile; 2000m from 1969; 3000m from 1976; 10,000m from 1986; 5000m from 1991)

1980	Tim Berrett	14:09.71
1981	Tim Berrett	13:23.76
1982	David Hucks	13:33.33
1983	Nathan Kavanagh	13:12.84
1984	not held	
1985	Paul Whitehouse	13:55.75
1986	Russell Hutchings	47:53.45
1987	Jon Vincent	48:53.17
1988	David Lawrence	51:55.14
1989	Stuart Tilbury	51:02.15
1990	Philip King	46:34.50
1991	Philip King	21:31.18
1992	Pierce O'Callaghan IRL	
	23:38.65 (2. Ben Allkins 24:36.06)	
1993	Jamie Costin IRL	23:48.29
	(2. Matt Dunne 26:04.23)	
1994	Scott Taylor	28:00.12
1995	Stuart Monk	24:39.7
1996	Matt Hales	23:49.89
1997	David Kidd IRL	22:57.2
	(2. Thomas Taylor 23:34.4)	
1998	Colin Griffin IRL	23:41.47
	(2. Nathan Adams 24:42.02)	
1999	Andy Parker	23:22.81
2000	Andy Parker	22:48.91
2001	Luke Finch	23:50.61
2002	Luke Finch	23:56.41
2003	Nick Ball	22:59.03
2004	Nick Ball	22:30.26
2005	Ben Wears	24:09.16
2006	Ben Wears	22:48.35
2007	Matthew Halliday	24:14.82
2008	Jonathan Hobbs	25:27.80
2009	Jonathan Hobbs	25:24.31
2010	Jamie Higgins	29:31.30
2011	Daniel Waples	27:10.59
2012	Daniel Watling	35:06.40
2013	Callum Wilkinson	23:28.80

WOMEN U17 1 MILE

1949	Zoe White	?
1950	Zoe White	8:49.4
1951	Irene McCormack	9:22.0
1952	Pauline Williams	9:39.0
1953-4	?	
1955	Pat Myatt	8:53.0
1956-60	not held	
1961	Jennifer Keen	9:11.4
1962	Jennifer Keen	8:45.6
1963	Sheila Higgleton	10:14.5
1964	Susan Dyer	8:36.0
1965	Jennifer Peck	9:01.8
1966	Jane Matthews	8:58.4
1967	Doris Froome	8:23.4
1968	Catherine Russell	8:45.2

U17 2000 METRES

1969	Barbara Brown	10:58.4
1970	Catherine Daniels	11:11.0
1971	Kim Braznell	10:31.6
1972	Marion Davis	12:20.0

U17 2500 METRES

1973	Pamela Branson	12:42.8
1974	Sylvia Saunders	12:47.8

U17 3000 METRES

1975	Bev Francis	16:27.0
1976	Elaine Cox	15:29.46
1977	Joanna Wickham	15:30.0
1978	Carol Brooke	16:43.8
1979	Jillian Mullins	15:47.5
1980	Jill Barrett	15:34.8
1981	Karen Nipper	14:59.32
1982	Helen Ringshaw	15:05.82
1983	Elizabeth Ryan	15:41.66
1984	Kim Macadam	15:24.3
1985	Susan Ashforth	14:35.5
1986	Nicola Massey	15:38.79
1987	Andrea Crofts	15:01.22
1988	Tracy Devlin	15:06.71
1989	Tracy Devlin	14:33.76

U17 5000 METRES

1990	Carla Jarvis	27:08.29
1991	Kate Horwill	26:48.37
1992	Lisa Crump	28:42.12
1993	Nina Howley	26:54.99
1994	Nina Howley	25:25.07
1995	Sarah Bennett	27:01.1
1996	Sarah Bennett	27:53.40
1997	Serena O'Keeffe IRL	25:00.6
	(2. Rebecca Tisshaw 25:52.8)	
1998	Serena O'Keeffe IRL	
	24:35.02 (2. Katie Ford 26:13.07)	
1999	Nicola Phillips	26:32.96
2000	Natalie Evans	27:24.88
2001	Bryna Chrismas	27:42.35
2002	Katie Stones	25:57.11
2003	Jenny Gagg	25:03.91
2004	Rebecca Mersh	24:47.75
2005	Laura Reynolds IRL	25:19.67
2006	Chelsea O'Rawe-Hobbs	26:44.55
2007	Fiona Dennehy IRL	26:52.49
2008	Emma Doherty	26:23.72
2009	Kate Veale IRL	23:27.58
2010	Heather Lewis	26:24.26
2011	Tasha Webster	26:10.69
2012	Tasha Webster	28:21.59
2013	Veronica Burke IRL	26:17.31
	(2. Heather Butcher 26:27.31)	

UNDER-15 BOYS 3000m

1991	Matthew Cross	16:08.72
1992	Robert Warren	19:35.37
1993	Matt Hales	15:45.2
1994	Matt Hales	14:51.12
1995	John Murphy	14:48.4
1996	Lloyd Finch	15:02.70
1997	Lloyd Finch	13:52.79
1998	Lloyd Finch	13:29.59
1999	James Davis	14:04.41
2000	Luke Finch	14:09.93
2001	Luke Davis	15:47.32
2002	Nick Ball	14:43.39
2003	Lewis Hayden	14:14.56
2004	Antonio Cirillo	15:49.32
2005	Antonio Cirillo	14:54.81
2006	Chris Ball	15:48.72
2007	Hamish Hall	14:48.86
2008	Maks Orzel	17:13.24
2009	Evan Lynch IRL	15:10.45
	(2. Ben Parsons 17:20.68)	
2010	Guy Thomas	17:55.55
2011	Cameron Corbishley	13:45.05
2012	Matthew Redfern	15:16.92
2013	Christopher Snook	15:53.25

JUNIOR GIRLS (U15) 2500m

1973	Dorothy Ilderton	13:26.2
1974	Elaine Cox	12:53.2
1975	Elaine Cox	13:09.4
1976	Karen Eden	13:34.27
1977	Karen Eden	13:17.0
1978	Jillian Mullins	13:07.6
1979	Angela Copeland	13:26.0
1980	Karen Bowers	12:43.0
1981	Lisa Langford	13:04.52
1982	Sally Clark	12:53.83
1983	Susan Ashforth	12:55.77
1984	Susan Ashforth	11:59.8
1985	Julie Snead	12:40.5
1986	Tracy Devlin	12:49.49
1987	Tracy Devlin	12:21.94

UNDER-15 GIRLS 3000m

1988	Nicola Greenfield	13:01.12	1996	Katie Ford	16:07.95	2005	Kathryn Granger	15:43.76
1989	Carla Jarvis	12:56.32	1997	Nicola Phillips	15:40.37	2006	Natalie Myers	16:08.65
1990	Nikki Parsons	16:28.92	1998	Natalie Evans	15:41.71	2007	Lauren Whelan	16:07.97
1991	Lucy Butterley	16:27.48	1999	Natalie Geens	16:03.49	2008	Katie Veale IRL	14:16.63
1992	Nina Howley	16:16.52	2000	Carol Burtonshaw IRL			(2. Kelsey Howard 16:46.58)	
1993	Sarah Bennett	15:47.0			16:43.43	2009	Katie Funnell	16:03.07
1994	Sarah Bennett	15:28.31	2001	Rebecca Mersh	16:03.25	2010	Emma Achurch	16:40.68
1995	Kelly Mann	15:41.0	2002	Rebecca Mersh	15:26.01	2011	Heather Butcher	15:55.65
			2003	Rebecca Mersh	15:09.10	2012	Heather Butcher	15:28.18
			2004	Kathryn Granger	16:04.35	2013	Sophie Lewis Ward	15:17.38

BRITISH ALL-TIME WALKS LISTS

MEN

3000 METRES TRACK

11:24.4	Mark Easton	24.05.63	1	Tonbridge	10 May 1989
11:28.4	Phil Vesty	5.01.63	1	Leicester	9 May 1984
11:31.0	Andrew Drake	6.02.65	1	Coventry	22 Jul 1990
11:31.8+	Tom Bosworth	17.01.90	2	Birmingham	29 Jun 2014
11:32.2	Ian McCombie	11.01.61	1	Derby	20 Jul 1988
11:33.4	Steve Partington	17.09.65	1	Douglas IOM	12 Jul 1995
11:34.0	Drake		1	Birmingham (Un)	24 Jun 1990
11:34.62	Daniel King	30.05.83	1	Bedford	30 May 2005
11:34.9	Easton		1	Woodford	19 Aug 1987
11:35.2	Vesty		1	Melbourne, AUS	13 Feb 1986
11:35.5	Andy Penn	31.03.67	1	Leamington	10 May 1997
11:36.7	Drake		1	Coventry	7 May 1989
11:38.07	Vesty		1	Swansea	13 Jul 1986
11:38.1	Drake		1	Solihull	19 May 1990
11:38.16	Alex Wright	19.12.90	1	Bedford	31 May 2010
11:39.54	Penn		1	Birmingham	22 May 1991
11:39.61	Drake		1	Wrexham	28 Jul 1990
11:40.0	Easton		1	Brighton	14 Feb 1989
11:41.0	Easton		1	Woodford	13 May 1987
11:41.0	Easton		1	Woking	23 Apr 1989
11:41.02	McCombie		2	Swansea	13 Jul 1986
11:41.73	McCombie		1	London (CP)	13 Jul 1985
11:42.5	Partington		1	Douglas IOM	18 Sep 1992
11:42.94	Vesty		1	London (CP)	23 Aug 1984
11:43.44	Bosworth		2	Bedford	31 May 2010
11:43.6	Partington		1	Douglas IOM	13 May 1992
11:44.68	Roger Mills (27/10)	11.02.48	1	London (CP)	7 Aug 1981
11:45.1	Chris Maddocks	28.03.57	1	Coventry	9 Aug 1987
11:45.77	Steve Johnson	10.06.60	1	Cwmbran	20 Jun 1987
11:49.0	Darrell Stone	2.02.68	2	Brighton	10 Jul 1990
11:49.48	Martin Rush	25.12.64	1	Birmingham	1 Jul 1984
11:49.64	Philip King	25.11.74	1	Bedford	29 May 1995
11:50.26	Luke Finch	21.09.85	4	Bedford	31 May 2010
11:50.55	Nick Ball	29.04.88	1	Bedford	29 May 2006
11:51.1	Paul Nihill	5.09.39	1	Motspur Park	5 Jun 1971
11:51.44	Dominic King	30.05.83	2	Bedford	29 May 2006
11:52.51	Sean Martindale (20)	8.11.66	2	Wrexham	28 Jul 1990
11:53.3	Martin Bell	9.04.61	1	Birmingham	9 Aug 1995
11:53.46	Steve Barry	25.10.50	1	Birmingham	21 Aug 1982
11:54.23	Tim Berrett	23.01.65	2	London (CP)	23 Jun 1984
11:55.0	Phil Embleton	28.12.48	1	Enfield	24 May 1971
11:55.7	Steve Hollier	27.02.76	1	Sutton Coldfield	12 May 2002
12:01.7	Gary Witton	25.08.73	1	Crawley	11 May 1996
12:02.2+	Brian Adams	13.03.49	1m	Leicester	28 Aug 1976
12:04.8	Paul Blagg	23.01.60	1	London (Col)	20 Jun 1990
12:05.0	Chris Smith	23.12.58	1	Leicester	17 May 1987
12:07.54	Matthew Hales (30)	6.10.79	1	Solihull	29 Jul 2000
12:08.8	Allan King	3.12.56	2	Birmingham	15 May 1985

1 MILE TRACK

5:58.4 Alex Wright 1 Leeds 5 Oct 11
5:58.9 Andy Penn 1 Rugby 13 Aug 97
5:59.1 Darrell Stone 1 Portsmouth 2 Jul 89
6:01.75 Roger Mills 2 London CP 15 Sep 78
6:01.8 Ian McCombie 1 Ilford 27 May 88
6:08.9 Steve Partington 1 Douglas 14 Jul 93
6:09.2 Phil Vesty 1 Leicester 23 Jun 82
6:09.96 Martin Bell 1 Solihull 22 Aug 93
6:10.01 Martin Rush 2 Solihull 22 Aug 93

Indoors
5:56.39 Tim Berrett 3 New York 2 Feb 90

109

12:11.5	Kevin Walmsley	6.09.67	2	Douglas IOM	15 May 1996
12:12.0	Chris Harvey	14.10.56	1	Manchester (Str)	1 Apr 1980
12:12.36	Gareth Holloway	2.02.70	1	Cardiff	23 May 1992
12:12.7	Pat Chichester	20.07.66	4	Birmingham	25 May 1988
12:13.0	Mike Smith	20.04.63	1	Leamington	23 Aug 1989
12:15.0	Darren Thorn	17.07.62	2	Leamington	23 Aug 1989
12:15.2	Steve Taylor	19.03.66	3	Douglas IOM	15 May 1996
12:15.6	Bob Hughes	27.10.47	1	Leicester	31 May 1971
12:16.41	Gordon Vale (40)	12.01.62	3	London (CP)	24 Jul 1982
12:16.5	Dave Hucks	2.09.65	2	High Wycombe	5 Aug 1984
12:16.7	Jamie O'Rawe	3.02.73	1	Ilford	6 Aug 2000
12:17.0+e	George Larner	7.03.75	1	Manchester	12 Jul 1904
12:17.6	Stuart Phillips	15.04.63	1	Woodford	14 Aug 1991
12:17.8	George Nibre	9.02.57	1	Enfield	9 Jul 1980
12:18.3	Roy Sheppard	17.08.59	1	Enfield	5 May 1984
12:19.0	Dave Staniforth	15.11.59	3	Corby	31 May 1987
12:20.0	Jimmy Ball	17.02.63	1	Horsham	5 Jul 1987

Uncertain performance

11:59.0	Kieron Butler	16.07.72	1	Melksham	9 Jun 1992

Indoors

11:23.99	Alex Wright	19.12.90	2	Athlone, IRL	27 Jan 2013
11:29.6	Tim Berrett	23.01.65	1	Boston (A), USA	21 Jan 1990
11:39.0+	Martin Rush	25.12.64	1m	Birmingham	8 Feb 1992
11:40.54	Rush		1	Birmingham	13 Feb 1993
11:43.57	Easton		2	Glasgow	3 Mar 1991
11:44.0+	Drake		1m	Turin, ITA	13 Feb 1991
11:44.78i	Bosworth (7/6)		2	Sheffield	5 Jan 2014
11:47.12	Philip King	25.11.74	1	Birmingham	26 Feb 1995
12:16.10	Martin Young	11.07.72	1	Birmingham	11 Feb 1996

2 MILES TRACK

12:52.6	Brian Adams	13.03.49	1	Leicester	28 Aug 1976
13:02.4	Stan Vickers	18.06.32	1	London (WC)	16 Jul 1960
13:09.6	Ken Matthews	21.06.34	2	London (WC)	16 Jul 1960
13:11.4	George Larner	7.03.75	1	Manchester	12 Jul 1904
13:12.2	Ian McCombie	11.01.61	1	Motspur Park	27 Jun 1984
13:16.0	Geoff Toone	19.01.47	1	Leicester	15 Jun 1968
13:16.0+	Paul Nihill	5.09.39	1k	London (CP)	14 May 1969

5000 METRES TRACK

19:16.82	Tom Bosworth	17.01.90	2	Birmingham	29 Jun 2014
19:27.39	Alex Wright	19.12.90	1	Birmingham	14 Jul 2013
19:29.87	Bosworth		1	Birmingham	31 Jul 2011
19:35.0	Darrell Stone	2.02.68	1	Brighton	16 May 1989
19:38.62	Bosworth		2	Birmingham	14 Jul 2013
19:48.14	Wright		1	Birmingham	24 Jun 2012
19:55.8+	Ian McCombie	11.01.61	1m	Jarrow	4 Jun 1989
19:57.91	Dominic King	30.05.83	1	Manchester (SC)	24 Jul 2004
19:57.95	Daniel King (9/6)	30.05.83	2	Manchester (SC)	24 Jul 2004
20:05.7	Philip King	25.11.74	4	Narbonne, FRA	29 Jul 1995
20:06.66	Matt Hales	6.10.79	3	Vittel, FRA	2 Sep 2000
20:22.0+	Steve Barry	25.10.50	m	London (WL)	20 Mar 1982
20:09.0	Steve Partington (10)	17.09.65	1	Douglas IOM	11 Mar 1992
20:13.0	Martin Bell	9.04.61	1	Enfield	2 May 1992
20:13.50	Sean Martindale	8.11.66	1	Crawley	22 Jul 1990
20:14.2	Paul Nihill	5.09.39	1	Östersund, SWE	12 Jul 1972
20:17.47	Paul Blagg	23.01.60	2	Crawley	22 Jul 1990
20:20.0	Chris Maddocks	28.03.57	1	Leamington	15 Aug 1987
20:20.0	Andrew Drake	6.02.65	1	Redditch	5 Sep 1987
20:24.0+	Phil Vesty	5.01.63	1m	Cwmbran	28 May 1984
20:26.7	Mike Parker	21.04.53	1	Brighton	22 Dec 1985
20:28.40	Steve Johnson	10.06.60	5	Cwmbran	9 Jul 1988
20:29.0	Les Morton	1.07.58	3	Coventry	19 Aug 1990

	(20)				
20:32.0+	Martin Rush	25.12.64	2m	Cwmbran	28 May 1984
20:36.0	Steve Hollier	27.02.76	1	Dartford	29 Sep 2002
20:37.4+	Mark Easton	24.05.63	2m	Birmingham	13 Aug 1989
20:46.0+	Andy Penn	31.03.67	3	Birmingham	27 Jul 1991
20:47.23	Lloyd Finch	26.10.83	1	Birmingham	14 Jul 2001
20:47.4	Phil Embleton	28.12.48	1	London (CP)	21 Aug 1971
20:54.8	Gareth Holloway	2.02.70	2	Cardiff	13 Aug 1991
20:55.01	Jamie Higgins	7.01.94	4	Birmingham	29 Jun 2014
20:55.4	Tim Berrett	23.01.65	1	London (BP)	9 Jun 1984
20:58.84	Luke Finch	21.09.85	4	Sligo, IRL	30 May 2004
	(30)				
20:15.0+sh	Steve Barry	25.10.50	1m	Kirkby	19 Mar 1983
Unconfirmed:	20:45.0 Roger Mills	11.02.48	1	-, NZL	1980
Indoors					
19:22.29	Martin Rush	25.12.64	1	Birmingham	8 Feb 1992
19:28.20	Andrew Drake	6.02.65	3	Turin, ITA	13 Feb 1991
19:36.92	Drake		1	Cosford	3 Feb 1991
19:42.90	Tim Berrett	23.01.65	1	New York, USA	23 Feb 1990
19:46.20	Stone		2	Birmingham	8 Feb 1992
19:50.52	Bosworth		3	Belfast	11 Feb 2012
20:01.65	Mark Easton	24.05.63	2	Glasgow	23 Feb 1990
20:08.04	Steve Barry	25.10.50	4	Budapest, HUN	5 Mar 1983
20:32.05	Andy Penn	31.03.67	4	Cosford	3 Feb 1991

10,000 METRES TRACK

40:06.65	Ian McCombie	11.01.61	1	Jarrow	4 Jun 1989
40:39.77	McCombie		1	Derby	5 Jun 1988
40:42.53	McCombie		3	Gateshead	28 Aug 1989
40:45.87	McCombie		1	Derby	25 May 1987
40:47.5+	McCombie		9m	Bergen (Fana), NOR	26 May 1990
40:52.49	McCombie		3	Birmingham	24 Jun 1989
40:53.60	Phil Vesty	5.01.63	1	Cwmbran	28 May 1984
40:55.6	Martin Rush	25.12.64	1	Bolton	14 Sep 1991
41:05.8	McCombie		1	Brighton	3 Feb 1985
41:06.57	Chris Maddocks	28.03.57	4	Portsmouth	20 Jun 1987
41:10.11	Darrell Stone	2.02.68	1	Birmingham	16 Jul 1995
41:11.66	Maddocks		2	Derby	25 May 1987
41:13.62	Steve Barry	25.10.50	3	London (CP)	19 Jun 1982
41:13.65	Martin Bell	9.04.61	1	Cardiff	22 Jul 1995
41:14.3	Mark Easton	24.05.63	1	Brighton	5 Feb 1989
41:14.38	Barry		1	Edinburgh	29 May 1983
41:14.61	Steve Partington	17.09.65	2	Birmingham	16 Jul 1995
41:14.7	Barry		1	London (WL)	20 Mar 1982
41:16.00	McCombie		1	Cardiff	2 Jun 1990
41:16.13	Bell		3	Birmingham	16 Jul 1995
41:16.14	McCombie		1	London (CP)	2 Aug 1987
41:16.36	McCombie		5	Gateshead	29 Jun 1990
41:16.4	Maddocks		1	Corby	10 Jul 1988
41:18.64	Andrew Drake	6.02.65	2	Derby	5 Jun 1988
41:18.94	Vesty		3	Derby	25 May 1987
41:22.0+	McCombie		9k	Bergen (Fana), NOR	15 May 1992
41:24.69	McCombie		1	Birmingham	27 Jul 1991
41:24.7	Rush		1	Corby	6 Jul 1986
41:25.90	McCombie		1	Antrim	26 May 1985
41:33.0	McCombie		1	Birmingham	17 Mar 1984
	(30/10)				
41:49.06	Sean Martindale	8.11.66	3	Antrim	26 Jun 1990
41:55.5+	Phil Embleton	28.12.48	1	London (Nh)	14 Apr 1971
41:59.10	Andy Penn	31.03.67	2	Birmingham	27 Jul 1991
42:06.35	Gordon Vale	12.01.62	1	Brighton	2 Aug 1981
42:07.11	Tom Bosworth	17.01.90	3	Dublin (S), IRL	6 Aug 2011
42:08.57	Paul Blagg	23.01.60	2	Gateshead	28 Aug 1989
42:17.1	Dominic King	30.05.83	1	Colchester	4 May 2002
42:25.06	Jamie Higgins	7.01.94	7	Rieti, ITA	20 Jul 2013
42:28.0	Philip King	25.11.74	1	Leamington	17 May 1995

42:34.6	Paul Nihill	5.09.39	1	Leicester	28 May 1972	
	(20)					
42:35.6	Ken Matthews	21.06.34	1	London (WC)	1 Aug 1960	
42:40.0	Brian Adams	13.03.49	1	London (WL)	29 Mar 1975	
42:41.6	Mick Greasley	26.04.54	1	Birmingham	25 May 1980	
42:42.18	Steve Johnson	10.06.60	4	Derby	5 Jun 1988	
42:44.0	George Nibre	9.02.57	2	Hornchurch	2 Apr 1980	
42:45.0	Tim Berrett	23.01.65	2	Montreal, CAN	22 Jul 1989	
42:54.6	Roger Mills	11.02.48	2	Birmingham	25 May 1980	
42:57+ no judge	Steve Hollier	27.02.76	1	Plymouth	9 Jan 2000	
42:57.14	Roy Sheppard	17.08.59	1	Hornchurch	30 Mar 1983	
43:03.4	Les Morton	1.07.58	2	Enfield	2 May 1992	
	(30)					
43:05.11	Chris Cheeseman	11.12.58	1	London (He)	29 Aug 1993	
43:08.59	Daniel King	30.05.83	1	Coventry	30 Aug 2003	
43:09.82	Lloyd Finch	26.10.83	1	Leamington	18 May 2002	
43:10.4	Gareth Holloway	2.02.70	3	Enfield	2 May 1992	
43:12.85	Matthew Hales	6.10.79	1	Birmingham	12 Aug 2000	
43:15.0	Chris Smith	23.12.58	2	Leicester	20 May 1987	
43:19.4	Chris Harvey	14.10.56	3	Birmingham	25 May 1980	
43:25.2	Jamie O'Rawe	3.02.73	1	Hornchurch	27 Mar 1996	
43:26.21	Adrian James	23.09.46	1	London (CP)	14 Jun 1980	
43:30.2	Stuart Phillips	15.04.63	2	Hornchurch	1 Apr 1992	
	(40)					
43:31.0	Darren Thorn	17.07.62	1	Leicester	31 Mar 1990	
43:34.50	Richard Dorman	13.01.61	3	Cwmbran	28 May 1984	
43:34.55	Mike Holmes	26.08.51	2	London (CP)	14 Jun 1980	
43:36.0	Jimmy Ball	17.02.63	1	Swindon	1987	
43:37.9	Allan King	3.12.56	4	Birmingham	25 May 1980	
43:39.0	Martin Young	11.07.72	1	Rugby	18 May 1996	
43:40.37	Pat Chichester	20.07.66	7	Derby	5 Jun 1988	
43:42.4+e	Roland Hardy	3.12.27	1m	London (WC)	31 May 1952	
43:43.6	Stan Vickers	18.06.32	2	London (WC)	1 Aug 1960	
43:47.0	Ray Hankin	23.03.49	1	Cudworth	15 Mar 1986	
	(50)					
43:50.94	Nick Ball	29.04.88	1	Bedford	23 Jul 2006	
43:51.8	Geoff Toone	19.01.47	1	Leicester	29 Nov 1969	
43:52.0	Dave Staniforth	15.11.59	2	Cudworth	15 Mar 1986	
43:54.25	Gareth Brown	10.05.68	9	Birmingham	7 Aug 1987	
43:57.0	Ron Wallwork	26.05.41	2	Leicester	30 May 1971	
44:02.95	Graham White	28.03.59	8	Derby	5 Jun 1988	
44:07.0	George Coleman	21.11.16	1	London (WC)	10 Oct 1956	
44:07.4	John Warhurst	1.10.44	1	Warley	28 May 1973	
44:09.2	Graham Morris	19.01.58	2	Hornchurch	31 Mar 1979	
44:12.0	Olly Flynn	30.06.50	3k	Woodford	1 Jun 1975	
	(60)					
44:13.50	Dave Jarman	2.02.50	2	London (CP)	31 Aug 1981	
44:15.75	Richard Oldale	26.01.66	3	Birmingham	15 Jun 1996	
44:16.0	Bob Dobson	4.11.42	1	Hornchurch	26 Nov 1978	
44:17.0	Shaun Lightman	15.04.43	1	Enfield	14 Apr 1971	
44:17.0	Dennis Jackson	29.06.45	1	Cudworth	18 Apr 1981	
44:19.69	Dave Hucks	2.09.65	3	Antrim	26 May 1985	
44:22.38	Jon Vincent	24.09.70	1	Leicester	1 Apr 1989	
44:25.6	Ian Richards	12.04.48	9	London (WL)	20 Mar 1982	
44:26.0	Amos Seddon	22.01.41	1	London (PH)	20 Sep 1980	
44:26.2	Bob Hughes	27.10.47	3	Enfield	30 May 1971	
	(70)					

Short course: 40:54.7 Steve Barry 25.10.50 1 Kirkby 19 Mar 1983
Unconfirmed: 44:22.3 Don Bearman 16.04.66 2 Horsham 27 Jan 2001

The track at Kirkby for the AAA Champs 10k race in 1983 was short by 4cm per lap but Barry must have walked full distance due to his constant lapping of field of 55+ competitors on the outside or in the 2nd lane.

10 KILOMETRES ROAD

40:17	Chris Maddocks	28.03.57	1	Burrator	30 Apr 1989
40:19	Tom Bosworth	17.01.90	2	Coventry	1 Mar 2014
40:24	Mark Easton	24.05.63	1	Bexley	21 Mar 1987
40:35+	Steve Barry	25.10.50	1m	Southport	14 May 1983
40:35	Maddocks		1	Dawlish	18 Oct 1992

40:40	Steve Partington	17.09.65	1hc	Douglas IOM		12 Jan 1992
40:44	Easton		1	Ilford		25 Jul 1989
40:44	Bosworth		m	Podebrady, CZE		12 Apr 2014
40:45	Darrell Stone	2.02.68	1	Redditch		8 Apr 1989
40:47	Stone		1	Bexley		10 Feb 1996
40:49	Partington		1	Douglas IOM		6 Feb 1994
40:53	Easton		1	Bexley		9 Dec 1989
40:55	Stone		1	East Molesey		14 Jan 1996
40:56+	Bosworth		2	Coventry		3 Mar 2012
41:01	Ian McCombie	11.01.61	1	Bexley		8 Dec 1984
41:08+	Martin Rush	25.12.64	m	Douglas IOM		30 Aug 1984
41:24	Alex Wright	19.12.90	1	London (VP)		3 Feb 2013
41:25+	Andrew Drake (10)	6.02.65	m	Eisenhüttenstadt, GER	17 Jun 2000
41:28+	Andy Penn	31.03.67	4m	Lancaster		9 May 1992

Where better than track best

41:51	Luke Finch	21.09.85	1	Coventry	4 Apr 2009
41:57	Tim Berrett	23.01.65	8	Hildesheim, GER	10 Jun 1989
41:57	Ben Wears	4.07.90	1	Coventry	4 Apr 2009
41:58	Steve Johnson	10.06.60	1	Leek Wootton	4 Mar 1989
42:02	Philip King	25.11.74	2	East Molesey	12 Jan 1997
42:08	Daniel King	30.05.83	1	Birmingham	18 Sep 2007
42:09	Sean Martindale	8.11.66	8	Søfteland, NOR	30 Apr 1989
42:11	Chris Cheeseman	11.12.58	2	East Molesey	9 Jan 2000
42:17+	Paul Nihill	5.09.39	m	Douglas IOM	30 Jul 1972
42:18+	Steve Hollier	27.02.76	2	Douglas IOM	19 Feb 2000
42:27	Roy Sheppard	17.08.59	1	Bexley	18 Feb 1984
42:35+	Roger Mills	11.02.48	m	Eschborn, GER	29 Sep 1979

Recorded during a road running race

40:48	Ian McCombie	11.01.61	1	York	15 Jan 1989

Unconfirmed: 42:28.0 Kieron Butler 16.07.72 1 Melksham   22 Jun 1993

7 MILES TRACK

48:22.2+	Ken Matthews	21.06.34	1m	Walton	6 Jun 1964
48:23.0	Matthews		1	London (Hu)	28 Mar 1964
48:24.0	Matthews		1	London (WC)	20 May 1961
49:03.0+	Paul Nihill	5.09.39	1m	London (He)	27 Sep 1969
49:28.6	Roland Hardy	3.12.27	1	London (WC)	31 May 1952
49:50.0+	Ron Wallwork	26.05.41	1m	Sheffield	16 Jul 1966
50:09.0+	Stan Vickers	18.06.32	1m	London (PH)	27 Sep 1958
50:16.2	Peter Fullager	19.04.43	1	London (WC)	28 May 1966
50:17.0+	Bill Sutherland	6.04.45			27 Sep 1969
50:19.0	George Coleman	21.11.16	1	London (WC)	13 Jul 1956
50:21.0	Arthur Jones	5.10.38	2	London (BP)	17 Apr 1968
50:22.6	Lol Allen (10)	25.04.21	2	London (WC)	15 Jul 1950

20 KILOMETRES

1:22:03	Ian McCombie	11.01.61	13	Seoul, KOR	23 Sep 1988
1:22:12	Chris Maddocks	28.03.57	1	Burrator	3 May 1992
1:22:20	Tom Bosworth	17.01.90	10	Podebrady, CZE	12 Apr 2014
1:22:35	Maddocks		15	L'Hospitalet, ESP	27 May 1989
1:22:37	McCombie		1	Thamesmead	11 May 1985
1:22:51	Steve Barry	25.10.50	1	Douglas IOM	26 Feb 1983
1:22:53	Bosworth		43	Taicang, CHN	3 May 2014
1:22:58	McCombie		18	L'Hospitalet, ESP	27 May 1989
1:23:05	Alex Wright	19.12.90	16	Lugano, SUI	17 Mar 2013
1:23:15	Barry		1	Southport	14 May 1983
1:23:24	McCombie		5	Potsdam, GER	24 May 1986
1:23:26	McCombie		1	Douglas IOM	28 Feb 1987
1:23:26.5t	McCombie		8	Bergen (Fana), NOR	26 May 1990
1:23:31	McCombie		1	Hoddesdon	21 May 1988
1:23:33	McCombie		1	Douglas IOM	27 Feb 1988
1:23:34	Andy Penn	31.03.67	1=	Douglas IOM	29 Feb 1992
1:23:34	Martin Rush	25.12.64	1=	Douglas IOM	29 Feb 1992
1:23:38	Maddocks		1	Lancaster	9 May 1992
1:23:45	Maddocks		2	Békéscsaba, HUN	10 Apr 1988
1:23:46	Maddocks		24	Seoul, KOR	23 Sep 1988

Time	Name		Perf	#	Venue	Date	
1:23:50	Maddocks			2	Békéscsaba, HUN	5 Apr 1987	**Most 20k times:**
1:23:51	McCombie			9	Rome, ITA	30 Aug 1987	**Under 1:25:00**
1:23:52	McCombie			1	Douglas IOM	1 Mar 1986	17 McCombie
1:23:58	Darrell Stone		2.02.68	1	Douglas IOM	24 Feb 1996	8 Maddocks
1:24:04	Mark Easton		24.05.63	2	Douglas IOM	25 Feb 1989	4 Partington
1:24:04.0t	Andrew Drake	(10)	6.02.65	10	Bergen (Fana), NOR	26 May 1990	4 Bosworth
1:24:06	Rush			11	Örnskoldsvik, SWE	29 Jun 1991	3 Barry
1:24:07.6t	Phil Vesty		5.01.63	1	Leicester	1 Dec 1984	3 Drake
1:24:08.3t	McCombie			9	Bergen (Fana), NOR	15 May 1992	3 Stone
1:24:09	Steve Partington		17.09.65	1	Dublin, IRL	24 Sep 1994	
1:24:11	Maddocks			2	Douglas IOM	28 Feb 1987	**Under 1:28:00**
1:24:13	McCombie			23	New York, USA	3 May 1987	37 McCombie
1:24:14	McCombie			1	Dartford	25 Feb 1984	34 Maddocks
1:24:18	McCombie			3	Naumburg, GER	1 May 1989	29 Stone
1:24:18	Partington			1	Castletown IOM	12 Dec 1990	16 Partington
1:24:22t	Ian McCombie			1	London (SP)	7 Jul 1986	13 Easton
1:24:25	Tim Berrett		23.01.65	4	Montreal, CAN	21 Apr 1990	11 Drake
1:24:25	Easton			14	Örnskoldsvik, SWE	29 Jun 1991	11 Penn
1:24:28	Partington			15	Örnskoldsvik, SWE	29 Jun 1991	11 Barry
1:24:30	Stone			15	Moscow, RUS	1 Jun 1996	9 Bell
1:24:33	Maddocks			27	New York, USA	3 May 1987	9 Vesty
1:24:33	McCombie			4	Trnava, SVK	8 May 1988	9 Bosworth
1:24:35	McCombie			1	York	27 Jun 1987	8 Rush
1:24:37	Barry			1	London (BP)	7 Apr 1984	
1:24:37	Penn			2	Lancaster	9 May 1992	
1:24:43	Drake			1	East Molesey	2 Mar 2002	
1:24:44	Bosworth			13	Podebrady, CZE	13 Apr 2013	
1:24:49	Stone			29	Beijing, CHN	29 Apr 1995	
1:24:49	Bosworth			14	La Coruña, ESP	9 Jun 2012	
1:24:50	Paul Nihill		5.09.39	1	Douglas IOM	30 Jul 1972	
1:24:53	Drake			2	York	27 Jun 1987	
1:24:53	Partington			3	Douglas IOM	29 Feb 1992	
1:24:58	Vesty			1	Douglas IOM	25 Feb 1984	
1:25:00	Barry			2	Bielefeld, GER	18 Jul 1982	
1:25:03	McCombie			2	Edinburgh	31 Jul 1986	
1:25:04	McCombie			9	La Coruña, ESP	13 Apr 1991	
1:25:05	Stone			14	La Coruña, ESP	6 Jun 1992	
1:25:09	Berrett			1	Hull, CAN	16 Apr 1989	
1:25:10	Drake			11	La Coruña, ESP	13 Apr 1991	
1:25:10	Maddocks			4	Douglas IOM	29 Feb 1992	
1:25:10	Stone (61/14)			1	Dublin, IRL	11 Sep 1999	
1:25:42	Martin Bell		9.04.61	3	Lancaster	9 May 1992	
1:25:53.6t	Sean Martindale		8.11.66	4	Bergen (Fana), NOR	28 Apr 1989	
1:26:02	Jamie Higgins		7.01.94	21	Podebrady, CZE	12 Apr 2014	
1:26:14	Daniel King		30.05.83	3	Lugano, SUI	9 Mar 2008	
1:26:53	Chris Cheeseman		11.12.58	2	Leamington	21 Mar 1999	
1:27:00	Roger Mills (20)		11.02.48	1	London (VP)	30 Jun 1980	
1:27:04t no judge	Steve Hollier		27.02.76	1=	Plymouth	9 Jan 2000	
	1:28:34			1	Sutton Coldfield	19 Jun 1999	
1:27:05	Mike Parker		21.04.53	1	London (VP)	5 Apr 1986	
1:27:16	Les Morton		1.07.58	4	Douglas IOM	25 Feb 1989	
1:27:30	Ben Wears		4.07.90	1	Macclesfield	15 May 2010	
1:27:35	Olly Flynn		30.06.50	1	Blackpool	3 Oct 1976	
1:27:43	Luke Finch		21.09.85	6	Bedford	20 Jun 2010	
1:27:46	Brian Adams		13.03.49	6	Grand-Quévilly, FRA	11 Oct 1975	
1:27:52	Dominic King		30.05.83	5	Dublin, IRL	27 Jun 2004	
1:27:59	Phil Embleton		28.12.48	1	London (BP)	3 Apr 1971	
1:28:02	Paul Blagg (30)		23.01.60	1	Dartford	27 Feb 1982	
1:28:15	Ken Matthews		21.06.34	1	London (VP)	23 Jul 1960	
1:28:26	Chris Harvey		14.10.56	29	Eschborn, GER	29 Sep 1979	
1:28:30	Allan King		3.12.56	4	Thamesmead	11 May 1985	
1:28:34	Chris Smith		23.12.58	5	Thamesmead	11 May 1985	

Time	Name	Date1	Pos	Location	Date2
1:28:37	Dave Jarman	2.02.50	4	London (VP)	30 Jun 1980
1:28:40	Matthew Hales	6.10.79	8	Leamington	21 Apr 2001
1:28:46	Jimmy Ball	17.02.63	1	London (TB)	4 Apr 1987
1:28:46	Steve Taylor	19.03.66	1	Castletown IOM	20 Dec 1992
1:28:46	Jamie O'Rawe	3.02.73	5	Leamington	21 Mar 1999
1:28:50	Amos Seddon (40)	22.01.41	1	London (VP)	3 Aug 1974
1:29:07	Philip King	25.11.74	4	Yverdon, SUI	20 Aug 1995
1:29:19	Stuart Phillips	15.04.63	1	Colchester	31 May 1992
1:29:24	George Nibre	9.02.57	1	Zürich, SUI	6 Apr 1980
1:29:27	Graham White	28.03.59	92	Podebrady, CZE	19 Apr 1997
1:29:29+	Steve Johnson	10.06.60	m	Douglas IOM	16 Apr 1989
1:29:37	John Warhurst	1.10.44	1	London (VP)	28 Jul 1973
1:29:42	Dennis Jackson	29.06.45	2	York	10 May 1986
1:29:48	Martin Young	11.07.72	8	Sligo, IRL	31 Mar 1996
1:29:49	Peter Marlow	20.04.41	4	London (VP)	3 Aug 1974
1:29:53	Don Bearman (50)	16.04.66	1	Basildon	11 May 2002
1:30:00	John Webb	21.12.36	6	Spremberg, GER	18 May 1968
1:30:02	Bob Dobson	4.11.42	5	London (VP)	3 Aug 1974
1:30:15	Gareth Brown	10.05.68	4	Leicester	13 May 1989
1:30:16	Roy Thorpe	18.05.34	3	London (VP)	28 Jul 1973
1:30:22	Roy Sheppard	17.08.59	2	Chelmsford	26 Apr 1980
1:30:27.38t	Steve Gower	7.10.50	3	London (CP)	10 Jun 1978
1:30:30	Graham Morris	19.01.58	1	Steyning	23 Feb 1980
1:30:35	Peter Fullager	19.04.43	2	London (BP)	4 Apr 1970
1:30:51	Mick Greasley	26.04.54	1	London Wall	4 May 1980
1:30:52	Mike Smith (60)	20.04.63	5	York	27 Jun 1987
1:30:52	Thomas Taylor	30.01.81	11	Bedford	20 Jun 2010
1:30:53	Gordon Vale	12.01.62	5	Hoddesdon	21 May 1988
1:31:01	Ron Wallwork	26.05.41	3	London (BP)	4 Apr 1970
1:31:10	Bill Sutherland	6.04.45	1	London (BP)	30 Aug 1969
1:31:10	Shaun Lightman	15.04.43	2	Enfield	30 Aug 1969
1:31:21	Dave Staniforth	15.11.59	5	York	10 May 1986
1:31:32	Richard Dorman	13.01.61	4	Redditch	12 May 1984
1:31:39	Darren Thorn	17.07.62	3	Birmingham	26 Aug 1989
1:31:40	Adrian James	23.09.46	3	Southport	10 May 1980
1:31:43	Stan Vickers (70)	18.06.32	2	London (VP)	23 Jul 1960
1:31:46	Mike Holmes	26.08.51	1	Douglas IOM	1 Mar 1980
1:31:53	Bryan Eley	28.01.39	4	Enfield	30 Aug 1969
1:31:56	Andrew Trigg	23.06.62	10	Thamesmead	11 May 1985
1:31:59	Gareth Holloway	2.02.70	24	La Coruña, ESP	6 Jun 1992
1:32:08+	Murray Lambden	14.10.56	1m	Douglas IOM	28 Feb 1981
1:32:15	Carl Lawton	20.01.48	5	Southend	15 May 1976
1:32:16	Ken Carter	7.03.47	3	Chelmsford	26 Apr 1980
1:32:18	Barry Graham	16.08.46	11	Thamesmead	11 May 1985
1:32:20	Dave Hucks	2.09.65	12	Thamesmead	11 May 1985
1:32:30	Bob Clark (80)	15.05.35	1	Zürich, SUI	23 Apr 1961
1:32:46	John Edgington	5.04.36	8	Tokyo, JPN	15 Oct 1964
1:32:48	Stuart Elms	30.04.46	7	Manchester (Str)	14 May 1977
1:33:00	Ian Brooks	21.04.45	5	Barcelona, ESP	25 Apr 1976
1:33:00	Ian Richards	12.04.48	3	London (VP)	12 Aug 1978
1:33:01	Rob Elliott	31.03.59	1	Guernsey	10 Jun 1982
1:33:03	Kevin Walmsley	6.09.67	8	Douglas IOM	22 Feb 1997
1:33:07	Alan Smallwood	11.01.42	1	Enfield	26 Aug 1972
1:33:08	Bob Hughes	27.10.47	1	Cwmbran	27 Jul 1968
1:33:10	Denis Holly	1.01.51	7	London (VP)	30 Jun 1980
1:33:11	Mike Dunion (90)	24.06.58	4	Chelmsford	26 Apr 1980
1:33:11	Kieron Butler	16.07.72	3	Burrator	3 May 1992
1:33:16	Edwin Ashforth	11.08.44	2	Sheffield	2 Apr 1983
1:33:17	Richard Oldale	26.01.66	4	Cardiff	21 Apr 1996
1:33:18	Tony Taylor	3.06.47	7	London (VP)	3 Aug 1974

Time	Name	Date	Extra	Place	Event Date
1:33:26	Scott Davis	3.04.75	27	Lugano, SUI	14 Mar 2010
1:33:28	Stuart Maidment	20.07.47	8	London (VP)	3 Aug 1974
1:33:29	John Paddick	31.08.43	10	Tokyo, JPN	15 Oct 1964
1:33:29+	Simon Moore	7.05.66	m	Leicester	5 May 1986
1:33:32	Dave Cotton	16.09.56	11	Manchester (Str)	14 May 1977
1:33:34	John Atterton (100)	12.05.48	17	Thamesmead	11 May 1985
1:33:37	Eric Hall	15.09.32	3	Ruislip	11 Apr 1959
1:33:41	Karl Atton	14.09.71	9	Leamington	21 Mar 1999
1:33:43	Roy Hart	23.01.36	2	Ruislip	4 Apr 1964
1:33:43	Eric Taylor	9.06.39	8	London (VP)	12 May 1973
1:33:45	Michael Kemp	23.12.79	10	Dublin, IRL	27 Sep 1997
1:33:47	Peter Kaneen	12.07.61	1	Dublin, IRL	17 Dec 2005
1:33:50	Bill Wright	20.09.48	2	Steyning	10 Apr 1976
1:33:51	Pat Chichester	20.07.66	4	Randers, DEN	8 Jun 1988
1:33:56	Peter Selby	16.03.43	1	London (BP)	5 Apr 1975
1:33:56	Don Cox	31.12.46	5	London Wall	22 Jul 1979
1:33:58	Mark O'Kane	7.03.91	39	Lugano, SUI	20 Mar 2011
1:34:00.6t	George Coleman	21.11.16	1	Alperton	29 Sep 1956
1:34:02	George Williams		3	Lugano, SUI	15 Oct 1961
1:34:05	Mark Wordsworth	18.11.59	2	Bexley	23 Feb 1980
1:34:05	Andy O'Rawe	8.09.63	4	Dublin, IRL	28 Sep 1996
1:34:06	Ray Middleton	9.08.36	6	Coventry	11 May 1968
1:34:07	Alan Buchanan	4.01.41	2	London (BP)	5 Apr 1975
1:34:11	Lou Mockett	2.03.39	10	London (VP)	3 Aug 1974
1:34:11	Peter Fawkes	24.08.49	1	Morecambe	9 Sep 1978
1:34:14	Allan Callow	4.09.45	8	London (VP)	28 Jul 1973
1:34:17	Phil Thorn	19.11.38	12	Spremberg, GER	18 May 1968
1:34:22	Nick Ball	29.04.88	1	East Molesey	25 Mar 2006
1:34:23.4t	George Chaplin	28.02.31	5	Brighton	1 Jul 1972
1:34:26	Olly Caviglioli ITA?	21.12.52	5	Enfield	28 Aug 1971
1:34:29	Ken Harding	23.06.29	1	Sutton Coldfield	7 Mar 1970
1:34:34	Bob Coates	8.01.41	9	London (BP)	4 Apr 1970
1:34:35	Arthur Thomson	22.04.36	2	London (RP)	8 Apr 1961
1:34:35	Ed Shillabeer	2.08.39	2	Dawlish	30 Dec 1983
1:34:37+	Graham Young	30.05.45	12m	Brisbane, AUS	7 Oct 1982
1:34:38	Noel Carmody	24.12.56	5	Leicester	12 May 1990
1:34:40	Mal Tolley	15.04.44	3	London (VP)	16 Jul 1966
1:34:40	Andrew Goudie	4.10.78	14	Leamington	21 Apr 2001
1:34:41	Roland Hardy	3.12.27	8	Melbourne, AUS	28 Nov 1956
1:34:42	Kevin Baker	12.12.57	1	London (BP)	6 Apr 1985
1:34:42	Stuart Kollmorgen	20.04.69	1	Hobart, AUS	19 Feb 2011
1:34:43	Peter Ryan	9.04.54	10	Southport	14 May 1983
1:34:44	Kirk Taylor	30.05.68	1	Cardiff	8 Jul 1989
1:34:45	Don Thompson	20.01.33	3	London (RP)	8 Apr 1961
1:34:49	Vaughan Thomas		2	London (RP)	6 Apr 1963
1:34:51	Arthur Jones (140)	5.10.38	4	Cwmbran	27 Jul 1968

Probable short courses

Time	Name	Date	Extra	Place	Event Date
1:23:27	Darrell Stone	2.02.68	11	Livorno, ITA	10 Jul 1993
1:25:36	Roger Mills	11.02.48	1	Clacton	10 Jun 1978
1:26:06	Ken Matthews	21.06.34	2	Moscow, RUS	6 Sep 1959
1:26:31	Les Morton	1.07.58	15	Livorno, ITA	10 Jul 1993
1:28:26	Peter Fullager	19.04.43	1	Zürich, SUI	13 Apr 1968
1:28:44	Stan Vickers	18.06.32	4	Moscow, RUS	6 Sep 1959
1:28:57	Ron Wallwork	26.05.41	1	Enfield	19 Sep 1970
1:30:11	Eric Taylor	9.06.39	1	Westbury	28 Mar 1970
1:31:02	Shaun Lightman	15.04.43	3	Enfield	19 Sep 1970
1:31:58	Tony Taylor	3.06.47	5	Morecambe	13 Sep 1969
1:32:57	Ray Middleton	9.08.36	5	Enfield	19 Sep 1970
1:33:00	Bob Coates	8.01.41	3	London (VP)	25 Jul 1970
1:33:12	Geoff Hunwicks	17.08.50	4	Clacton	10 Jun 1978
1:33:31	Harold Whitlock	16.12.03		Stockholm, SWE	1937
1:33:33	Alec Banyard	27.02.42	2	Morecambe	14 Sep 1968
1:33:47	Brian Armstrong	1.04.48	6	Clacton	10 Jun 1978
1:33:59	Dave Smyth	29.11.35	2	Westbury	28 Mar 1970
1:34:09	Mike Harcombe		3	Westbury	28 Mar 1970

1:34:23	Phil Etches	19.04.48	7	Morecambe	13 Sep 1969

30 KILOMETRES

2:07:56	Ian McCombie	11.01.61	1	Edinburgh	27 Apr 1986
2:09:20	McCombie		3	Auckland, NZL	2 Feb 1990
2:10:16	Steve Barry	25.10.50	1	Brisbane, AUS	7 Oct 1983
2:10:36	McCombie		3	Edinburgh	31 Jul 1986
2:11:09	Chris Maddocks	28.03.57	1	Douglas IOM	23 Feb 1985
2:11:30	Darrell Stone	2.02.68	4	Victoria, CAN	25 Aug 1994
2:11:38	Maddocks		1	Leeds	3 Sep 1989
2:11:43	McCombie		2	Leeds	3 Sep 1989
2:11:53	Maddocks		2	Edinburgh	27 Apr 1986
2:12:42	Maddocks		4	Edinburgh	31 Jul 1986
2:12:57	Tim Berrett	23.01.65	9	Sesto San Giovanni, ITA	1 May 1990
2:13:29	Martin Rush	25.12.64	3	Edinburgh	27 Apr 1986
2:13:33	Mark Easton	24.05.63	3	Leeds	3 Sep 1989
2:13:54+	Maddocks		m	Laval, FRA	25 Jun 1989
2:13:58	McCombie		2	Douglas IOM	23 Feb 1985
2:14:15	Steve Partington	17.09.65	7	Victoria, CAN	25 Aug 1994
2:14:16	Easton		1	Douglas IOM	26 Feb 1994
	(17/8)				
2:14:41	Les Morton	1.07.58	1	Cardiff	28 Apr 1991
2:15:01+	Andrew Drake (10)	6.02.65	1m	Sutton Coldfield	22 Apr 1989
2:15:44	Paul Blagg	23.01.60	4	Edinburgh	27 Apr 1986
2:16:49	Sean Martindale	8.11.66	4	Leeds	3 Sep 1989
2:17:36	Steve Johnson	10.06.60	1	Douglas IOM	16 Apr 1989
2:18:23+	Dennis Jackson	29.06.45	2m	Leicester	15 Jun 1985
2:18:35	Andy Penn	31.03.67	1	Cardiff	16 May 1993
2:19:12	Phil Vesty	5.01.63	9	Sesto San Giovanni, ITA	1 May 1985
2:19:42	Murray Lambden	14.10.56	1	Douglas IOM	28 Feb 1981
2:20:13	Barry Graham	16.08.46	6	Edinburgh	27 Apr 1986
2:21:09	Allan King	3.12.56	1	Leicester	17 Apr 1999
2:21:10	Brian Dowrick	20.01.63	1	Cardiff	29 Mar 1992
	(20)				
2:21:14	Darren Thorn	17.07.62	7	Edinburgh	27 Apr 1986
2:21:34	Steve Taylor	19.03.66	14	Victoria, CAN	25 Aug 1994
2:21:54	Olly Flynn	30.06.50	1	Sheffield	17 Jun 1978
2:21:54	Roger Mills	11.02.48	7	Brisbane, AUS	7 Oct 1982
2:22:21	Martin Bell	9.04.61	2	Cardiff	8 May 1994
2:22:26	Brian Adams	13.03.49	2	Sheffield	17 Jun 1978
2:22:26	Simon Moore	7.05.66	1	Leicester	5 May 1986
2:22:30+	Daniel King	30.05.83	9m	Dudince, SVK	29 Mar 2008
2:23:04	George Nibre	9.02.57	1	London Wall	10 Feb 1980
2:23:06	Stuart Phillips	15.04.63	3	Cardiff	29 Mar 1992
	(30)				
2:23:38	Amos Seddon	22.01.41	2	London Wall	10 Feb 1980
2:23:52	Graham White	28.03.59	4	Cardiff	8 May 1994
2:23:54+	Paul Nihill	5.09.39	m	Munich, GER	3 Sep 1972
2:24:13+	Mick Greasley	26.04.54	1m	York	20 Jun 1981
2:24:14+	Mike Smith	20.04.63	1m	Leicester	27 Mar 1989
2:24:18.2t	Roy Thorpe	18.05.34	1	Hamburg, GER	25 May 1974
2:24:19+	Bob Dobson	4.11.42	2m	York	20 Jun 1981
2:24:20+	Adrian James	23.09.46	m	Eschborn, GER	30 Sep 1979
2:24:22.8t	John Warhurst	1.10.44	m	Hamburg, GER	25 May 1974
2:24:28	Rob Elliott	31.03.59	10	Brisbane, AUS	7 Oct 1982
2:24:32.8t	Peter Fullager (41)	19.04.43	m	Lugano, SUI	8 Oct 1967

Irregular conditions
2:11:54	Chris Maddocks	28.3.57	1	Plymouth	31 Dec 1989
Ex-UK:	2:13:57 Alex Wright	19.12.90	1	Dublin	22 Dec 2013

35 KILOMETRES

2:36:19	Chris Maddocks	28.03.57	5	Örnsköldsvik, SWE	29 Jun 1991
2:37:20	Maddocks		6	Laval, FRA	25 Jun 1989
2:37:27	Les Morton	1.07.58	7	Örnsköldsvik, SWE	29 Jun 1991
2:38:01	Andrew Drake	6.02.65	1	Sutton Coldfield	22 Apr 1989
2:38:11	Martin Rush	25.12.64	6	La Coruña, ESP	6 Jun 1992

2:38:46	Maddocks		7	La Coruña, ESP	6 Jun 1992	
2:40:04	Amos Seddon	22.01.41	1	London (VP)	21 Jun 1980	
2:40:37	Mike Smith	20.04.63	2	Sutton Coldfield	22 Apr 1989	
2:40:38	Morton		14	Grassau, GER	17 Jun 1990	
2:40:49	Darrell Stone	2.02.68	11	Fougères, FRA	11 Jun 1995	
	(10/7)					
2:41:03	Dennis Jackson	29.06.45	1	Leicester	15 Jun 1985	
2:42:13	Mark Easton	24.05.63	25	Eschborn, GER	12 Jun 1993	
2:43:17	Paul Blagg	23.01.60	3	Sønder Omme, DEN	6 Jul 1991	
	(10)					
2:45:20	Allan King	3.12.56	15	Békéscsaba, HUN	28 Mar 1993	
2:47:21	Barry Graham	16.08.46	1	York	20 Apr 1981	
2:48:10	George Nibre	9.02.57	5	London (VP)	21 Jun 1980	
2:48:30	Bob Dobson	4.11.42	1	York	20 Jun 1981	
2:48:41	Dave Jarman	2.02.50	1	Kenilworth	19 Jun 1982	
2:48:50	Graham White	28.03.59	30	Livorno, ITA	12 Jun 1994	
2:49:08	Darren Thorn	17.07.62	3	Plymouth	22 Jun 1986	
2:49:28	Mick Greasley	26.04.54	2	York	20 Jun 1981	
2:49:37	Murray Lambden	14.10.56	3	Valencia, ESP	9 May 1982	
2:49:53+e	Paul Nihill	5.09.39	m	Munich	3 Sep 1972	
	(20)					
2:50:43+e	Ian Richards	12.04.48	m	London Wall	4 May 1980	
2:50:55	John Warhurst	1.10.44	4	Hillingdon	25 Sep 1971	
2:51:03	Roy Thorpe	18.05.34	1	Salzgitter. GER	6 Jun 1976	
2:51:20	Chris Cheeseman	11.12.58	1	Dartford	6 May 2000	
2:51:51	Carl Lawton	20.01.48	5	Kenilworth	19 Jun 1982	
2:51:59+	Daniel King	30.05.83	3m	Stockholm	10 Oct 2007	
2:52:08	Roger Mills	11.02.48	1	Leicester	16 Jun 1979	
2:52:15	Stuart Phillips	15.04.63	20	Békéscsaba, HUN	28 Mar 1993	
2:52:17	Ian Harvey	23.10.64	3	Sutton Coldfield	22 Apr 1989	
2:52:30	Dave Cotton	16.09.56	1	Sutton Coldfield	1 Jul 1978	
2:52:47	Steve Hollier (31)	27.02.76	9	Catania, ITA	30 May 1999	

50 KILOMETRES

3:51:37	Chris Maddocks	28.03.57	1	Burrator	28 Oct 1990	**Most 50k times:**
3:53:14	Maddocks	(2)	1	Constanta, ROM	25 Nov 1995	**Under 4:10:00**
3:57:10	Maddocks	(3)	1	Sint-Oedenrode, NED	12 Mar 2000	22 Morton
3:57:48	Les Morton	1.07.58	1	Burrator	30 Apr 1989	11 Maddocks
3:58:25	Morton	(2)	5	Puerto Pollensa, ESP	20 Mar 1988	7 Easton
3:58:36	Morton	(3)	1	Leicester	11 Oct 1992	6 Blagg
3:59:30	Morton	(4)	27	Seoul, KOR	30 Sep 1988	4 Jackson
3:59:55	Paul Blagg	23.01.60	19	Rome, ITA	5 Sep 1987	3 Dobson
4:00:02	Maddocks	(4)	2	Leicester	11 Oct 1992	3 James
4:00:07	Blagg	(2)	28	Seoul, KOR	30 Sep 1988	
4:00:47	Morton	(5)	5	Madrid, ESP	16 Mar 1986	**Under 4:20:00**
4:01:36	Morton	(6)	1	Stockport	1 Jul 1995	33 Morton
4:02:00	Maddocks	(5)	6	Vilanova, ESP	18 Mar 1984	17 Maddocks
4:02:07	Morton	(7)	1	Redditch	8 Apr 1990	14 Dobson
4:02:11	Morton	(8)	20	San Jose, USA	2 Jun 1991	13 Blagg
4:02:38	Maddocks	(6)	9	Bergen, NOR	25 Sep 1983	12 Jackson
4:02:39	Morton	(9)	1	Basildon	6 Apr 1991	10 James
4:02:47	Maddocks	(7)	2	Barendrecht, NED	8 Oct 1995	9 Easton
4:03:08	Dennis Jackson	29.06.45	8	Madrid, ESP	16 Mar 1986	9 Cheeseman
4:03:30	Morton	(10)	25	L'Hospitalet, ESP	28 May 1989	9 Richards
						8 Hollier
4:03:53	Mark Easton	24.05.63	28	Dudince, SVK	25 Apr 1998	7 Graham
4:03:55	Morton	(11)	1	Horsham	16 Oct 1993	7 Dom. King
4:04:09	Blagg	(3)	25	San Jose, USA	2 Jun 1991	6 Middleton
4:04:15	Morton	(12)	1	York	27 Jun 1987	5 Nihill
4:04:35	Morton	(13)	1	Leicester	27 May 1989	
4:04:44	Jackson	(2)	12	Potsdam, GER	25 May 1986	
4:04:49	Daniel King	30.05.83	11	Dudince, SVK	29 Mar 2008	
4:05:14	Maddocks	(8)	1	Paris, FRA	13 Sep 1980	
4:05:17	Easton	(2)	1	Stockport	27 Jun 1998	
4:05:28	Morton	(14)	11	Split, CRO	31 Aug 1990	
4:05:36	Dan King		1	Tilburg, NED	6 Oct 2013	

4:05:42	Maddocks		42	Podebrady, CZE	20 Apr 1997
4:05:44.6t	Blagg		3	Bergen (Fana), NOR	26 May 1990
4:05:47.3t	Maddocks		1	Birmingham	22 Sep 1984
4:05:53	Morton		13	Potsdam, GER	25 May 1986
4:06:01	Easton		42	Beijing, CHN	30 Apr 1995
4:06:14	Barry Graham	16.08.46	1	Basildon	20 Apr 1985
4:06:22	Blagg		27	New York, USA	2 May 1987
4:06:34	Dominic King	30.05.83	19	Dudince, SVK	24 Mar 2012
4:06:36	Blagg		14	Potsdam, GER	25 May 1986
4:06:43	Maddocks		1	Gdynia, POL	20 Apr 1980
4:06:46.6t	Morton		2	Bergen (Fana), NOR	25 May 1995
4:06:56	Morton		23	Stuttgart, GER	21 Aug 1993
4:07:18	Steve Hollier	27.02.76	28	Eisenhüttenstadt, GER	18 Jun 2000
4:07:23	Bob Dobson (10)	4.11.42	1	Lassing, AUT	21 Oct 1979
4:07:33	Easton		2	Sint-Oedenrode, NED	12 Mar 2000
4:07:45	Easton		1	Stockport	30 Aug 1997
4:07:49	Chris Cheeseman	11.12.58	57	Mézidon-Canon, FRA	2 May 1999
4:07:57	Ian Richards	12.04.48	3	Gdynia, POL	20 Apr 1980
4:07:58	Dennis Jackson (50/12)		16	Bergen, NOR	25 Sep 1983
4:08:41	Adrian James	23.09.46	1	Basildon	12 Apr 1980
4:09:22	Mike Smith	20.04.63	2	Leicester	27 Mar 1989
4:10:23	Darrell Stone	2.02.68	1	Burrator	6 May 1990
4:10:42	Amos Seddon	22.01.41	6	Llobregat, ESP	9 Mar 1980
4:11:32	Paul Nihill	5.09.39	2	Tokyo, JPN	18 Oct 1964
4:12:00	Sean Martindale	8.11.66	2	Horsham	16 Oct 1993
4:12:02	Martin Rush	25.12.64	4	Borås, SWE	28 Jul 1991
4:12:19	Don Thompson (20)	20.01.33	1	Baddesley	20 Jun 1959
4:12:37	John Warhurst	1.10.44	5	Bremen, GER	27 May 1972
4:12:50	Darren Thorn	17.07.62	2	Burrator	6 May 1990
4:13:18	Graham White	28.03.59	3	Stockport	27 Jun 1998
4:13:25	Allan King	3.12.56	2	York	16 Apr 1983
4:14:03	Tom Misson	11.05.30	2	Baddesley	20 Jun 1959
4:14:25	Dave Cotton	16.09.56	1	Manchester (Str)	15 Jul 1978
4:15:14	Shaun Lightman	15.04.43	12	Lugano, SUI	13 Oct 1973
4:15:22	Brian Adams	13.03.49	3	Sheffield	17 Sep 1978
4:15:52	Ray Middleton	9.08.36	6	Bremen, GER	27 May 1972
4:16:30	Karl Atton (30)	14.09.71	67	Podebrady, CZE	20 Apr 1997
4:16:45	Gareth Brown	10.05.68	4	Manchester (Wy)	21 Apr 2002
4:16:47	George Nibre	9.02.57	9	Llobregat, ESP	9 Mar 1980
4:17:24	Andrew Drake	6.02.65	1	Leamington	18 Oct 1987
4:17:34	Gordon Vale	12.01.62	3	Budapest, HUN	9 Oct 1983
4:17:40	Steve Partington	17.09.65	3	Dublin, IRL	26 Jun 2005
4:17:52	Stuart Elms	30.04.46	1	Basildon	17 Apr 1976
4:18:30	Peter Ryan	9.04.54	1	Basildon	10 Apr 1982
4:19:00	Carl Lawton	20.01.48	3	Redditch	17 Jul 1971
4:19:13	Bryan Eley	28.01.39	1	Redditch	19 Jul 1969
4:19:26	Roger Mills (40)	11.02.48	3	Basildon	9 Apr 1983
4:19:55	Mike Holmes	26.08.51	3	Redditch	4 Aug 1973
4:19:57	Barry Ingarfield	13.08.38	4	Lassing, AUT	21 Oct 1979
4:20:05	George Chaplin	28.02.31	7	Bremen, GER	27 May 1972
4:20:22	Scott Davis	3.04.75	2	Yverdon, SUI	13 Sep 2009
4:20:43	Tim Watt	19.09.66	6	Rotterdam, NED	8 Oct 1995
4:20:48	Andrew Trigg	23.06.62	1	Burrator	1 May 1988
4:20:51	Murray Lambden	14.10.56	11	Bielefeld, GER	18 Jul 1982
4:21:02	Ron Wallwork	26.05.41	4	Redditch	17 Jul 1971
4:22:05	Mel McCann	9.01.48	1	Sheffield	14 Sep 1986
4:22:41.0t	Charley Fogg (50)	14.03.34	6	Woodford	1 Jun 1975
4:23:12	Peter Hodkinson	5.11.44	5	Coventry	21 Jul 1979
4:23:22	Chris Berwick	1.05.46	2	Enfield	12 Jul 1986
4:23:32	John Lees	23.02.45	4	Tarragona, ESP	19 Mar 1978
4:23:43	Roy Thorpe	18.05.34	1	Birmingham	17 Jul 1976

Time	Name	Date	Pos	Venue	Event Date	
4:23:50	Paul Jarman	10.12.48	5	Sleaford	18 Jul 1981	**100 KILOMETRES**
4:24:02	Howard Timms	9.07.44	2	Badminton	15 Jul 1972	9:34:25 Tony Geal
4:24:13	John Paddick	31.08.43	1	London Wall	9 Mar 1980	Grand-Quévilly
4:24:40	Stuart Phillips	15.04.63	5	Leicester	11 Oct 1992	2 Jun 1979
4:24:54+	Andy Penn	31.03.67	9m	Scanzorosciate, ITA	19 Oct 2003	9:36:23 Graham
4:25:18	Tony Geal (60)	28.07.52	5	London Wall	4 May 1980	Young & 9:38:38 Murray Lambden
4:25:31	Graham Young	30.05.45	7	Sleaford	18 Jul 1981	both at Stoke Man-
4:25:45+	John Eddershaw	21.07.33	1m	Dawlish	3 May 1981	deville 26 Sep 1981
4:26:10	Brian Dowrick	20.01.63	1	Burrator	2 May 1993	**100 MILES**
4:26:29	Reg Gardner	19.04.50	5	Luxembourg, LUX	12 May 1985	16:50:28
4:26:32	Dave Rowland	25.09.55	4	Dunkirk, FRA	24 May 1987	Richard Brown at
4:27:21	Alec Banyard	27.02.42	4	London (He)	20 Jul 1974	Sint-Oedenrode,
4:27:48	Peter Selby	16.03.43	4	Birmingham	17 Jul 1976	NED 23 May 1993
4:28:06	Ed Shillabeer	2.08.39	12	Békéscsaba, HUN	20 Apr 1986	16:55:44
4:28:08	John Moullin	8.09.41	2	Dunkirk, FRA	20 May 1973	John Moullin at
4:28:44	Ken Mason (70)	7.03.37	6	Baddesley	15 Jun 1963	Ewhurst 27 Jun 1971 **24 HOURS**
4:28:54	Ken Smith	3.12.35	2	Basildon	9 Apr 1977	219.570
4:28:57	Ian Brooks	21.04.45	7	Redditch	17 Jul 1971	Derek Harrison at
4:29:15	Peter Fullager	19.04.43	2	Warribee, AUS	26 Sep 1970	Rouen 21 May 1978
4:29:31	Ray Hankin	23.03.49	1	Bradford	26 May 1986	
4:29:40	Mick Greasley	26.04.54	11	Manchester (Str)	15 Jul 1978	
4:30:00+	Albert Johnson	1.05.31	m	Brighton	13 Aug 1960	
4:30:26	Peter Kaneen	12.07.61	5	Copenhagen, DEN	8 Oct 2005	
4:30:34	Ken Harding	23.06.29	7	Redditch	4 Aug 1973	
4:30:38	Harold Whitlock	16.12.03	1	Derby	4 Jul 1936	
4:30:57	Guy Goodair (80)	28.09.36	6	Enfield	20 Jun 1964	
4:31:02	Joe Hopkins	19.02.02	2	Derby	4 Jul 1936	
4:31:09+	Clive Thomas	.60	2m	Dawlish	4 May 1985	
4:31:41	Eric Hall	15.09.32	2	Enfield	16 Jun 1956	
4:31:52	Chris Smith	23.12.58	1	Basildon	11 Apr 1987	
4:31:54	Ian Harvey	23.10.64	3	Redditch	8 Apr 1990	
4:32:08	Geoff Hunwicks	17.08.50	4	Basildon	17 Apr 1976	
4:32:21	Rex Whitlock	8.09.10	4	Helsinki, FIN	21 Jul 1952	
4:32:42	Don Bearman	16.04.66	3	London (VP)	9 Sep 2000	
4:33:00	Denis Holly	1.01.51	10	Coventry	21 Jul 1979	
4:33:01	Jonathan Cocker (90)	26.09.71	4	Stockport	1 Jul 1995	
4:33:01+	Kevin Walmsley	6.09.67	1m	Isle of Man	28 Apr 1996	
4:33:05	Dave Staniforth	15.11.59	4	Redditch	8 Apr 1990	
4:33:12	Roy Posner	13.03.50	4	Dunkirk, FRA	20 May 1973	
4:33:25	Phil Thorn	19.11.38	5	Ewell	20 Jul 1968	
4:33:32	Fred Bentley	18.08.09	3	Derby	4 Jul 1936	
4:33:38	Roger Lancefield	24.09.42	11	Coventry	21 Jul 1979	
4:33:42	Colin Bradley	2.02.56	7	Dunkirk, FRA	24 May 1987	
4:33:49	Denis Vale	4.02.27	7	Baddesley	15 Jun 1963	
4:33:51	Allan Worth	12.09.58	4	Leicester	27 Mar 1989	
4:34:02	Russell Rawlings (100)	12.03.61	1	Bradford	27 May 1985	
4:34:05	Peter Markham	11.07.35	4	Basildon	9 Apr 1977	
4:34:07	Ray Hall	25.06.33	8	Baddesley	15 Jun 1963	
4:34:16	Steve Johnson	10.06.60	3	Horsham	16 Oct 1993	
4:35:19	John Nye	14.09.43	6	London (He)	20 Jul 1974	
4:35:20	Colin Young	20.01.35	9	Baddesley	15 Jun 1963	
4:35:36	Tommy Green	30.03.94	1	London (Cr)	12 Jul 1930	
4:35:45	Gordon Brown		8	Enfield	20 Jun 1964	
4:36:02	Lloyd Johnson	7.04.00	2	Bournville	19 Jun 1948	
4:36:02	Dave Berry	18.02.49	10	Redditch	4 Aug 1973	
4:36:09	Nigel Thompson		6	Podebrady, CZE	13 Aug 1961	
4:36:17	John Llewellyn (111)	26.06.45	5	Basildon	20 Apr 1985	

Short courses

4:09:15	Don Thompson	20.01.33	4	Pescara, ITA	10 Oct 1965	
4:26:40	Albert Johnson	1.05.31	1	Bradford	26 May 1958	
4:27:00+e	David Watts	11.02.45	2m	Southend	19 May 1965	

WOMEN – 3000 METRES 1500m TRACK

Time	Name	Date	Pos	Venue	Event Date	1500m TRACK
12:22.62+	Jo Jackson/Atkinson	17.01.85	1m	Sydney, AUS	14 Feb 2009	6:35.20 Cattermole
12:40.98	Jackson		1	Bedford	26 May 2008	1 Perth 18 Dec 00
12:44.63+	Jackson		1	Birmingham	12 Jul 2009	6:48.5 Menendez 1
12:49.16	Betty Sworowski	12.03.61	1	Wrexham	28 Jul 1990	Tullamore 15 Aug 04
12:50.61	Lisa Kehler	15.03.67	1	Solihull	29 Jul 2000	**1 MILE TRACK**
12:56.03+	Jackson		1	Birmingham	13 Jul 2008	6:56.2 Jo Jackson
12:57.08	Jackson		1	Bedford	31 May 2010	1 Leeds 7 Oct 09
12:57.20	Jackson		1	Bedford	25 Aug 2012	7:08.9 C Charnock
12:59.0 mx	Kehler		1	Rugby	1 Jul 2000	1 Rugby 22 Aug 00
12:59.1	Sworowski		1	Leamington	19 Aug 1989	7:12.2 Bethan Davies
12:59.3	Vicky Lupton	17.04.72	1	Sheffield	13 May 1995	1 Leeds 2 Oct 13
13:00.50+	Sworowski		1m	Cardiff	5 Jun 1990	
13:02.5 mx	Kehler		1	Woodford	17 Jun 1998	
13:02.9	Sworowski		1	Sheffield	18 May 1991	
13:03.3	Sworowski		1	Cleckheaton	19 May 1990	
13:03.4	Lupton		2	Sheffield	18 May 1991	
13:03.76+	Kehler		1m	Birmingham	13 Jul 2002	
13:06.27	Lupton		1	Bedford	27 May 1996	
13:06.6+	Sworowski		1m	Gateshead	28 Aug 1989	
	(19/4)					
13:13.3	Cal Partington	27.06.66	1	Douglas IOM	12 Jul 1995	
13:14.73	Niobe Menendez	1.09.66	1	Ashford	11 Aug 2001	
13:16.0	Julie Drake	21.05.69	1	Brighton	11 Dec 1990	
13:16.23	Verity Snook	13.11.70	2	Bedford	27 May 1996	
13:21.01+	Heather Lewis	25.10.93	1m	Birmingham	29 Jun 2014	
13:21.5	Catherine Charnock	3.05.75	1	Whitehaven	8 May 1999	
	(10)					
13:25.2	Carol Tyson	15.12.57	1	Östersund, SWE	6 Jul 1979	
13:28.0	Helen Elleker	21.03.56	1	Crawley	22 Jul 1990	
13:37.1	Beverley Allen	16.03.59	1	Brighton	16 May 1987	
13:42.10	Sylvia Black	16.04.58	2	Birmingham	23 May 1990	
13:43.0	Melanie Wright	5.04.64	1	Coventry	5 Jul 1994	
13:44.0	Virginia Birch	1.07.55	1	Brighton	19 Jun 1984	
13:46.3+	Marion Fawkes	3.12.48	1m	Östersund, SWE	30 Jun 1979	
13:48.0	Sarah Brown	28.09.64	2	Brighton	16 May 1987	
13:49.64mx	Sophie Hales	30.03.85	1	Bedford	31 May 2004	
	13:57.45		2	Bedford	28 May 2007	
13:50.52mx	Rebecca Mersh	28.01.89	2	Bedford	31 May 2004	
	14:18.93		4	Manchester (SC)	24 Jul 2004	
	(20)					
13:52.0	Lillian Millen	5.03.45	1	Barrow	7 May 1983	
13:52.6	Sara-Jane Cattermole	29.01.77	1	Perth, AUS	1 Mar 2002	
13:53.79mx	Kate Horwill	26.01.75	2	Bedford	30 May 2005	
	13:57.0		1	Brierley Hill	10 Oct 2004	
13:53.8	Sharon Tonks	18.04.70	1	Stourport	12 May 2002	
13:56.0	Irene Bateman	13.11.47	2	London (PH)	20 Sep 1980	
13:57.8	Jill Barrett	13.07.64	1	London (He)	2 Jun 1984	
14:02.29	Karen Ratcliffe	1.06.61	1	Birmingham	19 May 1993	
14:02.3	Bethan Davies	7.11.90	1	Coventry	24 Aug 2013	
14:02.8+	Nicky Jackson	1.05.65	3m	Derby	25 May 1987	
14:04.1	Susan Ashforth	5.02.70	1	Cudworth	19 May 1985	
	(30)					
14:05.1	Karen Kneale	23.04.69	1	Douglas IOM	11 Jun 1995	
14:05.83	Tasha Webster	28.09.95	1	Hereford	31 May 2012	
14:08.0	Andrea Crofts	7.09.70	3	Coventry	19 Aug 1990	
14:09.81	Amy Hales	16.03.82	1	Hull	19 Sep 1998	
14:11.1	Liz Corran	23.09.55	2	Douglas IOM	11 Jun 1995	
14:11.8	Carolyn Brown	24.05.74	1	Douglas IOM	18 Sep 1992	
14:12.9	Elaine Callanin	13.09.60	2	Brierley Hill	9 Oct 1994	
14:13.0	Judy Farr	24.01.42	7	Östersund, SWE	6 Jul 1979	
14:15.0	Joanne Pope	17.01.71	1	Brighton	9 Mar 1993	
14:17.74	Kim Braznell	28.02.56	3	Birmingham	20 May 1995	
	(40)					
14:18.0	Gillian Edgar	26.06.64	4	Bergen, NOR	28 May 1981	
14:21.01	Jane Gibson	26.01.73	2	Birmingham	30 Jun 2001	

14:21.26	Laura Whelan	7.1.93	1	Dublin	25 May 2014
14:21.90	Katie Stones	22.11.85	2	Hull	15 Sep 2001
14:22.42	Wendy Bennett	21.12.65	3	Birmingham	30 Jun 2001
14:23.48	Debbie Wallen	28.05.79	2	Hexham	14 Jun 1998
14:24.14	Ellie Dooley	6.10.95	1	Leeds	10 Aug 2013
14:24.6	Becky Tisshaw	8.02.81	3	Dublin (M), IRL	19 Jul 1997
14:25.09	Lisa Crump	30.03.76	1	Bedford	31 May 1999
14:28.2	Karen Dunster (50)	18.05.69	1	Portsmouth	19 May 1991

Indoors

13:08.64	Niobe Menendez	1.09.66	2	Cardiff	2 Feb 2002
13:09.21	Bethan Davies	7.11.90	1	Cardiff	15 Dec 2013
13:11.80	Heather Lewis	25.10.93	1	Birmingham	16 Feb 2014
13:12.01	Julie Drake	21.05.69	8h2	Toronto, CAN	12 Mar 1993
13:29.46	Ellie Dooley	6.10.95	2	Birmingham	16 Feb 2014
13:36.43mx	Sophie Hales	30.03.85	1	Birmingham	29 Feb 2004
13:38.05mx	Katie Stones	22.11.85	2	Birmingham	29 Feb 2004
14:01.67	Rebecca Mersh	28.1.89	3	Birmingham	29 Feb 2004
14:04.97	Michelle Turner	24.06.72	3	Birmingham	16 Feb 2014
14:17.96	Katie Ford	21.10.81	3	Birmingham	28 Feb 1998
14:18.43	Emma Achurch	9.07.97	4	Birmingham	16 Feb 2014

5000 METRES TRACK

20:46.58	Jo Jackson/Atkinson	17.01.85	1	Sydney, AUS	14 Feb 2009
21:01.24	Jackson		1	Brisbane, AUS	7 Feb 2009
21:21.67	Jackson		1	Birmingham	12 Jul 2009
21:30.75	Jackson		1	Birmingham	13 Jul 2008
21:42.32	Jackson		1	Birmingham	31 Jul 2011
21:42.51	Lisa Kehler	15.03.67	1	Birmingham	13 Jul 2002
21:45.98	Jackson		1	Birmingham	24 Jun 2012
21:49.4	Jackson		1	Leeds	2 Jul 2011
21:52.38	Vicky Lupton	17.04.72	1	Sheffield (W)	9 Aug 1995
21:52.95	Jackson		1	Birmingham	27 Jun 2010
21:57.68	Kehler		2	Antrim	25 Jun 1990
22:01.53	Kehler		2	Birmingham	26 Jul 1998
22:02.06	Betty Sworowski	12.03.61	1	Gateshead	28 Aug 1989
22:03.65	Jackson		1	Manchester (SC)	29 Jul 2007
22:08.69	Kehler		1	Derby	30 May 1998
22:09.87	Heather Lewis	25.10.93	1	Birmingham	29 Jun 2014
22:11.30	Sworowski		2	Gateshead	29 Jun 1990
22:12.21	Lupton		1	Birmingham	28 Jun 1992
22:12.31	Jackson		1	Sydney, AUS	9 Feb 2008
22:15.4	Lupton		1	Cudworth	3 Sep 1995
22:19.04	Kehler		1	Derby	25 May 1987
22:20.03	Kehler		1	Birmingham	16 Jul 1995
22:22.7	Sworowski		1	Cudworth	16 Jul 1989
22:22.94+	Kehler		1k	Birmingham	13 Aug 2000
22:23.2	Lupton		1	Enfield	2 May 1992
22:23.35	Sworowski		1	Birmingham	4 Aug 1990
22:23.80	Lupton		2	Birmingham	16 Jul 1995
22:29.04	Sworowski		1	Birmingham	27 Jul 1991
22:30.59	Sworowski		1	Birmingham	13 Aug 1989
22:31.59	Sworowski		1	Cardiff	2 Jun 1990
22:33.4	Jackson (31/5)		1	Leeds	3 Sep 2009
22:37.47	Julie Drake	21.05.69	2	Birmingham	17 Jul 1993
22:41.19	Cal Partington	27.06.66	3	Birmingham	16 Jul 1995
22:51.23	Helen Elleker	21.03.56	4	Antrim	25 Jun 1990
23:11.2	Carol Tyson	15.12.57	1	Östersund, SWE	30 Jun 1979
23:11.7	Catherine Charnock (10)	3.05.75	1	Leeds	19 Jun 1999
23:15.04	Beverley Allen	16.03.59	2	Derby	25 May 1987
23:19.2	Marion Fawkes	3.12.48	2	Östersund, SWE	30 Jun 1979
23:20.00	Virginia Birch	1.07.55	1	Antrim	25 May 1985
23:21.08	Bethan Davies	7.11.90	1	Birmingham	14 Jul 2013
23:22.52	Verity Snook	13.11.70	1	Horsham	19 Jun 1994

Time	Name	DOB		Place	Date
23:34.43	Sylvia Black	16.04.58	1	Birmingham	5 Jul 1992
23:35.54	Nicky Jackson	1.05.65	4	Derby	25 May 1987
23:38.3	Irene Bateman	13.11.47	2	Brighton	28 Jun 1981
23:46.30	Niobe Menendez	1.09.66	1	Birmingham	14 Jul 2001
23:46.7	Lillian Millen	5.03.45	3	Brighton	28 Jun 1981
(20)					
23:47.6	Melanie Wright	5.04.64	1	Solihull	29 May 1994
23:51.1	Jill Barrett	13.07.64	14	Bergen (Fana), NOR	5 May 1984
23:55.27	Susan Ashforth	5.02.70	2	Antrim	25 May 1985
24:00.0	Sarah Brown	28.09.64	2	Brighton	21 May 1991
24:03.61	Katie Stones	22.11.85	3	Manchester (SC)	10 Jul 2005
24:04.21	Ellie Dooley	6.10.95	3	Birmingham	14 Jul 2013
24:05.49	Sharon Tonks	18.04.70	2	Birmingham	13 Jul 2002
24:06.6	Rebecca Mersh	28.01.89	2	Sheffield (W)	23 Apr 2005
24:09.66	Elaine Callanin	13.09.60	7	Birmingham	16 Jul 1995
24:12.11	Karen Ratcliffe	1.06.61	7	Birmingham	17 Jul 1993
(30)					
24:14.96	Emma Achurch	9.07.97	3	Birmingham	29 Jun 2014
24:16.4	Kim Braznell	28.02.56	1	Solihull	4 Jun 1995
24:17.19	Sophie Hales	30.03.85	2	Bedford	24 Jun 2007
24:18.6	Brenda Lupton	5.10.52	19	Bergen (Fana), NOR	5 May 1984
24:19.0	Vicky Lawrence	18.11.69	2	London (BP)	13 Jun 1987
24:24	Wendy Bennett	21.12.65	1	Tamworth	22 Sep 2001
24:24.31	Andrea Crofts	7.09.70	5	Jarrow	4 Jun 1989
24:26.41	Lisa Crump	30.03.76	3	Birmingham	25 Jul 1999
24:27.73	Carolyn Brown	24.05.74	4	Horsham	29 Aug 1992
24:28.60	Debbie Wallen	28.05.79	6	Birmingham	26 Jul 1998
(40)					
24:32.92	Karen Nipper	22.12.64	4	Copenhagen, DEN	21 Jul 1984
24:34.6	Tracy Devlin	20.11.72	2	Moss, NOR	17 Sep 1989
24:35.0	Joanne Pope	17.01.71	2	Brighton	16 Dec 1990
24:35.16	Angela Hodd	3.07.70	7	Derby	25 May 1987
24:35.55	Amy Hales	16.03.82	1	Bedford	4 Jul 1999
24:37.4	Kate Horwill	26.01.75	2	Tamworth	22 May 2005
24:37.7	Judy Farr	24.01.42	1	Gothenburg, SWE	13 Aug 1977
24:40.69	Karen Kneale	23.04.69	1	Cudworth	4 Aug 1996
24:40.91	Liz Corran	23.09.55	2	Cudworth	4 Aug 1996
24:45.4	Karen Eden	4.11.62	3	Warley	9 Jul 1978
(50)					
24:48.19	Nina Howley	22.01.78	2	Bedford	28 Jul 1996
24:53.39	Lisa Simpson	18.04.68	8	Derby	25 May 1987
24:56.34mx	Jenny Gagg	20.02.88	2	Birmingham	15 Aug 2004
25:00.36			3	Manchester (SC)	3 Jul 2004
24:56.69	Nikki Huckerby	27.02.78	2	Solihull	24 May 1998
24:57	Michelle Turner	24.06.72	1	Tamworth	18 May 2013
24:57	Jasmine Nicholls	23.08.95	1	Tamworth	18 May 2013
24:59.04	Helen Ringshaw	22.07.66	2	Haugesund, NOR	29 Jul 1984
25:00.79	Gill Watson	26.05.64	9	Birmingham	16 Jul 1995
25:03.0	Sue Wilson	2.06.58	2	Brighton	18 Dec 1988
25:03.72	Karen Dunster	18.05.69	2	Stoke-on-Trent	26 Jun 1988
(60)					
25:09.2	Betty Jenkins	13.01.38	3	Warley	16 Sep 1972
25:11.33	Sally Warren	29.01.78	4	Liverpool	22 Jul 2000
25:11.46	Nicola Phillips	23.04.83	8	Neubrandenburg, GER	21 Aug 1999
25:13.8	Carla Jarvis	5.08.75	1	Derby	2 Jun 1991
25:16.2	Jane Gibson	26.01.73	1	Douglas IOM	26 Sep 2001
25:20.0	Katie Ford	21.10.81	1	Sheffield	10 Sep 1997
25:21.00	Theresa Ashman	16.06.73	7	Cardiff	8 Jun 1971
25:25.1	Sandra Brown	1.04.49	8	Enfield	2 May 1992
25:25.80	Kim Macadam	22.03.69	7	Antrim	25 May 1985
25:26.41	Becky Tisshaw	8.02.81	2	Bedford	6 Jul 1997
(70)					
25:26.6	Gillan Edgar	26.06.64	13	Bergen, NOR	30 May 1981
25:28.28	Elizabeth Ryan	9.03.67	8	Cwmbran	27 May 1984
25:29.35	Gill Trower	3.08.53	7	Birmingham	25 Jul 1987
25:30.3	Elaine Worth	15.01.58	2	Birmingham	7 Jun 1980

25:31.14	Zena Lindley	20.05.73	10	Jarrow	4 Jun 1989
25:32.50	Susan Gibson	7.05.52	9	Derby	25 May 1987
25:33.94	Kerry Woodcock	5.04.72	3	Stoke-on-Trent	26 Jun 1988
25:34.0	Sally Wish	15.04.58	5	Copenhagen, DEN	1 Sep 1973
25:34.1	Sarah Bennett	27.07.80	2	Sheffield	31 May 1997
25:34.13	Lauren Whelan (80)	7.01.93	4	Birmingham	24 Jun 2012
25:36.56	Miranda Heathcote	18.09.72	5	Birmingham	14 Jul 2001
25:38.4	Pamela Branson	10.03.58	2	Warley	4 Aug 1974
25:50.83	Claire Reeves	31.07.84	1	Leamington	18 May 2002
25:52.5	Cath Reader	19.10.54	9	Enfield	2 May 1992
25:53.0	Christine Coleman	14.01.47	3	Leicester	3 Nov 1973
25:53.4	Nicole Lacey	20.03.86	2	Montreuil-sous-Bois, FRA	2 Oct 2006
25:54.58	Fiona Edgington	2.01.64	8	Birmingham	4 Aug 1990
25:55.0mx	Suzie Pratt	24.06.70	4	Leicester	25 Mar 1986
25:58.4	Brenda Cook	17.10.35	5	Warley	16 Sep 1972

5 KILOMETRES ROAD

21:36	Vicky Lupton	17.04.72	1	Sheffield	18 Jul 1992
21:50	Betty Sworowski	12.03.61	7	L'Hospitalet, ESP	6 May 1990
21:55	Kehler	15.03.67	1hc	Earlsdon	13 Jul 1998
22:01	Kehler		1	Birmingham	9 Dec 1989
22:09	Kehler	(2)	1	Redditch	8 Apr 1989
22:10	Kehler	(3)	10	Duisburg, GER	29 Aug 1989
22:17	Kehler	(4)	1	Cardiff	4 Nov 1989
22:18+	Jackson	(3)	m	Beijing, CHN	21 Aug 2008
22:20	Kehler	(5)	1	Sutton Coldfield	6 Jul 2002
22:22	Kehler	(6)	1	Tamworth	28 Oct 1995
22:22+	Jackson	(4)	8m	La Coruña, ESP	19 Jun 2010
22:24+	Betty Sworowski	(2)	1m	Redditch	11 Nov 1989
22:24	Kehler	(7)	1	York	9 May 1990
22:30	Vicky Lupton	(2)	1	Holmewood	13 Apr 1996
22:30+	Jackson	(5)	1m	Coventry	11 Sep 2010
22:31+	Jackson	(6)	1m	London (LV)	6 Sep 2008
22:32+	Kehler (17/4)	(8)	7m	Naumburg, GER	1 May 1990

Where better than track best

22:45+	Verity Snook	13.11.70	6=m	Victoria, CAN	25 Aug 1994
22:51	Marion Fawkes	3.12.48	1	Eschborn, GER	29 Sep 1979
22:59	Carol Tyson	15.12.57	2	Eschborn, GER	29 Sep 1979
23:00+	Beverley Allen	16.03.59	14m	Rome, ITA	1 Sep 1987
23:09	Catherine Charnock	3.05.75	1	Stockport	5 Jun 1999
23:13	Sylvia Black	16.04.58	1	Stoneleigh	13 Feb 1993
23:17+	Julie Drake	21.05.69	13m	Grassau, GER	16 Jun 1990
23:24	Melanie Wright	5.04.64	2	Holmewood	9 Apr 1995
23:25	Irene Bateman	13.11.47	6	Eschborn, GER	29 Sep 1979
23:32+	Sara-Jane Cattermole	29.01.77	1m	Murdoch, AUS	23 Jul 2000
23:35	Lisa Simpson	18.04.68	1	Cardiff	31 Oct 1987
23:38	Jill Barrett	13.07.64	1	Redditch	12 May 1984
23:42	Lillian Millen	5.03.45	1	Sheffield	23 Apr 1983
23:42 B	Kate Horwill	26.01.75	1	Worcester	17 Oct 2004
	24:01		1	Tamworth	27 Feb 2005
23:43	Sophie Hales	30.03.85	1	Bexley	11 Feb 2006
23:45hc	Elaine Callanin	13.09.60	1hc	Earlsdon	28 Jan 1995
23:53	Sharon Tonks	18.04.70	2	Sutton Coldfield	6 Jul 2002
23:53	Katie Stones	22.11.85	3	Leamington	15 Mar 2003
23:54	Vicky Lawrence	18.11.69	1	Paris, FRA	26 Sep 1987
23:57	Sarah Brown	28.09.64	2	London (BP)	6 Dec 1980
24:00	Andrea Crofts	7.09.70	1	Birmingham	1 Dec 1990
24:03	Karen Ratcliffe	1.06.61	2	Sutton Coldfield	12 Feb 1994
24:05	Brenda Lupton	5.10.52	1	Morecambe	18 Sep 1982
24:05	Emma Achurch	9.07.97	1	Coventry	1 Mar 2014
24:13	Gillian Edgar	26.06.64	3	Milan, ITA	3 May 1981
24:20	Karen Eden	4.11.62	2	Melksham	3 Dec 1978
24:20	Lisa Crump	30.03.76	7	Sheffield	12 Apr 1997
24:21	Judy Farr	24.01.42	1	Enfield	11 Nov 1978

24:21	Karen Kneale	23.04.69	1	Douglas IOM	14 May 1995
24:23	Joanne Pope	17.01.71	2	London (BP)	23 Mar 1991
24:23	Gemma Bridge	17.05.93	1	Tamworth	24 Nov 2013
24:25	Karen Nipper	22.12.64	6	Thamesmead	9 Feb 1985
24:25	Nikki Huckerby	27.02.78	8	Sheffield	12 Apr 1997
24:27	Jenny Gagg	20.02.88	1	Leamington	6 Mar 2004
24:33	Karen Dunster	18.05.69	1	Swindon	17 Oct 1987
24:36	Helen Ringshaw	22.07.66	4	London (BP)	5 Mar 1984
24:40	Kim Macadam	22.03.69	2	Redditch	13 Apr 1986
24:44	Jane Gibson	26.01.73	4	Peel IOM	16 Aug 1999
24:48	Katie Ford	21.10.81	16	Senigallia, ITA	30 May 1998
24:51	Liz Corran	23.09.55	2	Douglas IOM	14 May 1995
24:57	Virginia O'Connell	8.11.64	1	London	1 Jan 1985
24:59	Theresa Ashman	16.06.73	1	Solihull	22 Feb 1992
24:59	Sarah Bennett	27.07.80	19	Senigallia, ITA	30 May 1998

Short course

22:48	Lillian Millen	5.03.45	1	Morecambe	10 Sep 1983
23:36un	Judy Farr	24.01.42	1	L'Hospitalet, ESP	17 Apr 1977
23:49	Katie Stones	22.11.85	1	Sheffield	22 Apr 2006
24:03	Brenda Lupton	5.10.52	3	Morecambe	10 Sep 1983

10 KILOMETRES ROAD

43:52	Jo Jackson/Atkinson	17.01.85	1	Coventry	6 Mar 2010	**Most 10k times:**
44:52	Jackson		1	Sheffield	19 Apr 2008	**Under 47:00**
44:57+	Jackson		8m	La Coruña, ESP	19 Jun 2010	22 Kehler
44:59	Jackson		1	London (VP)	11 Sep 2011	20 Atkinson
45:02	Jackson		1	Coventry	1 Mar 2014	11 Sworowski
45:03	Lisa Kehler	15.03.67	3	Kuala Lumpur, MAS	19 Sep 1998	8 Lupton
45:04+	Jackson		28m	Beijing, CHN	21 Aug 2008	4 Drake
45:09.57t	Kehler		1	Birmingham	13 Aug 2000	
45:18	Kehler		1	Rotterdam, NED	15 May 1998	**Under 48:00**
45:18.8t	Vicky Lupton	17.04.72	1	Watford	2 Sep 1995	40 Kehler
45:20	Jackson		1	London (LV)	6 Sep 2008	27 Atkinson
45:31	Jackson		1	Coventry	11 Sep 2010	26 Lupton
45:39+	Jackson		2m	Lugano, SUI	8 Mar 2009	19 Sworowski
45:42	Kehler		11	New York, USA	3 May 1987	10 Drake
45:42	Kehler		18	Budapest, HUN	20 Aug 1998	10 Snook
45:42	Jackson		1	Leamington	8 Mar 2008	7 Elleker
45:44+	Jackson		5m	Sesto San Giovanni, ITA	1 May 2010	5 Partington
45:48	Lupton		5	Victoria, CAN	25 Aug 1994	
45:53	Kehler		1	Dublin, IRL	15 Jun 2002	
45:53.9t	Julie Drake	21.05.69	5	Bergen (Fana), NOR	26 May 1990	
45:54	Kehler		27	Dudince, SVK	25 Apr 1998	
45:59	Betty Sworowski	12.03.61	20	Tokyo, JPN	24 Aug 1991	
45:59	Drake		7	Békéscsaba, HUN	28 Mar 1993	
46:00	Kehler		35	Beijing, CHN	29 Apr 1995	
46:01	Sworowski		9	Sesto San Giovanni, ITA	1 May 1991	
46:01	Kehler		6	Victoria, CAN	25 Aug 1994	
46:02	Kehler		15	L'Hospitalet, ESP	27 May 1989	
46:02	Kehler		6	Naumburg, GER	1 May 1990	
46:04	Lupton		1	Lancaster	9 May 1992	
46:06	Verity Snook	13.11.70	7	Victoria, CAN	25 Aug 1994	
46:06	Kehler		35	Gothenburg, SWE	7 Aug 1995	
46:09	Kehler		1	Békéscsaba, HUN	5 Apr 1987	
46:13+	Jackson		1	London	30 May 2011	
46:21	Lupton		22	Eschborn, GER	12 Jun 1993	
46:22+	Jackson (35/7)		1m	Melbourne, AUS	23 Feb 2008	
46:26	Cal Partington	27.06.66	1	Stockport	1 Jul 1995	
46:25.2t	Helen Elleker	21.03.56	6	Bergen (Fana), NOR	26 May 1990	
46:38	Niobe Menendez (10)	1.09.66	2	Dublin, IRL	15 Jun 2002	
46:42	Bethan Davies	7.11.90	2	Coventry	1 Mar 2014	
46:59	Heather Lewis	25.10.93	3	Coventry	1 Mar 2014	
47:05	Sara-Jane Cattermole	29.01.77	1	Cambridge, AUS	15 Jul 2001	

47:51	Catherine Charnock	3.05.75	1	Leicester	5 Sep 1999
47:56.3t	Virginia Birch	1.07.55	4	Boras, SWE	15 Jun 1985
47:58	Nicky Jackson	1.05.65	2	York	27 Jun 1987
47:58.3t	Beverley Allen	16.03.59	3	Plymouth	21 Jun 1986
47:59	Sylvia Black	16.04.58	1	Cardiff	29 Mar 1992
48:11.4t	Marion Fawkes	3.12.48	1	Harnosand, SWE	8 Jul 1979
48:18	Melanie Wright	5.04.64	2	Lancaster	9 May 1992
	(20)				
48:30	Karen Ratcliffe	1.06.61	2	Horsham	16 Apr 1994
48:34.5t	Carol Tyson	15.12.57	1	Manchester (Str)	22 Aug 1981
48:36	Kim Braznell	28.02.56	1	Sheffield	25 Apr 1998
48:40	Sharon Tonks	18.04.70	1	Leamington	23 Mar 2002
48:47	Irene Bateman	13.11.47	1	York	20 Jun 1981
48:56.5t	Sarah Brown	28.09.64	2	Brighton	18 Apr 1991
48:58	Wendy Bennett	21.12.65	1	Worcester	20 Oct 2001
49:10	Vicky Lawrence	18.11.69	4	Ham	14 Mar 1987
49:12	Elaine Callanin	13.09.60	2	York	20 Jun 1981
49:14	Carolyn Brown	24.05.74	1	Douglas IOM	29 Mar 1992
	(30)				
49:26	Ellie Dooley	6.10.95	4	Coventry	1 Mar 2014
49:33	Lisa Simpson	18.04.68	5	Ham	14 Mar 1987
49:33	Michelle Turner	24.06.72	1	Andreas Village, IOM	17 Nov 2013
49:35	Lillian Millen	5.03.45	1	Chorley	2 Jun 1984
49:37	Karen Kneale	23.04.69	1	St. Johns IOM	26 May 1996
49:38	Kate Horwill	26.01.75	1	Tamworth	12 Dec 1999
49:40	Sophie Hales	30.03.85	1	Leamington	6 Mar 2004
49:47	Jill Barrett	13.07.64	25	Bergen, NOR	24 Sep 1983
49:50	Lisa Crump	30.03.76	2	Tamworth	3 Dec 2000
49:55un	Andrea Crofts	7.09.70	1	Solihull	17 Nov 1990
	(40)				
50:10.2t	Brenda Lupton	5.10.52	2	Birmingham	17 Mar 1984
50:20	Emma Achurch	9.07.97	1	London (VP)	2 Feb 2014
50:29	Katie Stones	22.11.85	12	Naumburg, GER	1 May 2004
50:39	Rebecca Mersh	28.01.89	1	Coventry	12 Mar 2006
50:46.0t	Judy Farr	24.01.42	3	London (WL)	25 Mar 1978
51:00.0t	Karen Nipper	22.12.64	1	Leicester	21 Feb 1981
51:03.0t	Liz Corran	23.09.55	4	Leicester	22 Apr 1995
51:07	Nikki Huckerby	27.02.78	5	Leicester	21 Mar 1998
51:07.6t	Joanne Pope	17.01.71	2	Brighton	2 Feb 1991
51:15	Lauren Whelan	7.01.93	3	Hobart, AUS	19 Feb 2011
	(50)				
51:18	Karen Dunster	18.05.69	1	Weymouth	9 Mar 1991
51:20	Sally Warren	29.01.78	2	Tamworth	13 Dec 1998
51:31.2t	Helen Ringshaw	22.07.66	3	Birmingham	17 Mar 1984
51:34	Jane Gibson	26.01.73	1	Peel IOM	18 Aug 1999
51:36	Nicola Phillips	23.04.83	8	Leamington	23 Apr 2000
52:00	Theresa Ashman	16.06.73	7	Lancaster	9 May 1992
52:04	Debbie Wallen	28.05.79	1	East Molesey	10 Jan 1999
52:12	Karen Eden	4.11.62	1	Northfield, USA	10 Mar 1979
52:13	Sue Wilson	2.06.58	1	Brighton	19 Nov 1988
52:15	Susan Gibson	7.05.52	11	Ham	14 Mar 1987
	(60)				
52:15	Sandra Brown	1.04.49	6	Cardiff	14 Mar 1993
52:18.8t	Jo Hesketh	16.06.69	1	Crawley	13 Sep 2003
52:29	Sarah Foster	11.02.89	3	East Molesey	9 Jan 2006
52:34	Claire Walker	8.10.72	4	Dublin, IRL	28 Sep 1996
52:43	Jasmine Nicholls	23.08.95	6	Coventry	1 Mar 2014
52:43.3t	Cath Reader	19.10.54	1	Hornchurch	1 Apr 1992
52:45	Tasha Webster	28.09.95	1	Coventry	4 Mar 2012
52:50.0t	Christine Coleman	14.01.47	7mx	Welwyn	21 Aug 1973
52:55	Katie Ford	21.10.81	10	Leicester	21 Mar 1998
52:57	Jenny Gagg	20.02.88	4	Vienna, AUT	5 Oct 2003
	(70)				
52:58	Claire Reeves	31.07.84	4	Dublin, IRL	15 Jun 2002
52:59.0t	Nicole Lacey	20.03.86	3	Montbéliard, FRA	26 Mar 2005
53:00.0t	Ruth Harper	15.04.62	2	Leicester	15 Mar 1986

Short courses

45:28	Vicky Lupton	17.04.72	12	Livorno, ITA	10 Jul 1993
45:30	Betty Sworowski	12.03.61	1	Redditch (31m sh)	11 Mar 1989
47:31	Beverley Allen	16.03.59	1	London (VP)	5 Apr 1986
47:40	Melanie Wright	5.04.64	13	Livorno, ITA	10 Jul 1993
51:03	Gill Trower	3.08.53	5	London (VP)	5 Apr 1986
51:43	Sue Wilson	2.06.58	6	Redditch	11 Mar 1989
52:26	Fiona Edgington	2.01.64	9	Redditch	11 Mar 1989
52:37	Pauline Leader	4.03.54	7	London (VP)	5 Apr 1986
52:53	Michelle Venables	3.03.73	11	Redditch	11 Mar 1989

Further best track times

46:23.08	Betty Sworowski	12.03.61	1	Stoke-on-Trent	4 Aug 1991
47:10.07	Verity Snook	13.11.70	1	Horsham	19 Jun 1993
48:20.0	Cal Partington	27.06.66	2	Bolton	7 May 1994
48:35.8	Melanie Wright	5.04.64	2	Watford	2 Sep 1995
48:57.6	Irene Bateman	13.11.47	1	London (WL)	20 Mar 1982
49:03.99	Bethan Davies	7.11.90	1	Bedford	16 Jun 2013
49:05.0	Sara-Jane Cattermole	29.01.77	1	Perth, AUS	29 Nov 1999
49:27.0	Sylvia Black	16.04.58	2	Leicester	22 Apr 1995
49:39.0	Karen Ratcliffe	1.06.61	1	Leamington	22 May 1991
49:41.0	Elaine Callanin	13.09.60	3	Leicester	22 Apr 1995
49:52.1	Niobe Menendez	1.09.66	1	Birmingham	29 Sep 2001
50:17.76	Heather Lewis	25.10.93	1	Bedford	16 Jun 2013
50:25.0mx	Lisa Simpson	18.04.68	13	Hornchurch	1 Apr 1987
51:54.5			3	Brighton	27 Sep 1986
50:28.0	Andrea Crofts	7.09.70	1	Leicester	21 Jul 1992
50:50.0	Nicky Jackson	1.05.65	9	Plymouth	21 Jun 1986
50:52.3	Kim Braznell	28.02.56	2	Enfield	31 Aug 1996
51:03.0	Karen Kneale	23.04.69	5	Leicester	22 Apr 1995
51:06.1	Lillian Millen	5.03.45	2	London (WL)	20 Mar 1982
51:13.4	Wendy Bennett	21.12.65	2	Birmingham	29 Sep 2001
51:59.49	Michelle Turner	24.06.72		Bedford	16 Jun 2013
52:07.36	Ellie Dooley	6.10.95	1	Bedford	16 Jun 2013
52:18.0B	Sophie Hales	30.03.85	1	Horsham	17 Feb 2007
52:43.3	Claire Walker	8.10.72	4	Enfield	31 Aug 1996
52:43.71	Sandra Brown	1.04.49	5	Horsham	19 Jun 1993
52:48.5	Kate Horwill	26.01.75	3	Douglas IOM	22 Aug 1992
52:54.26	Lauren Whelan	7.01.93	4	Bedford	20 Jun 2010

Short track

48:52.5	Irene Bateman	13.11.47	1	Kirkby	19 Mar 1983
50:11.2	Jill Barrett	13.07.64	2	Kirkby	19 Mar 1983

20 KILOMETRES

1:30:41	Jo Jackson/Atkinson	17.01.85	7	La Coruña, ESP	19 Jun 2010
1:31:16	Jackson		1	Lugano, SUI	8 Mar 2009
1:31:33	Jackson		22	Beijing, CHN	21 Aug 2008
1:31:40	Jackson		1	Melbourne, AUS	23 Feb 2008
1:31:50	Jackson		1	London	30 May 2011
1:32:05	Jackson		3	Sesto San Giovanni, ITA	1 May 2010
1:32:37	Jackson		4	Lugano, SUI	14 Mar 2010
1:32:40	Jackson		1	Leamington	15 Jun 2008
1:33:33	Jackson		10	Barcelona, ESP	28 Jul 2010
1:33:43	Jackson		12	Lugano, SUI	16 Mar 2014
1:33:43	Jackson		48	Taicang, CHN	3 May 2014
1:33:53	Jackson		12	Olhao, POR	21 May 2011
1:33:57	Lisa Kehler	15.03.67	23	Eisenhüttenstadt, GER	17 Jun 2000
1:34:22	Jackson		1	Delhi, IND	9 Oct 2010
1:35:25	Jackson		12	La Coruña, ESP	9 Jun 2012
1:35:32	Jackson		23	Daegu, KOR	31 Aug 2011
1:35:35	Kehler		14	Leamington	23 Apr 2000
1:35:57	Jackson		1	Shrewsbury	12 Apr 2009
1:36:28	Jackson		7	Debrecen, HUN	13 Jul 2007
1:36:40	Sara-Jane Cattermole	29.01.77	1	Perth, AUS	4 Mar 2000
1:36:45	Kehler		2	Manchester (SC)	28 Jul 2002
1:37:18	Jackson		1	Douglas IOM	10 Mar 2007
1:37:31	Cattermole		1	Perth, AUS	23 Jan 2000

Most 20k times:
Under 1:40:00
24 Atkinson
7 Cattermole
6 Kehler

Under 1:45:00
33 Atkinson
20 Cattermole
12 Kehler
10 Menendez
6 V Lupton

Time	Name	DOB	#	Location	Date
1:37:44	Vicky Lupton	17.04.72	1	Leamington	27 Jun 1999
1:37:47	Kehler		33	Sydney, AUS	28 Sep 2000
1:37:56	Jackson		45	Cheboksary, RUS	11 May 2008
1:38:00	Cattermole		1	Murdoch, AUS	2 Jan 2005
1:38:25	Cattermole		1	Perth, AUS	31 Oct 1999
1:38:29	Catherine Charnock	3.05.75	2	Dublin, IRL	11 Sep 1999
1:38:29	Jackson		42	Saransk, RUS	13 May 2012
1:38:34	Jackson		1	Coventry	14 Apr 2007
1:38:56	Jackson (33/5)		38	Leamington	20 May 2007
1:39:38	Heather Lewis	25.10.93	1	York	8 Jun 2014
1:39:59	Niobe Menendez	1.09.66	4	Manchester (Wy)	21 Apr 2002
1:40:45	Irene Bateman	13.11.47	1	Basildon	9 Apr 1983
1:41:44	Bethan Davies	7.11.90	8	Dublin, IRL	29 Jun 2013
1:42:02hc	Lillian Millen	5.03.45	2	Macclesfield	9 Apr 1983
1:44:42	(10)		1	London (BP)	2 Apr 1983
1:43:29	Sharon Tonks	18.04.70	2	East Molesey	3 Mar 2002
1:43:50	Betty Sworowski	12.03.61	1	Sheffield	22 Feb 1988
1:43:52	Sylvia Black	16.04.58	1	Sutton Coldfield	14 Jun 1997
1:44:19	Katie Stones	22.11.85	2	Douglas IOM	25 Feb 2006
1:44:29	Kim Braznell	28.02.56	4	Leamington	21 Mar 1999
1:44:30	Wendy Bennett	21.12.65	2	Leamington	26 Apr 2003
1:44:54	Cal Partington	27.06.66	1	York	23 Mar 2002
1:45:11	Elaine Callanin	13.09.60	1	Horsham	16 Oct 1993
1:45:23	Michelle Turner	24.06.72	31	Lugano, SUI	16 Mar 2014
1:45:40	Carolyn Brown (20)	24.05.74	1	Andreas Village, IOM	29 Jan 2006
1:45:58	Kate Horwill	26.01.75	4	Leamington	16 Apr 2005
1:46:35	Karen Ratcliffe	1.06.61	8	Manchester (Wy)	21 Apr 2002
1:46:48	Lisa Crump	30.03.76	4	Leamington	27 Jun 1999
1:47:10	Liz Corran	23.09.55	2	Bruges, BEL	29 Jun 1996
1:47:21	Debbie Wallen	28.05.79	1	Leicester	17 Apr 1999
1:47:39	Jane Gibson	26.01.73	14	Dublin, IRL	16 Jun 2001
1:47:50	Jo Hesketh	16.06.69	1	Sheriff Hutton	5 Jul 2003
1:48:00	Brenda Lupton	5.10.52	1	Sheffield	4 Sep 1983
1:48:22	Cath Reader	19.10.54	1	Colchester	31 May 1992
1:48:29	Sandra Brown (30)	1.04.49	1	London (WP)	2 Mar 1991
1:48:46	Julie Drake	21.05.69	3	Horsham	16 Oct 1993
1:49:12	Nikki Huckerby	27.02.78	10	Orleans, FRA	26 Sep 1999
1:49:18	Helen Sharratt	18.12.72	4	Horsham	16 Oct 1993
1:49:32	Nicola Phillips	23.04.83	4	Leamington	26 Apr 2003
1:49:40	Verity Snook	13.11.70	2	Coventry	30 Jul 2005
1:50:16	Sophie Hales	30.03.85	3	Douglas IOM	10 Mar 2007
1:50:56	Marie Jackson	18.10.60	6	Leamington	16 Apr 2005
1:51:38	Sarah Brown	28.09.64	3	Holmewood	3 Sep 1994
1:51:57	Diane Bradley	13.09.61	5	Leamington	15 Jun 2008
1:52:20	Helen Elleker (40)	21.03.56	2	Sheffield	4 Sep 1983

Short courses

Time	Name	DOB	#	Location	Date
1:35:52	Sara-Jane Cattermole	29.01.77	1	Perth, AUS 180m sh	4 Jun 2000
1:36:59	Julie Drake	21.05.69	1	Blackheath	22 May 1993
1:42:10	Sharon Tonks	18.04.70	1	Yverdon, SUI	6 Aug 2000

50 KILOMETRES

Time	Name	DOB	#	Location	Date
4:50:31	Sandra Brown	1.04.49	1	Basildon	13 Jul 1991
4:56:27	Brown		1	Basildon	13 Aug 1994
5:01:52	Lillian Millen	5.03.45	1	York	16 Apr 1983
5:02:48	Brown		1	Basildon	5 Apr 1997
5:03:26	Brown		1	Chelmsford	24 Sep 1983
5:05:31	Brown		1	Yelverton	30 Apr 1989
5:09:41	Millen		1	Sleaford	18 Jul 1981
5:11:11	Brown		1	Dawlish	6 May 1984
5:13:03+	Irene Corlett	18.01.43	1m	Isle of Man	29 Apr 1984
5:22:04	Cath Reader	19.10.54	1	Burrator	2 May 1993
5:27:00+	Jane Gibson	26.1.73	1	Isle of Man	20 Jun 1999
5:30:34+	Brenda Lupton	5.10.52	1	Bradford	27 May 1991

100 KILOMETRES
11:17:42.1t Sandra Brown at Étréchy, FRA 28 Oct 1990

100 MILES
18:36:29 Sandra Brown at Leicester 29 Jul 1984
18:54:05 Irene Corlett at Leicester 21 Aug 1982

24 HOURS
196,000 Sandra Brown at Bazencourt 29 Mar 1992